ORA ET LABORA

VOLUME IV

First Printing, 2023

ISBN 978-0-6451039-7-7

Ordo Templi Orientis
GPO Box 1193
Canberra, ACT 2601
AUSTRALIA

Every effort has been made to determine the ownership of all photos and secure proper permissions. If any errors have inadvertently occurred, we apologise and will correct such in subsequent printings.

www.otoaustralia.org.au
ora-et-labora.site

Editor: Brendan Walls
Cover Design: Ben Hay (honeyrogue.com)
Layout: Padraig Maclain

Ora et Labora

An OTO Research Journal

March MMXXIII e.v.

Volume IV

Grand Lodge of Australia

Ordo Templi Orientis

In Perpetuity Publishing

Contents

EDITORIAL   1

THE LIFE OF THE SUN, THE JOY OF THE EARTH: AN   7
ORIENTATION FOR PRACTICE AND AWARENESS IN THE
M∴M∴M∴
Ian Drummond (Australia)

THE MYTHOLOGY OF THE EUCHARIST   13
Soror Shalimar (Australia)

THE SOLAR MYTH AND THE PATH OF INITIATION   105
Cosimo Salvatorelli (Italy)

VIAOV: THE MONOMYTH OF ALEISTER CROWLEY   123
Sinisha Tzar (Croatia)

THE THERION FILE   149
William Peters (Germany)

A WORLD OF DIFFERENCE   177
Daniel Brand Corish (Australia)

THE LEFT HAND PATH   193
Frater S.P. (Ireland)

LIBER SAMEKH   217
Garry McSweeney (Australia)

THE KONAMI CODE: CROWLEY, CARD GAMES AND   229
THE OCCULT.
N. F. Robinson (Australia)

THE BIRTH OF HELL: FORMULAE OF INITIATION IN   249
THE BOOK OF TWO WAYS AND THE CEREMONY OF
THE DEATH OF ASAR
Shokufeh Alwazi (Germany)

READING BD SPELL 30: THE MINDFUL HEART OF   299
ANKH-EF-EN-KHONSU
Rev. Cosmé Hallelujah (Goa)

APOKALYPSIS III: DEPTH REVELATION   375
Steve King (Australia)

INTRODUCTION TO LARRY SITSKY'S MUSIC   481
(PIANO AND CHORUS) FOR ECCLESIAE GNOSTICAE
CATHOLICAE CANON MISSAE
Joel Brady (Australia)

MUSIC (PIANO AND CHORUS) FOR ECCLESIAE   499
GNOSTICAE CATHOLICAE CANON MISSAE
Larry Sitsky (Australia)

CONTRIBUTOR BIOGRAPHIES   545

EDITORIAL

Do what thou wilt shall be the whole of the Law.

Welcome to Volume 4 of *Ora Et Labora*! As in previous volumes, we were overwhelmed with incredible contributions from all over the world. The scholar-practitioner community is growing! The range of ideas and sheer vitality of Volume 4 is ample proof that the project remains as necessary as it was when we launched it in the midst of the pandemic.

I've written about the origin and mission of *Ora Et Labora* in previous volumes, but another underlying cultural archetype informing our approach came from an early conversation with Grand Master Shiva. The model: *SST Records*, the American independent record label formed in 1978 in Long Beach, California by Greg Ginn of *Black Flag* infamy[1]. Music writer Michael

---

[1] Side note – Henry Rollins of *Black Flag* was interviewed by Aussie punk promoter Jeff Halls in the 90s and it was later published in Oceania Lodge's *Beastly* publication. Rollins is probably still scratching his head about winding up in an OTO journal!

Azerrad wrote, "Ginn took his label from a cash-strapped, cop-hassled store-front operation to easily the most influential and popular underground indie of the Eighties"[2]

The IPP editorial team and OTO executive, grabbed the enthusiasm and passion of the *SST* model and applied that to our publishing program. *Best of Oz* and *Ora Et Labora* could be seen as the first *Black Flag* and *Minutemen* seven-inch records. The idea was to build a stable of writers and thinkers, nurture the scene, learn as we go, DIY and die daily. Eventually making way for longer cuts, deep dives... double albums.... Think: *Black Flag's* "The Process of Weeding Out", or *Husker Du's* "Zen Arcade". In terms of books: Monographs. Future focused, kicking out the jams, building scenes, and extending the hand to friends and allies in the fight. I found an old Slack message from Shiva:

> "SST is the magick formula. What's the acronym? I can only think of Super-Sized Thelema right now..."

Super-Sized is right, at close to 600 pages!

The supercharged SST model is refined and informed by the Grand Master's practical experience in educational

---

[2] Azerrad, Michael. *Our Band Could Be Your Life*. Little, Brown and Company, 2001.

models, experience design, user experience, and design thinking. Many of his teachings in this space were shared with Australian OTO leadership during the OTOX (OTO Experience) workshop and seminars of 2018 e.v. The fundamentals of UX (User Experience), UI (User Interface) processes and design thinking were taught, discussed and practically worked through, which led to a subtle realignment in thinking throughout the Australian Kingdom, particularly on the nature of the interaction points between the Order, its members, and the broader community. The foundations of these teachings, which form the core of both IPP, and the Australian OTO Executive is 'radical collaboration, openness and trust' - or in OTO terms, 'Peace, Tolerance and Truth'. One of the fruits of the reoriented thinking arising from the OTOX workshops is the outwardly focused, interconnective, networked approach to producing books like the one you are holding now.

> "Setting an audacious goal, understanding the problem, and identifying a solution are the necessary first steps towards social impact at scale."[3]

Once the idea and inspiration is correctly aligned with the higher values, the practical considerations takes care of themselves. For example, the 'in perpetuity' model means our Grand Lodge team are not weighed down by

---

[3] Chang, Ann Mei *Lean Impact*, Wiley 2019.

warehousing and distribution burdens, which would siphon off considerable energy from other pressing work. We were, and are, also willing to abandon *Ora Et Labora*, should it lose impact, or its' own unique self-perpetuating energy. One of the main mantras of the *Lean Impact* approach is "Start Small, Iterate Fast" which recalls CHAPTER LXIII of the Tao Te Ching:

> Do great things while they are yet small, hard things while they are yet easy; for all things, how great or hard soever, have a beginning when they are little and easy. So thus the wise man accomplisheth the greatest tasks without undertaking anything important.[4]

The marketing and advertising of these books also takes care of itself, as we have put the relationship with our readers and contributors above everything else. Developing good-faith trust and bonds with you, who in your enthusiasm to share and discuss, spread the word. None of this is accidental. *Ora* was not as much about sales as it was reach, building community and investing trust and respect in that community. This was all part of Shiva's original brief: take the most integral aspects of digital and social media marketing and apply the concepts to fraternal community building. So naturally, none of this is possible without the army of people supporting *Ora Et Labora*; those who pre-order,

---

[4] Crowley (trans) *Tao Te Ching*, Weiser, 1995.

those who tell friends, those who post about it on socials, those who drive their own passionate campaigns, those who review it, those who read it!

Our contributors are the most professional, thoughtful, responsive and committed people I've had the pleasure of working with. Thank you for your essays, entrusting us to read them, comment on, and edit them. We are so happy to present your work.

Thank you to proof-readers Lisa Campbell-Smith, Stephanie Williams, Peter Holmes; and the Editorial Board, Padraig MacIain, Joel Brady, Federica Tagliabue, Jindalae Sherman and Daniel Corish. For this edition, we were proud to invite Percy Mindnich from Berlin to the Editorial Board as our international guest editor. He's been a delight to work with, as was his predecessor Patrizia Ebner from Austria, our very first international guest editor. We thank Patrizia for her work on Volume 3.

Love is the law, love under will.

Brendan Walls

Grand Secretary General

OTO Grand Lodge of Australia

THE LIFE OF THE SUN, THE JOY OF THE EARTH:

An orientation for practice and awareness in the M∴M∴M∴

IAN DRUMMOND

"The basis of all is the oil of the olive. The olive is, traditionally, the gift of Minerva, the Wisdom of God, the Logos" (Liber ABA, Part II, Ch.5, The Holy Oil)

Like the olive oil which serves as the basis of the holy oil, the Minerval ceremony is the base of the Mysteria Mystica Maxima (M∴M∴M∴) of OTO. The ceremony itself is said to ritually enact "the object of the pure soul in determining to formulate itself consciously, or, as I may say, to understand itself. It chooses to enter into relations with the solar system."[1] It can be viewed as establishing a particularly Thelemic orientation for ongoing practice and awareness throughout the initiate's life.

As described above, the Minerval ceremony presents a prelude and precondition to the Miracle of Incarnation,

---

[1] Crowley, *Confessions*

7

and addresses a fundamental existential question, *"Where do I come from and where am I going?"* Any answer to this question shapes a world view and provides an orientation for a spiritual view and practice. Here very brief comparisons with the Hermetic *Poimandres* and the general approach of Buddhadharma are instructive, bringing into focus a distinct Thelemic Mysterium[2].

The *Poimandres* describes the descent of the Primal Man into Nature as a process of attraction and love:

> "When the man saw in the water the form like himself as it was in nature, he loved it and wished to inhabit it; wish and action came in the same moment, and he inhabited the unreasoning form. Nature took hold of her beloved, hugging him all about and embraced him, for they were lovers."[3]

Buddhadharma (more particularly in tantra) has a vivid and practical approach to death and incarnation (cf. the

---

[2] In Plato's *Phaedo*, the incarnation of the pure soul is presented as captivity in a perceptual prison: "Every seeker after wisdom knows that up to the time when philosophy takes it over his soul is a helpless prisoner, chained hand and foot in the body, compelled to view reality not directly but only through its prison bars, and wallowing in utter ignorance."

[3] Poimandres v.14 in Copenhaver, B. P. (1995). *Hermetica: The Greek Corpus Hermeticum and the Latin Asclepius in a new English translation, with notes and introduction.* Cambridge University Press.

serpentine curve explained in *De Lege Libellum*)[4]. Incarnation in this view occurs at conception and is understood on a physiological and psychological basis. The 'intermediate being' or incarnating consciousness is drawn by the passions of its parents into a process of elemental solidification and foetal development. The emphasis here is on the root cause of incarnation in *samsara* through karmic causes based on ignorance and attachment. It should also be noted, the same process is presented as a tantric physiological basis for practice and liberation – the red and white vital essences[5].

---

[4]The serpentine curve "which reaches out to infinity, and its zeros but mark the changes from the plus to minus, and minus to plus, coefficients of its equation." *De Lege Libellum*

[5] "According to tantra, in an embodied existence, the white vital essence originates from the semen of the father, and the red vital essence, from the ovum of the mother, which have merged at the time of sexual intercourse to form the physical basis for the consciousness of the intermediate being conceived in their midst. Throughout foetal development, these essences remain at the navel, the energy-centre from where the body develops. At birth, they separate; the white settles at the head, and the red, four fingers below the navel." "The subtle vital essences are present in both males and female, but the white is predominant in the male; the red, in the female. They pervade and abide in all parts of the body, the white being mainly in the channel-wheel of the head; the red, mainly in the channel-wheel of the genitals and that of the navel." Elio Guarisco, Introduction p. 30-31, Jamgon Kongtrul (Guarisco, E., & McLeod, Ingrid trans.) (2005). *The treasury of knowledge: book six, part four: Systems of Buddhist Tantra*. Snow Lion Publications .

Extending and adapting this tantric physiology, we could creatively speculate the ritual development of a physiology of the Thelemic Mysteria, with the key formulae of *Do what thou wilt shall be the whole of the Law* and *Love is the law, love under will* establishing the field of ongoing initiation in the M∴M∴M∴. Indeed, in contrast with the comparative examples above, the pure soul is neither incarnated (nor imprisoned!) through a blind attraction or passion but by *love under will*[6]. That is, the way is indicated for the pure soul, as in the description of the Minerval ceremony above, to *"formulate itself consciously."*

The formulation of the pure soul can be understood in further alchemical, Qabalistic and practical magical terms, as suggested by the Arcanum of Arcana, ON – a word, whose "significance is taught, gradually, in the OTO."[7] In the *Book of Thoth*, The Master Therion notes the arrangement of the Atu O (Ayin = 70) and N (Nun = 50) = 120 (Samekh) may be summed up "as a hieroglyph of the processes by which idea manifests as form."[8] The alchemical process of incarnation is also

---

[6] Yet is this ultimately so far from the Poimandres? In the Message of the Master Therion, *love under will* "is to be taken as meaning that while Will is the Law, the nature of that Will is Love."

[7] "ON is an Arcanum of Arcana; its significance is taught, gradually, in the OTO." *Liber Samekh*, n.1

[8] "On the Tree of Life, Atu XIII and XV are symmetrically placed; they lead from Tiphareth, the human consciousness, to the spheres

suggested by the title of these Atu in sequence – the Lord of the Gate of Matter, the Lord of the Gate of Death, and the Bringer Forth of Life[9].

As a pure soul, now manifest in form, we have attained the labour and heroism of incarnation and our true Will is fixed to an inevitable goal in Tiphareth, the Sun. As Soldiers of Freedom what then is our engine of war? The body, material and energetic (which are one), and the sensual world itself, as in the Eucharist of four and five elements[10].

To our initial existential question of, *Where do I come from and where am I going?* we can add, *What is the means and motive force for the journey ahead?* As in the Creed of the *Gnostic Mass* "meat and drink are

---

in which Thought (on the one hand) and Bliss (on the other) are developed. Between them, Atu XIV leads similarly to the sphere which formulates Existence. (See note on Atu X and arrangement.) These three cards may therefore be summed up as a hieroglyph of the processes by which idea manifests as form." *Book of Thoth,* p.105

[9] In further alchemical terms the subject of the Minerval can be seen as the scintilla, the spark around which the corpus (body) of nature is formed. The scintilla, the star, astrum, or pure soul, is fixed, "for love's sake" and "the chance of union", to incarnate existence. The task of the alchemist is to melt this corpus in preparation of a tincture.

[10] See *Liber ABA*, Part III Ch.XX, Of The Eucharist and of The Art of Alchemy

transmuted in us daily into spiritual substance". Here too then, the spiritual is made one with the material. As we are orientated to a valorisation of our incarnate and conditioned existence, each meal, our regular and necessary sustenance of food and drink, can recapitulate this primary orientation in *love under will.*

As the Holy Oil represents "the Aspiration of the Magician"[11], so too can the base of the M∴M∴M∴ shape our individual spiritual aspiration toward an awareness of the liberatory potentials of the human body, its senses, food and drink, and their energetic transformations. With presence and practice, it can initiate a literal orientation to the life of the Sun and the joy of the Earth, in the great serpentine curve, the Path in Eternity.

---

[11]*Liber ABA*, Part II, Ch.5, The Holy Oil

THE MYTHOLOGY OF THE EUCHARIST

An Introduction to the Cakes of Light.

SOROR SHALIMAR

Foreword by Frater Shiva X°

This essay by the late Soror Shalimar (1966-2022) was written over 1995 and published in the January 1996 inaugural edition of the then Oceania Lodge/Australian OTO journal, The Waratah. *The paper condensed a lot of Shalimar's research from the early 90s. We were living together and later married over this time, and the subject matter was something we had been interested in and actively exploring since we first met in the late 80s.*

During those years we were a junior Priest and Priestess of OTO's Ecclesia Gnostica Catholica. We were entranced by Joseph Campbell's 'Power of Myth' TV series, and had devoured his The Masks of God *books (Primitive Mythology, Oriental Mythology, Occidental Mythology, Creative Mythology) on top of what you might call the 'standard' curriculum. The Frater Superior's reports in the then OTO international newsletter,* The Magical Link, *had also turned us on to fascinating other studies, such as Jaan Puhvel's* Comparative Mythology, *Ioan Couliano's* The

13

Tree of Gnosis, *and David Ulansey's* The Origins of the Mithraic Mysteries. *OTO HQ was also pumping out the Crowley books. All in all it was a rich, vibrant, energetic and electric time, and a bustle of activity for the Sydney OTO. We had many late night soirees post-Mass discussing all of the above, notably with the redoubtable Frater In Vino Veritas.*

While a natural creative, empath and clairvoyant, Shalimar had solid scientific training as a registered nurse. A specialist in psychiatric nursing, she had a professional and personal interest in the deepest recesses of the psyche. She was an avid student and she could write, bringing all of the above together in this essay. Shalimar also wrote this as she wanted to raise the profile in this media of women writer-practitioners of the OTO, hoping to encourage others to do the same. At the time she certainly succeeded. 'The Mythology of the Eucharist' was widely applauded globally. For its day there was nothing quite like it, from the OTO at least.

The comparative method Shalimar employed is not to everyone's liking nor is it without scholarly criticism as an ethnographic method. Some of the references cited here are certainly now dated and critiqued in more sophisticated areas of knowledge. This was over 25 years ago. Shalimar's thesis, however, remains in my view fascinating and worth the study. For those overwhelmed or lost in the density of symbolism, it might be helpful to take a step back after each section and ask yourself what is its relationship to the Cakes of Light, before proceeding. Keep in mind that Shalimar was a Priestess-practitioner-scholar, and for her (and us) the work that went into this research was all part of an elaborate amplification *process, in the Jung-Campbell sense. We were at the time using the amplificatory process of associations based on comparative mythology to interpret the transformation symbolism in the Mass* (Liber XV). *Such a process takes you outside of otherwise personal or 'textbook' associations and meanings to discover connections to universal cultural themes. I believe the approach and how Shalimar went about it made her such an authentic priestess.*

Shalimar made some references in the original essay to a published Crowley paper that we now know was intended as a private, high-degree instruction. I have edited out these references for publication here.

* * *

One of the simplest and most complete of Magick ceremonies is the Eucharist. Crowley suggested that historically, the Eucharist consisted of, 'taking common things, transmuting them into things divine, and consuming them' (*Book 4*, p.267). Crowley further states that a Eucharist of some sort should be consumed daily by every Magician, and that it should be regarded as the main sustenance of the Magicians' Magical Life. By doing so, 'The Magician becomes filled with God, fed upon God, intoxicated with God' (*Book 4*, p.269). During *Liber XV*, The Gnostic Catholic Mass (*Book 4*, p.572), the Eucharist of two elements—the wafer or

Cake of Light, and wine, is ritually consumed by the Priest and congregation.

The purpose of this study is to introduce the notion of the Eucharist via an exploration of mythology. In this way we can draw attention to the Thelemic Eucharist by examining the symbolism of the ingredients comprising the Cakes of Light. These ingredients are outlined in *Liber AL vel Legis*, III:23, 'For perfume mix meal & honey & thick leavings of red wine: then oil of Abramelin and olive oil, and afterwards soften & smooth down with rich fresh blood.' They are commented upon by Crowley in *The Law Is For All*, (p.283-285). This study is not intended to be a definitive treatise on the Cakes of Light, or on the administering of the Thelemic Eucharist in general. It should be noted that Hymenaeus Beta, in his Editor's Notes to *Book 4* (p. 715, n.233), states that the *proper* production and use of the Cakes of Light is gradually taught in A∴A∴ and O.T.O.

Section 1: Grains.

Breads and Cakes

Life-foods, including grains, wine, fruits [especially those rich in seeds, as they were considered symbols of fecundity, that is, pomegranates, apples, figs and lemons], eggs, honey, water, milk, and blood, often made up ritual meals and offerings served to various gods and goddesses. Breads and cakes are well documented as such offerings (Drawer, p.7).

The Sumerian Goddess Inanna, Queen of Earth, was the goddess of the grain and the vine. Cakes called, 'the baked cakes of the Goddess Inanna,' were baked upon her altars in ritual ovens (Baring and Cashford, p. 195). The Canaanite Goddess Astarte/Anath, known as the 'Queen of Heaven', was likewise offered cakes baked upon her altars. It is highly probable that these cakes may have been moulded into, or imprinted with the image of the goddess, as a stone mould discovered in Israel dating from c.1600 B.C. would suggest (Patai, p.64). These cakes can, perhaps, be seen as a precursor to the Christian Eucharist, in which the host is 'mystically' transformed into the 'Body of Christ', and eaten. The burning of ritual incense, the offering up of cakes, and the pouring of libations of wine, were central to the worship of Astarte/Anath (Jeremiah 7:17-18; 44:15-19). As well, special honey and sesame cakes shaped like female genitals were offered to the Goddess Demeter, whom worshippers called 'the pure Mother Bee', at her Thesmorphia Festival (Graves, 1955, Vol.1, p.72).

The ritual process of grinding many grains into the unity of flour or meal, the mixing of the flour with water or oil, the adding of salt or honey, and the subsequent kneading, and baking of the dough in ritual ovens can be seen as a particularly sacred act. Even domestic bread [that is, not intended for sacramental use], is honoured by Arabs above all other foods. Its name in Egypt is 'life', and to deny it to a beggar, or ask payment for it in the desert, is a sin. Bread is seen as the union of many grains into a single substance and, when broken and divided amongst many, becomes a symbol of life shared (Drower, p.44).

The bread oven was a principle feature of Old European shrines. Miniature shrine models have been discovered in Western Ukraine that depict one or more figures engaged in the activities of grinding grain and kneading dough. It is thought that these bread ovens were once identified with the goddess herself, as some appear to have anthropomorphic features including eyes, and an opening representing the mouth or vagina of the pregnant goddess, as evidenced by the dome-shape of the oven. According to Gimbutas (p.70), the burial of the dough in the oven-womb-tomb of the goddess is analogous to a seed being planted in the earth[1]. It was therefore considered natural to expect new life [or rebirth, leading to immortality], to emerge as a result of this process. Further, the breads and cakes baked in ritual ovens were seen to personify the goddess (and in later times, the god)[2], to which they were offered, and to likewise confer new life to those partaking of the sacrament.

---

[1] The Hebrew word qubba means: 'dome; vault; tomb' which is synonymous with 'womb' (Drawer, p.71; p.77).

[2] In Egypt and Jerusalem, bread is still baked in wood-fuelled ovens attached to the churches. The oven-house is called a 'Bethlehem' – House of Bread/House of God (Drawer, p-52).

The Cycle of Birth, Death, and Rebirth.

The Goddess Myths:

The sowing, growth, and harvesting of vegetation, especially of grains, represents birth and death, as well as death and rebirth. This cycle of death and rebirth can be taken as a parable: life can be dormant, but is indestructible, (it is remembered that vegetation is essentially energy and, as such, energy cannot be lost, only transformed).

The Great Mother Goddess of Crete was worshipped as the Great Mother of Life, Death, and Regeneration; the Goddess of the Animals; and the Mistress of the Sea and of the Fruits of the Earth (Baring and Cashford, p. 107). According to Baring and Cashford (pp. 131-134), archaeological research has so far uncovered no image of a male god in Neolithic Crete. The male aspect of the goddess, who was at that time androgynous, was believed to have been symbolised by the crescent horns of the bull, ram or stag. In the Minoan Age of Crete, the male aspect appears to have separated from the goddess, but is not yet independent of her. It seems probable that the male child-god was in some way related to the cycles of the agricultural year. As harvesting was most likely a male activity, the ritual harvesting of corn and wheat may have intended to identify the male god with the annual death and rebirth of the vegetation crops. In this way, the god brings about the form of life that has to change, while the goddess remains as the principle of life that never dies, and continually renews itself through its changing forms. Willetts, in *Cretan Cults and Festivals* (p.81), comments that the god, 'represents the element of discontinuity, of growth, decay, and renewal in the vegetation cycle, as the goddess represents continuity. Because he shares in the mortality of the seed, he is an annually dying god'.

During the Bronze Age, the goddess is one, yet becomes many; she is single yet marries; she is virgin and mother; she may even take her son or brother as consort. As before, however, she gives life and takes it away (Baring and Cashford, pp. 145-147). The goddess has many names and many stories, but one central theme is unvarying throughout the Near East: the goddess becomes separated from the one she loves, who dies, or seems to die, and falls into a darkness called the Underworld. This separation is reflected in Nature as the loss of light and fertility (that is, the dark phase of the moon, or the season of winter). The goddess descends into the darkness so that her loved one may return to the light, and life may continue.

In Sumeria, Inanna descends to the world below to meet her sister Ereshkigal, Queen of the Underworld. She returns to the world above, and sends her consort Dumuzi, Lord of the Abyss, to take her place.

In Babylonia, Ishtar yearly journeys to awaken her son-lover, Tammuz, from his sleep in the darkness beneath the earth, and to bring him up to the light.

In Egypt, Isis marries her brother Osiris, and loses him through death at the hands of his brother Set. The whole earth is barren until Isis finds, and brings back together the dismembered pieces of his body [all except for his penis, which was swallowed by a fish]. The loss and finding of Osiris was manifest in the waning and waxing of the moon. Plutarch writes that Osiris was 28 years of age, and that his dismembering into 14 pieces referred allegorically to the 14 days of the waning moon, from the full to the new moon (cited in Baring and Cashford, p.239).

In Canaan, the god Baal enters the Underworld to confront the powers of death, personified by his brother Mot. Mot defeats him, and Baal's sister, the goddess Anath, journeys down to fetch his body for burial. She kills Mot, and scatters his body 'like grains in the field'.

In Greek myth, Demeter loses her daughter Persephone to the god of the Underworld, Hades, who seizes her from the fight to be his bride. Demeter's mourning leaves the earth barren, and only when her daughter is returned to her in spring does the earth grow fruitful again.

This theme continues through the myths of the Iron Age. The goddess Cybele of Anatolia, according to one version of her story, loved the shepherd Attis, but he however falls in love with a nymph. Driven insane by the jealous goddess, Attis castrates himself with a stone or sickle, and dies. As the goddess mourns him, a pine tree springs from his body, and flowers arise from his blood. [This idea is depicted in the Biblical 'creation of Eve.' Eve is born out of the side of the sleeping Adam while the 'phallic tree', in line with Adam's genitals, bursts into flower as though he had truly given birth to Eve like a mother. This 'phallic tree' has been suggested by some alchemical scholars to be symbolic of the umbilical cord, which attaches the unborn child to its mother.] (see Fig. 1 & 2)

The Greek goddess Aphrodite loses her lover Adonis, Lord of Vegetation, who is gored to death by a wild boar whilst hunting[3]. The goddess asks Zeus to allow him to return to life from spring to autumn, the fertile seasons of the year.

---

[3] The pig or boar, along with the ass, were employed to thresh the corn, grinding it into the ploughed soil to release the seeds, and thereby sowing the fields. Ploughing and sowing are often used as allegories for sexual fertilising. Pigs and asses are therefore seen as agents of change, and death was often imagined through the pig or boar.

Figure 2: Phallic Cord of the Universal Tree

Figure 1: The Cosmic Tree of Alchemy

Finally Jesus, son of the Virgin Mary, dies and descends into Hell for three days, the number of days of darkness when the moon is no longer visible. In the Christian myth, Jesus is rescued by his Heavenly Father. His return from the Underworld after three days coincides with the seasonal change from winter into spring – Easter Sunday is celebrated on the Sunday following the first full moon after the Spring Equinox in the Northern Hemisphere[4].

The pattern of these myths may have been inspired by humanity's relationship with the moon. For countless thousands of years, people have seen the light of the moon growing to fullness, then giving way to the darkness, and being reborn again and again in a continuous cycle. The moon was an image of the sky that was always changing, yet was always the same. What endured was the cycle, whose totality could never be seen at any one moment (Baring and Cashford, p.147).

The Dying Gods

Osiris was originally a Nature god, and embodied the spirit of vegetation. He was later worshipped throughout Egypt as the God of the Dead. The phases in the life of the grain were understood as the god within the grain dying, and coming to life again. When the first stalks of grain were ritually cut, there was weeping and wailing, as though the body of the god

---

[4]Crowley states that Christ rose on the third day for the reason that it takes three days for the planet Mercury to become visible after separating from the orb of the sun. He notes that Mercury and Venus, the planets between the Earth and the sun, can be seen as the Mother and the Son mediating between us and the Father-Sun {The Paris Working, 1st. Jan.,1914 e.v.)

was also being dismembered, and the reapers would invoke Isis to lament with them (Viaud, p. 16).

In the New Kingdom [c.1550-1070 B.C.], moulds of the god Osiris were filled with Nile silt, planted with barley seeds, and placed in the burial chambers of Royal Tombs. These Osiris-beds, sprouting with grain, ensured that the deceased would be resurrected in the same way that Osiris was reborn in the grain (Drower, p.41). Similarily, in the countries bordering the Mediterranean, the Adonis-cult inspired the making of Gardens of Adonis. Fast-growing, fast-dying plants like lettuce, fennel, barley and wheat, were sown in baskets filled with shallow earth. They were then heated in the sun, and tended for eight days but, having no deep roots, they soon withered and were thrown into the sea along with images or effigies of Adonis (Drower, p.41; Baring and Cashford, p.363). Drower further notes that a comparable ritual takes place in Sicily during the Christian Holy Week. Upon beds of sand are placed coloured pots of wheat, called 'Sepolcri', which had been forced into pale growth by being grown in dark cellars. On Holy Tuesday, the figure of Christ was lifted from the crucifix and lain upon the Sepolcri. These rituals, based upon the symbolic nature of wheat and other grains, can be taken as an allegory, that from death comes life.

Ritual Castration

The Son-Lover was often identified with the stalks of grain, or with trees. The ritual cutting or harvesting of the grain signified the yearly death of the Son-Lover. The harvesting or castration of the male gods is a common theme in many myths and was often accomplished by using the sickle (the Sickle of Demeter), with its crescent moon or double-horn shape[5].

Uranus [Heaven] was castrated, his power being usurped, by his son Cronus at the request of his mother Gaia [Earth]. Cronus used a sharp sickle or 'harpe' or, according to Puhvel (p.27), a jagged sickle[6]. His severed

---

[5] Hephaestus, the son of Hera and Zeus, was born with gross deformities, being lame in both legs and with a dislocated hip [lameness as with blindness are often allegories for castration, just as the hip or jawbone can represent the penis or phallus. Crowley identifies the phallus with the thigh (Book of Thoth, p.66)]. Hephaestus was the Blacksmith of Olympus, making weapons and armoury for the goddesses and gods, including Demeters sickle, used for harvesting both crops and genitals (Guirand, p.128).

The sickle is the traditional weapon of Saturn-Binah, attributed to the 32nd path on the Tree of Life. It implies the power of Time to reap the harvest of man's life and work. Binah is also attributed to the bee, and it is the Queen Bee alone who is endowed with a sickle-shaped implement for the purpose of castrating her lover during their nuptial flight [see Section 2: Honey- Life of the Bees].

[6] Freuds discovery of what he termed the 'Oedipus Complex', underlined the connection between sexuality and anxiety (1984,

genitals were cast into the sea to be reborn as the Virgin Aphrodite Uraia, 'Celestial Aphrodite', Queen of Heaven (Baring and Cashford, p.353). According to another version, Uranus was the consort of the Celestial Aphrodite. In this way, Uranus was seen as Son-Lover of Celestial Aphrodite, who died, fertilised her by his death or castration, and begot himself again (Campbell 1987, p.235).

The sickle was used by Attis, in some versions of his story, to castrate himself, whilst the priests of Cybele emasculated themselves with flint knives. In another myth, Adonis-Tammuz, consort of the goddess Aphrodite-Ishtar, was gorged by a wild boar in the loin whilst out hunting [an allegory for castration], and was either rendered impotent, or killed (Campbell, 1987, p. 176). Aphrodite was, however, able to conceive a son, Priapus, from her castrated lover [an obvious compensation for his fathers' emasculated state, as Priapus was endowed with an enormous penis]. In another version, the severed penis of Adonis became his

---

pp.316-319). He asserted that the root of sexuality was intimately linked with the fear of incest and the fear of castration. Fear of castration is frequently expressed in dreams, endowed with oral, vaginal and uterine features, and forming a fear of being devoured by the 'vagina dentata' or toothed vagina of the 'evil mother' (Rank, p.89). The toothed- vagina can be seen as the toothed-mouth, with both oral and vaginal characteristics, and may account for Puhvel's reference to the jagged, or toothed sickle.

son, Priapus, the ithyphallic Greek personification of the phallus (Graves, 1955, Vol.l, pp.69-72)[7].

The Eye of Horus

Egyptian Set, the ass-headed god of the hot desert winds, was the god of the South [Saturn: The Underworld[8]]. According to Budge (1969, Vol.2, p.59),

---

[7] In another way, therefore, castration can be identified with the sexual sacrifice involved in the principle of regeneration, that is the process of ejaculation and impregnation which Crowley termed 'the sacrifice of the Man, who transfers life to his descendants'

(*Book 4*, p.169). This is well enough stylised from its more pagan origins in the Christian conception of the Trinity, where the Son reveals the Father. In Crowley's 'Gnostic Mass', a Thelemic rite, this is further developed when the Priest, during Part VIII "Of the Mystic Marriage and Consummation of the Elements', intones in Greek, 'The Father is the Son through the Holy Spirit' (in Book 4, p.584). If the Holy Spirit is identified with the Khabs or Point, that is, the original, individual, eternal essence, then it is fairly easy to further identify this creative spark within semen, for, 'the whole race-consciousness, that which is omnipotent, omniscient, omnipresent is hidden therein' (Crowley, Comment to Ch.8, *The Book of Lies*, p.27). The Father sacrifices his life-blood to live on 'in thy child' —the Son of God. [This is why the heterosexual formula must be considered central to the Order of Nature, as the success of the race depends on it.]

[8] See also Atu XV, The Devil, attributed to Capricorn, which is ruled by Saturn. The Devil is attributed to the Hebrew letter Ayin, which means 'Eye'. The 'eye' is also related to the Ajna Chakra, or third-eye, 'Eye of Shiva'; the Phallus; Baphomet, the ass-headed idol of the Knights Templars; Satan [Set, Abrasax, Adad, Adonis,

Set was a sacrificial deity of the cult of Horus and Osiris. Set and Horus were represented as alternating or seasonal year gods, who fought and castrated one another, each being successively baptised in the blood of the others' 'Phallic Eye'. After castrating Set, Horus was said to spread his blood upon the fields to render them fertile.

> 'Horus is purified with the Eye of his brother Set;
> Set is purified with the Eye of his brother Horus'
> -Pyramid Texts.

The All-Seeing Eye of Ancient Egypt belonged to the Goddess Maat [the Mother syllable maa meant 'to see', and its hieroglyph was an eye (Budge, 1977, p.55)]. At a later time, the All-Seeing Eye became identified with Horus, the 'Eye of Horus'[9].

Attis, Adonai, Aphophis (Crowley, *Book 4*, p. 165)], Ahathor; Pan—Pan Pamphage Pangenetor, The All Devourer, All Begetter.

[9] 'He is the Open Eye of the exalted Sun...: also that Secret Eye which makes an image of God, the Light, and gives it power to utter oracles, enlightening the mind. Thus he is Man from God....' (Crowley, *Book 4*, p,166). The Secret Eye makes an image of God. Man is an image of the Macrocosm [God], centred around a point [the Secret Eye] of consciousness. In another way: The Point/Eye is Hadit: The image is Nuit The Point/Eye is Khabs: The image is Khu The Point/Eye is Phallus: The image is Kteis See also the 'Eye in the Triangle'. The Biblical Samson's 'blindness' and hair-cutting at the hands of Delilah and the Philistines (Judges 16:17-18), can be identified as mystic metaphors for castration. The shearing of the

The Green Man Of Spring

'The fool stirs within all of us at the return of Spring, and because we are a little bewildered, a little embarrassed, it has been thought a salutary custom to externalise the subconscious impulse by ceremonial means' (Crowley, *Book of Thoth*, p.56).

The Green Man is the personification of the mysteries that produce the phenomena of Spring.

Spring Festivals, customarily held on the first of May [the month sacred to Mary, the Virgin Mother...], celebrated the 'sacred marriage' between the elected May Queen and the Green Man [identified variously with Dummuzi, Tammuz, Attis...], enacting the ritual of the regeneration of life. During the May Day festival, according to Baring and Cashford (p.410- 411), the May Pole was erected [Phallus], and decorated with garlands of flowers and ribbons [Kteis].

The image of the Green Man appears as Mercurius in alchemical literature. Mercurius' power for self-generation, self-transformation, and self-destruction, was described by the alchemists, who understood this

---

sun god's hair or 'rays', resulted in his emasculation, or loss of power. [Samson can be viewed as a Sun god, and will be discussed at length in Section 2.] Freud also asserts that hair-cutting is synonymous with castration, especially in dreams (1984, p.357).

energy to be the divine life in all of Nature; ever changing, yet ever the same. Jung (1963, p.201), describes how the vision of the Green Man appeared to him in 1939, at the time when he was becoming immersed in alchemy, and working towards a reinterpretation of the meaning of the Christian symbols:

> 'One night I awoke and saw, bathed in bright light at the foot of my bed, the figure of Christ on the Cross. It was not quite life-size, but extremely distinct; and I saw that his body was made of greenish gold…'

The green figure of Christ turning to gold [as with all Dying Gods or Vegetation Gods], reflects as much the ripening of the soul, as it does the image of wheat ripening from green to gold.

The Green Knight

The Celtic myth of Percival can be said to represent the ancient and essential magical myths of Regeneration and Renewal. The Celts were concerned with the relationship between the rightful kingship and the Sovereignty of the Land [seen as the goddess of the Land, or the Land itself]. In order for there to exist a fertile kingdom, there must likewise be a vital and fecund relationship between the Land and the mortal king. In Celtic myth, this relationship, for whatever reason, has been disrupted. It becomes the Hero's task to restore this relationship (Godwin, pp.14-16). The Green Knight of the Arthurian Legends rides into King Arthur's court demanding that one of his Knights should strike his head from his shoulders. The Green Knight personifies the ancient sacrificed year god, or Dying God, and the deeper mysteries of life and death. However often the Green Knight lost his head, he could never die. Gawain responded to his challenge and beheads the Green Knight, who picks up his head and leaves the court. Gawain was instructed to wait one year, and then to go through the initiation of overcoming his fear of death at the hands of the Green Knight (Banns and Cashford, p.412; Campbell, 1988, p.152).

The Grail Legends follow similar themes to the myths previously outlined, including the lameness of the Fisher King, and the Green Knight, which was only briefly touched upon. Unfortunately, a detailed study of these myths are beyond the scope of this study.

In conclusion, the cycles of Birth, Death, and Rebirth, in relation to vegetation as well as to the 'religious experience' as portrayed by the Goddesses and Gods of ancient myths and religions, are seen to be of universal significance. To reiterate, the parable that, from death comes life, 'Verily verily, I say to you, Except a corn of wheat fall to the ground and die, it abideth alone; but if it die, it bringeth forth much fruit.', (John 12:24).

Section 2: Honey.

The Vedas speak of honey as the food of the Spirits. In Germanic myths, the fermented honey drink mead was drunk by the gods and heroes of Valhalla. The Greeks connected honey with chthonian rites [that is, of the earth, Underworld, or rites of death and rebirth], and corpses were often embalmed and preserved in honey, in the belief that it was a resurrection fluid.

Honey was considered a mythical food because, among other reasons, it was extracted by innocent bees, from innocent blossoms that were touched, but not destroyed. 'Even as a bee gathers honey from a flower and departs without injuring the flower or its colour or scent, so let a sage dwell in his village.' (*The Dhammapada*, IV: 6, in Radhakrishnan and Moore, Ed., p.296)

As Maeterlinck so well expresses, 'This secret spring comes from the beautiful honey, itself but a ray of heat transformed, that returns now to its first condition. It circulates in the hive like generous blood' (p.294), that is, as liquefied light.

Bernard of Clairvaux believed that the bee signified the Holy Ghost. Christian art in the Middle Ages depicted the Virgin Mary as a Beehive, who carried Jesus in her womb of sweetness. From the passage below, it would appear that the symbol of the Bee forms an integral part of Christian doctrine; 'The Holie Church of Rome herself doth compare the incomprehensible generation of the Sonne of God from His Father, together with His birth out of the pure and undefiled Virgine Marie, unto the Bees which were in verie deede a great blasphemie, if the bees were not of so great valour and virtue,'[or value and dignity], (*'Beehive and the Romish Church':* *Hones' Ancient Mysteries Described,* p.283, cited in Jennings, p.52).

The Life of the Bee

'The Life of the Bee', by French philosopher and apiarist Maurice Maeterlinck, is a mesmerising, poetic exploration of the honey bee. Maeterlinck writes that the beehive is rigidly structured and determined by what can be termed the Spirit of the Hive. The bee colony consists of the worker bees: those who forage and collect pollen; those who clean or guard the hive; those who tend and feed the bee larvae; and those who protect the Queen Bee. The worker bees are capable, under extreme duress, of producing a few male eggs if the Queen Bee is suddenly killed or otherwise unable to reproduce. They remain for the majority, however, as *neuters,* having as such no gender. The male bees or drones, who greatly outnumber the worker bees, do not work, visit no flowers, and are forever drunk on the honey which they take no part in producing. They appear to have but one purpose, that being to unite with the Virgin Princess, and only a few ever accomplish this task.

The construction of the beehive is a living work of art. The bees whose job it is to build the inner hive will climb to the top of the hive [be it in a tree hollow, or a man-made structure]. From there they form a thick, triangular curtain or inverted cone, 'whose apex attains the summit of the cupola, and whose widening base descends to one half or two thirds of the entire height of the hive', (Maeterlinck, p. 146). Each bee, in turn, will move to the top of the dome and dislodge her waxen scales, creating symmetrically perfect hexagonal cells. The bees produce their wax from honey, the 'soul of the honey, that itself is the spirit of flowers'. Eventually they succeed in creating a conical or, 'inverted city, hanging down from the sky, and not rising from the bosom of earth like a city of men' (Maeterlinck, pp.147, 149).

The Queen Bee, though born of the same egg, is at least two times larger than the worker bees; lays 2000 to 2500 eggs per day; and lives for six to eight years, while the worker bees live only 30 to 40 days. For the first two days of life, all bee larvae feed on milk consisting of pollen and Royal Jelly, a substance secreted by the nursery bees from glands on top of their heads. After two days, only the Queen Bee is fed Royal Jelly, and it is this alone which is responsible for creating her. The Queen Bee is equipped with a curved scimitar [attributed to Saturn-Binah], whilst the worker bees have only straight 'stings' or appendages. They will use their stings to massacre the entire male population of the hive once the Queen has been successfully impregnated during her nuptial flight.

Although virgin, the future Queen Bee is not sterile. Parthenogenesis, a 'precaution' of Nature, allows her to produce male offspring without the need of fertilisation by the male, [see Atu IX, The Hermit, who too is endowed with the gift of Parthenogenesis (Crowley, 777, Table XLV, p. 12]. It is only after her 'nuptial flight', where she unites with her chosen lover, that she is capable of producing female offspring. During her nuptial flight, the virgin Queen unites with, and tears from her lover, his penis [that is, castrates him] along with his entrails and sacs containing his seminal fluid, thereby killing him. She keeps the seminal fluid, which contains spermatozoa, alive in the spermatheca gland, under her ovaries.

'Around the virgin queen, and dwelling with her in the hive, are hundreds of exuberant males, forever drunk on honey; the sole reason for their existence being one act of love. But, notwithstanding the 'incessant contact of two desires that elsewhere invariably triumph over every obstacle, the union never takes place in the hive…While she lives in their midst the lovers about her know not what she is. They seek her in space, in the remote depths of the horizon…One might almost believe that those wonderful eyes of theirs, which cover their head as though with a glittering helmet, do not recognise or desire her save when she soars in the blue…; and from these ten thousand, one alone will be the chosen, for the unique kiss of an instant that shall

wed him to death no less than to happiness'
(Maeterlinck, pp.244-245).

'...for the male has given her all he possesses, and
much more than she requires. She retains only, in her
spermatheca, the seminal liquid where millions of
germs are floating which, until her last day, will issue
one by one, as the eggs pass by, and in the obscurity of
her body accomplish the mysterious union of the male
and female element...Through a curious inversion, it is
she who furnishes the male principle, and the drone
who provides the female.' (Maeterlinck, p 263).

Bees — Symbols Of Regeneration

Bees and butterflies belong together as images of the
Great Goddess of Regeneration. This was, in part, due
to the ancient belief that bees arose out of the dead
carcass of a bull, and from there on associating the
Goddess with bees and bulls, as well as the moon, whose
crescent shape found reference in the horns of the bull
(Baring and Cashford, p. 118).

In the 3rd century A.D., Porphry writes of the Goddess
of Greece:

'The ancients gave the name of Melissae [bees] to the
priestesses of Demeter who were initiates of the
chthonian goddess; the name Melitodes to Kore
herself: the Moon [Artemis] too, whose province it was

to bring to the birth, they called Mellisa, because the
moon being a bull and its ascension the bull, bees are
begotten of bulls. And souls that pass to earth are bull
begotten,' (cited in Baring and Cashford, p. 118).

In the Biblical *Book of Judges* (14:5-9), we read the story
of Samson and the Lion[10]. In a letter from Crowley to
Grady McMurtry, this story is discussed: 'Interesting
about bees. I cannot be sure whether you refer to the

---

[10] Deborah [chapters 4 and 5 of the Book of Judges], was a
successful military leader, a law giver, and was described as a
Prophetess. According to some accounts, Deborah was called a
Judge, 'Prophet' in the Bible to disguise the fact that she was one of
the remaining vestiges of the governing Matriarchs of Israel, [see
Judges 4:4]. It is speculated that, since Deborah means 'bee' in
Hebrew, that she was previously associated with the Bee Goddess of
Mycenaean Crete, or Anatolia [that is, with Ashera, Aphrodite,
Demeter...] (Sobol, p.138). Samson is a rather enigmatic figure.
Samson, in Hebrew, is spelt shin-mem-shin-vau- nun final, which
adds to 1346; 1+3+4+6=14. Samson, in the Chaldean language, is
spelt shin-mem-shin-yod (Wigram, ed.,p.43), which adds to 650;
6+5+0=11. According to the Sepher Sephiroth (Crowley, in 777,
p.2.), both numbers 11 and 14 correspond in meaning to 'gold',
[and interestingly, 'gold' is attributed to 11 in the Chaldean
language, and to 14 in the Hebrew]— the 'gold' is of the Sun or
Son. SaM enumerates to 340, which means 'lion' (*Sepher Sephiroth*,
p.37); while SaMS- Shemesh [Hebrew for Sun] enumerates to 640,
which can mean 'The Cup of Consolidations' - the Holy Grail, as
well as 'the Sphere of Tiphareth, The Sun; Palm of the Hand; and
Palm Tree', (Sepher Sephiroth, p.56). ON enumerates as
70+50=120, which is a name of GOD, (Sepher Sephiroth, p.18). In
this way, Samson is the 'Son of the Sun'.

9th Degree story in the Book of Judges where Samson killed a lion with the jawbone of an ass, he returns the next day and finds himself hungry; going to the carcass of the lion, he finds that the bees have swarmed in it, and gets their honey. This is only one of several stories in the Old Testament where the 9th Degree is definitely advertised.' (Letter from Crowley to McMurtry, April 10th, 1946.)

The story continues with Samson putting forth a riddle to the Philistines of Timnath during a seven day feast for his new bride, herself a Philistine. He said of the eater came forth meat, and out of the strong came forth sweetness. And could not in three days expound the riddle, (Judges 14:14). On the seventh day, the Philistines ordered Samson's wife to entice her husband to disclose the answer to the riddle, which she finally succeeded in doing. Before the sun went down on the seventh day, the men of the city answered Samson, 'What is sweeter than honey? and what is stronger than a lion? And he said unto them, if ye had not plowed with my heifer, ye had not found out my riddle', (Judges 14:18). This mysterious 'riddle' was interpreted by Crowley in a sexual and alchemical sense.

Bulls and Bees

There is an extraordinary likeness between the female uterus and Fallopian tubes, and the head and horns of the bull. This similarity, according to Cameron (pp.4-5), was likely to have been discovered with the development of the excarnation process of burial [the removal of the flesh from bones prior to burial, perhaps for ritual embalming]. The Fallopian tubes normally turn downwards in relation to the uterus. However, when the body is lying flat, as would be the case during the excarnation process, they would turn upwards, thereby revealing their similarity to the crescent horns of the bull, as well as the crescent moon. Further, both woman and the bison have a normal pregnancy spanning nine months, which could also account for their association. From this evidence, it can be understood how the prominence of the bull, in this symbolic system of regeneration, comes not from its strength and masculinity, as in the Indo-European myths, but rather from the similarity between the bull's head and horns, and the generative organs of the female (Gimbutas, p.266).

The Bee Goddess

The earliest known image of the Bee Goddess was discovered in Western Ukraine, dating from 3700-3500 B.C. Upon a bull's head carved from bone, was scratched the stylised silhouette of the 'hourglass' or 'double-axe' shaped Bee Goddess (Gimbutas, p.270). The double-axe symbol of the Bronze Age was, according to Gimbutas (p.321), an hourglass-shaped goddess of Death and Regeneration, symbolising the double-wings of the butterfly or bee, and embodying the principle of transformation.

The ancient Greeks understood the principle of life from death through the image of Aphrodite as a Bee. The image appears to have been inherited from the Bee Goddess of Crete, who was linked to the art of soothsaying or prophecy, as were the bee-maidens or Thriae who taught prophecy to Apollo.[11].

The tombs at Mycenae were shaped as 'beehives', as was the 'Omphalos' at Delphi, where Apollo ruled with his oracular priestess, the Pythia, who was also called the Delphic Bee. Harrison (p.398-400), believes that the Omphalos was the grave mound of the sacred python, or Snake of Delphi, which Apollo slew.

The symbol of Aphrodite at the Sicilian Mount Eryx was a golden honeycomb. Her priestesses, as were the

---

[11] In the Greek Homeric Hymn to Hermes [8th Cent. B.C.], Apollo speaks of three female seers or 'Fates', as three bee-maidens who had nursed him as a child, and were to be his gift to Hermes. [Hermes, on the day of his birth, stole Apollo's cattle. As recompense, Hermes gave Apollo the lyre he had just crafted. However, Apollo was still more enchanted by Hermes windpipes, that he offered to trade his golden herdsman's staff for the pipes. Hermes accepted, but only on the condition that he, too be instructed in the art of prophecy (Guirand, p. 123)] In relation to the 'Thriae' or Fates: the Greek word for fete [the power supposed to predetermine events; the goddess of destiny], death, and goddess of death, is e kef; the word for heart and breast is 'to kef; while the word for honeycomb is 'to kerion'. The common root, ker, unites the images of honeycomb, goddess, death, fete, and the heart, which is made comprehensible only when it is remembered that the goddess was once imagined as a bee (Baring and Cashford p. 119).

priestesses of Demeter, were known as 'Mellisae', or Queen Bees (Graves, 1955, Vol.l, p.72).

Honeycomb is mentioned in the Biblical passage of 1 Samuel 14:25-29 and 43- 44, where Jonathan destroys the Philistine garrison. After the battle, there was discovered 'honey upon the ground'. Jonathan, not having heard that his father Saul had forbidden them to eat until evening, stuck the end of his rod into the honeycomb, and then put his hand to his mouth, 'and his eyes were enlightened'. His father, on hearing that he had tasted of the honey, condemned him to die. However, he was rescued by his comrades. The sexual symbolism is quite evident. The 'rod' appears to symbolise the penis, whilst the 'honeycomb' would relate to the Sanctuary of Aphrodite, being the vagina, with its secretions oozing out in a similar way to honey dripping from the honeycomb.

In The Greek Qabalah the number 535 represents both the word 'vagina' and 'comb'. The meaning of the word 'comb' can easily be extended to include 'honeycomb', which thereby links the two. As well, Crowley (*The Gospel according to St. Bernard Shaw*, Ed. King, p.229), talks about perfecting the method of extracting most efficiently, 'the honey from this Comb'. This is a reference to a Sex Magick Operation, to which no further comment will be made. It is included only to illustrate the hidden meaning of the 'honeycomb' mentioned in the above Biblical passage.

With the bee, or hymenoptera ['veil-winged'], further reference is made to the 'hymen of the female anatomy, that being the thin veil of membrane covering the vaginal orifice. The hymen or veil was said to cover the inner sanctum of the Goddess Aphrodites temple. Defloration [deflowering], was the ritual penetration of, or 'renting of the veil', conducted under the 'hymeneal rules' of the Goddess Hymen, thought to be an aspect of Aphrodite, who was the patroness of the wedding night and honeymoon. It was understood that the honeymoon spanned at least one lunar month, which would include one menstrual period; this was believed to be the real source of what was euphemistically termed 'moon honey' (Graves, 1975, p. 166).

[According to Hindu belief, the bridegroom comes into contact with the 'source of life' by copulating with his bride during her menstruation. It is said that Siva was helpless unless his phallus was 'baptised in blood' from the vagina of Kali-Maja in the Tantric rites of Maharutti (Edwards, p.50).]

Fleurs-de-Lys as Bees

Fleurs-de-Lys; 'Lucifers' [Light Bringers]; Lucifer; Lisses; Luces; Lucy; Lily; Lux [Light]; Bees; Scarabs; Scara-bees; Bourbon Lilies; Imperial Bees of Charlemange, and of Napoleon the First and Third, (Jennings, p.47).

According to Jennings (p. 50), the lilies on the French
Coat of Arms were originally represented as 'insects'
spotted on the blue field, or 'sky'. The motto placed
under the lilies reads:

> *Lilia non laborant, neque nent.*
> 'Lilia non laborant' [the lilies do not toil, like bees],
> neque nent' [neither do they spin, like spiders].
>
> 'Consider the lilies of the field, how they grow; they
> toil not, neither do they spin: yet I say to you, that even
> Solomon, in all his glory was not arrayed', [not exalted,
> dignified], 'like one of these.', (Matt. 6:28).

Jennings (p.51), states that the Fleur-de-Lys is the Lotus
[water rose], the flower sacred to the Lux or Sun. The
three lotuses or 'lisses' were the French Coat of Arms
and, according to Jennings (pp. 51,263), also represented
the three persons of the triple generative power; the
triple powers of Nature – the producer, the means of
production, and that which produces; and the Three
Nails of the Passion [the three nails of Christ on the
Cross], which is reminiscent of the Crux Ansata, the
Hebrew letter Tau, and the triple- Tau of the
Freemasons.

Crowley on Bees

Crowley makes allusions to bees and the Fleur-de-Lys, however veiled, in the *Book of Thoth* and *Liber 418, The Vision and the Voice*, and suggests a Fleur-de-Lys design on the crimson altar cloth specified for the Gnostic Mass (*Liber XV*). Bees and honey are referred to in the 21st Aethyr, where he ascribes the Bee to Binah (*Liber 418*, p.78). Bees also feature on Atu III, The Empress; Atu IV, The Emperor; the alchemical cards Atu VI, The Lovers and Atu XIV, Art; as well as Atu XVII, The Star. According to Frieda Harris (1942), the inclusion of the bees on these cards was probably referring to the bees of the Secret Doctrines of the Indian Upanishads[12].

In discussing Atu III, The Empress, Crowley writes, 'beneath the throne is a floor of tapestry, embroidered with fleurs-de-lys and fishes; they seem to be adoring the Secret Rose, which is indicated at the base of the throne... In this card all symbols are cognate...There is here no contradiction: such opposition as there seems to be is only the opposition necessary to balance' (*Book of Thoth*, p.76). Crowley later identifies the Fleur de-Lys with the phallus, which would appear to contradict

---

[12] As the bees, my dear, prepare honey by collecting the essences of different trees and reducing the essence to a unity, [...] as they are not able to discriminate 'I am the essence of this tree', 'I am the essence of that tree'- even so, indeed, my dear, all creatures here, though they reach Being, know not 'We have reached Being'[...] 'That which is the finest essence- this whole world has that as itself. That is Reality. Thou art that [Tat tvam Asi], Svetaketu...', (Radhaknshnan and Moore, Eds., pp.68-69).

what we already know of the Fleur de-Lys, having emerged from the Bee, attributed to Binah (*Book of Thoth* p.277). The Fleur-de-Lys on the Empress card are drawn with 'fish'. Since, as Crowley states, all symbols are cognate, it would follow that the fish and the Fleur-de-Lys are related, and that both symbols must contain within both masculine and feminine principles, [as is necessary above the Abyss, where each idea must be balanced by its opposite].

The symbol of the Fish is one of the oldest symbols of Christ. The fish is attributed to Atu XIII Death, and is also the Hebrew letter Nun. Nun is attributed to the zodiacal sign of Scorpio, ruled by Mars. The sign of Scorpio is divided into three parts; the lowest is symbolised by the Scorpion; the middle is symbolised by the Serpent; whilst the highest aspect is the Eagle, representing exaltation beyond solid matter.

The Serpent is the Lord of Life and Death, the principle symbol of male generative energy. Crowley notes that the Serpent of the Garden of Eden, NChSh, has a value of 358, as does MShICh, the Messiah. Accordingly, the Serpent, in the Secret Doctrine, is the Redeemer or Messiah. 'The Fish is identical in essence with the Serpent; for Fish = NVN = Scorpio = Serpent, but Fish is also the Vesica, or Womb, and Christ, and so forth. This symbol resumes the Whole Secret Doctrine' (*Book of*

Thoth, p.100)[13]. In this way, the Fish and the Serpent are the same; so too the Fishes and the Fleur-de-Lys; the Bees and the Serpents [see the 'marriage' of the Bees and Serpents depicted on Atu XIV, Art].

The Serpent is also identified with the Goddess Kundalini, the coiled Serpent at the base of the spine who must unite with her Lord Siva in the cranium[14]. The Eye of Horus [see earlier notes] is identified with the Eye of Siva in Atu XVI, The Tower (*Book of Thoth*, p.108). These represent both the Phallic Eye and the Third Eye or Ajna Chakra [and the relationship between the two]. In his comments to the 2nd Aethyr, Crowley identifies the 'Mark of the Beast' to the Ajna Chakra,

---

[13] Qoph-100; the 'back of the head'- the cerebellum, where the creative or reproductive force is primarily situated. Qoph is represented by Atu XVII, The Moon, which is attributed to Pisces, symbolic of the positive and negative currents of fluidic energy – the male ichthus or pesce, and the female vesica seeking respectively 'the anode and kathode'. The number 100 mystically indicates the magical formula of the Universe (Crowley, Book 4, p.174).

[14] Campbell (1987, p.164), notes that two spiritual channels [the ida and pingala] on either side of the central channel of the spine [the susumna, which is compressed at the base by kundalini, the magical power, a sleeping serpent, (Crowley, Book 4, p.76), are called the lunar and solar Channels. He goes on to identify their relationship to the centre or susumna, with the twin serpents entwined about the staff of Hermes [the Caduceus]. In this way, therefore, the Serpent contains within itself both the masculine and feminine principles.

the 'Beast' being the 'Lord of the City of the Pyramids', or Binah (*Liber 418*, p.225). Whilst the implications here become too involved for this study, it can be noted that the Serpents dual function as Lord of Life and Death, can be taken as sexual and yogic, which correlate to the magical and mystical, and the masculine and feminine. These are all represented in the Fleur-de-Lys.

Binah, or the City of the Pyramids, can be related to the 'Beehive'. The bees collect the various essences or pollen from the many different flowers to make honey. As quoted earlier, 'the bees...prepare honey by collecting the essences of different trees and reducing the essence to a unity.' This pollen could be seen as both the 'Blood of the Saints' of Thelemic Mysticism, or the 'sperm', or 'life of the race' of the regenerative principle. This relates the hive to the Grail and to the womb-tomb[15]. The giving of the last drop of one's blood to the 'Cup of Babalon' is like the giving of pollen to the hive of the Queen Bee. The gathering of the Many [or two] essences— or pollen, into the Cup or hive, is the mystical formula of Two to One, or 210, the Greek gematria for NOX, called 'the Mystical Night of PAN' (refer to Crowley, *The Book of Lies*, Comment to Chapter 1, p. 13). As Duquette notes of the traditional 'IO PAN invocation, the I [the lingam] joined with O

---

[15] And in one womb, wherein all men are begotten and wherein they shall rest, Mystery of Mystery, in Her name Babalon', (Crowley, *Liber XV*, The Creed, in Book 4, p.573).

[the yoni] is a simple yet explicit invitation for the God who transcends duality to couple with the devotee', (*Magick of Thelema*, p.85). This annihilation is what Crowley called 'charioteering'— the orgasm of sex and /or mystical attainment. The success of the race through reproduction and/or through creative genius. The honey can be seen as representing this union of the individual life and the universal life at a particular stage in the process.

Another approach is to consider the Bees in relation to Hermes [Mercury] as the 'Psychopomp' – The Conductor of the Souls through the lower regions or the Underworld. Neoplatonic philosophers called Hermes the 'Logos'— the Word of God made flesh; the 'God within'; the creative spark [See Atu IX, The Hermit, which is attributed to Virgo, and exalted in Mercury). From this position, the honey or 'essence' could be identified with 'semen', which can be thought of as the 'soul'. This reiterates the point previous made by Crowley (Comment to Chapter 8, The Book of Lies, p. 27), for 'the whole race consciousness, that which is omnipotent, omniscient, omnipresent is hidden therein'. The soul is therefore guided by the bees, or in another way 'the soul is the bee' [the word Psyche in Greek means both soul and butterfly, which is consonant with the bee in Greek and Cretan myth].

Through the relationship of the soul to semen, we could further imagine the 'soul' personifying the Fleur-de-Lys, as a stylised glyph of the phallus and testes. Similarly, the soul as the 'psyche would find the Fleur-de-Lys being analogous with the feminine bee of Binah. This idea is best expressed by Crowley in his comments on Atu VIII, Adjustment (*Book of Thoth*, p.86). Adjustment holds the Magic Sword or Phallus in both hands, and the Balance or Testes [the Judex and Testes of Final Judgment] upon her shoulders. She is the 'Woman Satisfied', the Justice of Nature, or Balance of Opposites.

Fleur-de-lys. Symbolic Representations

There are numerous images that would appear cognate in semblance to the Fleur-de-Lys. The Double-Headed Eagle of the Freemasons and alchemists is an excellent example. In Roman art, the ascending eagle bears the souls of the dead to Heaven after cremation of the body (Strong, p. 182). The Eagle in the Middle Ages became a symbol rebirth and baptism, as well as of Christ and His ascension to Heaven. The alchemical depiction of the Christos [the anointed one], crucified upon the Double-Headed Eagle is particularly evocative. It portrays the 'red death marriage in Heaven', one of the final stages of the Great Work of the alchemists. (See Fig. 3)

*Figure 3: A bleeding Christ splitting in the sign
of the double eagle on the cross of death*

In Minoan Crete, the 'Double-Axe' [representing the bee or butterfly] is often depicted between the horns of the bull, as are columns of vegetation and flowers. Bovine sculptures have been discovered with a hole between the horns of the bull, and, as evidenced by Mycenaean art, fresh vegetation and flowers have been placed there to exemplify the 'life power' inherent in the bull (Gimbutas, p.270). Consequently, the bovine horns may be seen to characterize the feminine principle of regeneration – that of the Dying Gods [We can also see the horns as representing the masculine principle, with the 'fountain' of flowery growth being feminine in nature.]

Another symbol deserving mention is the hand gesture known as 'the Fig', the Ficus, or Il Fico [Latin]. The gesture is formed by thrusting the thumb between index and middle fingers of the closed hand. This gesture has been variously understood in Mediterranean countries as a defence against the 'Evil-Eye' [the eye of the phallus?]; an obscene insult; and as a sexual symbol. It is this gesture that the Priest and the Deacon are required to use whilst officiating in the Gnostic Catholic Mass The Ficus can be seen variously as the male genitals [phallus and testes, often used as a symbol to personify Priapus]; the female and male genitals in union; or as the female genitals, which may be used as a defence against the 'evil phallic eye' (Dumezil, Vol.1 p.367). It follows, therefore, that the gesture of the Ficus can be thought of as glyph of the Fleur-de-Lys, wherein both masculine and feminine principals exist.

In summary, Honey, the essence of the flowers which is produced by the bees deep inside their dim, obscured hives, along with the bees themselves, have been portrayed in myths as being of supreme mystical importance. The purpose of this study was to illustrate the logical [though somewhat diverse] transformations undertaken by the ancient bee symbol as the Bee Goddess, through to the Fleur-de-Lys, with its manifold Christian, Hermetic and Thelemic attributions.

Section 3: Wine

Thick leavings of red wine and fresh blood are both ingredients in the Cakes of Light. Whilst they are obviously quite different fluids, much of the symbolism and mystery ascribed to them are interchangeable. For this reason, reference will be made variously to wine and/or blood in the following section on wine, and later in the section concerned with blood. The purpose of the following section is to outline the myth of Dionysus, the God of the Vine and Vegetation, and to then explore the various images of wine as depicted in religious rituals, in alchemical literature, as well as in the writings of Crowley.

Dionysus

Dionysus is also known as Bacchus, Iaccus, Dionysus-Zagreus, Sabazios, Liber Pater, and Bassarius. Dionysus was the god of the Vine and Vegetation; Ecstasy; Intoxication and Madness; and Death and Resurrection. Crowley thought Dionysus was probably an ecstatic 'from the East', whose Rites formed the Central Mystery of the Christian religion. He therefore identified Dionysus with Christ (*Book 4*, p. 147).

Numerous versions of the Dionysus myth, however, he can be seen to appear in three successive forms as: Phanes-Dionysus, the bisexual God of Light, Dionysus-Zagreus; and Dionysus, the Dithyrambos, or the Twice Born.

[The following is paraphrased from *Red Flame*, Issue No. 2, pp. 127–128, and Baring and Cashford, pp.305–310.] Phanes, the 'Revealer', created a daughter, Nyx [Night], with whom he begot Gaia [Earth] and Uranus [Heaven], Gaia and Uranus begot the Fates, the Centimani, the Cyclops, and the Titans, whose leader was Cronus [Saturn]. In the revolt of the Titans against Uranus, Cronus succeeded in becoming the Ruler of the World. He subsequently begot the remaining gods, whose ruler was Zeus. Zeus assumed the rulership of the world by 'swallowing' his great grandfather Phanes, thereby assimilating his power. Zeus then took the form of a Serpent and begot Dionysus' Zagreus, the 'Horned Child', upon Persephone. Persephone was the daughter of Zeus by Demeter, though some versions hold that Demeter was the mother of Zeus. Dionysus was therefore the fruit of the marriage of Heaven [Zeus] and Earth [Persephone or Demeter], (Crowley, *Book of Thoth*, p.65).

Zeus bequeathed rulership of the World and the Underworld to Dionysus-Zagreus whilst he was still a child. This angered the Titans and Zeus's wife Hera, who, according to one account, bribed the Kouretes, the armed, orgiastic dancers and guardians of the child Dionysus, into distracting him with toys and crystal mirrors (Harrison, p.23). Meanwhile, the Titans concealed themselves with a covering of white gypsum, and then crept up and tore Dionysus-Zagreus to pieces, devouring his body (Harrison, p.17). Zeus was enraged, and destroyed the Titans with his Thunderbolts. From their ashes, commingled with those of Dionysus-Zagreus, the human race was born. Athena, the Goddess of Wisdom, had witnessed the murder, and had managed to rescue the child's heart, which she immediately brought to Zeus. He consumed the heart, and then went to Semele,[16] the daughter of Cadmus, King of Thebes, and begot upon her the 'third' Dionysus.

Hera, jealous of Zeus' union with Semele, disguises herself as Semele's nurse, and persuades her to make Zeus show himself to her in all his Olympian glory. Though he tried to resist her demands, he finally conceded. Semele was unable to endure his dazzling brilliance, and was consumed by the flames which emanated from him. Other versions hold that Semele was still carrying the child Dionysus, and that he was rescued by Zeus and sewn into his thigh [that is, his phallus], where he remained hidden until puberty.

---

[16] According to Puhvel (pp.136-137), Semele is the Thracian word for Earth, and therefore stands for a non-Greek deity. Puhvel speculates that this might provide a glimpse of lost Thracian myth, where the Earth Goddess is struck and consumed by the lightning of the Heaven God in the course of bearing Sabazios, the Thracian name for Dionysus. Sabazios literally means 'selfbeing' and 'free', just as Liber Pater [the Roman representation of Dionysus], means 'free' and 'unrestricted'.

Dionysus is known as the Dithyrambos, the 'twice-born', or 'he-of-the-Two-fold-Door', as he had been born twice, once as Dionysus-Zagreus, and again as Dionysus. Harrison (pp.33-35) speculates that the 'immortal fire' which consumed Semele, may reflect an initiation rite of purgation, or a 'Baptism by Fire' for the child Dionysus. Having been born of Semele, he endured a 'Baptism by Fire' at the hands of his father, Zeus, and was given a second 'divine' birth from the Phallus of Zeus, in order that he might be free of the mortality of his mother.[17]

Zeus entrusted the child Dionysus to the care of the Nymphs at Nysa, who nurtured him through his childhood. When fully grown, he learned the methods of cultivating the vine, and wine making. Hera continued to seek out Dionysus, eventually striking him

---

[17] The theme of initiation or 'baptism by fire' runs through many myths. Isis, whilst mourning and searching for Osiris, discovers that his sarcophagus has been imbedded in a tree trunk which stood in the Palace of Queen Arstarte of Byblos. She is made the nurse of Queen Asarte's child. She offers the child her finger to suck instead of her breast, and at night places him in a fire to burn away all that was mortal. One night, the Queen saw her child in the flames and screamed, and from that moment deprived her child of the treasures of immortality (Baring and Cashford, p.229). This story occurs again with Demeter, as she searches the earth for her daughter Persephone. She attempts to render the child Demophoon [a name which means 'Slayer of the People'], immortal by placing him amongst the flames, but is again prevented from doing so when the child's mother intervenes (Baring and Cashford, p.369).

down with madness, causing him to aimlessly wander the earth. In some versions, Dionysus rides an ass, his sacred animal, which associates him with Priapus [Priapus is said to be the son of Aphrodite and Dionysus, or variously, Adonis, Hermes, Pan, Zeus]. His riding of the ass identifies him with Christ, who entered Jerusalem on Palm Sunday upon an ass.

In Phrygia, he was cured of his madness by the Great Mother Goddess his grandmother, Rhea [known also as Cybele or Magna Mater], who initiated him into her mysteries. He then set out to teach viticulture, and to establish his cult amongst the peoples of the world. He was accompanied by a retinue of female maenads, male satyrs, and Silenus, his fat, aged, drunken companion and wise teacher.

The worship of Dionysus included the drinking of wine [the vine being sacred to Dionysus], and the consumption of the raw flesh of sacrificial animals, usually fawns, goats, or bulls. In this ritual, known as the 'Omophagia, the animals were torn apart and consumed in commemoration of the dismemberment of Dionysus–Zagreus at the hands of the Titans. According to Harrison (pp. 156-157), the animals were not killed to appease the gods, but to 'become god', that is, to become 'Dionysus'. The animals used in the Omophagia were those sacred to Dionysus, so that they were seen to partake of his nature. They were also ritually killed in the same way that Dionysus–Zagreus had been killed. Therefore, through this ritual of 'sympathetic magic', the animals became the God Dionysus. When the worshippers consumed the raw flesh and wine, they consumed the Body and Blood of Dionysus.

Fermentation Of Wine

We are told to use 'thick leavings of red wine' for making the Cakes of Light. Crowley asserts in The Law Is For All (p.284), that: 'leavings: the 'beeswing' of port should be good'. 'Beeswing' is defined as, 'the second crust, consisting of shiny filmy scales of tartar, forming in port and some other wines after long keeping' (The Shorter Oxford English Dictionary, Vol 1, p.174).

Wine is created through the process of fermentation or 'putrefaction'. Putrefaction is the term given by the alchemists to a series of chemical changes which develop the final form of 'life' from the 'original latent seed in the Orphic Egg' (Crowley, Book of Thoth, p.99). When a substance, especially a liquid, is allowed to ferment or decay, it will issue forth bubbles of gas, known as effervescence, as well as generate heat due to the chemical reactions occurring. This results in alterations to the properties of the substance. For example, grape juice, which is sweet, undergoes fermentation to become wine, which has a dry, sour taste, and an intoxicating quality.

Putrefaction Images In The Thoth Tarot

The Hermit, Atu IX, symbolises Fertility in its most exalted sense. Virgo [attributed to the Hermit], represents the most receptive, feminine form of Earth, and is said to 'form the Crust over Hades' (Crowley, *Book of Thoth*, p.89). The Hermit recalls the myth of Persephone, who abided for one third of every year with her husband Hades, Lord of the Underworld. During this time [that is late autumn and winter], her mother Demeter, due to her great sorrow at losing her daughter, caused the earth to remain barren. The fields of the earth are left to decay, thereby fertilising the soil for the next season's crops, whilst the fruit of the vine is allowed to ferment, giving birth to wine.

Death, Atu XIII, is attributed to the Hebrew letter Nun, which means fish – the symbol of life beneath the waters, and illustrates the concept of putrefaction. Three essential aspects or stages of putrefaction are expressed within the Scorpion, Serpent and Eagle, which are depicted on the Death card, and which together expound the spiritual formula of incarnation (Crowley, *Book 4*, p. 174). The Scorpion who, in a desperate situation, will commit suicide by biting its poisoned tail, represents putrefaction in its lowest aspect. 'The Serpent is the Secret Nature of Man, that is Life Death, and maketh his way through the Generations in Silence' (Crowley, *Liber Aleph*, p. 157). The Serpent is ascribed to Atu XIII, as well as to Atu XI, Lust. The Lust card is

attributed to the sign of Leo, and to the Hebrew letter
Teth, which means Serpent - 'the Serpent and the Lion'.
The Serpent of Atu XIII characterises the masculine
energy [while Atu XI embodies the unbridled Lust of
Babalon], and describes the solution [dissolving] or
dissolution [decomposition] stages of the putrefaction
process. This therefore links Death to Lust, and likewise
unites the marriage of the Lion and the Serpent to Atu
XII— The Hanged Man [attributed to the Hebrew letter
Mem, which means Water], which alludes to the
Sacrament of the Holy Grail.[18]

The Eagle symbolises exaltation above solid or earthy
matter. During certain chemical reactions, the purest,
most subtle elements, are observed to be given off as gas
or vapour, or as effervescence [that is, as bubbles]. In
outlining the 'Dance of Death', where new life emerges
from the dead and decaying, Crowley writes,

---

[18] Crowley explains, concerning the 'Bloody Sacrifice', that warm
blooded animals should be used, with the exception of the Serpent
[it should be noted that snakes, as we know them, are cold
blooded], and the magical beetles of *Liber AL vel Legis* III:25. The
Serpent is not 'really' killed. It is seethed [that is, boiled or
fermented], in an 'appropriate vessel', from where it will issue in
due season, refreshed and modified, yet still essentially itself. This
involves the transmission of life and wisdom from a vehicle which
has 'fulfilled its formula', to one capable of further extension (Book
4, p.210). The meaning of the above passage is fairly apparent, with
the Serpent, as previously considered, representing the
Spermatozoan, and the 'appropriate vessel' suggesting the female
uterus.

concerning Atu XIII, 'With the sweep of his scythe he creates bubbles in which are beginning to take shape the new forms which he creates in his dance...' (*Book of Thoth*, p.100).

Rising from the Cauldron of Atu XIV – Art or Temperance where the process of putrefaction is taking place is a stream of light which divides into two rainbows. This is significant, in that there is observed, as a result of putrefaction, a 'phenomena of many coloured lights', which may equate with the rainbow (Crowley, *Book of Thoth*, p.103). Crowley suggests using the 'beeswing' of port for the Cakes of Light, which has previously been defined as a 'crust,' comprised of shiny scales of tartar. The 'beeswing' may, accordingly, be the many-coloured, or 'rainbow' coloured scales of the putrefaction process. The Crust of Hades, as with the Crust of the barren, putrefying Earth, and the 'Crust of the Beeswing of port', cloaks the fermenting Wine of Hades, symbolized by Persephone, the 'fermenting Womb of Hades.' The concept is further echoed in: *Visita Interiora Trrae Rectificando Invenies Occultum Lapidem* [Visit the interior parts of the Earth: by Rectification thou shalt find the hidden stone]. Rectification means to purify or refine by repeated distillation. It implies the 'right leading' of the new living substance in the path of the True Will (Crowley, *Book 4*, p.104).

Water And Wine

Wine, as sacred to Dionysus, can be used to invoke ecstasy by intoxication on manifold levels. Many religions, however, make use of unfermented wines, or wine mingled with water- the 'water of life', in their ritual sacraments.

Unfermented wine is used during the Mandaean marriage ceremony of Southern Iraq. The Priest fills a drinking bowl with water collected from a running source. He then places fresh grapes or raisins [symbolic of female fertility] and dates [symbolic of male fertility], into the water, and presses them with his fingers until the water becomes well coloured. According to Drower (p.62), this process may, in a literal sense, 'turn water into wine'. This is a reference to the Biblical story of the wedding at Cana, where Jesus performs the 'miracle' of turning water into wine.[19]

---

[19] Crowley makes mention of the miracle at Cana (*The Gospel according to St. Bernard Shaw*, King, Ed., p. 161). He asserts that Jesus, as 'the Vine' ['I am the true Vine', John 15:1], transmutes the 'rain of Heaven [the water], into the juice of the grape [the wine]. He concludes, that this 'miracle' is identical to what Dionysus, as the Vine, brings about.

Crowley subsequently correlates the Lesser Mystery of the wedding at Cana, where Jesus turned water into wine, with the Greater Mystery of the Last Supper, where He turns the wine into His Blood (*The Gospel according to St. Bernard Shaw*, King, Ed., p.166).

Coptic priests ritually mix sacramental wine with water, although it seems unlikely that this is to reduce the intoxicating quality of the wine. The 'commingling' of the water and wine most likely reflects the 'holy union', or 'sacred marriage' of the female and male principles. These are represented by the goddess and god; Queen and King; Celestial Bride and Celestial Bridegroom; and the union of conception and procreation (Drower, p.68).

In some Gnostic Traditions, it is believed that the water poured into the bowl symbolises fecundation, and that the wine is the blood in the Womb of the virgin Mother. The water can be identified with 'semen', and the wine with the mystery of the Womb. 'When thou sayest, 'water into wine', semen falleth into the womb, for the wine is the blood', (trans, from the Mandaean *Alma rishaia Rba*, cited in Drower, p.68).

The Coptic priests assert that the ritual of commingling was inspired by the Biblical passage John 19:34: 'But one of the soldiers pierced His side with a spear, and immediately blood and water came out.'

Drower maintains that the Melkites, the Greek and Russian Orthodox, as well as the Coptics, recite this verse before the wine is poured into the chalice, and as the water is added, thereby manifesting the Holy Union.

Jung (1984, p. 105) asserts that the mixing of water with wine referred to an ancient custom of not drinking undiluted wine. The mixing of water and wine in the Roman Eucharist, according to Yves, Bishop of Chartres [1116], signified that the 'Divinity' [wine], is mingled with 'humanity' [water]. St. Cyprian, Bishop of Carthage [d.258], believed that the wine referred to Christ, and the water to the congregation as the 'Body of Christ'. St. John Chrysostom [Patriarch of Constantinople, d. 407], postulated that, in drinking the wine, Christ drank His own blood. This concept may be an interpretation in regards to the Biblical verse John 19:34. By the same token, one might also say that Christ eats His own flesh, as with the orgiastic Omophagia of the Dionysian cults, where sacrificial animals were torn to pieces and eaten raw.

Alchemical Wine

The commingling of water and wine; milk and blood; white and red water, wine or tinctures, features prominently in alchemical literature. The alchemist Senior, 1593 (cited in Fabricius, p.24), reveals the following regarding the Alchemical Water: 'Make one water out of two waters...You should have two waters, the one white, the other red...: This is the water in which the powers of whiteness and redness are united.'

Basil Valentine's woodcut engraving (1603, cited in Fabricius, p.78), depicts the mermaid goddess being born out of the Sea, holding her breasts from which issue two streams, whereby She fills the ocean the Water of Life, the Great Sea of Binah with 'milk and also red blood' [The alchemists called her the Siren of the Philosophers' 'born of our deep sea [Maria], who pours milk and blood from her paps.] This can also be viewed as the White and Red tinctures; the Silver and Gold; Lunar and Solar; or Water and Wine [Blood].

Figure 4: A maternal sea of blood and milk

In another way, the 'water of life' may refer to the 'amniotic fluid' of the pregnant uterus — the Salty Sea of Binah. Crowley notes that Mem, the Hebrew letter meaning water, attributed to Atu XII, the Hanged Man, is the amniotic fluid, the 'Flood', wherein is the life-bearing Ark (*Book 4*, p.158, n.l). (see Fig.4.)

The following passage further elucidates the alchemical imagery surrounding the mermaid goddess:

'I am a goddess for beauty and extraction famous, born out of our proper sea which compasseth the whole earth and is ever restless. Out of my breasts I pour forth milk and blood; boil these two till they are turned into silver and gold...Thy parents are the Sun and Moon; in thee there is water and wine, gold also and silver upon earth... Torture the Eagle till she weeps and the Lion become weakened and bleed to death. The blood of this Lion incorporated with the tears of this Eagle is the treasure of the Earth,' (Regardie, p. 251).

In the Hebrew Tetragrammaton [YHVH], the Red Lion represents the Y [Father], while the White Eagle represents the first H [Mother]. The YH are conceived to characterise the two cosmic principles, the two rivers of scarlet blood issuing from the mermaid's breast into the Sea of Life. This passage mentions two substances used in the preparation of the alchemical 'gold': the Serpent or Blood of the Red Lion and Tears or Gluten of the White Eagle. The Serpent is attributed to the V [Son] of Tetragrammaton, while the Gluten is assigned to the H final [Daughter]. The Serpent and Gluten is assigned to the Eagle and the Lion (Regardie, pp. 284-255; this concept will be further explored in Section 5).

Wine in the Thoth Tarot

Atu VI, The Lovers, and Atu XIV, Art or Temperance, [to temper wine with water, which is likewise the dissolving of the Red Lion in the White Eagle], together constitute the comprehensive alchemical maxim: 'Solve et Coagula [Dissolve and Coagulate]. Detailed discussion of the symbolism of the Tarot cards is beyond the scope of this study. However, it is interesting to observe the positions of these two cards upon the Tree of Life. The Lovers follow the path from the Great Salty Sea of Binah through the Abyss to Tiphareth, the Sun, whilst Art unites the Moon of Yesod with the Sun of Tiphareth. We can, in this way, imagine the 'mermaid goddess' being born [or Coagulated] from the Great Sea of Binah [or Amniotic Fluid], from where the two waters, those of Luna and Sol, or Water and Wine, are united [or Dissolved]. Furthermore, Atu XIV, Art, represents the 'Consummation of the Sacred Marriage' which took place in Atu VI, The Lovers. As illustrated, the black and white figures of the King and Queen have become united into a single androgyne figure [which is said to be the goal of the Great Work of the Alchemists]; the Bees and Serpents have made an 'alliance', appearing together on the robe of the androgyne; the Red Lion has become White, while the White Eagle has become Red; and the Lion has exchanged his 'red blood' for the Eagle's 'white gluten', which is consequently being 'mingled' [Solve et Coagula], in the Cauldron (Crowley, *Book of Thoth*, p.102).

Crowley, in his commentary on Atu XII, the Hanged Man, writes of the alchemical nature of the Water and Blood as 'Wine' (*Book of Thoth*, pp.98-99). The 'wine' issuing from the side of Christ upon the Cross was collected by 'the Beloved Disciple and His Virgin Mother Mary' in a cup or chalice, thereafter known as the Holy Grail. This 'sacrament', according to Crowley, is exalted in the Zenith in Cancer, which corresponds with Atu VII, The Chariot. The Chariot, ascribed to the Hebrew letter Cheth, which means 'furnace' [or womb], and 'cup' [or Grail], also numerates in the Hebrew to 418, which is equivalent to the Thelemic Word 'Abrahadabra'— the Great Work. The path of the Chariot on the Tree of Life descends from Binah, through the Abyss of Water [which can be imagined as Blood], to Geburah [attributed to the planet Mars]. In this way, the influence of the Supernals [those sephirah above the Abyss], is enabled to inspire and energise 'Man'. The sole function of the Charioteer is to bear the Holy Grail.

While no conclusive explanation can be given as to what Crowley intended by 'thick leavings of red wine' or 'beeswing of port', various ideas have been examined in this section on wine. An interesting article appeared in the *Magical Link* (Frater Tristan, Vol. 1, No.5, May 1981), concerning the method of producing essential salts and VITRIOL from wine for use in the Cakes of Light. To produce these VITRIOL salts, rub the inside of a chalice [preferably gold plated] with Oil of Abramelin. Place red wine in the chalice, and cover with a cloth. After one lunar cycle, the wine should have evaporated, leaving a thick syrup which will taste both sticky sweet and salty — its true mercurial nature. If this syrup is left for several months, a solid salt wafer [salt of the second earth] will form, being but one aspect of the Secret Stone. This syrup [thick leavings of wine] or salt wafer [the Crust of Hades, or beeswing of port], can be used in the Cakes of Light. However, as mentioned earlier, their proper production is gradually taught in A∴A∴ and O.T.O.

Section 4: Oil And Perfume

Any reasonably concise book on herbs and essential oils should be able to deliver a reasonable account of the attributions ascribed to the essential oils comprising the Oil of Abramelin, an ingredient in the Cakes of Light. This section will instead outline the significance of oil as a 'perfume', and its use for anointing and baptising, and finally, 'oil' as a Biblical and alchemical synonym for 'semen' will be explored.

Oil of Abramelin

'Holy Oil', according to Crowley, is the 'aspiration of the Magician' (*Book 4*, p.60). It consecrates the magician to the performance of the Great Work, and should also be used to consecrate all of the furniture and instruments of the Temple. The Holy Oil, or Oil of Abramelin as it is known, is a compound of four essential oils. Its basis is olive oil, which is attributed to Minerva, the Wisdom of God, or the Logos [the Word of God]. In this are dissolved oil of myrrh, oil of cinnamon, and oil of galangal. Crowley attributes myrrh to Binah, the Great Mother; cinnamon to Tiphareth, the Sun-Son; while galangal represents both Kether and Malkuth, the First and the Last, the One and the Many, for in this mixture of oils, they become One. Abramelin Oil therefore represents the whole Tree of Life, with the essences of the ten Sephiroth being blended into 'the Perfect Gold'.

Oil in Tantric Texts

Numerous references in the Bible, Alchemical, and Tantric texts, as well as in Crowley's writings, are made to oils, ointments, perfumes, and semen. The substances are often said to be used ritually to 'anoint', 'baptise', 'Christen', perfume, and to make holy various objects [for example, Temple furniture], or parts of the body. Further references are made to the mixing of this 'Oil' with perfume, as well as with wine, which as previously mentioned, can be synonymous with Blood [especially menstrual blood].

In Hindu Tantra, according to Rawson (1982, p.31), orgasm can be seen as analogous to the ancient traditions of Hindu sacrifice. This 'sacrifice' consisted of pouring oil, fat, or butter onto an altar fire, into which other things may also be sacrificed. Tantra equates the male ejaculation with the oil being poured out; the friction of the sexual organs during coitus with the rubbing together of two sticks to ignite the fire; the vagina of the female partner, who should be menstruating so that her own vital energies are at their peak, with the altar onto which the 'offering' is poured; the fire with sexual enjoyment; and the female partner with the Great Goddess. Rawson also notes, (1986, p.29) that in Hindu Temples, the Lingam of the 'God', or the erect penis of his statue, was anointed with 'Holy Oil' for easier penetration of his 'Goddess Bride', which was impersonated by one of the Temple prostitutes.

Perfumed Oils

Perfumed oils are also used during ritual intercourse in order to stimulate various parts of the body, as well as to intoxicate with the perfume. Indian tradition holds that on different days of the month, a woman's sexual sensitivity, which is determined by her monthly cycle, needs to be triggered by special attention to certain areas of her body. This can be achieved by anointing parts of her body with perfumed oils, by reciting symbolic mantras, and by touching the various body areas (Rawson, 1982, p.89).

Drower also writes (pp.81-82), that scented myrtle flowers, branches and leaves, are used in all Mandaen rituals. Wreathes of myrtle flowers are worn by the

priests as 'crowns'. These wreathes are also placed on the
heads of men and women at Baptism, upon the heads of
the dying, and are worn by the bride and bridegroom
during the marriage ceremony. The Mandaens believe
perfume to be the 'vital essence' (the quintessence) or
'spirit' of the plants and herbs.

Frazer writes (cited in Drower, p.82), 'In the eyes of a
people who, like the Hebrews, identified the principle of
life with the breath, the mere act of smelling a perfume
might easily assume a spiritual aspect; a scented breath
inhaled might seem an accession of life; an addition
made to the essence of the soul.'

Alchemical Oil

According to Mylius (1622, p.260, cited in Fabricius,
p.86), the 'second water' or 'sap' of the Philosophical
Tree or Arbor Vitae, is described as 'an oily water, and
[it] is the philosophical stone, from which branches
multiply into infinity'.

In alchemy, 'oil' can be seen as a synonym for 'the
quintessence'. 'The spirit of the quintessence, called the
tincture, fermentum, anima, or oil, which is the very
next matter to the philosophical stone' (*Artis Aurif*,
1572, p.250, cited in Fabricius, p. 188).

Carl Jung (1938, p.109), sees the quintessence or 'quinta
essentia' as the essential fifth part [in addition to earth,
water, air, and fire], embodying the 'Spirit of
Immortality'. Medieval alchemists described the quinta

essentia as a blue elixir, which was able to confer spiritual illumination and resurrection of the body.

Baptism With Oil (And Water)

Sterling writes in *The Canon* (1981, pp.285-286) that infant baptism was unknown in the early Christian Church. One preparing for Baptism was required to undergo years of instruction to gain knowledge and to participate in the deeper mysteries of the Church. The ritual of Baptism was considered second only to the celebration of the Eucharistic Mass. It originally consisted of the immersion of the body in river, fountain or spring, which was usually preceded by the anointing with chrism or oil. Sometimes they were anointed twice, once with oil [probably olive oil], and after being immersed in the water, with chrism, which is oil [olive oil] mingled with scented balms, and consecrated by the priest.

St. Cyril is cited in *The Canon* (p.286) as saying: 'When ye were stripped ye were anointed with exorcised oil, from the very hairs of your head to your feet... After these things ye were lead to the holy pool of Divine Baptism, as Christ was carried from the cross to the Sepulchre. ...And descended three times into the water, and ascended again'. He goes on to explain that the three immersions refer to the three days passed by Christ in 'the womb of the Earth', for, 'at the self-same moment ye died and were born; and that water of salvation was at once your grave and your mother.

The modern Roman Catholic Church continues to use Holy Oils. Holy Oil is usually blessed olive oil, and is employed for the Sacrament of Extreme Unction, where the sick and dying are anointed (James 5:14; Mark 6:13). Chrism, which is olive oil mixed with perfumed balms, is used for Baptisms, Confirmations and other such consecrations and blessings.

Anointing With Holy Oil

Traditional Israelite anointing oil, or Holy Oil, is composed of myrrh, cinnamon, sweet calmus, cassia, and olive oil (Exodus 30:23-25). Allegro (p.81) suggests that these aromatic oils may have represented the 'powerful semen' of God.[20] He further speculates that the Holy Oil, when rubbed on the skin, could have

---

[20] Allegro (p.85), speculates that both the Semitic and Greek words for 'Christ', the 'anointed or smeared one', derived from the Sumerian terms for semen and resinous saps, MASh and ShEM. Allegro goes on to explain that, used as descriptive titles in the Sumerian language, 'MASh-man would be a term used to describe an exorcist or priest who drives away demons, while a 'ShEM-man' would be a compounder of perfumes, the equivalent of the Old Testament mixer of the holy anointing oils. The Hebrew word MShICh—'Messiah' means the anointed one, as does the Greek word 'Christos'. Interestingly, the Hebrew word NChSh, which means Serpent, enumerates to 358 in the Hebrew Qabalah, as does MShICh—Messiah (Crowley, *Sepher Sephiroth*, p. 39, in 777). In this way, the Messiah, or 'anointed one' would appear to correspond in some fashion with the Serpent [the Serpent in the Garden of Eden, or the Serpent as an allegory for Spermatozoa].

produced an intoxicating belief in the 'self-omniscience' referred to in the New Testament. He is referring here to the Biblical passage John 2:20; 27: 'But ye have an unction [oil] from the Holy One, and ye know all things', 'But the anointing which ye have received of him abideth in you, and ye need not that any man teach you: but as the same anointing teacheth you all things, and is truth, and is no lie, and even as it hath taught you, ye shall abide in him.. In this way, the 'Christian' or 'smeared or anointed one' receives knowledge of all things' by the 'anointing from the Holy One'.

With the institution of Kingship in Israel, anointing, rather than coronation, became the ceremony in which the new king took office. Laws (p.30) postulates that, once kingship had been established, the ritual of anointing was most likely performed by the priests. The priest Zadock anointed Solomon in 1 Kings 1:39, 'And Zadock the priest took a horn of oil out of the Tabernacle, and anointed Solomon'. Samuel, a prophet and probably a priest, is said to have anointed Saul in 1 Sam. 10:1, 'Then Samuel took a vial of oil, and poured it upon his head'. The anointing of the kings appears to have symbolised their special relationship with God, and was looked on as the moment when they received God's Spirit [or Holy Spirit]. The subsequent anointing of the priests probably began during the Post-exile period of Israel, when the High Priests assumed many of the leadership functions that had previously belonged to the Kings. This occurs in Exodus 30:30, 'And thou shalt anoint Aaron and his sons and consecrate them, that they may minister unto me in the priests office'.

Jesus himself is described as having been 'anointed' with the Holy Ghost and with 'power', (Acts 10:38). It is further asserted in Acts 11:16, that Jesus had said, 'John indeed baptised [or anointed] with water; but ye shall be baptised with the Holy Ghost.'

Anointing the head with oil can sometimes be used as a euphemism for anointing or smearing the 'crown of the penis' with oil or semen. Many Biblical Books, especially the Book of Psalms and the Song of Solomon, rely heavily on analogy and allegory, and are over-brimming with sexual euphemisms. For example; Ps. 141:5, 'It shall be an excellent oil, which shall not break my head'; Ps. 133:2-3, 'It is like the precious ointment upon the head, that ran down upon the beard', [or pubic hair? beard of the Macroprosopus?]; and Ps. 92:10, 'But my horn shalt thou exalt like the horn of a unicorn: I shall be anointed with fresh oil'.

In Psalm 23:5, it is written, 'Thou prepares! a table before me in the presence of mine enemies: thou anointest my head with oil; my cup runneth over'. This can be [creatively] interpreted to read, 'Thou anointest my penis with semen; my womb overfloweth'.

Again in Psalm 45:7-8, 'Therefore God, thy God, hath anointed thee with the oil of gladness above thy fellows. All thy garments smell of myrrh, and aloes, and cassia, out of the ivory palaces, whereby they have made me glad'. The 'oil of gladness' could euphemistically refer to semen, whilst the 'spiced wine' flows from out of the 'ivory palaces' or vagina. Several passages in the Bible mention the mixture of oil and wine [semen and blood], and 'spiced wine'. In the Song of Sol. 8:2, it reads, 'I would cause thee to drink of spiced wine of the juice of my pomegranate' [or uterus], and in Song of Sol. 4:10, 'How much better is thy love than wine! and the smell of thine ointments than all spices!'.

Section 5: Blood

> 'The best blood is of the moon, monthly: then the fresh blood of a child, or dropping from the host of heaven: then of enemies; then of the priest or of the worshipers; then last of some beast, no matter what'
> Liber AL vel Legis, III:24.

Crowley comments in *The Law Is For All* (p.284), that menstrual blood should be used for the Cakes of Light, but that Dragon's blood might also be used. The 'blood of a child' is said to be Babalon and the Beast conjoined, symbolised by the Egg and Serpent hieroglyph [or the ovum and sperm united]. Crowley further notes that the 'dragon's blood' is also a form of Baphomet, but that it differs from the child in that it is the Lion-Serpent in its original form.

Menstrual Blood

An understanding of the succession of aeons is imperative at this stage in order to illustrate how certain ideas or concepts have dramatically changed in relation to the aeons. For example, menstrual blood, once thought to be 'wise-blood' capable of 'creation' independent of male fertilisation, came to be considered unclean and unholy, requiring strict taboos to protect men from its demonic powers. Throughout time, the secret of Nature has been the union of opposites. Although Nature has remained intrinsically unchanged, our understanding of Nature has been altered in relation to the succession of the Aeons.

In the Aeon of Isis, the Matriarchal Age, the principle of Parthenogenesis was held to be true. The Virgin [the Hermit card of the Tarot, attributed to the Hebrew letter Yod, is assigned to the Zodiacal sign of Virgo], contains within herself the principle of Growth— the epicene [of both sexes] Hermetic Seed. The Aeon of Isis was uncomplicated. However, according to Crowley, the spiritual principles were ignored in preference to the material side (*Book 4*, p.164).

The Aeon of Osiris, the Patriarchal Age, acknowledged that both sexes were necessary for Creation. The Parthenogenesis idea persisted, but had become the formula for incorporating demons, or 'divine kings'. The worship of Osiris, the Father, was centred on suffering and death [typical of the Dying Gods], where the 'spiritual' strives to ignore the 'material' [or feminine aspect].

In the current Aeon [that is, of Horus, the Crowned and Conquering Child], we aim towards incorporating the two sexes in each individual. The Aeon of Horus therefore focuses on the worship of the 'spiritual' made one with the material' (Crowley, *Book 4*, pp.164-165, 443).

The Aeon Of Isis

From the earliest recorded times, the mysterious magic of creation was thought to reside in the wise-blood [that is, menstrual blood], which women issued forth without pain or injury, forever in harmony with the cycles of the moon. It was widely believed that this blood, if retained within the womb, coagulated to create a child. In Hindu myths, the Great Mother gives birth to the cosmos.[21] Her 'substance' [menstrual blood], becomes thickened and forms a 'curd' or 'clot', which then solidifies into a 'crust' [see earlier reference to the Crust of Hades in Section 3] (Avalon, p.305).

---

[21] According to the Mahanirvanatantra Texts, the Great Mother is represented by Kali, who personifies the colour 'black'; 'just as all colours disappears in black, so all names and forms disappear in her'. She gives birth to the cosmos parthenogenetically, and contains the masculine principle within herself, [as does the Queen Bee and the Hermit of Atu IX].

Menstrual blood was believed to carry the 'spirit of sovereign authority', as it was the medium of transmission of life among the clan or tribe. This concept is clearly defined in India, where menstrual blood is known as the 'Kula Flower' or 'Kula Nectar'.[22] It represents the life of the woman's children, and her bond with the past maternal spirit of her clan (Mahanirvanatantra, p.88).

When a girl first menstruates, she is said to have 'borne the flower' [the English meaning of 'flower' is also 'that which flows']. In the Yonitantra Texts, the menstrual 'flux' is known as the 'flower' or 'puspa' (Mookerjee, p.42). The Bible also describes menstrual blood as the 'flower' (Lev. 15:24), being the precursor of the 'fruit of the womb' [see also Rev. 22:2]. As the flower mysteriously contains its future fruit, so too menstrual blood was believed to contain the 'soul' of the future generations.

'The fruit of the womb is nourished only by the Mother's blood' (Daustenius, cited in Silberer, p. 136).

---

[22] 'Kula' means 'family; form; Supreme Consciousness of the Universe' (Svoboda, p.309). Dyczkowski (pp.59, 61), explains that both the Kula [Sakti] and Akula [Siva] are combined in the Kaula doctrine, where Ultimate Reality is Kaula— the fusion of the opposites. He writes (pp.81-82), that the triangle represents the divine matrix [yoni] from whose centre, in Her aroused state during sexual union, flows 'Kula', the blissful 'power of emission' through which the cosmic order is generated.

This was the central idea that encapsulated the matrilineal concept of the clan.

The mystical powers of the gods: longevity, authority, and creativity, were thought to have come from a 'magical elixir' which was, as a rule, of a feminine nature. The Rig Veda describes the Soma Rasa, the juice of the 'Soma Plant', as Amrita, which is akin to the Greek Ambrosia [Soma means 'body' in Greek, while Rasa is a Sanskrit word meaning 'joy juice', which is 'full of sweetness' (Rawson, 1982, p.88, 102)]. Soma, according to Hindu myths, was variously produced by the churning of the 'primal sea' [that is, of Kali's 'Ocean of Blood' or 'Sea of Milk', or the 'Great Salty Sea of Binah'...]; secreted by the 'Moon-Cow' or 'Moon'; or carried in the 'white pot' [or belly] of Mohini, the Enchantress. It is also claimed that the Hindu Goddess Lakshmi gave Soma to Indra to make him King of the Gods, thereby conferring upon him wisdom, power, and the capacity for pregnancy (O'Flaherty, p.148).

Tantric doctrines describe how Soma [or Amrita], the 'drink of immortality', is manufactured within the 'alchemical laboratory' of the body through the fires of sustained sexual excitement [the uterus is understood, in the Tantric Texts, to be the furnace or oven, while the testes are likened to test-tubes]. It is recognised by the Tantrikas that Soma or Amrita involves the 'pituitary-pineal-hypothalamic complex', which is stimulated during sustained sexual excitation to release a variety of hormones and endorphins into the bloodstream. It is these chemicals, produced by the endocrine glands and mucous membranes, that are held to be the key to rejuvenation, the key to immortality (Mumford, p.57).

Egyptian Pharaohs were said to become 'immortal' by drinking the 'Blood of Isis', a Soma-like ambrosia called 'Sa', whose hieroglyph was the same as that of the vulva — a yonic loop similar to the Ankh, or Cross of Life (Budge, 1969, Vol.l, p.43). Mumford (p. 13) speculates that the Ankh represents the male phallus [the vertical line] united with the female uterus and vagina, represented by the horizontal line and oval. Crowley asserts that the Tau [or cross] and the circle make one form of the Rosy Cross— the uniting of subject and object, which is the Great Work (Book 4, p.51). This is otherwise depicted as the Lingam-Yoni; as the Ankh or Crux Ansata; or as the 'Marriage Feast', Mystic Marriage, the Union of Opposites.

In Persia, the elixir of immortality was 'Amrita'. It was sometimes the milk of the Goddess, or sacred blood, but it was always associated with the moon. As Zimmer writes (p.60); 'Dew and rain becoming vegetable sap, sap becoming the milk of the cow, and the milk then becoming converted into blood: Amrita, water, sap, milk and blood represent but different states of the one elixir. The vessel or cup of this immortal fluid is the moon'.

The Aeon Of Osiris

Since menstrual blood held such a central position in matrilineal theologies it was understandable that the later patriarchal religions showed almost hysterical fear of it. Women in many cultures are secluded or 'tabooed' during their period of menstruation and childbirth. This was thought to neutralise the dangerous influences supposed to emanate from them [this was especially so during a girls first menstruation]. Pliny, in his book *Natural History* (cited in Graves, 1975, p.166), details the dangers arising from menstrual blood. He stated that the touch of a menstruating woman turned wine into vinegar; blighted crops; killed seedlings; dimmed mirrors; blunted razors; killed bees, or drove them from their hives; and caused animals to miscarry.

The Zoroastrians believed that any man who lay with a menstruating woman would beget a demon. It was believed that the first onset of menses was caused by copulating with a serpent (Campbell, 1987, p. 199). [This theme prevailed in Minoan Crete, where women and serpents were held to be sacred.]

The Phrygian Ophiogenesis, 'Snake-Born People', imagined their first male ancestor as the 'Great Serpent', who dwelt in the 'Garden of Paradise' (Harrison, p. 129, 399). The Virgin Hera [Earth], whose virgin form was Hebe, a Greek spelling of Eve, parthenogenetically conceived the oracular Serpent, 'Python', of the 'Womb-Tomb- Temple' or Omphalos of Delphi (Graves and

Patai, p.712). It is widely held that Eve's firstborn son Cain was not begotten of Adam, but by the Great Serpent in the 'Garden of Eden' (Crowley, *Book of Thoth*, p.80).

The Bible mentions similar taboos associated with menstruating women. Leviticus, Chapter 15, outlines the reasons why menstruating women should be avoided, and why the uncontrolled emissions of semen was considered a 'waste' or a 'sin', and instructs on methods of atoning for the breaking of these taboos and sins. Christians appeared to readily accept the patriarchal horror of menstruating women, and women in general. St. Jerome wrote (cited in Morris, p.106), that, 'Nothing is so unclean as a woman in her periods; what she touches she causes to become unclean'. As late as 1684, it was still ordered that women in their 'fluxes' [that is, menstruating], and women just after childbirth who were still bleeding, must remain outside of the church doors (Morris, p.106, 110).

Dragon's Blood

Dragons Blood is the resinous exudation or sap of the fruits of the Daemomorops Draco Palmaceae [Dragon's Blood Palm]. It is used to colour varnishes, toothpaste, and for dying horn to imitate tortoise shell. The trunk of the giant Dracaena Draco of the East Indies and Canary Islands, cracks and emits the red resinous Dragon's Blood, which is used for the embalming of corpses (Grieve, pp.262-263)

It is unlikely that Crowley was referring to this resin as 'Dragon's Blood'. However, tree sap can be an allegory for the 'blood of life' as it is the blood of the tree. It is said that the Philosopher's Tree, the 'Arbour Vitae' of alchemy, has 'blood' in its veins. When exuding, the sap of the tree coagulates into the 'immortal fruit which has life and blood' (Jung, 1967).

> 'This most precious tree, of whose fruit he who eats shall never hunger'
> (*Ars Chemica*, 1566, in Fabricius, p.86).

> 'The dragon is dead without fighting,
> It swells and grows, emitting a sulphurous vapour, and,
> Like a sponge, it produces sap; its
> Meat has the power of silver and gold.'
> (from *Quinta Essentia*, Vol.II, cited in Fabricius, p.202)

This obscure verse appears to describe the 'dragon as the union of the Sun and the Moon [Gold and Silver; Male and Female...], which, having embedded itself upon the uterine wall, grows or swells, and 'ferments', emitting a 'sulphurous vapour' [foetus in Latin means 'stench', while fetus means 'pregnant; producing fruit']. The placenta [which means 'cake' in Latin], has been alchemically described as a 'blood-filled sponge' that nourishes the 'meat' of the union of the Sun and Moon. From this, we can postulate that 'Dragon's Blood' is the end result of the sexual union of the Male and Female.

However, as Crowley implicitly states, it differs from the 'child' in that it is the 'Lion- Serpent' in its original form.

[The Lion-Serpent relates to the Hebrew letter Teth, the Tarot trump Atu XI, Lust, as well as to the Hebrew letter Nun and Atu XIII, Death, which has previously been discussed at length. The Lion-Serpent can further be linked to Atu XII, The Hanged Man, attributed to the Hebrew letter Mem, meaning water, or 'amniotic fluid', which alludes to the Sacrament of the Holy Grail. This idea requires considerable personal research and meditation.]

Pythagorean Triangle

The Pythagorean Triangle is a summary of the Great Work. It can be related to alchemy in that Osiris and Horus are Solar divinities, and Isis is a Lunar divinity. The triangle is seen as representing the Great Work in that it seeks to unite the Sun and the Moon.

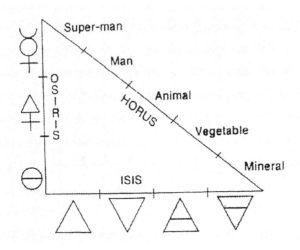

The angle formed by the junction of the Osiris and Isis lines results in a 90 degree right angle. The Hebrew value of Mem — water, variously spelt as Mim, is 90 (Crowley, 777, p.25).[23] Therefore, the right angle uniting the lines of Osiris and Isis may be represented by the alchemical aphorism: 'Our Sun and our Moon are conjoined in our Water' (Case, p.49).

As it is understood, 'Our Water' must not be mistaken for what we consider to be water, rather it is that to which is cryptically referred in the Biblical verse of 1 John 5:8 'There are three that bear witness in earth, the

---

[23] 'MIM— the Secret is hidden between the Waters that are above and the Waters that are beneath. (Symbol, the Ark containing the secret of Life borne upon the Bosom of the Deluge beneath the Clouds)', (Crowley, 777, p.25).

Spirit, and the water, and the blood; and these three agree in one.'[24]

The 'Spirit' mentioned in 1 John 5:8 is the 'Life-breath', represented by the descending line of Osiris. The 'Water' is the generative potency, representing the union of the Father and Mother, or the Sun and Moon. The 'Blood' is the union of Spirit and Water, or rather, the consequence of their union. The Blood is that which is manifest in the ascending scale of the evolution of forms [see diagram].

Moses reportedly said that 'life is in the blood' ['The Blood is the life' Deut. 12:23]. That 'life' is in the blood figures well with modern physiology. Without going into unnecessary detail, the crucial stages of oogenesis in the female ovaries, and spermatogenesis in the male testes, will be outlined (Seeley, Stephens and Tate, pp.858- 898). From this, the relationship between the Life-breath or Spirit, Water and Blood, will be made comprehensible.

Primordial germ cells are primitive, undifferentiated body cells, from which spermatocytes and oocytes develop. The spermatocytes and oocytes correspond to normal body cells in every way except that they have

---

[24] Crowley writes in the *Book of Thoth* (p. 98), that, 'It is to water that the Adepts have always looked for the continuation (in some sense or another) and to the prolongation and perhaps renovation of life'.

been segregated and embedded in the germinal epithelium of the ovaries and testes during embryonic development. This segregation is achieved by the migration of a group of cells from the wall of the embryos yolk sac, to the genital ridge of the embryo, which will later develop into the germinal epithelium of the ovaries or testes. In this 'transition', which represents the individual's primal birth, the cell goes from death to eternal life', that is, it transcends the so called 'death' of the normal body cell, to have 'eternal life' as the primordial germ cell, with its possibility of continuing the unbroken 'thread of life' [that is, as an ovum or spermatozoan]. Here again, the formula of continued life is death. Each individual's spermatozoan and ovum [that is, the union of the sperm and ovum from which they were created], can theoretically be traced back to their ultimate cell of origin. The actual birth of the primordial germ cell is effected in the embryonic organism of the individual's mother and father, and enclosed, in turn, in the pregnant uterus of the individual's grandmother and great-grandmother....

The germinal epithelium of the testes is, according to alchemical literature, considered a 'fountain of life', in that it forms part of the endless thread of life stretching back to the beginning of life on this planet (Fabricius, p. 161). Numerous Biblical passages make mention to the 'fountain of blood' or of water. The menstruating woman in Leviticus (Lev. 21:18) for example, is said to have, 'uncovered the fountain of her blood'. It can be speculated that the 'fountain of life' is synonymous with the 'fountain of blood', and that blood might well refer to semen as well as to menstrual blood, given that semen is essentially 'distilled blood'.[25]

Alchemical literature further identifies the germinal epithelium of the ovaries with a 'rose garden', [the Rose Garden of the Philosophers] (Fabricius, p. 161). The Latin word for 'Rose' is rosa; for 'Rosegarden' the word is rosaria or rosorum; whilst the Latin for 'dew' is ros. From these Latin similarities, it can be postulated that the Rosegarden of the ovaries would in some way contain also the 'Dew' [which has elsewhere been identified with semen].

The Song of Solomon, or 'Song of Songs' is said, by Christian theologians, to be an allegorical tribute of Christ's love for His Church, the Lady Ecclesia.

---

[25] Simon Magus (in Hippolyrus, Elenchos vi.p.4f, cited in Jung, 1984, p.133), speaks of an incorruptible essence potentially present in every human being, the divine 'pneuma. Simon says of this pneuma: I and thou, thou before me. I, who am after thee'. It is a force that 'generates itself, that causes itself to grow; it is its own mother, sister, bride, daughter; its own son, mother, father; a unity, a root of the whole'. It is the very ground of existence, the procreative urge, which is of a fiery origin. Fire is related to blood, being warm, and of the colour of blood. According to Jung, blood turns into semen in men, and into milk in women. One might speculate that this milk may refer to the white vaginal secretions or 'gluten', euphemistically called 'milk'.

However, when the metaphors are unravelled, they are revealed to be of an explicitly sexual nature.

'A garden enclosed is my sister, my spouse: a spring shut up, a fountain sealed.' (Song of Sol.4:12). The 'hortus conclusus' or 'enclosed garden [Rosegarden of the alchemists], can be identified with the female genitalia, whereby her spouse may enter paradise" [the word 'paradise' is derived from the Hebrew word pardes, which means 'garden']. Solomon intends to 'unseal' her, or unlock the door to her garden, and to 'drink of spiced wine of the juice of my pomegranate' (Song of Sol. 8:2). The pomegranate [Hebrew word rimmon], is a traditional female genital symbol, from the Hebrew word Rim, 'to give birth' (Graves, 1955, Vol.l, pp.59-60). [The Pillars of King Solomon's temple were ornamented with female genital symbols, including lilies and pomegranates (1 Kings 7:18-20; 2 Kings 5:18). The pomegranate, with its red juice and numerous seeds, was a symbol of uterine fertility.]

The 'spiced wine' may refer to the secretions of the Goddess, representing the 'blood of life', that is, the menstrual blood mingled or spiced with vaginal secretions [or semen?], of which only kings and gods could taste (Mahanirvana Tantra, p.273).

Solomon's bride, the Shulamite continues, 'Let my beloved come into his garden, and eat his pleasant fruits' (Song of Sol. 4:16). Solomon answers, 'I am come into my garden, my sister, my spouse: I have gathered my

myrrh and my spice; I have eaten my honeycomb with
my honey; I have drunk my wine with my milk; Open
to me, my sister, my love, my dove, my undefiled: for
my head is filled with dew, and my locks with the 'drops
of the night,' (Song of Sol.5:1-2). According to
Pritchard (p. 97), the King's 'dew-filled head' was a
symbol of the erect penis.

The Placental Cake

The following recipe for 'Mercurial Wine', which is said
to intoxicate the alchemist while 'dissolving their
bodies', is given in the *Rosarium* (1550, cited in
Fabricius, p.19): 'Sap of the moon plant, water of life,
quintessence, ardent wine, mercurius vegetabilis: all
these things are one thing. The sap of the moon plant is
made of our wine which is known to few of our sons…'

The 'Moon plant' can be seen to represent the blood-
rich placenta, called the 'Arbor Vitae' or Tree of Life.
The Arbor Vitae, as spoken of in Daniel 4:12, is a tree of
which 'all flesh was fed of it'.

Crowley advises using the 'blood of the moon,
monthly', for making the Cakes of Light, referring to
the female menses. During the menstruation cycle, the
uterus prepares itself for the possibility of conception by
developing a blood-rich 'spongy' lining, covering the
inner surface of the uterus [this thick layer of blood-
filled sponge may allude, in some fashion, to the 'thick
leavings' of wine, where wine is seen as a synonym for

blood]. If conception and impregnation does not occur, this blood is shed as menses. However, if conception is successful, the uterine lining continues to develop into a placenta. 'Placenta', in Latin, means cake; the 'Placenta of Light' ['Placenta of Life' 'Body of Light'...], gives us much food for thought.

Body Of Light—The Bloody Sacrifice

The Egyptian concept of the 'ba', the soul image of man, was that of a spiritual double. The ba was immortal, and its hieroglyph was a star. The ancient Greeks called the inner spiritual body the 'psyche', which means butterfly or soul; the Romans called it the genius, while the Persians called it the 'fravauli'. Paracelsus believed that a half, corporeal body, which he termed the 'astral body' [corpus astrale], lives beside the body of flesh, and is its mirror image (Fabricius, pp.194-195).

According to Eliphas Levi, the 'Astral Light' was the mediator or 'menstruum' between the inner will of the magician, and the outer world of the elements (Hymenaeus Beta, Ed., *Book 4*, p.x/v-x/vi). Crowley explained (*The International*, Nov. 1917. e.v.), that, to "get into the astral body" means to allow the consciousness to rest in a vehicle of fine matter, and detaching from the gross body, to move about'. It is this which Crowley terms the 'Body of Light'. It follows that this 'consciousness' is therefore able to pick up any 'ready material' as a basis or vehicle in order to 'incarnate'.

> 'Mind is a disease of semen.
> All that a man is or maybe is hidden therein.'

> 'Race consciousness; that which is omnipotent, omniscient, and omnipresent, is concealed within the glyph of the Serpent, or sperm.'
> (Crowley, *Book of Lies*, Chap. 8, and it's Comment, pp.26-27.)

Crowley held that the offering of blood [that is, the 'Bloody Sacrifice'], was the only menstruum strong enough to make the Body of Light mechanically solid'. It follows that blood can provide the 'ready material' for the consciousness [the sperm] to incarnate in. Crowley stated that, for nearly all purposes, human sacrifice was the best offering. By this he was referring to self-sacrifice through meditation, and alluding to the sacrifice of the self through certain sex-magick practices (*Book 4*, p.208). Crowley was often misrepresented on the subject of blood-sacrifices. For example, 'A male child of perfect innocence and high intelligence is the most satisfactory and suitable victim,' was taken literally by many vocal detractors of Crowley.

Biologically, the male child possesses a pair of XY sex-chromosomes in each body cell, which are responsible for the child being of the male sex, whereas the female possesses a pair of XX sex-chromosomes. It is the Y-chromosome that overall determines the sex of the child (note that Atu IX, The Hermit, is attributed to the Hebrew letter Yod, which is represented by the English letter Y).[26]

The 'sacrifice' of the male child is, in one way, the conscious act of not allowing the 'union' to develop. The sperm is not permitted to become united with the ovum and to take root, but is perhaps ritually consumed so as to allow the development of the 'magical child' or 'Body of Light'. In *The Eucharist* (Le Chevalier Clement de Saint Marcq, trans, by Jessel and Fr. Y.V., no pagination), Saint Epiphanius gives a description of a particular Gnostic Eucharistic ceremony. He states that the men and women eat reciprocally the seed of the human species, whilst turning towards the altar and saying to the 'High One': 'Offerimus tibi donum corpus Christi', ['We offer you in sacrifice the body of Jesus Christ!']. Filoramo (pp. 183-184) cites Epiphanius as further stating that, along with the eating of the seed or 'sperm' as the 'Body of Christ', the assembled congregation would also offer up unclean menstrual blood, saying 'Behold the blood of Christ...' He asserts

---

[26] The Medieval German Bishop and alchemist Albertus Magnus identified the goal of the Royal An of alchemy as, Y— the original, bisexual man, 'All things agree in the One which is cleft in two'. This body is said to be masculine, while it's soul is feminine, although the reverse is sometimes true (Fabricius, p.92).

that their sexual practices were not designed for the begetting of children, but for mere pleasure. However, if a woman does become pregnant, Epiphanius maintains that the embryo is removed and crushed with a mortar and pestle, mixed with honey, pepper and other spices, and perfumed oils, and ritually eaten by the congregation. This may relate the Bloody Sacrifice to the Eucharistic Cakes of Light, which represent the essence of the Universe. By consuming them daily, one becomes imbued with the consciousness of the Universe, thereby becoming master of the Universe. As we ritually consume the blood of our own bodies, we are partaking of our own 'essence', our 'Divine God', which is also the Blood of our Ancestors, the Blood of the Saints, the Holy Grail of Babalon.

Conclusion:

From death comes life. One must die in order to be reborn; refreshed and reinvigorated. 'Life-foods' and 'life-fluids' are representative of powers which bestow, nourish, increase, preserve, and reproduce or regenerate life. The Cakes of Light, as illustrated throughout this study, are composed of such life-foods. The ingredients, as outlined in *Liber AL vel Legis* III:23, includes: meal, or wheaten flour, where vegetation, especially grains, can be seen as the union of Heaven and Earth; honey, where the bees collect the essence of the flower and transforms it into 'pure light'; wine, being the fermented essence or 'blood' of the vine; olive oil and the essential perfumed oils which constitute the Oil of Abramelin—cinnamon, myrrh, galangal, and olive oil in fixed proportions, which are the essences of the fruits and flowers; and finally fresh blood, which is life itself.

The purpose of this study, as previously explained, was not to deliver a definitive treatise on the proper production of the Cakes of Light. It was intended to shed light on, and encourage further study of the myths, alchemy, and traditional religious significance of the Eucharist, by focusing on the Thelemic Eucharist— the Cakes of Light.

Bibliography:

Allegro, J. M.,1970, The Sacred Mushroom and the Cross, Abacus: London.

Avalon, A., 1978, Shakti and Shakta, Dover Publications: New York

Baring, A. and Cashford, G.,1991, Myth of the Goddess: Evolution of an Image, Viking Arkana: London.

Barry, K.1984, The Greek QabalahPailas Athene Press: Auckland.

Budge, E. A.,1969, Gods of the Egyptians (2 Vol.), Dover Publications: New York.

Budge, E. A., 1977, Egyptian Language, Dover Publications: New York.

Cameron, D.,1981, Symbols of Birth and Death in the Neolithic Era, Kenyon-Deane: London.

Campbell, J.,1987, The Masks of God: Occidental MythologyAskana-. New York.

Campbell, J.,1988, The Power of Myth, Doubleday: New York.

Case, P. F.,1992, The True and Invisible Rosicrucian Order, Samuel Weiser: Maine.

Crowley, A.,1991, Liber Aleph vel CXI, Samuel Weiser: Maine.

Crowley, A.,1946, letter to Grady Mcmurtry, 10 April, in Thelema Lodge Calendar, May 1993 e.v.: Berkeley

Crowley, A., 1994, Magick: Book IV, edited, annotated and introduced by Hymenaeus Beta, Samuel Weiser: Maine.

Crowley, A.,1982, 777, Samuel Weiser: Maine.

Crowley, A., 1988, The Book Of Lies, Samuel Weiser: Maine.

Crowley, A.,1989, The Book Of Thoth, Samuel Weiser: Maine.

Crowley, A., 1974, 'The Gospel according to St. Bernard Shaw', in Crowley on Christ, Ed. E King, The C.W. Daniel Company: London.

Crowley, A.,1917, The Revival of Magick, in The International, August, 1917e.v.

Crowley, A., 1991, The Law Is For All, New Falcon Publications: Arizona.

Crowley, A.,1990, The Paris Working, O.T.O. Electronic Program: CA.

Crowley, A.,1972, The Vision And The Voice, Liber 418, Sangreal Foundation Inc: Texas.

Drawer, E. S.,1956, Water Into Wine, John Murray: London.

Dumezil, G.,1970, Archaic Roman Religion (2 Vol.), University of Chicago Press: Chicago.

DuQuette, L. M.,1993, The Magick Of Thelema, Samuel Weiser: Maine.

Dyczkowski, M. S.,1989, The Canon of the Saivagama, Motilal Banarsidass: Delhi.

Edwardes, A., 1965, The Jewel in the Lotus, Lancer Books: New York.

Fabricius, J, 1976, Alchemy, Rosenkilde and Bagger: Copenhagen.

Filoramo, G-, 1994, A History of Gnosticism, trans, by A. Alcock, Blackwell Publishers: Cambridge, MA.

Freud, S.,1984, On Sexuality, Penguin Books: Vic.

Gimbutas, M.,1989, The Language of the Goddess, Harper and Row: San Francisco.

Godwin, M.,1994, The Holy Grail, Labyrinth: London.

Graves R.,1955, The Greek Myths (2 Vol.), Penguin Books: New York.

Graves' R.,1975, The White Goddess, Faber and Faber Books: London.

Graves' R.'and Patai, R.,1983, Hebrew Myths-.The Book of Genesis, Greenwich House; New York.

Grieve, M.,1982, A Modem Herbal, Penguin Books: Vic.

Guirand, F.,1970, 'Greek Mythology', in New Larousse Encyclopedia of Mythology, The Hamlyn Publishing Group: Sydney.

Harris, E, 1942, Catalogue for Exhibition of78 Paintings of the Tarot Cards.

Harrison, J., 1989, Themis, Merlin Press: London.

Holy Bible, Authorised King James Version, Oxford University Press: Oxford.

Jennings, H.,1966, The Rosicrucians, Health Research: CA.

Jung, C. G.,1963, Memories, Dreams and Reflections, Routledge and Kegan Paul: London.

Jung, C. G.,1938, Psychology and Religion, Yale University Press: New Haven.

Jung, C. G.,1984, Psychology and Western Religion, Princeton University Press: New Jersey.

Laws, S., 1993, Anoint, in The Oxford Companion to the Bible, Oxford University Press: Oxford.

Le Chevalier Clement de Saint Marcq, 1995, The Eucharist, trans, by R. Jessel and Frater Y.V., Pangenetor Lodge Publications: Berkeley, CA.

Liber AL vel Legis, in A. Crowley, Magick, Book IV, Samuel Weiser: Maine.

Maeterlinck, M.,1914, The Life of the Bee, Dodd, Mead and Company: New York.

Mahanirvanatantra (Sir John Woodroffe, Trans.), 1972, Dover Publications: New York.

Mookerjee, A.,1988, Kali The Feminine Force, Destiny Books: New York.

Morris, J., 1973, The Lady Was a Bishop, Macmillan: New York.

Mumford, J., 1977, Sexual Occultism, Compendium: Victoria.

O Flaherty, W. D.,1975, Hindu Myths. Penguin Books: Harmondsworth, England.

Patai, R., 1990, The Hebrew Goddess, 3rd. edition, Wayne State University Press: Detroit.

Pritchard, J.B.,1974, Solomon and Sheba, Phaidon Press: London.

Puhvel, J., 1987, Comparative Mythology, The John Hopkins University Press: Baltimore.

Radhakrishnan, S. and Moore, C.A., 1989, A Source Book in Indian Philosophy, Princeton University Press: New Jersey.

Rank, G.,1958, The Myth of the Birth of the Hero, Vintage-Books: New York

Rawson, E.1968, Erotic Art of the East, G.P.Putnan's Sons: New York.

Rawson, P.,1982, The Art of Tantra, Thames and Hudson: London.

Red Flame, Vol.2, Pangenetor Lodge: Berkeley.

Regardie, I..1989, The Tree of Life, Samuel Weiser: Maine.

Seeley, R. Stephens, T„ and Tate, P.,1989, Anatomy and Physiology, Mosby College Publishing: St.Louis.

Silberer, H., 1971, Hidden Symbolism of Alchemy and the Occult Arts, Dover Publicatons: New York.

Sobol, D. J.,1972, The Amazons of Greek Mythology, A.S. Barnes & Co. Inc: New Jersey.

Sterling, W.,1981, The Canon, Research into Lost Knowledge Organisation: London.

Strong, E.S.,1969, Apotheosis and After Life, Books For Libraries Press: New York.

Svoboda, R.,1993, Aghora II: Kundalini, Brotherhood of Light: Albuquerque.

The Shorter Oxford English Dictionary, 2 Vol., 1987, Carendon Press: Oxford.

Viaud, J., 1970, 'Egyptian Mythology', in New Larousse Encyclopedia of Mythology, the Hamlyn Publishing Group: Sydney.

Willetts, R. F.,1962, Cretan Cults and Festivals, Routledge and Kegan Paul: London.

Zimmer, H., 1946, Myths and Symbols in Indian Art and Civilization, Princeton University Press: New Jersey.

THE SOLAR MYTH AND THE PATH OF INITIATION

COSIMO SALVATORELLI

Do what thou wilt shall be the whole of the Law.

This Knowledge is not for all men, few indeed are called, but of these few many are chosen.
- Liber Porta Lucis, v.9[1]

We can conceive of Ordo Templi Orientis as a system of knowledge. In the beginning of his involvement with OTO, Crowley considered OTO preparatory training for the A∴A∴. In 1910 after the artistic and social experiment The Rites of Eleusis performed by A∴A∴ aspirants (some of whom joined OTO in 1912), Crowley understood that the OTO could become an experimental forge whereby the *Great Work* might be attempted under the auspices of the so-called "Invisible Church". The Word of the Law which is Thelema connected two great schools: the A∴A∴ and the OTO, giving birth to the "Duplexity" experiment. Two different methods but in harmony with each other. After two World Wars, history tells us that OTO, in the care

---

[1] *Liber Porta Lucis*, in *The Holy Books of Thelema*, York Beach 1983, pg. 37

of Karl Germer, successor of Aleister Crowley, faced extinction, avoided only by Grady McMurtry, who gathered within the Order a multitude of esoteric science lovers. A clear definition of this system of consciousness became increasingly obscured. In 1944 Crowley wrote:

> But it is true that with regard to the O.T.O. there is no similar manual of instruction [as in *One Star in Sight*][2].

> In the Manifesto, and other Official Pronunciamenti, there are, it is true, what ought to be adequate data; but I quite understand that they are not as ordered and classified as one would wish:[3]

Today, OTO can be defined as a serious initiatic and religious order whose initiation program trains every member of its body in the magical secrets that can make him Master of Life, i.e. a Master of Magick. The acquisition of this expertise is developed through the initiation rituals, and the tools unique to the individual initiate of this School. Basically every member of OTO instructs himself through the formulas of the New Aeon. Not proved through examinations, nor having an

---

[2] Crowley, Magick, Book 4, Parts I-III, ed rev., Rome 2020, page 405

[3] *Magick Without Tears*, chapter XIII: System of the O.T.O., 1988., page 122

instructor in the Order, every initiate of OTO doesn't merely instruct himself, but he experiences life in a unique and individual way, undergoing the founding principle in *The Book of the Law*: "Success is thy proof".[4]

The word *"success"* comes from the Latin "successus" which means "good result", "happy outcome". It is composed of *sub* + *cedere* from the indo-european root *"ked"* which means "going" and also "surrender". The candidate through his own *Ingenium* tries to discover the aim of his life and then to identify himself with it. Moreover, the etymology of *Ingenium* is formed by the particle "in" and "genium", meaning the creative quality that enables him to travel unmarked paths. OTO is an experiment dedicated to the destruction of the Old Temple, so that a new one can be built.

In OTO the initiate experiences the core of the journey reported in the Myths: Heracles who chooses a life of perpetual service, Moses who proclaims IHVH's law, Perseus who faces Medusa, Teseus who challenges the Minotaur or the self-slain Ankh-af-na-Khonsu[5] who faces the depths in order to do his will among the living.

But all these myths are constantly alive in every man's life every time he decides to go in search of himself.

---

[4] *Liber AL* III, 42

[5] Priest of the Egyptian god Mentu who lived in Thebes during the 26th dynasty. Crowley believed him to be one of his previous incarnations.

The authentic researcher who is able to create a personal relation with the initiation myth will get the reward: success, which is progress, the expansion of life.

> The man of earth is the adherent. The lover giveth his life unto the work among men. The hermit goeth solitary, and giveth only of his light unto men.[6]

Psychologically the figure of the hero can be conceived as a process of growth of consciousness. The process of initiation in the OTO celebrates the realization of the individual unity.

The most common feature in the life of heroes is the motif of double parents. Heracles' fathers, for example, are Amphitrion and Jupiter. Moses has biological parents and adoptive ones, Christ, apart from Joseph and Mary, has an invisible parent, the Holy Spirit. Every hero has birth parents and a transpersonal parent who initiates him. The drive towards expansion of consciousness has therefore a twofold source: a human, personal element and a transpersonal, divine one. Another recurring motif in the hero's life is the source of power which he conveys. We often call it vital force or *kuṇḍalinī*, the serpent coiled at the base of the mūlādhāra cakra which in its unfolding vitalizes the thousand petal lotus. We can actually see in Heracles' myth two serpents sent by

---

[6] The Cry of the 13th Aethyr [ZIM], in The Vision and the Voice, op. cit.

the goddess Hera, which are strangled by the hero while he is still in his cradle or the miracles on his path toward Egypt, while a still young Jesus is escaping from Herod's persecution. This miraculous power can be defined as a drive, the desire for individuation. Every human being is provided with it, and like every hero, is exposed to threats, since the drive to discover oneself as unique and unrepeatable, contrary to conventional standards, doesn't find external support. The surrounding environment slightly resists, since this approach represents a threat for both the world of gods and that of humans.

Through knowledge of himself and the exploration of his mental states the initiate discovers to be the bearer of a kind of "passion" which is Vital Force. He is the goat that flits from rock to rock to reach the top of the mountain. The achievement consists thereby in becoming conscious of that "*Capricorni Pneumatici*"[7] with a fiery nature and already abiding within us. This awareness simply helps us become the Lord of it. We learn from the myth that the Oracle of Delphi through Jupiter declares that Heracles, in order to master this aggressive, stubborn and insubordinate force which springs as a fury, has to undergo twelve labors and the discipline of service. In the OTO system this Bhakti

---

[7] *Liber A'ash vel Capricorni Pnuematici*, in *The Holy Books of Thelema*, York Beach 1983, pg. 205

Yoga is called union through devotion. The common thread is therefore service through renunciation.

This attitude was previously called "mystic", a term indicating union through renunciation of a theoretical comprehension of divinity and the research of an experience-based path which requires abandoning all those contents that prevent the complete realization of the union itself. In OTO the work of renunciation and devotion enables to refine more and more that vital force since It has to be refined in order to be effective:

> There is a light so strenuous that it is not perceived as light. Wolf's bane is not as sharp as steel; yet it pierceth the body more subtly.[8]

The myth of Heracles is probably the first and best example of the hero where service anticipates, the version discussed by Isaiah who describes IHVH's suffering servant. We also see a connection with the Biblical teaching: "whoever among you wants to be the first, must be the servant of all".

Heracles is an example of a psychological truth: giving without worrying about receiving. To Delphi's Oracle question about how to refine that vital force, we can answer: being at the service of the process of expansion of consciousness. Heracles's twelve labors can therefore

---

[8] Liber LXV, I, 12-13.

be considered as a series of encounters with our inner world in its different aspects.

The first of Heracles' task is killing and skinning the Lion of Nemea who devastates the country. The lion is precisely that warlike and instinctive force. Heracles not only has to kill the lion but he also has to skin and flay him. He succeeds in killing the lion strangling him and then he flays him with the claws of the lion himself. Killing the beast with his own claws recalls the ancient alchemic aphorism: "dissolve the water with water" or "calcinate the fire with fire". It is as if the vital force, fierce, aggressive and gross, has to be transformed by the hero using vitality itself. It's not the intellectual process which allows it, since it does not have the driving force necessary, but that force which abides intimately inside us.

> "Even for five hundred and eleven times nightly for one and forty days did I cry aloud unto the Lord the affirmation of His Unity".[9]

The keystone is active action, an intentional movement towards an unknown goal. Indeed, we know that only by using one's own energies can the work be accomplished.

---

[9] Liber Ararita, III, 1.

Heracles then clothes himself with the Lion's skin with the jaws sticking out over his head. He uses it as a sort of cloak of invulnerability. He learns to come to terms with the instinctual primordial force, to accept it, until it doesn't threaten to overwhelm him but protects him, because he recognizes it and now it belongs to him. This Force is now at the service of consciousness. In Nietzsche's *Homeric Agony*[10] the philosopher explains that the Lion of Nemea represents cruelty: Heracles overcoming the Lion overcomes his own cruelty, subjecting it to the balanced service of discovering himself.

The second of Heracles' tasks is overtaking the Hydra of Lerna, a poison breathing monster with two heads that regenerate themselves when they are cut off. Heracles, thanks to the support of another human being, his nephew Iolaus, figures out a method for defeating the Hydra: while Heracles cuts off the monster's head, Iolaus immediately cauterizes it, preventing its regrowth. The Hydra can represent the Animal Soul, that instinctual and automatic part which obstructs the Great Work.

Yet this process is very subtle, since the Hydra's head is not only cut off, but also cauterized, and this has to do

---

[10] F. Nietzsche, *The State of the Greeks. The Homeric Agony,* Avellino 2006

with the emotional intensity that is satisfied: handling Fire with Fire.

Heracles finally uses the poison of the hydra for dipping his arrows in it. It is as if the fulfillment of the animal soul released a poison which is a remedy for initiates shooting the Arrow.

The third labor is catching the Cerynean hind, a female deer with brass hooves and golden horns, sacred to Artemis. Thus we have the masculine principle, the horns, associated with the feminine one, the goddess. In this adventure Heracles has to meet and conquer Artemis' principle which enables him to expand his consciousness. The hind of Ceryneia is then captured by virtue of the arrow dipped in Hydra's poison. It is as if the juice of the Animal Soul, its essence, facilitated the fixation of the feminine principle of inspiration. In *The Book of Thoth* Artemis is Atu II, "The Priestess of the Silver Star". The fixation of the principle of inspiration descending from the Crown, the intimate essence, is a recurring motif in the path of initiation.

Going on with the stream of the knowledge of oneself through aspiration, during the fourth labor Heracles has to catch the Erymanthian boar, the creature who killed Adonis and also Attis, son and lover of the Great Mother Cybele. The boar can be conceived as the rough creative power, phallic, of the Great Mother. Overcoming the Erymanthian boar can mean that the hero gets in touch with a certain aspect of the primordial feminine power and masters it. The primordial aspect of the feminine manifests itself through the figure of the terrible mother and is expressed with the fear of denial and judgment.

Cleaning King Augeas' stables, in just one day, is the fifth labor for Heracles, which he accomplishes causing the thick manure of the oxen to deviate through the river Alphaeus. The oxen had accumulated an enormous amount of manure suggesting the abandonment of instinctual processes. The Strength of the hero lies in dealing with them, taking care of them and giving them due meaning. Crowley in *The Wake World* describes in this way the path of Samekh, the letter attributed to ATU XIV, Art:

> Then there was another passage called the Arrow by Day, and there was a most lovely lady all shining with the sun, and moon, and stars, who was lighting a great bowl of water with one hand, by dropping dew on it out of a cup, and with the other she was putting out a terrible fire with a torch. She had a red lion and a white eagle that she had always had ever since she was a little girl. She had found them in a nasty pit full of all kinds of filth, and they were very savage; but by always treating them kindly they had grown up faithful and good. This should be a lesson to all of us never to be unkind to our pets.[11]

---

[11] Crowley, *Konx Om Pax*.

The sixth labor is getting rid of the birds of Lake Stymphalia, enormous creatures with brass beak and feathers and poisonous excrements, who live in a swamp which is neither earth nor water. Heracles drives them away with rattles, tools that in ancient times were used for banishing evil spirits. If chattering and babbling can be used for smoothing the fear of silence, we can think of rattles as the sound of pure will through which the Law is spread, becoming its vehicle.

Thus far we have seen how the hero, after clashing with the unconquered masculine force, has to submit himself to the extreme in the service of the feminine, a concept we find in the principles of medieval chivalry, where the knight dedicated himself to the service of his lover.

After pushing away the Stymphalian birds, the hero undertakes the seventh labor: the capture of the Cretan bull which involves the symbolism resumed in the myth of Theseus. The struggle against the Nemean Lion is the first encounter with the refinement of vital force, fierce, aggressive and still gross. The bull, together with the lion, represents an aspect of the instinctual masculine force and one of Jupiter's manifestations. The bull is linked to the Mithraic cults of sacrifice that we find for example through the biblical account of Exodus where the Jewish people, waiting for Moses to come back from Mount Sinai, make Aaron build a golden image of a bull in order to adore it. In Mesopotamia it was known as the Heavenly Bull, in Egypt as Apis, in the Greek world we have the famous Minotaur, for the Canaanite it is Moloch. In Christianity the bull refers to the Passion of Christ, the sacrifice the Redeemer offered for sinful humanity. Even the lion is a symbol of Resurrection (in the ancient world the lion was believed to sleep with open eyes). The initiate has to dissolve his old synapsis or to dissolve his vision of outer and inner world, based on the principles of dying gods, in order to radiate Light, Life, Love and Liberty, the four arms of the Law. In *Liber Aleph*[12] Crowley associates the Bull with the virtue of Will and Jñāna Yoga, a training which enables to experiment with different kinds of Dhyāna or mental depth. Heracles succeeds in defeating the Bull by strangling it, hence taking off oxygen, breath, which is Vital Force. It is as if our Strength at this stage of initiation ceases to give life and form to the principles of dying gods and becomes Life, the steady and restless Will whose letter in the Hebrew alphabet is Vau, six, the number of the Sun, the substance of being. In Hinduism the Bull is sacred to Shiva who is the Phallus and if Will operates through love, the Phallus is dissolved in the Cup.

Heracles' eighth labor involves the man eating Mares of Diomedes. We have seen how the initiate begins to enter the depth of the mind in order to direct that subtle vital force, and this is like an introverted work concealing a

---

[12] *The Equinox*, III (6)

hidden danger: the encounter with man-eaters, Mares or the destructive and devouring aspect of the unconscious.

The myth tells that Ares had a son named Diomed who had fiery mares breathing fire and flames from their nostrils. Diomed fed these mares with traders sailing Thracian shores. In this labor we are dealing with the god of war's son; in fact Diomed enacts aggression, cruelty and sadism, attributes of an Ares who is not mitigated by the Sun and thus unbalanced. The internalisation of vital force enables to get in touch with the most telluric elements, those least able to be harnessed, but the initiate has to do everything on the basis of the principle of philosophy, which is love for knowledge, which is Wisdom, which is Logos, the aim of individual life which enables humanity to follow the river of continuity of existence. At this stage the initiate doesn't stop at the onanistic activity of self-exploration, but he goes on with his work of union between this human self and the Star. Moreover we begin to catch a glimpse of the New Aeon paradigm shift where the Christian statement "Magister Iesus Christus Deus et Homo" is totally abrogated since the new Understanding reads: "Deus est Homo". We don't have Spirit on one side and Matter on the other, but Unity.

In this labor Heracles kills Diomed and feeds the mares with him, and then he brings them aboard the ship. He doesn't sever the aggressive force that is Ares, but the one of his son, the unbalanced one.

The next labor is slightly different because the hero is asked to take Ares' golden belt worn by Hippolyta, queen of the Amazons. The word "amazon" means "without breast" and the history tells that these women amputate their right breast in order to be better archers; moreover, they used to break male children's legs in order to turn them into cripples: this was meant to underline the exclusion of the male principle.

Some state that according to Greek etymology the word amazon means "without a male", as a moon without the sun. The name "Hippolyta" means "free mare". The myth tells that when Heracles arrived in the kingdom of the Amazons, against all the odds, he was graciously welcomed by Hippolyta who, as soon as she understood the purpose of his travel, accepted him and gave him her belt. But during the night once again Hera opposed; the goddess incited the Amazons, telling them the hero wanted to kidnap their beautiful queen. All the women lashed out at Heracles who, after a long fight, managed to defeat them, killing Hippolyta and stealing the belt from her. Here we see the first attempt of the lunar queen to unite herself with the hero through the belt. This is a wedding promise that still doesn't come true since the tender part, yin, is killed by the strong part, yang, because of the aggressiveness of the many.

And in order to subdue this multitude, Heracles has to undergo another ordeal: following the path of the Sun to where humanity sees it disappearing. It is as if

Heracles, overcoming the boundary of the horizon, overcomes the night also, identifying himself with the Sun. In this labor Heracles first defeats the giant Antaeus, son of Poseidon and Gaea, who has a weak point: his strength fails when he is raised. It is as if at this stage the hero subjects the fatal image of nature and the inertia of incarnation in order to conquer the oxen and go beyond. The strength he achieved defeating the giant enables him to create an inaccessible gate. The god Helios lends his boat to Heracles to get to Erytheia island: therefore the identification with the Sun begins. In this way Heracles conquers the red oxen, charging them on the solar boat. In this labor we find the bovine again. The ox is however different from the bull. The vital force and its various aspects are like laborious oxen who enable the hero to weave the dance of life on Earth.

The second last labor of Heracles is to go and pick three golden apples in the Hesperides garden, guarded by a dragon wrapped around the tree – an environment that obviously reminds us of the Garden of Eden. Heracles has to invoke the Titan Atlas to localize the garden, and in order to do it, he helps him to hold up the heavens while Atlas picks up the apples. The Titan then refuses to take back the heavens and Heracles, pretending to agree, asks Atlas to hold up the heavens one last time while he bends his head. At that moment Heracles tricks Atlas and runs away with the apples, achieving the task. This labor also indicates the struggle against the principles of dying gods: holding up the weight of the heavens sounds like being crucified in order to save humanity.

It should be also noticed that the labors of Heracles are characterized by recognizable geographical locations except the last three which are mythical places forbidden to an ordinary human being, even if he is full of good intentions. In this labor the dragon is killed again with a poisoned arrow, the arrow of aspiration. And this arrow enables the picking up of the three golden apples that can be conceived as the supernal triad on the Tree of Life.

It is both the dragon and the garden of the tree. As Horatius writes in the Satyrs: "The banquet should begin with eggs and finish with apples because after eating the apple one should make love."

It is the symbol of femininity associated with Venus, the goddess born from sea foam and Lady of Nature. It is as if the initiate who attains the three apples recognizes a nature in itself free from the veils of illusion. He is a circle inside which are hidden the seeds of Life. He does Nothing and he is simply as he is.

Finally Heracles puts an end to his duty with the capture of Cerberus, the dog of Hell. This seems to be the negative version of the previous activity. The heavenly garden of the Hesperides represents the positive aspect of the contact with the center, the Star, but here we see a descent to the infernal regions instead of an ascension to heaven. Heracles brings Cerberus up to the earth, exposing him to consciousness, so that the horror of the dark side of the Self becomes visible and is not questioned anymore. Cerberus has three heads, as the apples of the Hesperides are three. This is linked to the fact that the aspects of the psyche are like Heracles' weapons: the sword comes from Hermes, the arch and arrows from Apollon, the armor from Hephaestus and the peplum from Athena. The club is the only weapon he builds by himself. We notice a similitude between the club and the Ace of Clubs which Crowley describes in *The Book of Thoth*: this card represents the essence of the element Fire in its beginning, a solar-phallic flame explosion from which thunderbolts emanate in every direction. These flames are Yod, disposed in the shape of the Tree of Life, the primordial Energy of the Divine manifested in matter in such an early passage that it is not formulated yet as Will. It is as if the labors of Heracles, and therefore of the initiate of OTO, are conceived to develop the Will or Vital Force, who in Ordo Templi Orientis gradually unveils itself through the experience of degrees which are his "labors".

Love is the law, love under will.

*translated by Francesca Passerone.

VIAOV: THE MONOMYTH OF ALEISTER CROWLEY

SINISHA TZAR

The Unlikely Peer

Although published more than sixty years ago, the appeal of *The Hero with a Thousand Faces*[1] still doesn't fade away.[2] To explain the long-lasting allure of this book, one must understand the fundamental idea behind it. Instead of writing yet another overview of various myths, American professor of literature Joseph Campbell offered a comparative take on the various hero stories, distilling an underlying cyclical pattern of the so-called Hero's Journey which, borrowing from James Joyce, he dubbed the 'monomyth'.

Before Campbell, there were Lord Raglan (1936) and Otto Rank (1909) who not only recognized a pattern-like mythological structure but offered its analysis. While Rank, of the Freudian background, focused on the childhood of the hero, understanding the myth as a blueprint of the family dynamics, Raglan interpreted similar material from the Frazerian myth-ritualist

---

[1] The Bollingen Series XVII, New York: Pantheon Books, 1949.

[2] "Amazon Best Sellers," accessed 01.10.22.

corner. In contrast, Campbell's hero is an individual or, to be more precise, his mind, presuming not just the conscious part but both Freudian and Jungian layers of unconsciousness.[3] Ultimately, *The Hero* talks not about Hercules, Gilgamesh, or Arjuna but of Joe/Jane Average on the road to the Godhead.

Campbell's intellectual position is, essentially, the one of perennialism, shared with other great scholars of his time such as Jung, Eliade, Scholem, and Corbin who were a part, as he was as well, of the Eranos circle.[4] His stance goes hand to hand with his cultural and historical position detected by Professor Karen L. King as American Romanticism, cherishing, among others, individuality, heroic selflessness, and democracy while holding 'that truth lies in the authentic experience of the inner self, a self that is not only sacred but divine'. As King plainly demonstrates, these traits of Campbell's thought are closely connected with his understanding of Gnosticism.[5] Therefore, the culmination of the Hero's journey is not the acquisition of mundane power, but

---

[3] R. A. Segal, "Introduction" in *In Quest of the Hero* (Princeton University Press, 1990), vii–xli, xxvi.

[4] W. J. Hanegraaff, *Esotericism and the Academy* (Cambridge University Press, 2013), 295–314.

[5] K. L. King, "Social Factors in Mythic Knowing" in *Paths to the Power of Myth* (Crossroad, 1990), 69.

deification as presented by the figures of Christ, Bodhisattva, Buddha, etc.

In this light, it is interesting to mention an individual whose name is usually not taken into consideration when monomyth is discussed: Aleister Crowley. It is in his acclaimed *Magick in Theory and Practice* (*MTP*)[6], published twenty years before Campbell's book, that one finds a pithy analysis of hero myth as a cyclical, phase-parted, archetypal, psychologically interpreted narrative describing the process of deification.[7] Therefore, the objective of this article is to present Crowley's treatment of the hero myth and compare it with Campbell's, which, so far, has not been done, with one honourable exception of a hint offered by Crowley's biographer Richard Kaczynski.[8]

IAO formula and the Hero

At the beginning of the 1920s, Crowley would find himself in a small Sicilian town in the vicinity of Palermo, Cefalù, conducting a sort of "monastic" experiment in his Abbey of Thelema. There he will, among other things, work on the *MTP* together with Mary Butts and write a chapter on the formula of IAO,

---

[6] Paris: Lecram Press, 1929.

[7] A. Crowley, M. Desti and L. Waddell, *Magick* (Weiser Books, 1997), 158–66.

[8] R. Kaczynski, *Perdurabo* (North Atlantic Books, 2010), 559.

here of crucial importance.[9] Although he was aware of the historical background of this divine name, he preferred to use it as a word that described a certain spiritual process, a formula. The process in question was initially concerning the symbolic Frazerian dying-and-rising procedure, through which initiates of the *Adeptus Minor* (5°=6°) degree in the Hermetic Order of Golden Dawn (H.O.G.D.) passed,[10] and the subsequent spiritual attainment of the union with the Divine Genius they strived to attain.[11]

However, Crowley's plan was not to simply rehash what he had learned years ago but to offer an update on the understanding of the IAO process appropriate for his own magical order the A∴A∴. Taking into consideration the Aeon of Horus and the attainment of Crossing the Abyss or the symbolic gulf between the Man and God, he arrives at an upgrade, the VIAOV formula. To explain its meaning, Crowley combines the Tarot correspondences, psychoanalytic lingo, sexual symbolism, and finally, mythological material while holding the IAO formula behind 'Almost all the legends

---

[9] *Crowley et al. 1997*, 158–66.

[10] Ibid, 159–60.

[11] I. Regardie, *The Golden Dawn* (Llewellyn Publications, 1989), 230.

of heroes...', which precisely confirms its place in the present discussion.[12]

It is important to note that while for Campbell, as the theorist of the myth, the Hero's journey occupies the central position, whereas for Crowley myth is just a tool to expand the understanding of the crucial spiritual attainments. Still, both concepts, monomyth and VIAOV formula, have very similar three-step unfolding. Campbell, relying on the previous work of folklorist van Gennep, adopts his *schéma des rites de passage* (separation, transition, incorporation)[13] and remodels it into separation (hero ventures forth), initiation (encounters forces), and return (bestows boon).[14] Crowley, similarly so, while going through the various myths, recognizes a narrative pattern we can summarize as a partition, crisis, rebirth, or according to his new interpretation, conception, gestation, and maturation. In the following article, the focus will be on Crowley's symbolical interpretation of each phase, trying to explain the underlying context of the formula to the best of my ability while relying on the Parzival example as the one which is most consistent, and finally,

---

[12] *Crowley et al. 1997*, 162.

[13] R. Rensma, *The Innateness of Myth* (Continuum, 2009), 107.

[14] J. Campbell, *The Hero with a Thousand Faces* (Princeton University Press, 2004), 28.

comparing the VIAOV with Campbell's monomyth theory.

Hero's Journey and Adept's Evolution

The basic understanding of the IAO formula is through the generative symbolism, starting with the archaic notion of parthenogenesis reserved for the matriarchal Aeon of Isis, moving to sexual reproduction of the patriarchal Aeon of Osiris, and continuing with autogamic symbolism of the current age presuming 'Two sexes in one person'. These, however, have nothing to do with the actual procreation modalities but describe the Great Work, or more precisely, the fundamental relation of the Adept with the aforementioned Divine Genius or Holy Guardian Angel, a term Crowley preferred to use.

Accordingly, we find in his later writing the instruction regarding the tarot card *Hierophant* which relates to the initial **V** phase, 'Offer thyself Virgin to the Knowledge and Conversation of thine Holy Guardian Angel!'. In this light, the design of the card with the central figure and four worshippers, or in later design Kerubs,[15] represents the initial four elemental grades of the A∴A∴ path and the one just above them, all understood as the preparation for the union with the Angel.[16] A suitable mythological parallel concerns the young Parzival shielded from the outside world by his overprotective

---

[15] A. Crowley, *The Book of Thoth* (Samuel Weiser, 1983), 78.

widowed mother, implying the need for the consciousness (*Ruach*) to gain independence from the inner forces represented by the Freudian mother figure.[17] Campbell too talks about the status quo of the hero-to-be and the need to separate from the world into the 'zone unknown', a call whose refusal denotes an 'infantile ego' bound by the mesmerizing power of the inner father and mother. The uncharted territory is unconsciousness itself and embarking on a quest can signify 'the coming of adolescence' as well as the 'dawn of religious illumination' or 'the awakening of the self'. An important role in this process is reserved for mythological figures of the Herald, who jump starts the adventure and of the Helper, often an old, male character (wizard, hermit, smith, etc.) of mercurial nature representing the 'protecting power of destiny'.[18]

Crowley elsewhere speaks of the Herald as well but as the personal Angel (lat. *aggelos,* 'messenger'), concerning

---

[16] *Dominus Liminis,* corresponding to the Spirit. Although the *Hierophant* card has no direct relation to this grade, in the H.O.G.D. initiating officer of the same name had a temple station matching the position of the grade on the Tree of Life, the outer side of *Paroketh* (*Regardie 1989,* 334). However, parallels to the A∴A∴ grades given here and further, are my own conclusion not backed by Crowley but still deduced from his exposition of the related symbols.

[17] *Crowley et al. 1997,* 160, 162.

[18] *Campbell 2004,* 45–67.

the letter *Yod*, here matching phase **I**.[19] Therefore, this step concerns the result of the previous preparation, or the union with the Angel, a major task for the *Adeptus Minor* initiate. The difference to Campbell is that Herald and Helper are here the same figure, likewise of mercurial nature, stemming from the secondary astrological correspondence of the matching Tarot card *Hermit*, the planet Mercury. The primary astrological correspondence, the zodiac sign Virgo, too confirms the connection to a personal Angel by indicating the soul duly prepared for the sacred union.[20] Therefore here, similarly to Campbell, the separation is related to a profound spiritual experience.

According to generative symbology, the **I** is the first manifestation of the paternal energy of the being, having both spermatic and phallic connotations. The former is derived from the shape of the Hebrew letter *Yod* (י) as the seed from which the letter *Vav* (ו) is formed while the latter is based on the shape of the

---

[19] A. Crowley, "Liber V Vel Reguli" in *Magick* (Weiser Books, 1997), 578. Written during the same Cefalù period, proving the commonality of Crowley's reasoning.

[20] Usually, the relation of the Angel and the Soul is explained by the IHVH formula based on *Vau-Heh* pair while the VIAOV formula is centred on the *Yod-Vau* link. Maybe the best way to look at this, is to consider *Yod* in VIAOV formula as the force (Hermit) which binds *Vau-Heh* (King and Queen) in the mystical marriage depicted on the *Lovers* card of Thoth deck, indicating the alchemical process *Solve,* soon to follow (*Crowley 1983*, 80, 82).

Latin letter I.[21] Ultimately, Crowley would merge spermatic symbology with the wand (phallus) in the image of spermatozoon, as a part of his own *Hermit* card design.[22] Here a psycho-biological development of the individual serves as a symbol for deep maturation, signifying that inner progress should be understood in terms of spiritual growth instead of perfection through suffering as in the previous Aeon.[23]

Accordingly, contact with the Angel 'as Unconscious Creature Self—the Spiritual Phallus' constitutes an 'occult puberty'.[24] This can be understood as the revelation of the 'Unconscious Will' of psychoanalysis or the 'True Will' of Crowley's teaching, the unique and authentic nature of the person one must discover and accept as the only Law to follow.[25] Alternatively, the I phase represents the manifestation of the Word of the

---

[21] *Crowley et al. 1997*, 161, 163-4.

[22] Still, *Yod* as the seed has the feminine aspect being expressed through the *Virgo* correspondence. Hence, *Yod* can be understood as a hermaphroditic potentiality in need of development. Similar symbolism of this letter, we find in *Zohar* as well (D. C. Matt, *The Zohar [Sefer Ha-Zohar]* (Stanford University Press, 2009), 2:178b).

[23] *Crowley et al. 1997*, 164.

[24] A. Crowley, "Liber Samekh" in *Magick* (Weiser Books, 1997), 523. Written in Cefalù as well.

[25] *Crowley et al. 1997*, 161, 163.

Angel.[26] This is a concept comparable to the Word of God, or divine plan of Stoicism, or Johannine Logos incarnated in the flesh. In Crowley's case, it can signify the Word of the Aeon, as the specific expression of the spiritual nature of the particular age, he was compelled to manifest. The matching mythological example, following the generative symbolism, is the one of the Wagnerian hero seizing the Holy Spear from the evil magician Klingsor or, along the more general Grail narrative, a hero venturing off into the wasteland (desert).[27]

Campbell too talks about an inhospitable place (desert, jungle, etc.) as the realm where the hero has to face psychological forces of libido and destrudo. Beforehand, the threshold guardian needs to be faced so that one can cross the border between God and man, abandoning the dualistic tendencies of the mind. The result is the release from ego as 'a form of self-annihilation' and a symbolic death in the World Womb that entails rebirth, as in the myth of Osiris. Once the crossover is made, the hero goes through many trials which are a preparation for the highest initiation.[28]

---

[26] "Reguli 1997," *Magick*, 578.

[27] *Crowley et al. 1997*, 161. Crowley's mention of Parzival in the desert can't be a Wagnerian reference since the motif of the wasteland is not present in the original version of *Parsifal* but we do find it elsewhere in the Grail literature.

One familiar with the A∴A∴ path will immediately recognize the parallel with the already noted Crossing of the Abyss, implying the annihilation of the ego and correlating with the motif of the threshold and desert as well.[29] More precisely, **A** phase could be taken to represent the grade of Babe of the Abyss, symbolically imagined as the baby growing inside the womb of its mother, the Great Goddess. Refraining from the dying-and-rising symbolism, Crowley here avoids stressing the destructive aspect of this phase by focusing on the symbol of eternal, indestructible life, the child not unlike the *puer aeternus*.[30]

More precisely, it is the child God Harpocrates who in Crowley's system is related to the most transcendent aspects of the Godhead, the Monad, and Nothingness, and with all the Tarot cards we encountered so far: the *Hierophant*, the *Hermit*, and the *Fool*.[31] This child God is pre-existent or unborn, further supported by the

---

[28] *Campbell 2004*, 71–86, 89.

[29] A. Crowley, *The Book of Lies* (Samuel Weiser, 1970), "Dust-Devils" (MB).

[30] Not in Jungian but in the original sense as we find it in Ovid (4.18), identified with Iacchus which has further symbolic consequences we can't explore here. Suffice it to say that the card *Fool* refers also to Iacchus (*Crowley 1983*, 65).

[31] All these connections can be confirmed by checking *The Book of Thoth* or 777.

explanation that it 'has formulated his Father, and made fertile his Mother'. Accordingly, Crowley here is not continuing various hero narratives but breaks down chronology and goes back to the points which are more fitting for the start than the middle point of the storyline. The suitable Wagnerian parallel is the one of Parzival as the 'pure fool', a motif from Scene 1 of Act I.[32]

Along with the generative metaphor, the next O phase is all about the maturation of the baby into 'Hermaphrodite fully grown' or Harpocrates into the adult Horus. In other words, it is a full realization of the androgynous potential of the letter *Yod*, matching the 'Two sexes in one person' designation and the Tarot card *Devil* with its historical link to the famous Baphomet of Eliphas Levi. Following the Parzival story-line, the fitting mythological parallel has the hero in Black Armour (Scene 1 of Act III) 'ready to return to Montsalvat'.[33]

Saturn ruling the Capricorn of the *Devil* card is connecting the O phase with the third emanation of the Tree of Life *Binah* and accompanying grade *Magister Templi* but its general description goes more in favour of the second emanation and the grade *Magus*.[34] However, *Chokmah* itself alludes to hermaphroditic nature

---

[32] *Crowley et al. 1997*, 161, 163.

[33] Ibid, 161–65.

according to Mathers, so in a certain sense, it contains both polarities,[35] known as the Mother and Father in the *Idrot* section of *Zohar*.[36] The idea of Father-Mother coupled, is a detail of the *Devil* card of Thoth deck as a female ring crowning the shaft of the phallus. Although highly abstract, this line of thinking is consonant with the kabbalistic symbolism of the androgynous phallus, its corona implying the feminine principle.[37] Having in mind that equally mercurial and hermaphroditic *Yod* signifies *Chokmah* as well, this confirms the O phase as the full realization (revelation) of the already mentioned hermaphroditic potential of the I phase. Therefore, we do find that the VIAOV formula corresponds precisely to *Chokmah*.[38]

Strangely enough, similar ideas we encounter in Campbell's description of the Initiation stage that comes in three distinctive variations, the 'bliss of infancy

---

[34] A. Crowley, V. B. Neuburg and M. Desti, *The Vision & the Voice* (Samuel Weiser, 1998), 266, fig. 14.

[35] S. L. M. Mathers, "Kabbalah" in *Kabbala denudata* (The Theosophical Publishing Company, 1912), 27. This claim, however, is not the brainchild of Mathers but derives from *Zohar* (290b).

[36] 2:123a

[37] E. R. Wolfson, *Circle in the Square* (State University of New York Press, 1995), 85–86.

[38] A. Crowley and I. Regardie, *777 and Other Qabalistic Writings of Aleister Crowley* (Samuel Weiser, 1996), 37 (CLXXXVII:2).

regained' in the Meeting with the Goddess, at-one-ment with Father, and *apotheosis*.[39] The first type presupposes a *hieros gamos* and rising above the infantile dualistic tendencies while the next, the initiation into the role of World Redeemer.[40] The last one somewhat unites the previous two, presuming androgyny as the final integration of opposites or the non-dual state before the Fall, to be restored.[41] The last type is best illustrated by the Tibetan image of Father-Mother (*Yab-Yum*).[42] Finally, the critical moment of the journey can be represented by the ultimate boon (elixir, soma, the grail, etc.), matching, to a certain extent, the Grail or Lance symbolism attached to *Binah* and *Chokmah* respectively.[43]

After the resolution of the critical point, the hero must return and share his insight(s) or reward with the common world. As the master of both realms, the hero passes back and forth with ease, understanding his role as 'the conscious vehicle of the terrible, wonderful Law,

---

[39] *Campbell 2004*, 34.

[40] Ibid, 100; 105; 322–23.

[41] Revealing among other things that Father is 'antecedent to the division of sex: the pronoun "He" was a manner of speech', an explanation fitting quite well with above mentioned idea of androgynous Father/Phallus (Ibid., 150).

[42] Ibid, 141–42; 150; 156–57.

[43] Ibid, 162–63.

whether his work be that of butcher, jockey, or king'. The final act is the restoration of the World.[44]

Crowley's matured child is the World redeemer as well. or 'Parzival as King and Priest in Montsalvat performing the miracle of redemption', the closing of Act III of *Parsifal*.[45] The idea of the Hero's return to the starting point, albeit changed by the adventure, is precisely the conclusion of the VIAOV formula, as can be seen from the identical opening and **closing V**. Cyclical change Crowley illustrated by giving a chemical metaphor of the transformation of copper into the monosulfide compound.[46] This again alludes to Crossing the Abyss since the process includes Sulphuric acid known as Oil of Vitriol in alchemy, close to the fabled Universal Solvent.[47] In other words, it signifies the destructive process of the adept's dissolution into the fundamental components, the Paracelsian *Tria Prima*, corresponding to the Supernals above the Abyss and to the three innermost parts of the soul.[48] Moreover, it seems that Vitriol in particular is linked to the Hierophant whose

---

[44] Ibid, 179; 212–13; 221–22.

[45] *Crowley et al. 1997*, 160.

[46] Ibid, 164.

[47] See symbolic interpretation of the oil of vitriol in the context of *LXV* I:16 (Ibid, 89).

[48] 777 *1996*, 23 (CXII:1–3), 21 (XCVII:1–3).

card represents the initial and the final step of the VIAOV formula.[49]

However, the *Solve* part of the alchemical process presumes the *Coagula* step as well, or the re-creation (coagulation) of the ego, back below the Abyss.[50] Following the generative symbolism, Crowley imagines autocopulation of the inner Androgyne i.e., Baphomet, begetting 'himself on himself as V again'.[51] To put it differently, once the non-dual root of the awareness is fully realized, the standard, working consciousness has to be reconstructed so the mission of the Master could continue among the 'sleeping ones'.

To further explain the point, Crowley utilizes kabbalistic symbolism and distinguishes the initial, plain V spelled *Vau-Vau* as usual, from the exalted **final V** spelled *Vau-Yod-Vau*.[52] The middle *Yod* alludes that Angel, initially encountered at the second stage, is now fully integrated/incorporated into the mundane *Vau*

---

[49] A. Crowley, "Liber Liberi Vel Lapidis Lazuli" in *Thelema* (Samuel Weiser, 1983), 23 (IV:42).

[50] H. P. Blavatsky and A. Crowley, "Liber LXXI" in *Commentaries on the Holy Books and other papers* (S. Weiser, 1996), 319 (III:57).

[51] The interesting parallel between the Hierophant figure of Atu V and Baphomet is the former's wand-left hand opposition which resembles the juxtaposition of the latter's hands precisely indicating *Solve et Coagula*.

[52] Cf. *777 1996*, 31 (LXVI: 31-32).

consciousness. The outcome of such attainment is that one becomes the 'master of the Event by giving him the understanding that whatever happens to him is the execution of his true will'.[53] Finally, we can conclude that the **closing V** suggests *Yod*-Logos incarnated in the flesh, matching Crowley's explanation of the corresponding *Hierophant* (*Pope*) card as representing incarnation.[54] From the perspective of the **final V**, the *Hierophant* card is a further development of the *Devil* card. In this light, we might add that one of the interpretations of the name 'Baphomet' is 'Baptism of Wisdom' which not only points to *Chokmah* (Wisdom) but is related to the 'miracle of incarnation'.[55]

---

[53] *Crowley et al. 1997*, 163.

[54] A. Crowley and E. Adams, *The General Principles of Astrology* (Weiser Books, 2002), 36. Campbell too, *nota bene*, considered 'transubstantiated word' as one form of the ultimate boon (*Larsen et al. 2002*, 306).

[55] A. Crowley, "Liber XV" in *Magick* (Weiser Books, 1997), 585. This is a too specific matter for the present paper. Its outline can be defined by listing the following points. Incarnation is related to the specific power of the Spirit, *Ire* which is expressed on the *Hierophant* card. Because of its position on the Tree of Life, the function of the Hierophant is explained as bringing down the fire of *Chokmah* (*Crowley 1983*, 15, 85). So, if we take Baphomet-Devil to be the representative of this emanation and the development of *Yod* (fire), as proposed above, we could say that the fire of **O** phase is manifested in the final **V** phase. The Hierophant's left-hand position and the fingers gesture of the number 2 pointed downward, could symbolize the incarnation (bringing down) of

Points of contact

Considering that Campbell elaborates on the Hero's journey to a great extent, some details of his monomyth don't correlate with the concise VIAOV formula. Still, the above-given comparison shows a good deal of the overlap between the two concepts. This begs the question, how can this be?

It is important to stress that, so far, there is no proof that Campbell was familiar with Crowley's work so early in his writing career. He would eventually possess the Thoth deck[56] and write on the topic of Tarot but this came at a later stage in his life.[57] It is clear from his work that Eastern traditions played a much bigger role than their Western counterpart, ancient or modern. Nevertheless, he was interested in astrology and visited famous American astrologer Evangeline Adams in 1925, who knew, worked with, and plagiarized Crowley almost a decade previous. In the same period, he would

---

the *Chokmah* (2), the Will, Word, etc... See Gunther's work where he elaborates on the sign of V to a much broader degree and in a somewhat different context (J. Daniel Gunther *The Angel & Abyss* (Ibis Press, 2014) pages 269–299).

[56] *OPUS Archives and Research Center*, Campbell (Joseph) Collection, CAMPBELL 105 artif.

[57] J. Campbell and R. Roberts, *Tarot Revelations* (Vernal Equinox Press, 1982 1979).

pick up from Fenwick Holmes, one of the key figures in the New Thought movement, a technique of discovering the common direction of one's interests, which could be compared to the idea of True Will to a certain extent.[58] Still, there is no trace of the actual influence of Crowley or other Western occultists of the time.

It is true that Crowley, at a certain point, did a series of lectures while staying in New York whose structure resembled the one of *MTP* but Campbell was far too young to attend those.[59] Finally, there is a question of the book itself which was, after all, published so many years before *The Hero*. Campbell did have a period of extensive reading, up to nine hours per day, between 1929 and 1934 while living in Woodstock, New York and it is an alluring thought that among the many tomes he digested *MTP* was included.[60] However, it is very doubtful that he would be able to get his hands on the copy because the distribution of the book was very limited. Watkins Books, a famous esoteric bookshop in London, did offer the book in 1931 for the price of 1 pound, 12 shillings, and 6 pennies which roughly

---

[58] *Larsen et al. 2002*, 67–68.

[59] *Kaczynski 2010*, 279.

[60] J. Campbell, P. Cousineau and S. L. Brown, *The Hero's Journey* (New World Library, 2003), 53.

amounts to 85£ of today's worth but that is the UK.[61] It seems that *MTP* was a rare and not much sought-after commodity in the States until the end of the 60s when the interest in Crowley was reignited, followed by the Grant-Symonds edition in the 70s. So, the possibility of the direct influence of the VIAOV formula on Campbell's monomyth can't be confirmed with any certainty.[62]

This leaves us with the only possible option; the influence of common sources. While the importance of Freud and Jung in the development monomyth is widely acknowledged, the role of these authors in Crowley's writing is only vaguely considered. However, Crowley did read both and as is evident from his interpretation of the (V)IAO(V) formula, incorporated some of the psychoanalytic ideas into his work. In this context, it is very telling that in the Cefalù period he interpreted the Harpocrates we encountered above, in the context of the personal Angel, as 'almost the "unconscious" of Freud'.[63] Therefore, it seems that both authors had a similar appreciation for mythological

---

[61] Watkins Catalogue for December 1931 (No. CXIII)

[62] I would like to express my sincere gratitude to the following individuals who were kind enough and provided the necessary information regarding the first edition of MTP and its availability in the States during the 1930s and 40s, so I could form the present conclusion: Richard Kaczynski, Martin P. Starr, Allen H. Greenfield and Carl from Watkins Books.

content and under the influence of Freud, Jung, and general mystical thought, came to a similar conclusion which they presented according to their areas of expertise, interest, and level of experience.[64]

---

[63] M. Pasi, "Varieties of Magical Experience: Aleister Crowley's Views on Occult Practice," *Magic, Ritual, and Witchcraft* 6, no. 2 (2011): 158n107.

[64] There is, of course, another author that should be taken into consideration; Otto Rank. However, unlike Campbell it is not clear whether Crowley was familiar with his work. One possible telling sign is Crowley's interpretation of mythological Waters as the amniotic fluid, an idea also present in Rank's book on the hero myth (55).

Bibliography

"Amazon Best Sellers: Best Sellers in Mythology & Folklore Encyclopedias." Accessed October 1, 2022. https://www.amazon.com/gp/bestsellers/books/11749. (*Amazon 2022*).

Blavatsky, Helena P., and Aleister Crowley. "Liber LXXI: The Voice of Silence." In *Commentaries on the Holy Books and Other Papers.* I. The Equinox IV. York Beach, Me.: S. Weiser, 1996. (*Liber 1996*).

Campbell, Joseph. *The Hero with a Thousand Faces.* Commemorative ed. Bollingen series 17. Princeton NJ: Princeton University Press, 2004. (*Campbell 2004*).

Campbell, Joseph, Phil Cousineau, and Stuart L. Brown. *The Hero's Journey: Joseph Campbell on His Life and Work.* 1st New World Library ed. The collected works of Joseph Campbell. Novato Calif.: New World Library, 2003. (*Campbell et al. 2003*).

Campbell, Joseph, and Richard Roberts. *Tarot Revelations.* 2nd ed. San Anselmo CA: Vernal Equinox Press, 1982 1979. (*Campbell et al. 1982*).

Crowley, Aleister. *The Book of Lies, Which Is Also Falsely Called Breaks; the Wanderings of Falsifications of the One Thought of Frater Perdurabo (Aleister Crowley), Which*

Thought Is Itself Untrue. A Reprint, with an Additional Commentary to Each Chapter. New York: Samuel Weiser, 1970. CCCXXXIII. (*Crowley 1970*).

———. "Liber Liberi Vel Lapidis Lazuli: Adumbratio Kabbalæ Ægyptiorum Sub Figurâ VII." In *Thelema: The Holy Books of Thelema*, 7–35. York Beach, Maine: Samuel Weiser, 1983. (*Liberi 1983*).

———. *The Book of Thoth: A Short Essay on the Tarot of the Egyptians.* V. The Equinox III. New York: Samuel Weiser, 1983. (*Crowley 1983*).

———. *Thelema: The Holy Books of Thelema.* York Beach, Maine: Samuel Weiser, 1983. (*Crowley 1983*).

———. "Liber Samekh: Theurgia Goetia Summa Congressus Cum Daemone." In *Magick: Liber ABA, Book Four, Parts I-IV*. Edited by Hymenaeus Beta. 2nd rev. ed., 513–43. Boston, Mass.: Weiser Books, 1997; Sub Figura DCCC. (*Samekh 1997*).

———. "Liber V Vel Reguli." In *Magick: Liber ABA, Book Four, Parts I-IV*. Edited by Hymenaeus Beta. 2nd rev. ed., 573–84. Boston, Mass.: Weiser Books, 1997. (*Reguli 1997*).

———. "Liber XV: O.T.O. Ecclesiae Gnosticae Catholicae Canon Missae." In *Magick: Liber ABA, Book Four, Parts I-IV*. Edited by Hymenaeus Beta. 2nd rev. ed., 584–98. Boston, Mass.: Weiser Books, 1997. (*Liber XV 1997*).

Crowley, Aleister, and Evangeline Adams. *The General Principles of Astrology: Liber DXXXVI*. Boston, MA: Weiser Books, 2002. (*Crowley et al. 2002*).

Crowley, Aleister, Mary Desti, and Leila Waddell. *Magick: Liber ABA, Book Four, Parts I-IV*. 2nd rev. ed. Edited by Hymenaeus Beta. Boston, Mass.: Weiser Books, 1997. (*Crowley et al. 1997*).

Crowley, Aleister, Victor B. Neuburg, and Mary Desti. *The Vision & the Voice: With Commentary and Other Papers*. II. The Equinox IV. York Beach, Me.: Samuel Weiser, 1998. (*Crowley et al. 1998*).

Crowley, Aleister, and Israel Regardie. *777 and Other Qabalistic Writings of Aleister Crowley: Including Gematria & Sepher Sephiroth*. York Beach, Me.: Samuel Weiser, 1996. (*777 1996*).

Gunther, J. Daniel. *The Angel and the Abyss: Comprising the Angel and the Abyss and the Hieroglyphic Triad, Being Books II & III of the Inward Journey*. Lake Worth: Ibis Press, 2014. (*Gunther 2014*).

Hanegraaff, Wouter J. *Esotericism and the Academy: Rejected Knowledge in Western Culture*. Cambridge, New York, Melbourne: Cambridge University Press, 2013. (*Hanegraaff 2013*).

Kaczynski, Richard. *Perdurabo: The Life of Aleister Crowley*. Rev. and expanded ed. Berkeley Calif.: North Atlantic Books, 2010. (*Kaczynski 2010*).

King, Karen L. "Social Factors in Mythic Knowing: Joseph Campbell and Christian Gnosis." In *Paths to the Power of Myth: Joseph Campbell and the Study of Religion*. Edited by Daniel C. Noel, 68–80. New York: Crossroad, 1990. (*Social 1990*).

Larsen, Stephen, and Robin Larsen. *Joseph Campbell: A Fire in the Mind*. Rochester Vt.: Inner Traditions, 2002. The authorized biography. (*Larsen et al. 2002*).

Mathers, S. L. MacGregor. "Kabbalah." In *Kabbala Denudata: The Kabbalah Unveiled, Containing the Following Books of the Zohar. 1. The Book of Concealed Mystery. 2. The Greater Holy Assembly. 3. The Lesser Holy Assembly*, 1–42. New York: The Theosophical Publishing Company, 1912. (*Kabbalah 1912*).

Matt, Daniel Chanan. *The Zohar = [Sefer Ha-Zohar]*. Pritzker ed. XII V. Stanford, Calif.: Stanford University Press, 2009. (*Matt 2009*).

OPUS Archives and Research Center, Campbell (Joseph) Collection, CAMPBELL 105 artif. https://gencat1.eloquent-systems.com/webcat/request/DoMenuRequest?SystemName=Opus+Archives+%26+Research+Center&UserName=WA+Public&Password=&UniqueID=0&TemplateProcessID=6000_854_854&bCachable=1&MenuName=Opus+Archives+%26+Research+Center&ControlPer=20&ControlLoc=T&eloquentref=opus_public, accessed October 27, 2022. (*Campbell Collection*).

Pasi, Marco. "Varieties of Magical Experience: Aleister Crowley's Views on Occult Practice." *Magic, Ritual, and Witchcraft* 6, no. 2 (2011): 123–62. (*Pasi 2011*).

Rank, Otto, ed. *The Myth of the Birth of the Hero: A Psychological Exploration of Myth*. Expanded and updated ed. Baltimore: Johns Hopkins University Press, 2004. (*Rank 2004*).

Regardie, Israel. *The Golden Dawn: A Complete Course in Practical Ceremonial Magic the Original Account of the Teachings, Rites, and Ceremonies of the Hermetic Order of the Golden Dawn (Stella Matutina)*. 6th edition, revised and enlarged. St. Paul MN: Llewellyn Publications, 1989. (*Regardie 1989*).

Rensma, Ritske. *The Innateness of Myth: A New Interpretation of Joseph Campbell's Reception of C.G. Jung*. Continuum advances in religious studies. London: Continuum, 2009. (*Rensma 2009*).

Segal, Robert Alan. "Introduction: In Quest of the Hero." In *In Quest of the Hero*, vii–xli. Mythos. Princeton, N.J.: Princeton University Press, 1990. (*Introduction 1990*).

Wolfson, Elliot R. *Circle in the Square: Studies in the Use of Gender in Kabbalistic Symbolism*. Albany: State University of New York Press, 1995. (*Wolfson 1995*).

THE THERION FILES

WILLIAM PETERS

Introduction

In February 1926 the Internationalen Theosophischen Verbrüderung (I.T.V.), published an article in its quarterly *Notices for Members*, ominously titled *Der Fall Therion (The Therion Case)*.[1] Founded by Franz Hartmann in 1897 and after 1910 headed by Hermann Rudolph, the I.T.V. grew to be one of the leading German theosophical organisations of its day, and by 1925 had over 2,000 members registered in forty local bodies across Germany.[2] The six page article was the organisation's public response to a controversy brewing since the previous summer which had been brought to a head by a missive many members had received the past December. In *An Open Letter to Hermann Rudolph*, the mysterious author Αλαστωρ (Alastor), reproached the I.T.V. chairman for betraying his theosophical "flock" by failing to instruct them of the arrival in Germany of the long heralded Theosophical World-Teacher. More

---

[1] "Der Fall Therion", *Mitteilungen für die Mitgliedern der Internationalen Theosophischen Verbrüderung*, 15 February, 1926, XVI Jahrg. Nr. 1., 6-12.

[2] Helmut Zander, *Anthroposophie in Deutschland Bd. 1* (Göttingen, Germany: Vandenhoeck & Ruprecht, 2007), 290.

controversially, the letter compared Rudolph to Caiaphas, a Jewish high priest who was said to have plotted to kill Jesus. In point of fact penned by Aleister Crowley, the *Open Letter* was an attempt to salvage something from Crowley's disappointing 1925 sojourn in Germany and, while the letter was written primarily for members of the I.T.V., the response of the organisation's Management Committee as detailed in *The Therion Case* had repercussions far beyond German theosophical circles.

The Conference at Hohenleuben

Aleister Crowley traveled to the German village of Hohenleuben in June 1925 at the invitation of German publisher, theosophist and occultist Heinrich Tränker who, attracted by the hamlet's peace and seclusion, had recently settled there after leaving nearby Leipzig. Though a member of long standing, in 1922 Tränker had resigned from the German section of the I.T.V., the Theosophische Gesellschaft Deutschland (T.G.D.), after a falling out with his former brethren.[3] Taking the name 'Frater Recnartus', he founded the Collegium Pansophicum, which he intended to develop as a hermetic teaching academy based on the principles of universal education proposed by 17th century Czech philosopher John Amos Comenius. The new order

---

[3] Volker Lechler, *Heinrich Tränker als Theosoph, Rosenkreuzer und Pansoph,* (Stuttgart: Volker Lechler, 2013), 103.

began publishing a journal, *Pansophia*, and established a body in the German capital, The Pansophic Lodge of Light Seeking Brothers Orient Berlin. Parallel to this, in 1921 Tränker had been named German national head of the Ordo Templi Orientis by OTO founder Theodor Reuss.[4] Following the latter's death in October 1923, though having never worked the Order's initiatory system nor having met Reuss in person, Tränker sought unsuccessfully to acquire Reuss' literary estate.[5] The following year, in correspondence with the Order's Canadian national head, Charles Stansfeld Jones, a plan was conceived to revivify the OTO by elevating Aleister Crowley, chartered by Reuss as British national head, to the position of Outer Head of the Order (vacant since Reuss' death), to align the Collegium Pansophicum with Crowley's new Thelemic teachings, and to establish an international headquarters in Germany for publishing and promulgation.

Preliminary agreements having been made, Tränker announced in the Spring 1925 issue of *Pansophia* that he would be publishing three translations of works by Frater Achad (Jones) later that year; *Q.B.L. or The Bride's Reception, The Egyptian Revival,* and *Crystal Vision*

---

[4] Helmut Möller and Ellic Howe, *Merlin Peregrinus : vom Untergrund des Abendlandes,* (Würzburg : Königshausen & Neumann, 1986), 248.

[5] Volker Lechler, *Heinrich Tränker als Theosoph, Rosenkreuzer und Pansoph,* 155.

Through Crystal Gazing.[6] And, just as the issue went to press, Tränker decided to include a translation of the Master Therion's *Mediterranean Manifesto*. This broadsheet, published months earlier by Crowley from his rooms at the Majestic Hotel in Tunis, initiated his campaign to have himself, in his role as the Master Therion, recognised as the Theosophical World-Teacher. A footnote indicated that the Summer Solstice issue of *Pansophia* would contain a biography of the Master, as well as "other essential commentaries".[7] Jones and Crowley's writings were to be translated into German by Tränker's publishing partner Karl Germer. The two had met in Leipzig six years earlier, sharing a common interest in the spiritual and esoteric, and when Tränker relocated to rural Hohenleuben in 1921 Germer soon followed, purchasing a house in nearby Weida. In these bucolic surroundings Germer worked with Tränker and Tränker's wife Helene to establish Pansophieverlag, the Collegium Pansophicum's publishing arm; Heinrich Tränker assumed editorial duties and Helene Tränker managed finances and distribution, while Germer produced translations and bankrolled the printing costs.

---

[6] Heinrich Tränker, *Mystischer Feuerschein : d. i. eine einfältige Lehre der hermetischen Bruderschaft im fixen Osten* (Leipzig: Pansophie-Verlag, 1925)

[7] Ibid.

Crowley, traveling by rail to Hohenleuben from Paris via Frankfurt, arrived on the Summer Solstice. He was met at the station by Germer who, having lived and worked in England before WWI, had the best command of English and would act as his interpreter and driver for the summer. Crowley and Germer had already been in contact by post regarding translation issues and financial matters. The master bedded down at Tränker's guesthouse, joined two weeks later by his companion Dorothy Olsen. "Lady Crowley", as she was introduced, had been delayed in Paris where, according to Helene Tränker, she'd been unable to settle her hotel bill until the necessary funds were wired by Germer.[8] Crowley's students Leah Hirsig and Norman Mudd, arriving with Dorothy Olsen, found accommodation with Germer and his wife Maria at their home in Weida.

Before long the Crowleys were joined at the *Torheit* ('Folly', as Tränker's guesthouse was known to locals), by Otto Gebhardi of Danzig, an old line freemason, theosophist and Tränker's mentor in the T.G.D. The seventy-three year old Gebhardi had also worked with Theodor Reuss and Franz Hartmann to establish what would eventually become the OTO, contributing to the *Oriflamme*, the Order's irregularly published journal. Accompanying Gebhardi was Martha Küntzel, a retired

---

[8] Volker Lechler, 'Aleister Crowley und die „Weida-Konferenz" aus der Sicht von Helene Tränker', *Gnostika 57*, (2015), 44-58.

schoolteacher from Leipzig. Küntzel had written two pamphlets for the I.T.V.'s Theosophische Kultur Verlag *Thoughts as Creators our Destiny*[9] and *The Education of the Child*[10] and often led theosophical study classes at local bodies across Germany. Like Gebhardi, she was a member of the I.T.V.'s Speaker Society and toured Germany giving lectures on topics such as "The Cultural Task of the Woman", "Salvation from Self", "The Way to True Peace", and "Occult Teaching in Folklore".[11]

With Crowley and his entourage settled in for the summer, a steady stream of pansophists, theosophists and other seekers made their way to Hohenleuben. For the thirty-five days Crowley was their guest Helene Tränker recalled that "every day at lunch and dinner we were at least five, usually seven or eight, and often ten people."[12] As plans for the future of their Pansophic Lodge of Light Seeking Brethren were being

---

[9] Martha Küntzel, *Die Gedanken als Schöpfer unseres Schicksals,* (Leipzig: Theosophisches Kultur-Verlag, 1923).

[10] Martha Küntzel, *Die Erziehung des Kindes,* (Leipzig: Theosophisches Kultur-Verlag, 1925).

[11] "Vortragsverband", *Mitteilungen für die Mitgliedern der Internationalen Theosophischen Verbrüderung*, 15 February, 1925, XV Jahrg. Nr. 1., 6.

[12] Volker Lechler, 'Aleister Crowley und die „Weida-Konferenz" aus der Sicht von Helene Tränker', 49.

considered, members from Berlin came to call, including film producer and painter Albin Grau and bookseller Eugen Grosche. Other visitors included I.T.V. Treasurer Georg Priem, and astrologer A. Frank Glahn.[13] Artist Oskar Hopfer, who was responsible for the artwork and graphics of *Pansophia* also made his way over to Hohenleuben from his parent's home in nearby Triebes.

The discussions in Hohenleuben revolved, and ultimately foundered, upon three topics; the organisation of the Ordo Templi Orientis, Collegium Pansophicum and affiliated organisations under Crowley's authority, the publication of Crowley and Jones' works from a new international headquarters in Germany, and the establishment of The Master Therion as the Theosophical World-Teacher. The last concern was gaining urgency as it was rumoured that Annie Besant planned to introduce Krishnamurti as the World-Teacher upon the Theosophical Society's 50th Anniversary later that year.

In the end, hopes of subsuming the German esoteric orders under Crowley's leadership came to naught. It was not only the reluctance of the German brethren to give up their independence, but also an ignorance bordering on hostility with which Tränker and the others greeted the new Thelemic creed. Tränker had

---

[13] Ibid., 48.

only just received a translation of 'The Book of Law', on
the 21st of June and, after his first reading of it, confided
to his wife that if he "had the translation of Liber Legis
before Crowley arrived, he would have never been
allowed to set foot in our house!"[14] Growing financial
disagreements and, according to Crowley, a dearth of
hospitality,[15] soon took their toll and, despite initial
plans to spend the entire summer as Tränker's guests,
Crowley and Dorothy Olsen relocated to Germer's
home at the end of July. By then Germer had fully cast
his lot with Crowley, as had Oskar Hopfer, finding in
him the spiritual mentor they had long been seeking.
Though Tränker seemed to find his way to a grudging
acceptance of Liber AL, the die was already cast and
despite long winded letters shuttling between Weida and
Hohenleuben, the two men were unable to reach terms
for further cooperation. Crowley wrote to Martha
Küntzel that despite Tränker's "natural gift of
illumination" there was no "substance in his
attainments" and his refusal to devote his full resources
to the work was part of his "Ordeal of the Abyss".[16] The
conflict also spelled the end for the Pansophic Lodge of

---

[14] Ibid., 53.

[15] Aleister Crowley, "Statement of the Relations between myself
(Aleister Crowley) and Heinrich Tränker", November, 1925, O.T.O
Archives.

[16] Aleister Crowley to Martha Küntzel, 7 September 1925, KBAR,
CMO.

the Light Seeking Brethren. Eugen Grosche and Albin Grau, having lost confidence in Tränker's esoteric authority, ceremonially dissolved their lodge. Immediately thereafter they reconstituted, sans Frater Recnartus, as the Fraternitas Saturni.[17] With their new order Grau and Grosche cleverly thread the needle; recognising the Master Therion as Prophet of the New Aeon, but declining submission to the authority of the more mundane Aleister Crowley.

Further publication of Crowley's works also fell victim to the discord with Tränker. While the biography of Master Therion and translations of Crowley's works did indeed appear in the summer issue of *Pansophia,* and *The Heart of the Master* was published under separate cover, translation and printing errors aggravated tensions between the parties. Crowley complained the texts chosen for inclusion were "advanced methods of meditation quite unintelligible even to students of long standing",[18] and that Tränker's printing of his work "without having any knowledge of it is bound to discredit that work in everybody's eyes." At the same time the Tränkers complained that customers were cancelling their subscriptions in response to the new issue, endangering a vital revenue stream for the

---

[17] Volker Lechler, *Die ersten Jahre der Fraternitas Saturni,* (Stuttgart: Verlag Volker Lechler, 2015), 69.

[18] Aleister Crowley to Martha Küntzel, 7 September 1925, KBAR, CMO.

Collegium Pansophicum. Plans for further cooperation were scrapped in a flurry of recriminations.

The World-Teacher

Despite the collapse of discussions with Tränker, Crowley would continue his World-Teacher campaign. Indeed, mid-August, before further cooperation became impossible, Crowley drew up and had Germer translate the campaign's next broadside; entitled *The Testimony of the Seekers*, the document was explicit in its message:

> The World-Teacher, whose appearance was heralded for this year, and who all true seekers, especially those of the Theosophical Society, have expected, has appeared at the appointed time in the person of the Master To Mega Therion.

> We, the undersigned, have seen with our own eyes and heard with our own ears, and know "certain without falsehood" that he is the Bearer of that Word for which the soul of mankind thirsts.

> The current issue of Pansophia provides enough of his teaching to allow all honest, intelligent and enlightened persons to confirm this testimony through their own judgement. We request all of these to examine the facts carefully and to announce their decision without allowing their judgement to be clouded by the

unsupported assertions of those who attempt – due to vanity or self-interest – to darken the Truth.

Signed by the Tränkers, Karl Germer, Otto Gebhardi, Martha Küntzel and Crowley's three English adherents, the document furthermore requested readers to distribute it as broadly as possible, providing Germer's address if further copies were necessary. Germer had 500 copies printed by Bernhard Sporn, whom Tränker regularly employed to print *Pansophia*. However, upon receipt the Tränkers immediately requested their signatures struck through, claiming they'd been led to believe the document was intended "only for the lodge's files".[19]

Despite – or perhaps because of – the recalcitrance of the Tränkers, Germer worked with Otto Gebhardi and Martha Küntzel to put the *Testimony* into as many hands as possible, sending it to subscribers of *Pansophia* as well as Gebhardi and Küntzel's theosophical contacts. Germer also sent it to Georg Priem of the I.T.V., along with an account of Tränker's perfidy. Priem returned the papers, thanking Germer but indicating he felt the information on Tränker too intimate and reading it would be indiscreet. He further suggested contacting Hermann Rudolph, whom Priem had briefed on his

---

[19] Volker Lechler, 'Aleister Crowley und die „Weida-Konferenz" aus der Sicht von Helene Tränker', 54.

conversations with Crowley, and provided Rudolph's Leipzig address.[20]

Martha Küntzel intended to distribute the document on her speaking engagements planned for that Autumn. While the topics of her lectures had long been decided, in personal conversations following her talks she could take the opportunity to share the good news of the Master's appearance. Surprisingly, she'd barely begun her September speaking engagements before she and Gebhardi received word that their permission to lecture on behalf of the Theosophical Society had been withdrawn. Even more surprising were the grounds for the action; their 'propaganda' on behalf of the Master Therion. This decision was formalised on the 1st of November by unanimous vote at a session of the I.T.V. Management Committee, which included Hermann Rudolph and Georg Priem.[21] Shortly afterward, in the autumn issue of the I.T.V. *Notices for Members*, an article on the I.T.V. Bylaws indicated that a few members (no names were provided) had misunderstood §37 – which held that speakers, as representatives of the organisation,

---

[20] Georg Priem to Karl Germer, 17 September, 1925, GStA PK, HA I, Rep. 238.

[21] Rudolph Kaupisch, et al., "Aus der Ausserordentlichen Verwaltungsausschusses-Sitzung", 1 November, 1925, GStA PK, HA I, Rep. 238.

must not "injure the principles of the fraternity" by propagandising for any specific master or teacher.[22]

This was a setback for the World-Teacher campaign. The Summer's grand plans had fallen prey to betrayal and conspiracy. Tränker had dashed Crowley's hopes for a German headquarters and now his representatives in the German Theosophical Society had been gagged. Crowley decided for a direct appeal to the German theosophists. Aware of their Christian sympathies and drawing upon his own deep familiarity with the Gospels, Crowley decided to cast himself as the victim of those who would keep mankind in darkness for their own self-interest.

The Open Letter

Open Letter to Hermann Rudolph

The Word of every World-Teacher marks a definite stage in human progress: but there is often some similarity in the conditions which each in turn must meet.

Hence the Master, who has appeared this summer in Germany, found not only men and women worthy and ready to receive him; but in Heinrich Tränker (Frater

---

[22] "Kommentar zur Normalsatzung", *Mitteilungen für die Mitgliedern der Internationalen Theosophischen Verbrüderung*, 15 November, 1925, XV Jahrg. Nr. 4., 68.

Recnartus) His Judas: – 'for Judas was a thief and kept the bag and stole that which was put therein.' – Has He found His Caiaphas in you?

O High Priest of the Pharisees, what account hast thou to render of thy stewardship?

For thou hast hid thy talent in a napkin.

Thou hast forbidden those who looked to you for guidance to perform any of those practices which thou knewest well are seemly for all who seek Attainment.

And what is thine excuse? That none should seek Attainment for himself, but love all Beings, and serve Mankind.

Thus thou hast aborted human growth towards the Light. Is it then fit that we should serve the Work in impotence and blindness?

It is the first and supreme Duty of every man and woman to attain to the Highest, that utmost Wisdom, Light and Power may be given to the Work of helping the Race.

But thine own case! Hadst thou but fanned that tiny spark of thine to flames thou hadst been such a Light unto thy people as had served them all to recognize this greater Light – the Light of the Love of the Master. Instead, thou hast cast weeds of vanity and lust of power upon thy glimmer, to stifle and to stupefy thy folk with smoke and stench.

Hadst thou but let thy minute germ increase, what harvest of ripe corn had waved in gold to greet the Sunlight of the arising Master! But thou hast sterilized thyself, like Klingsor and bound the wounded Knights in thine enchantment.

More, to the obstinate blindness of the official Caiaphas, thou hast now added the persecuting fury of the bigot Saul of Tharsus.

When the most noble, venerable, and distinguished of thy Brethren, the most enlightened and beloved of all thy Sisters, leapt with pure hearts aflame and eyes "by pity enlightened" to proclaim the glad news that the World-Teacher so long sought was indeed arisen among us, thy vanity thrust through to the heart, thou hurlest forth against them – the latchet of whose shoes thou are not worthy to unloose – the thunders of thine excommunication.

Mayest thou like Saul be stricken down upon thy way by sheer illumination from on high! Mayst thou be blasted like a withered tree – to bloom again a nobler

Paul, apostle of the Master's Word to them that sit afar
off in darkness and in the shadow of death.

Though it was doubtful that Hermann Rudolph would
"bloom again" after its reading, the letter was sure to
attract wide attention in the I.T.V. community and the
inclusion of references from Wagner's *Parsifal* might
appeal to those untouched by the Christian imagery.

For the letter's translation Crowley turned to Emerich
Reeck, a German author and translator he'd met in
Frankfurt en route to Hohenleuben. The two hit it off
and Reeck presented Crowley with a copy of *Die Seele
am Galgen (Souls on the Gallows)*,[23] his newly published
translation of stories by Lord Dunsany. Crowley was
well acquainted with Dunsany's work, having published
Dunsany's poem *The Sphinx at Gizeh* in his journal *The
Equinox*, in which he later reviewed Dunsany's *A
Dreamer's Tales*. Reeck was also in contact with German
author Hanns Heinz Ewers, whom Crowley knew from
his time in New York during WWI. Crowley was
impressed enough with Reeck to draw up a contract,
assigning him German translation and publication rights
for Crowley's literary corpus, excluding "all work
treating strictly of Magick and Mysticism from the

---

[23] Edward John Moreton Drax Plunkett Dunsany, Baron and
Emerich Reeck, *Die Seele am Galgen : ein Buch von Menschen,
Göttern und Geistern,* (Frankfurt a. M : Rütten & Loening, 1924).

technical standpoint, also dramatic work and scenarios for the screen".[24]

Crowley sent Reeck the Open Letter for translation on the 8th of October as he prepared to leave for Tunisia with Dorothy Olsen. Norman Mudd and Leah Hirsig remained in Weida with the Germers, while Otto Gebhardi and Martha Küntzel returned to her home in Leipzig. Frustratingly, when Reeck's translation finally arrived weeks later, it proved so unsatisfactory that Germer, Mudd, and Hirsig were forced to begin anew, using Germer's Elberfeld German Bible to better retain the letter's biblical phraseology.[25]

Finding a printer also proved difficult. Though he'd been willing to print the *Testimony of the Seekers,* Bernhard Sporn refused to print the *Open Letter,* as Tränker, the letter's Judas, was one of his regular clients.[26] To further complicate matters, Leah Hirsig was quite pregnant and Germer, following Crowley to Tunis, was on the verge of selling off the Weida house. Despite these obstacles, with Martha Küntzel's assistance the letter's translation was finished and a printer found

---

[24] Aleister Crowley and Emerich Reeck, "Memorandum of Agreement", 1 July, 1925, Yorke Collection, Warburg Institute, University of London.

[25] Norman Mudd to Martha Küntzel, 3 November, 1925, Yorke Collection, Warburg Institute, University of London.

[26] Ibid.

in Leipzig who ran off 1500 copies. At the beginning of December these were folded into envelopes and mailed to theosophists across Germany.

The Response

Responses were quick to arrive. Within the week Germer received a letter from Ernst Voss, member of the I.T.V. Management Committee. In a paragraph by paragraph rebuttal addressed to "Mr. Alastor", Voss denied any connection with Tränker, defended Hermann Rudolph's character and derided the idea of the I.T.V. endorsing any Master or World-Teacher.[27] Other letters arrived from theosophists unfamiliar with the background of the controversy, supportive of Hermann Rudolph but inquiring "who is Alastor and which is the Message of the Master?"[28] or inquiring if the "venerable Sister" mentioned in the letter was actually Annie Besant![29]

The I.T.V.'s official response to Küntzel and Gebhardi was more succinct. On the 5th of December both were sent a terse communication:

---

[27] Ernst Voss to Alastor, 07 December, 1925, Yorke Collection, Warburg Institute, University of London.

[28] L. Chobola to Karl Germer, 15 December, 1925, Yorke Collection, Warburg Institute, University of London.

[29] Hedwig David to Alastor, 15 December, 1925, Yorke Collection, Warburg Institute, University of London.

"Today's session of the Administrative Committee has received the attached Open Letter of Alastor to Hermann Rudolph. We request a written response within 10 days as to your position, as a member of the Theosophical Society Leipzig, to this open letter."[30]

Otto Gebhardi replied promptly, writing to committee member Rudolf Kaupisch to disclaim any part in the drafting of the letter "which has been composed by the Master Therion and has been handed over to me by Herr Germer and Professor Mudd at Weida for distribution".[31] Despite Gebhardi's claim he was not responsible for the content, Kaupisch accepted this as an admission of guilt and wrote the two members, suggesting they resign from the I.T.V.[32]

Martha Küntzel, offended by the committee's "dictatorial demand" and Kaupisch's suggestion, responded sharply. In a letter dated December 18th she noted that every member is allowed "full freedom of

---

[30] Der Verwaltungsausschuss der Theosophische Gesellschaft to Martha Küntzel, 05 December, 1925 GStA PK, HA I, Rep. 238. This is incorrectly dated 5 November 1925.

[31] Otto Gebhardi to Rudolph Kaupisch, 9 December, 1925, Yorke Collection, Warburg Institute, University of London.

[32] Martha Küntzel, "To the Managing Committee of the Theosophical Society in Leipzig", 18 December, 1925, Yorke Collection, Warburg Institute, University of London.

opinion and …. perfect religious liberty"[33]. She quoted the I.T.V.'s "Notices for Members" from the previous August, in which Hermann Rudolph himself wrote "We have been preparing for the coming of a new World-Teacher" and "members are destined to prepare the way for the coming Adept, the Messenger of the White Lodge, who will be the personification of Love and Wisdom and will lead humanity to the new Aeon. Every one may do his best in this work, according to his knowledge and ability!"[34]

She then reminded the committee that Hermann Rudolph had not only ignored an invitation to meet the Master Therion but spoke of him disdainfully, misrepresenting him as a "Pansophical Master" and portraying herself and Gebhardi as "Sectarians". She noted Rudolph had rudely examined Dorothea Walker, a Scottish I.T.V. member, about the Master Therion, afterwards proclaiming "I do not suffer any contradiction!" Küntzel wrote that she feared for the welfare of the German Theosophical Society under Rudolph's leadership, that "Evolution will not make a halt before your Statutes", finally stating that neither she nor Gebhardi would resign from the I.T.V.[35] She then

---

[33] Ibid.

[34] "29. Jahresbericht der Theosophischen Gesellschaft Leipzig", *Mitteilungen für die Mitgliedern der Internationalen Theosophischen Verbrüderung*, 15 August, 1925, XV Jahrg. Nr. 3., 46.

posted this response to all her theosophical contacts in Germany.

The committee responded the next day, declaring that as "Alastor-Therion" had never met Rudolph, Küntzel's "open and hidden attacks" revealed her as the 'spiritual' author of the *Open Letter*. It insisted her "faith" was not at issue, but her support for the letter's printing and distribution and her broken promises not to 'agitate' for her master during her lecture tours. Furthermore, Kaupisch had only advanced his suggestion that Gebhardi and Küntzel resign after a public reading of the letter to the Leipzig group inspired a unanimous motion to bar the two members. Hermann Rudolph, it was claimed, had sought only to protect the principles of the I.T.V. even as he refused the invitation "to create an inner circle of secret leaders in direct contact with the Secret Chiefs", and it was noted that Küntzel had praised Tränker and his teachings until his falling out with Therion.[36]

The battle lines were now clear and actions quickly followed on both sides.

---

[35] Martha Küntzel, "To the Managing Committee of the Theosophical Society in Leipzig", 18 December, 1925, Yorke Collection, Warburg Institute, University of London.

[36] Hermann Fischer, Rudolph Kaupisch, Hermann Rudolph, "Antwort auf das von Martha Küntzel an den Vorstand der T.G. in Leipzig gerichtete Schreiben vom 19. Dezember 1925" 22 December, 1925, GStA PK, HA I, Rep. 238.

At a special session on December 22nd, the Management Committee of the Theosophical Society in Leipzig voted to bar Gebhardi and revoke Küntzel's membership. Word having reached Dorothea Walker in Scotland, she wrote to the Management Committee on the 26th in support of Küntzel and Gebhardi, noting "the great privilege I consider was bestowed upon me by various meetings with this Adept named Therion", and suggested that Rudolph's failure to accept the invitation "was an error of judgement on his part and has therefore disabled his usual capacity to see clearly."[37] Then, on the 28th, Kaupisch posted a circular to German theosophical groups explaining the committee's position, characterising the attack on Hermann Rudolph as an attack on the committee and the German Theosophical Society itself.[38] On the same day, however, Walter Wacker, a committee member in Chemnitz, wrote protesting the barring of Küntzel and Gebhardi as he felt the evidence that they had injured the interests of the society was unconvincing.[39]

---

[37] Dorothea Walker, "To the Management Committee of the International Theosophical Brotherhood in Leipzig", 26 December, 1925, GStA PK, HA I, Rep. 238.

[38] Rudolph Kaupisch, "Erklärung auf den 'offenen Brief' von Alastor an Hermann Rudolph", 28 December, 1925, Yorke Collection, Warburg Institute, University of London.

[39] Walter Wacker to Rudolph Kaupisch, 28 December, 1925, GStA PK, HA I, Rep. 238.

The situation grew alarming as theosophists beyond Leipzig began taking an interest. In hopes of ending the issue, on the 2nd of January Kaupisch circulated a motion to be voted upon at a meeting of the Management Committee scheduled for the 12th. The motion acknowledged receipt of Alastor's *Open Letter* and expressed solidarity with Hermann Rudolph, noting the actions of the Theosophical Society in Leipzig and the communications with Küntzel and Gebhardi. It proposed that by their behaviour, Otto Gebhardi and Martha Küntzel had offended the principles of the I.T.V. and forfeited their claim to membership. However, in consideration of their ages and their previous work on behalf of the I.T.V., the committee would not exercise their right to expel either of the two, as long as there were no further "incidents". When the day came, all but one of the committee's twenty members voted to pass the motion and Gebhardi and Küntzel were notified of the results.[40]

If they thought the issue closed, the committee members were soon disabused of the notion. In a response written on the 18th of January, Gebhardi and Küntzel claimed that Rudolph and Kaupisch had stated falsehoods and made misrepresentations in their prior communications. In fact, the letter claimed, Küntzel had never praised Tränker as a "most holy Brother" and that

---

[40] Rudolph Kaupisch to Martha Küntzel, 15 January, 1926, GStA PK, HA I, Rep. 238.

the invitation to Rudolph made no mention of "Secret Chiefs". Furthermore, it was claimed that as several members of the committee had no understanding of the context of these events and yet were pressured to vote, the motion violated the regulations of the I.T.V.[41]

After consideration, on the 6th of February the committee responded to her allegations, listing witnesses who could testify that Küntzel had broken her promises not to propagandise for Therion on her speaking tours and had praised Tränker as enlightened. They insisted that the invitation made to Hermann Rudolph to meet Therion had indeed referred to "Secret Masters" and offered to produce the letter itself.[42] Before either Gebhardi or Küntzel had a chance to respond, the committee convened a special session and on the 13th of February at 8:30 p.m. passed a motion expelling Otto Gebhardi and Martha Küntzel from the T.G.D.[43] The decision and its background were then published as *The Therion Case* in February's *Notices for Members*, issued a mere two days later.

---

[41] Martha Küntzel, "Antwort auf dass vom Vorstand der T.G. Leipzig gesandte Schreiben vom 2.I.1926" 18 January, 1926, GStA PK, HA I, Rep. 238.

[42] Rudolph Kaupisch, et al., "Entgegnung" 6 February, 1926, GStA PK, HA I, Rep. 238.

[43] Georg Priem, et al., "Ordentliche Sitzung des Verwaltungs-Ausschusses der T.G. Deutschland", 13 February, 1926, GStA PK, HA I, Rep. 238.

Even then, the matter was not quite finished. Robert Syring, General Secretary of the T.G.D., disagreed with the decision (his was the one vote against the motion of the 12th of January) and, after his efforts to bring the matter up again for discussion at the organisation's Easter Conference were stymied, resigned from his office.[44] In Tunis, Crowley penned another announcement from Alastor, this time to the Theosophical Society itself, now titling himself 'The Avenger',[45] (though there is no evidence that this second broadsheet was translated or distributed in Germany). For her part, Martha Küntzel wrote for support to Hugo Vollrath, head of the Supranational Theosophical Society, a competing theosophical group which had split from the I.T.V. in 1923, knowing that there was no love lost between Vollrath and Hermann Rudolph. She also hoped to interest him in publishing Crowley's qabalistic reference work 777 through his Theosophical Publishing House.[46] In August of 1926 Crowley sent Martha Küntzel another polemic against Hermann Rudolph. In *The Arraignment of Hermann Rudolph before*

---

[44] Georg Priem, et al., "Ausserordentliche Sitzung des Verwaltungs-Ausschusses der T.G.D", 4 April, 1926, GStA PK, HA I, Rep. 238.

[45] Aleister Crowley, "The WORLD TEACHER to the Theosophical Society" February 1926, Yorke Collection, Warburg Institute, University of London.

[46] Martha Küntzel, "An den Vorstand des Theosophischen Verlagshaus", 6 September, 1926, GStA PK, HA I, Rep. 238.

the Court of Honour the I.T.V. leader is portrayed as a cowardly autocrat whose true spiritual experience is negligible, whose writings are full of errors, and who refused an invitation to meet with the World-Teacher in hopes of maintaining his leadership position through intimidation and intrigue.[47] Küntzel planned to translate portions of the six page document, add additional material and mail out a hundred copies.[48] But, as the year wore on, it was increasingly clear that their hopes of appealing the decision of the management committee were misplaced.

Their expulsion from the T.G.D. and the I.T.V. was a heavy blow – not only to Gebhardi and Küntzel personally, until then sought after speakers and respected members of the German theosophical community – but also to the Master Therion's World-Teacher Campaign. With Crowley now in Tunisia and his most established German students ostracised by their fellows, a new strategy would be required to spread his message. It became clear that Thelema in Germany would be best propagated outside the established theosophical and pansophical communities. The new wine demanded new vessels. With this in mind, a new publishing house

---

[47] Aleister Crowley, "The Arraignment of Hermann Rudolph before the Court of Honour", August 1926, Yorke Collection, Warburg Institute, University of London.

[48] Martha Küntzel to Aleister Crowley, 13 August, 1926, Yorke Collection, Warburg Institute, University of London.

was formed in the spring of 1927, the Thelema-Verlag-Gesellschaft; with Crowley, Germer, Gebhardi, Küntzel, Oskar Hopfer and Bernhard Sporn sharing ownership. Gebhardi and Küntzel immediately set about bringing Crowley's mystical and magical works into the German language. Martha Küntzel translated from the English while Gebhardi, drawing upon his own experience as a freemason, theosophist, and spiritual seeker, edited the resulting translations for a German readership. Hopfer, now also a student of the Master Therion, created graphics for the new editions and Sporn oversaw their printing. While only nine of the fifteen publications announced by Thelema-Verlag-Gesellschaft were eventually published, Gebhardi and Küntzel's translations, published and unpublished, also formed a great part of the publishing output of Hermann Metzger's Psychosophische Gesellschaft in Switzerland some four decades later, thus playing a major role in the promulgation of Crowley's teachings in the German speaking countries. Despite the setbacks of that summer in Weida and a failure to enflame the hearts of the I.T.V. leadership, The Message of the Master Therion would spread well beyond the established theosophical communities to inspire new generations of seekers.

A WORLD OF DIFFERENCE

Love in the New Aeon

DANIEL BRANT CORISH

"The Book of the Law solves the sexual problem completely. Each individual has an absolute right to satisfy his sexual instinct as is physiologically proper for him. The one injunction is to treat all such acts as sacraments. One should not eat as the brutes, but in order to enable one to do one's will. The same applies to sex. We must use every faculty to further the one object of our existence.

The sexual instinct thus freed from its bonds will no more be liable to assume monstrous shapes." — Aleister Crowley, The Confessions of Aleister Crowley[1]

Introduction

The name Aleister Crowley has become synonymous with both occultism and sex, but he was hardly alone in discussing the sexual mysteries at the secret heart of the

---

[1]*The Confessions of Aleister Crowley*, Aleister Crowley, Chapter 87, Page 851, Edited by John Symonds and Kenneth Grant, Jonathan Cape, 1969

Occult Revival of the late nineteenth and early twentieth centuries. This brief essay will compare his *New Aeon*[2] teachings on sex with those of other well-known occultists, demonstrating how Crowley's philosophies are both unique and of greater relevance to us today.

Blavatsky

> "Never—physically speaking—has there ever existed a girl or woman colder than I. I had a volcano in constant eruption in my brain, and a glacier at the foot of the mountain."

So wrote Helena Petrovna Blavatsky (1831—1891) professing her asexuality in *The Secret Doctrine*. Despite this, however, she discussed the subject of sex extensively throughout her 1888 masterwork. While not going so far as to expect her readers to become celibates, Blavatsky taught that sexual union should only ever take place in order to reproduce the species. According to her, non-procreative sex had resulted in both the expulsion of Adam and Eve from the Garden of Eden and the destruction of Atlantis,[3]

---

[2] *The Aeon of Horus* was inaugurated in 1904 with the writing of *Liber AL vel Legis*.

[3] It is reasonable to assume that she did not believe this in a literal sense.

"Creative powers in man were the gift of divine wisdom, not the result of sin. This is clearly instanced in the paradoxical behaviour of Jehovah, who first *curses* Adam and Eve (or Humanity) for the supposed committed crime, and then *blesses* his 'chosen people' by saying 'Be fruitful and multiply, and replenish the earth.' […] Nor was the curse of KARMA called down upon [the Atlanteans] for seeking *natural* union, as all the mindless animal-world does in its proper seasons; but, for abusing the creative power, for desecrating the divine gift, and wasting the life-essence for no purpose except bestial personal gratification."

Aleister Crowley respected Blavatsky, so much so that he considered her to have attained to the high grade of Magister Templi, and yet he disagreed with her on many points. Her position on non-procreative sex most certainly did not match his own, as shown in the following excerpt from *The New Comment* to *Liber AL vel Legis*,[4]

"We [Thelemites are] particularly careful to deny that the object of love is the gross physiological object which happens to be Nature's excuse for it. Generation is a sacrament of the physical Rite, by which we create ourselves anew in our own image, weave in a new

---

[4] *The Law is for All*, Aleister Crowley, Part One: 50-51, page 109, New Falcon, 1991

flesh-tapestry the Romance of our own Soul's History. But also Love is a sacrament of trans-substantiation whereby we initiate our own souls; it is the Wine of Intoxication as well as the Bread of Nourishment. Nor is he for priest designed Who partakes only in one kind.

We therefore heartily cherish those forms of Love in which no question of generation arises; we use the stimulating effects of physical enthusiasm to inspire us morally and spiritually. Experience teaches that passions thus employed do serve to refine and to exalt the whole being of man or woman. Nuith indicates the sole condition: 'But always unto me.'"[5]

Also among her views, Blavatsky deemed marriage to be "the only remedy against immorality," and advisable in all cases where the spiritual seeker was not ready to embrace a life of sexless asceticism. This opinion that non-monogamous sexual relationships should be

---

[5] "There are four gates to one palace; the floor of that palace is of silver and gold; lapis lazuli & jasper are there; and all rare scents; jasmine & rose, and the emblems of death. Let him enter in turn or at once the four gates; let him stand on the floor of the palace. Will he not sink? Amn. Ho! warrior, if thy servant sink? But there are means and means. Be goodly therefore: dress ye all in fine apparel; eat rich foods and drink sweet wines and wines that foam! Also, take your fill and will of love as ye will, when, where and with whom ye will! But always unto me." *Liber AL vel Legis I:51*

avoided is shared by all of the personalities featuring in this essay except for Aleister Crowley, who alone did not consider devotion to a single partner the only road open to the occultist, or more accurately, to the Thelemite.

> "[...] we find that almost the only love-affairs which breed no annoyance, and leave no scar, are those between people who have accepted the Law of Thelema, and broken for good with the tabus of the slave-gods. The true artist, loving his art and nothing else, can enjoy a series of spontaneous liaisons, all his life long, yet never suffer himself, or cause any other to suffer.

> Of such liaisons Beauty[6] is ever the child; the wholesome attitude of the clean simple mind, free from all complications alien to Love, assures it."[7]

Randolph

Blavatsky and her contemporary Paschal Beverly Randolph (1825 – 1875) were in accord that sex should only take place within the confines of marriage, but there was much on which they were not aligned. Blavatsky stated plainly in *The Secret Doctrine* that "All,

---

[6] Beauty in Hebrew is *Tiphareth*, also the name of the sixth Sefirah on the Qabalistic Tree of Life.

[7] *The Law is for All*, Aleister Crowley, Part Three: 56, Page 315, New Falcon, 1991

sexual intercourse is forbidden in practical occultism." Randolph, on the other hand, was a pioneer in the field of what is commonly referred to today as Sex Magic.

In his *The Ansairetic Mystery*,[8] Randolph instructed on the powers, both positive and negative, of the orgasm,

> "In the orgasmal moment there is no middle-ground; for we either rise toward heaven or descend hellward. At its close, we are either better or worse—generally worse—than before [...] The ejective moment, therefore, is the most divine and tremendously important one in the human career as an independent entity; for not only may we launch Genius, Power, Beauty, Deformity, Crime, Idiocy, Shame or Glory on the world's great sea of Life, in the person of the children we may then produce, but we may plunge our own souls neck-deep in Hell's horrid slime, or else mount the Azure as coequal associate Gods; for then the mystic Soul swings wide its Golden gates, opens its portals to the whole vast Universe and through them come trooping either Angels of Light or the Grizzly Presence from the dark corners of the Spaces. Therefore, human copulation is either ascentive and ennobling, or descensive and degrading [...]"[9]

---

[8] Named from Western mistranslations of *Nusayri*, a Middle Eastern ethnoreligious group, better known today as *Alawites*, associated with Gnostic sex rituals by Orientalist writers.

Randolph also warned against *onanism*, claiming that it "saps the vitality of soul, body, spirit, mind and morals."[10] This term is derived from the biblical figure Onan,[11] slain by Yahweh for committing the sin of coitus interruptus, rather than fulfilling his obligation to impregnate the wife of his heirless brother, though interpreted as being careless with his seed by early Christian writers. Onanism would also become a synonym for masturbation from the eighteenth century onwards.

One would be hard pressed to find an occultist unopposed to onanism. Aleister Crowley addressed the subject as well,

> "It must be obvious to the most embryonic tyro in alchemy that if there be any material substance soever endowed with magical properties, one must class, *primus inter pares*, that vehicle of essential humanity which is the first matter of that Great Work wherein

---

[9] *Paschal Beverly Randolph*, John Patrick Deveney, Appendix A-The Ansairetic Mystery, Page 317, State University of New York Press, 1997

[10] *After Death: The Immortality of Man*, Paschal Beverly Randolph, Philosophical Publishing Co., 1970

[11] "And Onan knew that the seed should not be his; and it came to pass, when he went in unto his brother's wife, that he spilled it on the ground, lest that he should give seed to his brother." *Genesis 38:9, King James Version*

our race shares the divine prerogative of creating man in its own image, male and female. […] Man is in actual possession of this supreme talisman. It is his 'pearl of great price,' in comparison with which all other jewels are but gew-gaws. It is his prime duty to preserve the integrity of this substance. He must not allow its quality to be impaired either by malnutrition or by disease. He must not destroy it like Origen[12] and Klingsor.[13] He must not waste it like Onan."[14]

Though in agreement that semen should not be wasted, in Crowley's magical outlook there were ways around this problem. Onanism could be avoided by employing emissions for spiritual or magical aims. In his *Magick In Theory and Practice*,[15] in a chapter concerned with ejaculation, veiled in terms of blood sacrifice—ironically safer from a legal perspective than discussing sexual secretions at the time of its writing—Crowley informs us, "But the bloody sacrifice, though more dangerous, is

---

[12] Early Christian theologian who denounced sexual relationships as inherently impure.

[13] Magician antagonist of Parsifal. Richard Wagner's Parsifal was given a sexual interpretation in *Parsifal and the Secret of the Graal Unveiled* by OTO co-founder Theodor Reuss.

[14] *The Law is for All*, Aleister Crowley, Part One: 52, Page 121, New Falcon, 1991

[15] *Magick in Theory and Practice*, Aleister Crowley, Chapter XII-Of the Bloody Sacrifice: And Matters Cognate, Page 96, Castle, 1991

more efficacious; and for nearly all purposes human sacrifice is the best. The truly great Magician will be able to use his own blood, or possibly that of a disciple, and that without sacrificing the physical life irrevocably." He then refers the reader to his Eucharistic ritual *The Mass of the Phoenix*. In a later chapter we are told,

"A Eucharist of some sort should most assuredly be consummated daily by every magician, and he should regard it as the main sustenance of his magical life. It is of more importance than any other magical ceremony, because it is a complete circle. The whole of the force expended is completely re-absorbed; yet the virtue is that vast gain represented by the abyss between Man and God.

The magician becomes filled with God, fed upon God, intoxicated with God. Little by little his body will become purified by the internal lustration of God; day by day his mortal frame, shedding its earthly elements, will become in very truth the Temple of the Holy Ghost. Day by day matter is replaced by Spirit, the human by the divine; ultimately the change will be complete; God manifest in flesh will be his name."[16]

---

[16] *Magick in Theory and Practice*, Aleister Crowley, Chapter XX-Of the Eucharist and the Art of Alchemy, Page 179, Castle, 1991

Accounts of spermo-gnosticism reach back to Saint
Epiphanius of Salamis' record of the Boroborites in the
Fourth Century. These Egyptian Gnostics purportedly
used menstrual blood and semen for their Eucharists,
holding these substances to be the blood and body of
Jesus Christ. Epiphanius also mentioned a text sacred to
the Borborites called *The Greater Questions of Mary* in
which Jesus engages in sexual intercourse before
consuming his own seed and declaring, "Thus must we
do, that we may live."[17]

Craddock

His views on non-monogamous sex notwithstanding,
Paschal Beverly Randolph was progressive for his time,
particularly in regards to his teaching that the male
orgasm ought coincide with that of the female. This
importance placed on the female orgasm was shared by
Ida Craddock (1857 – 1902) who taught in 1900's *The
Wedding Night*,

> "A woman's orgasm is as important for her health as a
> man's is for his. And the bridegroom who hastens
> through the act without giving the bride the necessary
> half-hour or hour to come to her own climax, is not
> only acting selfishly; he is also sowing the seeds of
> future ill-health and permanent invalidism in his wife."

---

[17] *The Panarion of Epiphanius of Salamis, Part 26. Epiphanius Against
the Gnostics, or Borborites*

Curiously, however, she considered orgasms brought on by the stimulation of the clitoris, even when occurring in the act of sexual union, to be masturbatory and thus taboo.

As with Blavatsky, Aleister Crowley thought highly of Craddock, writing in a review of her 1894 work *Heavenly Bridegrooms*,

> "I am very far from agreeing with all that this most talented woman sets forth in her paper, but she certainly obtained initiated knowledge of extraordinary depth. [...] This book is of incalculable value to every student of occult matters. No Magick library is complete without it."[18]

References to the female orgasm are not easily found in Aleister Crowley's veiled sexual teachings unlike those given in the plainer language of Randolph and Craddock. It is possible that, in Crowley's belief, a woman's orgasm—whether occurring several times, once or not at all—is not of the same consequence, magically speaking, as that of the male, of whom greater self-control is necessary prior to allowing his own climax.

---

[18] *The Equinox, Volume III, Number 1*, The Tank, Page 280, Samuel Weiser, 1973

Fortune

In correspondence with Crowley, Dion Fortune (1890 – 1945) plainly confirmed the influence of his writings on her own and even her acceptance that it was indeed the Aeon of the Child, but she did not embrace all of his views. Fortune warned that visiting brothels subjects a man to detrimental psychic forces, whereas Crowley was unafraid to employ prostitutes in sexual workings. She also held the opinion, typical of her time, that homosexuality was a pathological condition stating in her *Esoteric Philosophy of Love and Marriage*,

> "We are equipped with physical bodies in which the configuration of the generative organs determines the part we shall play in the polarity of life; we are born male or female and have to abide by the decision of our conception, the phenomena of the hermaphrodite and homosexual being regarded as pathological by the esoteric as well as the exoteric scientist."[19]

The fact of Aleister Crowley's bisexuality is well established, and doubtless played a part in the greater diversity of sexual expression permissible within his own magical world view. According to Crowley, his participation in homosexual sex acts in the Algerian desert with disciple Victor Neuburg resulted in no less

---

[19] *Esoteric Philosophy of Love and Marriage*, Dion Fortune, Chapter 12, Page 42, Aquarian Press, 1974

important an event than undergoing the *Ordeal of the Abyss*, as chronicled in *The Confessions of Aleister Crowley*[20] (although, a different account of the experience was supposedly related by Neuburg to Arthur Calder-Marshal, in which, as opposed to summoning the demon Choronzon, the pair called forth, "a spirit who wished to be known as P.472 [...] a foreman builder from Ur of the Chaldees, still earthbound").[21] In any event, the Thelemic perspective on homosexuality, also explained by Crowley in *The New Comment*, is antithetical to that of Dion Fortune,

> "Every one should discover, by experience of every kind, the extent and intention of his own sexual Universe. He must be taught that all roads are equally royal, and that the only question for him is 'Which road is mine?' All details are equally likely to be of the essence of his personal plan, all equally 'right' in themselves, his own choice of the one as correct as, and independent of, his neighbour's preference for the other.

---

[20] *The Confessions of Aleister Crowley*, Aleister Crowley, Chapter 66, Page 611, Edited by John Symonds and Kenneth Grant, Jonathan Cape, 1969

[21] *The Magic of My Youth*, Arthur Calder-Marshall, Chapter One, Page 35, Cardinal/Sphere Books, 1990

He must not be ashamed or afraid of being homosexual
if he happens to be so at heart; he must not attempt to
violate his own true nature because public opinion, or
mediaeval morality, or religious prejudice would wish
he were otherwise."[22]

Conclusion

The opinions held by Aleister Crowley's predecessors
and contemporaries concerning sex generally reflect the
stricter moral conservatism of the late nineteenth and
early twentieth centuries. These teachings are more at
odds with modern sexual morality than those of
Crowley, whose views, revolutionary for their time,
have managed to remain relevant into the twenty-first
century when less restrictive sexual attitudes are the
norm.

---

[22] *The Law is for All*, Aleister Crowley, Part One: 50–51, Page 111,
New Falcon, 1991

Select Bibliography

The Secret Doctrine, H. P. Blavatsky, Theosophical University Press, 1977

Sexual Magic, Paschal Beverly Randolph, Magickal Childe Publishing, 1988

Sexual Outlaw, Erotic Mystic, The Essential Ida Craddock, Vere Chappell, Red Wheel/Weiser, 2010

Esoteric Philosophy of Love and Marriage, Dion Fortune, The Aquarian Press, 1974

The Law is for All, Aleister Crowley, New Falcon, 1991

Magick in Theory and Practice, Aleister Crowley, Castle, 1991

The Confessions of Aleister Crowley, Aleister Crowley, Edited by John Symonds and Kenneth Grant, Jonathan Cape, 1969

THE LEFT-HAND PATH

FRATER S.P.

The "Left-Hand Path" is a term well known within contemporary occultism, as is its inherently suggested opposite, the "Right-Hand Path." That these terms have their origin as translations of Sanskrit ones (Vāmamārga/Vāmācāra and Dakṣiṇamārga/Dakṣiṇācāra respectively) originally used in an Indian Tantrik[1] context is not an obscure fact either. However, it is the case that these terms, and their original context, were misunderstood by influential (in fact pivotal) figures in Western occultism, and as a result, what exists today as "Left-Hand Path" practices and organisations within Western occultism (and, by extension, what is considered "Right-Hand Path" by such practitioners and organisations) can differ crucially, both conceptually and practically, from the Indian Tantrik approaches to worship which bore the Sanskrit designations from which these terms were adapted. In this essay, I will give an overview of the origins of these terms as found within Western occultism, before examining the nature of "left-handed" and "right-handed" approaches within

---

[1] Given the IAST transliteration scheme used to spell romanised Sanskrit words, this spelling of the word is more correct than that of "tantric."

Indian Tantra (in particular, within the tradition of Śrī Vidyā, a Tantrik Hindu tradition of which I am myself an initiate, and which has its origins in classical nondual Śaiva-Śākta Tantra), and offering some points of comparison with aspects of Thelemic Magick, which I hope may provoke some thought or reflection upon our own tradition and its practices.

While the Theosophical work of Helena Petrovna Blavatsky in general displayed an appreciation of the rich religious heritage of the colonised people of India (similarly to how the Celtic Revival would represent an appreciation of cultural heritage of the colonised people of Ireland), her depiction of the "adepts" or "brothers" of the "left path," and of Tantriks more generally,[2] as perverse, self-serving and corrupting sorcerers (essentially identified as black magicians), at odds with those who serve the forces of good (identified as "right

---

[2] The conflation of the Left-Hand Path and Tantra in general remains ongoing within Western occultism, though it is not entirely accurate. With regard to Indian Tantra, it's more accurate to say that while the left-handed approaches to worship are indeed Tantrik, not all Tantrik practices are left-handed. For example, one can easily find Yantra Puja rituals which use Tantrik Mantras, but which make no use of taboo substances. Indeed, these right-handed Dakshinachara approaches are approaches to Tantrik practice: within Indian tradition, both the right and left-handed approaches exist within the scope of Tantra. It is not correct, therefore, to refer to the Right-Hand Path as non-Tantrik.

hand adepts"), builds upon the attitudes of missionaries such as William Ward and orientalists such as Horace Hayman Wilson: the former's horror at the Tantrik practices he encountered confirmed this opinion of Hinduism as the religion of "effeminate and dissolute people,"[3] and provided justification for the so-called "civilising mission," while Wilson would find in the Tantras "all that is abominable in the present state of Hindu religion."[4] It is notable, though not at all surprising, that for all of these individuals, the most deplorable aspects of these Tantrik rites and texts are the worship of the Divine in the form of the human body (particularly that of a female who may even be unclothed) along with the use of substances and activities which induce pleasure.

The narrative, presented by Blavatsky, of Adepts of the Right-Hand Path as champions of the Ancient Wisdom Tradition involved in mystical war with the depraved, self-serving and corrupting Black Magicians of the Left-Hand Path is a deeply influential one, escaping even the obscurity of occultism to influence popular culture (with this struggle of the Lodges of Magic, peppered with a little further inspiration from Crowley's *Moonchild* and Parson's Babalon Working, becoming the

---

[3] Ward, William. A View of the History, Literature and Religion of the Hindoos, 1817.

[4] Wilson, Horace Hayman. Sketch of the Religious Sects of the Hindus, 1828.

central storyline of Mark Frost and David Lynch's TV
and film series *Twin Peaks*). This narrative, and its
terminology, appears throughout Crowley's work, with
a reference to "the Brothers of the Left-hand Path"
present even within one of the Holy Books of Thelema,
Liber Trigrammaton.[5] This antagonistic dichotomy is
present in the work of other early 20th century
occultists also, such as Dion Fortune, who posits similar
explanations of the left-hand path initiate as "self-
centred," "often deluding themselves," "dangerous," and

---

[5] I must admit, as both an initiate of an Indian Tantrik tradition and
an aspirant to the A∴A∴, to have struggled with this. As an initiate
of a Kaulachara tradition, which incorporates "left-handed"
approaches to worship, the Left-hand Path—in the Tantrik sense—is
not malevolent sorcery based around spiritual pride, egotism, or
unwillingness to surrender: quite the opposite, in fact. The presence
of a term based upon, and perpetuating, misunderstanding, and
which originally denigrated a tradition which I am personally
engaged with, has been troubling to me, and I have even ruminated
on the status of that text in particular. I have wondered if all the
Class A texts are equally inspired? Are some divinely revealed,
while others are more the fruit of sublime Gnana Yoga? Or perhaps
the Divine speaks through us only using the vocabulary we already
have. Homonyms are also a feature of language. And so I wonder
on... But then I realise that all of this pulls me away from the
imminent totality that is the Goddess, and I recall that the Weapon
of the Practicus is the Cup, not the Dagger, and further that all
opposites should be fused in the Fire of the forge of Devotion to the
Divine, just as the One Word has Seven letters. And I recall the
words of Liber AL vel Legis, I:22 and I:52.

aiming at "self-gratification," in contrast to the "God-centred" initiate of the right-hand path.[6] Fortune, likely accidentally, does however hit on a detail which is actually more akin in spirit to one aspect of the original Indian Tantrik left-handed approach when she warns that "the use of drugs for raising consciousness" is a distinctive feature of left-hand practice; indeed, the use of substances which are prohibited by society is a defining feature of left-handed practice in Indian Tantra, the primary taboo intoxicant used in Tantrik ritual being alcohol, traditionally prohibited by Vedik orthodoxy (it should be borne in mind that it is the fact that the intoxicant is prohibited that is of primary importance with regard to left-handed Tantrik practice: if the intoxicant is not prohibited by the authorities of one's religion and one's society, it will lack its power in the essential context of transgression within ritual with the aim of self-transformation through a taboo breaking act of religious virtuosity). I believe an examination of what the original Sanskrit terms refer to reveals that, despite the misunderstandings of the late 19th and early 20th century occultists of the West (as brilliant as some were and as influential as they have been), what the right-handed and left-handed approaches of Tantra—the Dakṣiṇamārga / Dakṣiṇācāra and the Vāmamārga /

---

[6] Fortune, Dion. Sane Occultism, 1929, republished as What Is Occultism?

Vāmācāra — actually contain will seem familiar to the student and practitioner of Thelemic Magick.

But before that, the issue of Tantra's influence on Crowley must be addressed, as there has been recent discussion, both academic and popular, which tends to overstate this to the point of exaggeration.[7] Aside from the understanding of the Kuṇḍalinī System, which appears to have been primarily informed by the *Śiva Saṃhitā* and the *Haṭha Yoga Pradīpikā*, alongside the techniques of Sri Sabhapati Swami, and then later the comments in Gerard Aumont's article on the Three Schools of Magick, there is not much on Tantra or Tantrik practice presented by Crowley. There are no

---

[7] A definition of the word Tantra might be useful at this point for some readers. One original meaning of the term "tantra" is that of "book," in particular, the scriptures, and, further, the systems of spiritual practice presented within them, which began to appear in the 6th century CE. The term can be interpreted etymologically to mean that which spreads ("tan:" "tanoti") wisdom which saves ("tra:" "trayanti") one from worldly harm while bestowing ultimate spiritual liberation (the root of "tan" could also be interpreted as "expand," and thus suggest an expansion of consciousness). In practice, and in the context of Indian traditions, Tantra often refers to the technique in which Mantra (sacred sounds, incantations, invocations) and Yantra (sacred geometry, symbols) are utilised for magical and mystical ends, most usually in the context of the ritual worship and propitiation of a particular Deity, the goal of which could be that of liberation, the experience of the manifestation of the Deity, or a more worldly end.

discussions of the contents of particular Tantras (Āgama scriptures), no mention of Dīkṣā (initiation into Tantrik practice), none of the Mantras discussed are Mūlamantras containing Bījas, no Yantras are presented, there is nothing on Pūjā rituals, and nothing on Tantrik philosophy, such as that of Trika Śaiva, whose ontology is most similar to that of Thelema.[8] I don't feel that it is controversial to say that Crowley was not really all that

---

[8] Tantra Illuminated by the Sanskrit scholar and Tantrik practitioner Christopher Wallis is perhaps the best introduction to the subject in the English language that I am aware of. The only issue with this book that I can find happens to be in its solitary mention of Aleister Crowley, where it is claimed that Crowley invented "sex magick" rites inspired by what he knew of Tantra. This is incorrect, in my view. Still, at least Wallis could spell Crowley's name correctly, unlike David Gordon White in his 2014 The Yoga Sutra of Patanjali: A Biography (disappointingly for such an excellent scholar, whose Kiss of the Yogini is surely worthy of the attention of every OTO initiate). I feel that these attempts to suggest that Crowley either introduced Tantra to the West, or fathered Western neo-tantra, and the association him with Pierre Bernard, are mistaken, as is the claim that Indian Tantra was the primary influence on his sexual magick rituals or instructions (the influence of Indian Tantra upon OTO founders such as Carl Kellner is another matter, but solid evidence would still be required to support this claim, and I have not to date been made aware of evidence that Kellner received Diksha—initiation—into Indian Tantrik practice, or that it was Indian Tantra specifically which was the primary influence on the OTO's particular technique of sexual magick, though I am of course open to correction on this should such definite evidence exist).

knowledgeable regarding Tantrik traditions, texts, or techniques.[9]

Nonetheless, it is hard to deny that while Crowley was unaware of the details of Indian Tantra, the magical and mystical techniques he developed and practiced in his own life often displayed striking similarities with those of certain Tantrik traditions, a kind of entirely intuitive affinity. This is a topic which is discussed excellently by Gordan Djurdjevic in his essay on *The Great Beast as a Tantric Hero* (in *Aleister Crowley and Western Esotericism* edited by Bogdan and Starr, Oxford University Press, 2012), who presents Crowley as a Vīra, despite Crowley's own likely unawareness of that very term, an

---

[9] I have also seen and heard it claimed that Tantra was an influence on the Hermetic Order of the Golden Dawn. Having spent some time studying a complete collection of original H.O.G.D./R.R. et A.C. instructions, including multiple copies of several documents and various notes by initiates of the original Order, I am fairly confident in saying that there is little, beyond the use of the elemental Tattvas, of Hindu origin, much less of Tantrik origin, in that material. What is there is filtered very much through the Theosophical perspective, which - as I have previously explained - does not contain a favourable opinion of Tantra (and I cannot imagine the likes of the Mathers approving of the Panchamakara, or other embodied and sexual aspects of Kaulachara practice, had they been aware of them). Indeed, a motivating factor for formation of the H.O.G.D. was arguably a desire to move away from the focus on Dharmic religions which the Theosophical Society presented, back towards a fundamental core of Judeo-Christian symbolism and practices inspired by Judeo-Christian ceremonial magic.

essay later revised in Djurdjevic's book *India and the Occult: The Influence of South Asian Spirituality on Modern Western Occultism* (Palgrave Macmillan, 2014), where he writes that Crowley's involvement with Tantra "shares primarily *functional* parallels with the tantric path" and that "[it] is feasible to recognize in the whole project of Crowley's magick an analogy with the approach of tantra, even if his formal knowledge of the latter was limited." Indeed, it does seem that both Thelema and Tantra present to the virtuosos of religion who engage with them largely identical general approaches to religious practice: for example, the deliberate exploration of those aspects of reality which one may be inclined to shirk from, in order to fully embrace the totality of experience, to unite fully with the universe.

Kenneth Grant would go on to explore the subject of Indian Tantra with more enthusiasm, even showing a greater understanding of Tantrik terminology than he had of Qabalistic and Thelemic terminology (of which he could display attempted elucidations which might be most charitably described as idiosyncratic). Enthusiasm was not exactly displayed by the elderly Crowley when presented with David Curwen's manuscript of the *Ānanda Laharī* containing a commentary from a Kaula Guru.[10] And after Crowley's death, it would be the

---

[10] Though very curiously, almost tantalisingly, Crowley's 1901 notebook titled "Shivaya Namaha Aum / Sepher Hain: The

further combination of Thelema and Tantra with the stuff of Western horror fiction in the mind of Grant which would provide a significant, if not primary, influence upon the Western "Left- Hand Path" forms of contemporary occultism, something altogether different

---

Beginning and End of Udghata, Abhavananda his Book," written by Crowley in Ceylon while learning Yoga under Allan Bennett, contains three pages of Sanskrit text in Devanagari script: one containing the first few shlokas of the Lalita Sahasranama, and the others six shlokas of the Ananda Lahari, both texts relevant to Sri Vidya Tantra and Kundalini Yoga. As of the time of my writing of these comments, however, it remains unknown whether these pages were written by Crowley or Bennett; a case might be made for assuming the latter as the writer, as the first page of text appears in a section containing information on the Gayatri Mantra and Mahasatipathana which is in "Bennett's hand" according to Gerald Yorke's notes, and also since, to my knowledge, Crowley makes no other reference to either the Lalita Sahasranama or the Ananda Lahari elsewhere in his work (excluding the Curwen correspondence). However, the presence of Hindustani in the Devanagari script in Crowley's poem Pentacost, in The Sword of Song, prevents certainty on this point (my thanks to Gordan Djurdjevic and Keith E. Cantú for their conversation, thoughts, and educated insight on this topic). For more on Curwen and Crowley, see *Brother Curwen, Brother Crowley: A Correspondence*, edited by Henrik Bogdan, Teitan Press, 2010.

The Ananda Lahari is part of the Saundarya Lahari, a particularly interesting text, since not only is it a sublimely composed hymn to the Goddess which elucidates on esoteric philosophy, it also has practical magical value: each of its 100 verses has its own Yantra and a specific function (ranging from obtaining riches and

from the Indian traditions, their practices, and their practitioners.

And so for the Ācāras (approaches) of Indian Tantra, within the Śrī Vidyā perspective. Tantra is a vast subject, and Sanātana Dharma[11] an even more massive one, so my explanations which follow will necessarily be simplications. I do not claim to be an expert of any sort either, and I will always defer to the far more knowledgeable authorities of the Indian traditions regarding this subject.

In order to understand the difference between the right-handed and left-handed approaches, we need to consider the important Deity Ardhanārīśvara, which is Śiva and Śakti in one body: the right side is Śiva, and the left side is Śakti (Śiva and Śakti are, respectively, Consciousness and Nature; the Seer and the Seen). Therefore we can say that the Right Hand Path is the worship of Divine conceived of as a God (masculine), and its practices are orthodox: its rituals do not make use of substances or actions considered taboo, and its practice does not

---

attracting lovers to realising ultimate truth and attaining ultimate bliss, and also including victory over enemies, mastery of music, the ability to control dreams, knowledge of science, among many others) which is achieved by a method including the chanting of the particular verse a certain number of times.

[11]"Eternal Dharma (or Order):" the Sanskrit term for what is called Hinduism. "Hinduism" is an exonym, "Sanatana Dharma" is an endonym.

challenge the status quo. The Left-Hand Path, then, is the worship of Divine conceived of as a Goddess (feminine), and its practices are heterodox: they make deliberate use of substances and actions considered taboo, and its practice therefore challenges the status quo (for the practitioner at the very least). The left-handed approaches involve forbidden substances and actions, since Śakti means "Power," and substances and actions considered taboo or impure have definite power for the individual who utilises them, at the very least from their inherently transgressive nature. We must recall, though, that Śiva and Śakti are in one body as Ardhanārīśvara: they are essentially One. The Right-Hand and Left-Hand paths both approach the same Deity, and they are both approaches within Tantrik practice.

Ardhanārīśvara is frequently depicted with four arms, and so we can consider the right and left-handed approaches as being not two, but four: Samayācāra, Dakṣiṇācāra, Kaulācārā, and Vāmācārā. Samayācāra and Dakṣiṇācāra are right-handed approaches, while Kaulācārā and Vāmācārā are left-handed approaches.

The right side of Ardhanārīśvara is Śiva, often depicted with one right hand open and the with the other right hand holding an implement (usually a trident). Thus we have two right-handed approaches, one without implements (Samayācāra) and one with (Dakṣiṇācāra).

In Samayācāra, all practices are done entirely internally, that is, the performance of all rituals is entirely visualised (ritual fire sacrifices are also a part of this approach, the open hand also suggests the sacrifice, but again these can be performed internally). As the ritual practices in the Samayācāra approach are performed entirely in the mind while in a meditative state, it obviously doesn't make use of substances or actions which are prohibited, for no substances or actions of any kind are made use of. The imagination has been devalued in Western thought until relatively recently, being merely considered the producer of entertainment or reverie. Indian thought, on the other hand, has valued the imagination. Indeed, there can be found within Indian religious traditions, such as those of Tantra, the idea that to do something in the imagination, with total concentration, can in fact be more powerful than such an action in reality. It is only relatively recently in Western culture that the idea that the imaginative faculty has any power at all has been folded into popular awareness, in the form of New Age successes emphasising visualisation, such as Ronda Byrnes' *The Secret*. The Samayācāra approach is considered a most advanced one within contemporary Tantrik traditions, such as that of Śrī Vidyā, given that it requires a great deal of experience with regular performance of the rituals and extended practices of meditation, along with significant abilities of concentration and visualisation (the rituals of Indian Tantra are often highly complex and demandingly repetitive). This approach reminds of that of Liber Samekh, an advanced ritual of Thelemic Magick, which is intended to be performed entirely astrally, which of course requires considerable skills of memorisation, visualisation, and concentration.[12]

Dakṣiṇācāra involves the orthodox performance of rituals involving a variety of implements, with no substances or actions which are considered taboo, prohibited, or impure being used. It should be recalled that the Dakṣiṇācāra approach is still within the context of wider Tantrik (that is esoteric or occult) practice:

---

[12] Indeed, the full, complete, and perfect performance of Liber Samekh in fact requires the use of all of the magical and meditative skills honed by all of the work of all the Elemental grades of the Collegio Externo G∴D∴ of the A∴A∴: The ritual is to be performed throughout in the "Body of Light," that is, astrally, and the mastery of the astral plane is the work of the Neophyte.

The Adept may be prepared "by the practices of Yoga," which are begun in earnest by the Zelator.

The Elemental invocations in the Four Quarters are preceded by an exercise in the expansion of consciousness, "[having] experience of success in the practices of Liber 536: Batrachophrenoboocosmomachia," which is given to the Practicus.

The Adept "may be prepared by Liber 175 (being Liber Astarté)," which is worked by the Philosophus.

This is all since the objective of Liber Samekh is nothing less than the Knowledge and Conversation of the Holy Guardian Angel.

Dakṣiṇācāra Pūjā rituals using Tantrik Mantras and Yantras absolutely exist and are a viable approach to worship, and in them symbolic substitutes for the taboo substances are used. Dakṣiṇācāra, the right-handed approach, is not non-Tantrik, rather it is an approach within Tantra. Equally, to view either the right-handed or the left-handed approach as better or worse than the other is neither accurate nor correct when it comes to the Indian Tantrik traditions, as it's more a matter of what is best for a particular practitioner at a particular point on their path, and the fact that the right-handed rituals do not inherently challenge the status quo does not mean that they are useless to the Tantrika.[13] I could liken this to the Hermetic Order of the Golden Dawn/R.R. et A.C. rituals (presented within *Liber O*) which represent a kind of orthodoxy within Western occultism which does not challenge the status quo of Christianity, but which still retain practical value for the aspirant in the New Aeon, at a certain stage of their practice at least.

Whereas the rituals of the Samayācāra worship the Divine in the form of the fire, and Dakṣiṇācāra in that of an idol or Yantra, the left-handed approach of Kaulācāra worships the Divine in the form of the living human body (which, whether male or female, is

---

[13] Tantrika = Tantrik practitioner.

worshipped as the Goddess) in its Śakti Pūjā.[14] In this there is an obvious similarity with the Gnostic Mass. The Kaulācāra may also make use of substances and acts considered prohibited or taboo, with the Pañcamakāra often being referred to in this regard. These are the "five Ms:" Madya (alcohol), Māṃsa (meat), Matsya (fish), Mudrā,[15] and Maithuna (sexual intercourse). The use of

---

[14] Further, the genitals are worshipped in a ritual of Yoni Puja or Lingam Puja.

[15] This word is harder to define in the context of the Panchamakara. The word "mudra" commonly means a hand-gesture with esoteric significance utilised at specific points in Tantrik rituals (not at all unlike the Signs used in Hermetic and Thelemic rituals), but those are not taboo within Tantrik ritual. The word is most commonly translated as meaning "parched grain", but this is also odd as it's not a prohibited substance. I have seen it suggested that it's probably some kind of unspecified aphrodisiac (certainly possible but still a rather unsatisfying definition), or perhaps that the grain is fermented to create alcohol, which is far more believable than the other theory I have seen positing the idea that the grain might contain ergot mould, which I consider to be highly improbable as there are likely very few who could remain in a state of detachment while meditating on their own gangrenous limbs! Other definitions I have heard for this "mudra" include money and fried snacks: the former perhaps vulgar, and the latter certainly unhealthy, but neither are taboo. Christopher Wallis in his Tantra Illuminated does say that originally there were just three Ms, but the Bengalis wanted to include fish, and four not being considered an auspicious number, added in the non-taboo fried grain simply to make them five in total. However, the most interesting definition is that given by Sri Amritananda

alcohol, meat, and fish as taboo items show the
culturally specific nature of the selection: a ritual use of
such substances isn't going to have the effect for a
westerner for whom drinking a beer and eating a
hamburger is no way a transgressive act (to achieve the
same effect they would have to make use of substances
either considered illicit or impure both within Western
society in general, and their own peer group more
particularly). Likewise, the sexual partner required in the
transgressive classical Indian Tantrik tradition could well
be one outside of one's marriage, of a lower caste, or
someone one is not attracted to (it's not a casual hook-
up just for pleasure's sake, rather it must be challenging).
Again, a definite similarity can be seen with the impact
transgressive sexual explorations and experiences had on
Crowley's spiritual development, and also in the
following remarks made within the essay which
accompanies the ritual instructions of *Liber V vel Reguli*:
"[the] Magician should devise for himself a definite
technique for destroying "evil." The essence of such a
practice will consist in training the mind and the body
to confront things which cause fear, pain, disgust,
shame and the like. He must learn to endure them, then

Natha Saraswati, in his Gifts from the Goddess (edited by Michael
Bowden, 45th Parallel Press, 2019), of this "mudra" as semen and
menstrual blood, or, in another sense, the pleasure obtained from
any given experience.

to become indifferent to them, then to analyze them until they give pleasure and instruction, and finally to appreciate them for their own sake, as aspects of Truth. When this has been done, he should abandon them, if they are really harmful in relation to health and comfort."[16]

As mentioned previously, the left-handed approach within Tantra is linked, via the iconography of Ardhanārīśvara, to worship of the Goddess (this interpretation is reinforced by the potential double meaning of "vāmā" as "woman" and "vāma" as "left"). The Goddess may take beautiful and benevolent or fierce and horrific forms, and it can also be noted the right hands of the popular image of Dakṣiṇa Kālī display gestures of dispelling fear and granting boons, while her left hands hold a severed head and a bloody sword. And so while the Kaulācāra in Śrī Vidyā tradition is focused on the worship of the beautiful

---

[16] It is notable, too, that Liber V vel Reguli was created by Crowley at his Abbey of Thelema in Cefalu, the location of some of his most transgressive experiences. For more on this and the similarity to Tantrik practice, see Gordan Djurdjevic's essay The Great Beast as a Tantric Hero (in Aleister Crowley and Western Esotericism edited by Bogdan and Starr). Note also that the ritual of Liber V vel Reguli makes use of symbols and actions all but prohibited by the Hermetic Order of the Golden Dawn / R.R. et A.C., in a purely ceremonial expression of the confronting and overcoming of taboos for spiritual ends.

Goddess, the Vāmācāra focuses on the Goddess in her terrible form. And while the Kaulācāra makes use of the living human body, the Vāmācāra makes use of human remains: transcendence is experienced either in the apotheosis of pleasure, or in the conquering of the fear of death.[17] The transgression is used for transcendence. In terms of non-dual philosophy, one puts one's money where one's mouth is, to use the idiom. The construct of the ego, the limited personality in the form of the social identity, is annihilated in that moment, burned up in the worship of the Goddess. And after that, the experience is integrated, and inner transformation effected. The intent is not to replace the previous limited personality and social identity with a new one: to use a prohibited intoxicant to destroy one's limited identity, only to replace it with a new identity (one based around regular use of the intoxicant), would be a complete failure (and a case of thinking the moon to be the finger pointing at it). It is about embracing the totality of experience, not fleeing from, or denying, any aspect of it. No aspect of the material world of physical manifestation is to be shunned, or indeed to be considered as anything less than perfect. Although the true nature of spiritual reality may be concealed from us

---

[17] In the Kalikula tradition of Indian Tantra, typically found more in the north of India, this path is referred to as Virachara: the path of the hero.

as a default in everyday life, this Great Illusion (Mahāmāyā) is in fact the Goddess (who we know to be the Universe, including the planet Earth).

The entry point into the bliss of transcendence, of the highest mystical communion, is available from any aspect of experience, if only we could realise this. Therefore bodily pleasure can be just as usefully employed as asceticism (and indeed the privilege of renunciation when used to escape from one's fears, to evade one's dislikes, or to shirk one's responsibilities can be seen to be considerably less useful, certainly not heroic; and here is where this perspective can be subversive to established social constructs and institutions built upon orthodoxy).

These paths are not mutually exclusive within Indian Tantrik traditions: Sampradāyas (schools or traditions) of Śrī Vidyā present Samayācāra, Dakṣiṇācāra, and Kaulācārā approaches.[18] It is not necessarily a case of

---

[18] The Sri Vidya tradition, being a tradition which still retains elements the of classical non-dual Shaiva Tantra of the first millennium of the common era, was retained among Smarta brahmins and perhaps sanitised somewhat with a focus on the right-handed Samayachara and Dakshinachara approaches, but the transgressive Kaulachara practices do remain, in theoretical forms at the very least. Sexual repression still wielding a strong influence over contemporary Indian culture, this is obviously not something which has been openly discussed in much detail by contemporary practitioners and authorities within the tradition, Sri Amritananda Natha Saraswati being one notable exception.

either, and exclusively, right-handed or left-handed practice. The distortion of the concepts of the Right-hand and Left-hand paths, away from being different, yet valid, approaches to the same divinity, into that of distinct, adversarial, and diametrically opposed occult groups has been made by Western occultists from Blavatsky through to contemporary "Left-Hand Path" practitioners, who, at the time of writing, are mainly composed of a variety of self-proclaimed Satanists and black magicians of a notable "edgelord" persuasion, to use a word from informal present-day parlance. These contemporary exponents of Western "Left-Hand Path" occultism, in marked contrast to those of Indian Tantra, encourage the deification of the self,[19] and worse still, in some cases encourage anti-social behaviour including acts of violence towards other humans, espouse bigotry and reactionary views, or even involvement with far-right political ideologies and extremist organisations. A far cry from the Indian Tantriks who strive to overcome the self, who endeavour to recognise the essential and divine consciousness which we are all share, and whose

---

[19] As opposed to seeking the annihilation of the self in the Beloved, or the total surrender of every part of one's self. Instead choosing to cling to the ego, to the idea of one's self as a separate identity, this kind of Western "Left-Hand Path" occultist does indeed become what Crowley would call a black magician, equally something Indian Tantrikas in left-handed—Kaulachara, Vamachara, Virachara — traditions would denounce.

transgressive practices actually strike at discriminatory structures (such as the caste system), rather than support them. And it should also be borne in mind that the Goddess approached through the left-handed rites of Indian Tantra, in terms of Her original mythology (as found in the Devīmāhātmyam and the Lalitopākhyāna), does not make pacts with demons, She destroys them.[20]

I hope that, despite the appearance of the term "Left-Hand Path" as a pejorative in our own tradition, it can be seen that the left-handed approaches of Indian Tantra do in fact bear some resemblance to approaches within Thelemic Magick and Mysticism. But lest there be any misunderstanding, I also urge respect for the original traditions. One's mastery of the practices of Thelemic Magick and Mysticism does not confer authority regarding Indian Tantrik traditions in any sense, nor does it confer legitimacy in practices reserved for initiates of those traditions (for example, the use of principal Mantras, such as the Mūlamantras, or "root Mantras," of Deities).[21] Nevertheless, I do believe that the continuing study of the world's esoteric traditions can provide us with thought provoking perspectives on our own spiritual practices and approaches to religion,

---

[20] And it is frequently explained by Shakta commentators that these demons represent the negative tendencies of one's self.

[21] Indeed, and as mentioned previously, the rituals of Indian Tantra are extremely complex and demandingly repetitive, when compared with those of Western occult traditions.

especially if we are already utilising concepts and techniques from such a tradition (such as those of the Kuṇḍalinī Yoga system, which originates from Indian Tantra).

In our worship of the Great Goddess, we must embrace all aspects of reality completely, to unite with all, and indeed ultimately surrender our all to Her. As Vivekananda said, the bird cannot fly with just one wing; and the balance, the equilibration, the marriage of opposites is an essential practice recommended by Crowley throughout his work. In the words of *Liber LXV*, "Go thou unto the outermost places and subdue all things. Subdue thy fear and thy disgust. Then— yield!"

LIBER SAMEKH

GARRY MCSWEENEY

"It is a curious thing that in the everyday, mundane world, millions of people are distracting themselves with all manner of technologies, social media platforms, sports results, TV dramas; the list is endless. They are not present. What are they distracting themselves from? Yet the moment the magician even starts to think about engaging in ritual, the moment the magician steps into a ritual space, suddenly the lower (let's be frank and call it the head) wants to be present, wants to be involved, wants to get in the bloody way. Is this sudden interest in being present a reaction against being in a setting where it (the head) is inevitably confronted with the reality that there is more to the world than what it thinks is going on? Mere speculation but definitely something to think about, and possibly something else to reflect on and distract oneself with."[1]

What should an effective ritual achieve? According to Tupman's view of ceremonial magic(k) "...the successful use of ritual would create a change in the spiritual condition of human beings and, by steps,

---

[1] Petersen, 2014, n.p

elevate them to an epiphany of spirituality."[2] The mundane consciousness should either be elevated or obliterated – the latter being arguably preferable to the former – though each practitioner will have their own unique position on this matter. Either way, to put it simply: the intellect and associated 'lower' ego faculties do not have the capacity for the 'higher' revelations afforded by genuine spiritual experience. Unfortunately, a lack of space does not permit the exploration of concepts such as sangsaric duality[3] ("There is no higher, there is no lower. There is beginning, there is no end." Etc.) or the unification of opposites above the abyss so the reader's indulgence is requested for the remainder of this essay.

So, working under the assumption that the mind is incapable of grasping the true face of divinity, sages and mages of all manner of religious and mystical persuasions developed various systems to occupy the mind while the higher faculties were engaged in a cheeky tete-a-tete with *insert name of preferred God/Goddess here* - and this is where Liber Samekh really comes into its own.

---

[2] Tupman, 2003, p. 3

[3] Sangsaric duality here refers to the idea of, for instance, one having a thought of something being 'bad', which means there must also be a concept of 'good'. This applies to other dualities; good and evil, delicious and tasteless, etc.

For some histories around Liber Samekh, the reader is referred to Feist and Yemeth. For the text itself, the reader is referred to Thelemapedia, Crowley's Magick, and the Hermetic Library, with particular consideration to the Crowley and Hermetic Library versions as these contain the commentary to Liber Samekh, which is also explored. The purpose of this essay is to look at Liber Samekh, a ritual that Crowley designed to assist Frater Progradior (Australia's very own Frank Bennett, Head of the Australian OTO in Sydney) to attain Knowledge and Conversation of the Holy Guardian Angel while in Cefalu, Sicily.

Sections A through to Section J give the practitioner the 'meat and bones' of the ritual; these are the parts concerned with the incantations, barbarous names, and magickal gestures that the magician must commit to memory. In Point III (Scholion on Sections G and Gg) Perdurabo notes that the adept "...ought not to allow his mind to loosen its grip...or even to forget its duty to the body and the sensible surroundings."[4] Continuing, he says

> "But he should have acquired, by previous practice, the faculty of detaching these elements of his consciousness from their articulate centre, so that they become (temporarily) independent responsible units, capable of receiving communications from headquarters at will,

---

[4] Hermetic Library, n.d, n.p

but perfectly able to take care of themselves without troubling their chief, and to report to him at the proper time."[5]

This suggests that there is a faculty (the Neschemah?) higher than the mundane mind which operates and interacts with the higher/divine while the lower/mundane mind is distracted with x, y, or z; these 'distractions' can include reflection on qabalistic correspondences, the recitation of barbarous names, mantras, or the performance of the general 'mechanics' of the ritual being performed. Pedurabo's 777[6] is an excellent tool for preoccupying an itinerant mind. Another alternative to the idea of a 'higher consciousness' is that through magickal disciplines and practices such as Liber Jugorum, the mundane mind becomes disciplined and cleansed sufficiently to become capable of processing the concept of entities, and experiences, existing which are greater than the ego and which cannot satisfactorily be explained away by mundane consciousness. This latter suggestion seems to fit very well with the reasoning behind why such discipline is demanded of the novice practitioner. It also fits with Perdurabo's comments on Samadhi (in one way, not dissimilar to the spiritual event referred to in Thelema as Crossing the Abyss) and the need for

---

[5] Hermetic Library, n.d, n.p

[6] Crowley, 2005

balance when approaching the divine (i.e – when the unbalanced mind experiences Samadhi, the unbalanced portions of mind become magnified, resulting in a religious experience that is distorted.) – "any idea not so equilibrated is below the Abyss, contains in itself an unmitigated duality or falsehood, and is to that extent qliphotic and dangerous."[7] We see the results of this in many religions, and indeed personal religious experiences, of today. Perdurabo further alludes to this need for balance in The Principles of Ritual warning that without this balanced approach the magician may find that his or her "...natural excess in that direction will be still further exaggerated."[8] This need for balance is so vital to the magician that Perdurabo again reiterates the importance of it in Chapter 8 entitled Of Equilibrium..."[9] Perhaps not coincidentally, he even quotes Liber Samekh[10] on this matter.

Mahayana Buddhism echoes this need for balance, as true balance cancels out the duality of phenomenal existence so the adept is left with a 'quality-less' experience of the 'Voidness', the 'Clear Light of Reality',

---

[7] Crowley, 1997, p. 182

[8] Ibid, pp. 144 – pp. 145

[9] Ibid, pp. 181 – pp. 182

[10] Ibid, p. 184

and the 'immaculate Mind'.[11] This is not to suggest that these supra-mundane experiences are nothing but rather they are no thing. This is not to define the experience by negation but the concept of 'netti-netti' does seem wholly applicable here; the experience is 'not this' and it is 'not that' in an intellectual sense. Any attempt by the mind to categorise and limit the experience will always be incomplete. The researcher summarises the experience as 'one cannot know god but one can be god'. This can also be expressed in the aphorism 'When god is present, I am not. When I am present, god is not'.

Returning to the initial proposal that the mind is incapable of experiencing divinity, and must therefore be distracted like a fractious child, it is proposed that this may be why there are allegedly 330 million gods and goddesses in the Hindu Pantheon according to Verse 7, Chapter 6, Verse 18, Chapter 47, and Verse 99, Chapter 62 of the Skanda Purana.[12] It is also worth considering that numerous deities can have many, many names such as the 1008 names of Kali.[13] The devoted practitioner could easily distract their mind solely with the sheer effort required in remembering, and reciting, all 1008 names of the Black Mother, let alone endeavouring to

---

[11] Ed. Evans-Wentz; 1997, pp. 202 – pp. 254

[12] Wisdom Library, 2019

[13] Narasimhaye, 2008

recall the 330 million names alluded to in the Skanda Purana.

This proposition can also be applied to the highly ritualised Japanese tea ceremony (also known as 'Sado' or 'Chado' - 'the way of tea'). Zen Buddhism is considered a primary influcnce on the development of the tea ceremony, with the seemingly simple act of serving and drinking tea combining into a highly ritualised process which is designed to promote tranquility, at-one-ment, and mindfulness. Given that the tea ceremony involves following numerous steps, it could be argued that the mind is gently led to a state of passivity or preoccupation by the many complex and highly prescribed stages of the ceremony which thereby allow the practitioner to "...gain inner peace while performing this ritualistic activity"[14]. In essence, the mind is stilled, or distracted; if stilled, the divine experience may be able to manifest in the space created by the absence of mental activity. Equally if the mind is distracted – or focused elsewhere – then the divine experience bypasses the mundane (which is concentrating on the ritual aspects of the ceremony). Irrespective of where the mind goes to, there a break in the participant's mental chatter which can allow for insight or revelation to occur.

---

[14] Acar, 2021, n.p

On another note, and returning to 777, while committing the various correspondences to memory will certainly provide the magician with ample material to distract the lower faculties during ritual (and otherwise), it is also an invaluable tool for meditation and reflection. As an example, why does Perdurabo link The Magician tarot card with the Christian church of Sardis, one of the seven churches of Asia as addressed by John in Revelation? Each practitioner should reflect on such correspondences and reach their own conclusions. For the researcher, these two particular correspondences are seen as an example of Perdurabo's enduring wit. Sardis was a church associated with incompleteness and the all too human failing of never finishing anything. "The church was essentially wasting its own time."[15] – was Perdurabo, with his tongue firmly in his cheek, insinuating that magicians never complete anything and are all wasting their time? When considering all of this, it is worth noting that at the age of eight Wickstrom was 'saved' by Billy Graham so it could be argued that anything that he has to say – indeed anything that anyone has to say – should be viewed with an exceptionally critical eye.

The original plan was to write this article as a purely academic piece but then the researcher recalled how that very same academic approach (often so very dry and so very dusty) to the occult, magick, and the lived religious

---

[15] Wickstrom, n.d, n.p

experience, seems to squeeze the very blood out of the topic which it claims, often quite falsely, to be viewing with a dispassionate and objective lens. Therefore it was decided that academic rigour would be retained but the essay would be written in an accessible manner.

In conclusion, this essay has explored the possibility that, sangsaric duality aside, there are higher and lower faculties which are engaged during magickal ritual. The lower faculties, incapable of processing experiences of the divine, need to be distracted while the higher faculties experience the full uninterrupted, and uncorrupted, glory of the ineffable.

These distractions are exemplified by both the 'meat and bones' of Liber Samekh and by various commentaries written by Perdurabo.

These distractions are also exemplified by the extensive correspondences of 777 or the innumerable gods of the Hindu and Buddhist pantheons.

These distractions are found in a variety of rituals including the tea ceremony of Zen Buddhism.

May all attain. Amen!

Bibliography

Acar, A., What is the Relationship between Zen and Tea Ceremony?, accessed 10th August 2022 via

https://mai-ko.com/travel/culture-in-japan/tea-ceremony/what-is-the-relationship-between-zen-and-tea-ceremony/

Crowley, A., 777, 2005, accessed 5th September 2022 via http://thelemapedia.org/index.php/Tree_of_Life:777

Crowley, A., Magick: Book 4. 2nd ed. York Beach, ME: Weiser 1997.

Evans-Wentz, E (ed)., The Tibetan Book of the Great Liberation. London: Oxford University Press 1977.

Feist, Harper., Liber Samekh – History and Development, USGL Education Committee 2022, accessed 10th June 2022 via https://edu.oto-usa.org/liber-samekh-history-and-development/

Hermetic Library (with commentary): Liber Samekh Theurgia Goetia Summa (Congressus Cum Daemone) sub figura DCCC n.d, accessed 8th June 2022 via https://hermetic.com/crowley/libers/lib800

Narasimhaye. Narasimhaye's Blog, 1008 Names of Maa Kali, 2008, accessed 14th June 2022 via https://narasimhaye.wordpress.com/2008/11/08/1008-names-of-maa-kali/

Petersen, Albert., personal correspondence, 6th June 2014.

Thelemapedia version (no commentary): Liber Samekh
n.d, accessed 9th June 2022 via
http://www.thelemapedia.org/index.php/Liber_Samekh

Tupman, T., Theatre Magick: Aleister Crowley and the
Rites of Eleusis, Ohio State University 2003, accessed
15th June 2022 via:
https://etd.ohiolink.edu/apexprod/rws_etd/send_file/sen
d?accession=osu1054580207&disposition=inline

Wickstrom, S., Sardis Church of the Living Dead, n.d,
accessed 9th September 2022 via
http://www.spwickstrom.com/sardis/

Wisdom Library: Skanda Purana, 2019, accessed 22nd
June 2022 via:
https://www.wisdomlib.org/hinduism/book/the-skanda-
purana/d/doc366034.html

Yemeth., Liber Samekh: The Knowledge and
Conversation of the Holy Guardian Angel (see
Historical Introduction) n.d, accessed 10th June 2022 via
https://openmagick.com/en/a/ceremonial-magick/liber-
samekh-the-knowledge-and-conversation-of-the-holy-
guardian-angel

THE KONAMI CODE

Crowley, Card Games and the Occult

N. F. ROBINSON

Dedicated to the memory of Kazuki Takahashi (1961–2022).

Aleister Crowley's position in the pop culture zeitgeist of the 20th century is beyond dispute – the magician has appeared in countless films, television shows, pieces of literature, comic books and theatrical plays. Some of these have had a huge impact on broader society's perception of the man (The Beatles' *Sgt. Pepper's Lonely Hearts Club Band*) while others have had considerably less of an impact (a brief cameo in 2003's animated television show *The Venture Bros*).

In this essay I will elaborate on one of the more significant of Crowley's appearances – in the popular children's media franchise, *Yu-Gi-Oh!* – and discuss what, if anything, it has to do with Crowley's own religious movement, Thelema.

Three years before it reached American shores, the *Yu-Gi-Oh! Trading Card Game* dominated the hearts of Japanese children and adults alike. On August 26th, 1999, the game's parent company, Konami Holdings

Corporation, hosted an official tournament at the prestigious Tokyo Dome. The invitation was open to any who owned the latest *Weekly Shonen Jump*, the young men's magazine that published Kazuki Takahashi's manga on which the game was based. Konami announced that the "Premium Pack," including a copy of the infamous card *Exodia the Forbidden One*, would be available only at this event.

In 1998, *Shonen Jump's* weekly circulation was roughly four million copies.[1] Tokyo Dome had a capacity limit of fifty-five thousand people. In retrospect, Konami was lucky that only sixty-five thousand showed up. The resulting riot hospitalized two and injured two dozen more. Konami issued an immediate apology.[2]

Aleister Crowley, working with the masterful Lady Frieda Harris, crafted his own deck of cards – *The Book of Thoth* deck. Like the Rider-Waite deck, the Thoth Tarot is based on the Golden Dawn system, which Crowley adapted to the Thelemic universe. It is still the preferred deck of Thelemites today. Crowley cheekily played with the theory that the Tarot contains all the wisdom of the mythical *Book of Thoth*, stolen from the Library of Alexandria, encoded yet preserved for the seeker, when he published his own volume, *The*

---

[1] *Japanese Magazine Publisher's Association*, 1998.

[2] M. Magnier, "Cartoon Craze Boils Over in Japan," *Los Angeles Times*, 1999.

Equinox: III, No. 5 (subtitled *The Book of Thoth: A Short Essay on the Tarot of the Egyptians*), in 1944.[3]

In the world of *Yu-Gi-Oh!*, an eccentric billionaire appropriates eldritch Egyptian hieroglyphic carvings to create *Duel Monsters*, the card game at the heart of the franchise and the inspiration for the real world *Yu-Gi-Oh! Trading Card Game*. Like the mythological-hermetic Thoth, he is also successful in encoding and preserving wisdom into a set of cards. In the greater narrative, transmuting profound Egyptian mysteries into a children's card game turns out to have disastrous, world-shattering consequences, to which he has the audacity to feign surprise.

Yu-Gi-Oh! doesn't just draw heavily on the ancient Egyptian mythology, though – it also frequently references Crowley's work, and many other esoteric traditions besides.[4]

Memories of the Old Kingdom

In the *Yu-Gi-Oh!* manga and anime adaptation, our young protagonist is shy Yugi Muto, a high-schooler obsessed with games of every type. In the manga's

---

[3] Crowley himself was careful only to confirm that the Tarot existed "in what may be called the classical form," as early as the 14th Century.

[4] It would take at least another 777 words to disentangle the Qabalistic references in *Yu-Gi-Oh!'s* "Timelord" archetype.

inciting incident, he solves the mystery of the "Millennium Puzzle," and is rewarded by becoming host to the ghost of an amnesiac, vengeful Pharaoh. In times of great need the Pharaoh is able to exert control over Yugi's body.[5] Yugi and his Pharaoh suffer through many conflicts and trials, but with the power of friendship and a belief in the "heart of the cards" manage to unravel the mystery of the billionaire's sorcery and reverse its impact on the world.

There are significant parallels to Crowley's experience. In 1904, on their honeymoon, Rose Kelly, despite her usual scepticism, drew her new husband to the Stele of Revealing. She claimed that Horus awaited him. Crowley soon heard the disembodied voice of Aiwass, minister of Hoor-Paar-Kraat, and the spirit would reveal to him the three chapters of *Liber AL vel Legis*, the central sacred text of Thelema.

> My scribe Ankh-af-na-khonsu, the priest of the princes, shall not in one letter change this book; but lest there be folly, he shall comment thereupon by the wisdom of Ra-Hoor-Khu-it.[6]

---

[5] While in this state, Yugi is shown with the *Ajna* chakra ablaze with golden light.

[6] *Liber AL vel Legis, I:36.*

Crowley signed the comment to *Liber AL vel Legis* under the magical name Ankh-f-n-khonsu and used that name in other capacities as the Prophet of Thelema. Kenneth Grant, in *Nightside of Eden*, would suggest that "Crowley claimed to have been a re-embodiment of the magical current represented by the priesthood to which Ankh-af-na-Khonsu belonged."[7] Crowley himself imagined a past life as the priest of the princes; like poor Yugi, our prophet believed himself to collaborate with a discarnate Egyptian spirit.

The *Yu-Gi-Oh!* anime and manga are rife with similar interactions with ancient Pharaonic royalty. Another of Yugi's antagonists – again, an eccentric billionaire – is later revealed to be the reincarnation of "Seto," a ruthless priest of Set. Set, in Egyptian mythology, is responsible for the butchering of Osiris, the husband and brother of Isis, and for combating Apophis, the great serpent of chaos. In the 5th-century BC, Herodotus would associate Set with Typhon, the evil son of Hera.[8]

Isis, Apophis, Osiris – three hugely important figures in western esotericism, each of them intimately connected to Set.

Seto created the "Tablet of Lost Memories," a stele depicting the duel between himself and the Pharaoh.

---

[7] Kenneth Grant, *Nightside of Eden,* 1977.

[8] Herodotus, *Histories.*

Above them are various fictional creatures and deities of the manga's universe, including the *Blue-Eyes White Dragon* and *Dark Magician*, and above this is the winged sun associated with Horus in his Old Kingdom form.[9] It is this stele that triggers memories of Kaiba's past life. Yugi epiphanizes that he, also, is the reincarnation of the Pharaoh.

The "Tablet of Lost Memories" bears remarkable physical similarities to the Stele of Revealing.

---

[9] J Hill, *ancientegyptonline.co.uk*, accessed on October 5th 2021.

Yu-Gi-Oh!'s "Tablet of Lost Memories."

The Stele of Revealing

The Heart of the Cards

These are general connections. The cards themselves reveal a deeper pattern of inspiration on Konami's part. Aleister Crowley himself has four separate depictions within the *Yu-Gi-Oh! Trading Card Game*.

Crowley, the Magistus of Grimoires and Aleister the Invoker.

In *Crowley, the Magistus of Grimoires*, we see a young, blue-haired – this is anime, after all! - interpretation of Aleister Crowley. He holds a staff and grimoire and wears a monocle, presumably because he is meant to be a British ceremonial magician of some standing.

Crowley, the Magistus of Grimoires is a "magistus" - a word bastardized from "trismegistus," referencing Hermes Trismegistus,[10] mythical father to hermeticism. *Crowley*, along with three colleagues, is shown in the *Trading Card Game* to strive to achieve command over the gods themselves. This may also be a further reference to the A∴A∴ grade of Master of the Temple (*Magister Templi*).

---

[10] Naturally, Trismegistus has his own card, unpictured.

This Crowley would eventually become the figure shown in *Aleister the Invoker*, wielding the same staff and monocle but holding a different book.

> Here, o my son, is the One Secret of Success in this Great Work: Invoke often.[11]

This is where things get exciting.

Invocation *and* Magical Meltdown.

We can see the results of *Crowley, the Magistus of Grimoire's* experiments on other cards. In *Invocation*, we see him utilizing a magical circle in his magic. The symbol within the circle bears similarities to the unicursal hexagram, the most recognizable symbol of Thelema. Another card, *Magical Meltdown*, shows him

---

[11] Aleister Crowley, *The Book of Wisdom and Folly*, 1962.

at the height of his powers. Amusingly, this card allows him to summon his monsters without fear of an opponent's meddling – is it his True Will to perform this magick?[12]

Invoked Caliga *and* Omega Summon.

In *Invoked Caliga*, we see *Aleister the Invoker* assuming the godform[13] of a great beast. As that beast, in *Omega Summon* he conjures more spirits to his aid. The original name of *Omega Summon*, in the original

---

[12] A proper unicursal hexagram, minus the five-pointed star, can be found on the card *The Seal of Orichalcos*, humorously used in the anime to imprison souls.

[13] Crowley speaks of godforms in *Liber O vel Manus et Sagittae*.

Japanese romanji, is *To Mega Serion*, or *To Mega Therion*. Aleister Crowley would refer to himself by this name throughout his life and is addressed as the Beast in *Liber AL vel Legis*.

> This book shall be translated into all tongues; but always with the original writing of the Beast; for in the chance shape of the letters and their position to one another: in these are mysteries that no Beast shall divine.[14]

Magistus Invocation *and* Aiwass, the Magistus Spell Spirit.

In *Magistus Invocation*, we see *Aleister* reaching for divinity. He is being gifted a book.

---

[14] *Liber AL vel Legis, III:47.*

This "god" that *Aleister* contacts is *Aiwass, the Magistus Spell Spirit*. This is massively significant. Modern media cribbing Crowley's life for Halloween stories is a well-worn tradition, but few properties include the non-corporeal intelligence behind *Liber AL vel Legis*. For a children's card game, it's an especially deep cut!

The Book of the Law *and* The Book of the Law.

Liber AL vel Legis isn't neglected. Though it is pictured differently to any printing of the volume available, *The Book of the Law* is included. It is hard not to be taken by the symbolism. The geometry of the Rose Cross of the Golden Dawn is alluded to on the book's cover. In the centre of this cross sits a deep blue jewel filled with stars, the infinite vastness of the night sky, evoking our Nuit, Lady of the Stars. Behind the book itself we see alchemical equipment: scales, mortar and pestle, glass flasks and a silver spoon, all of which have surface relevance to Crowley's history.

Aleister the Invoker of Madness.

In *Aleister, Invoker of Madness*, we see him at his worst, wide-eyed and struggling. He does not carry *The Book of the Law*, though he wears gloves bearing the same faux unicursal hexagram and behind him is the light of

Aiwass. In *Crowley the First Propheseer,*[15] the *Trading Card Game* recognizes Crowley's role as Prophet of Thelema. We also see the results of his excesses – he is comatose and sealed within a prison of glass.[16]

Millennium Puzzles

As of 2021, the *Yu-Gi-Oh!* franchise is estimated to have grossed over 17 billion dollars. The *Yu-Gi-Oh!* empire consists of ten animated series, three films, more than two dozen videogames, and two separate trading card games based on one of those video games. As of January 2021, Konami has sold more than thirty-five billion cards worldwide.[17] Though in recent years the company has seemingly given up on film and video games, pivoting instead to slots and pachinko machines, *Yu-Gi-Oh!* has shown no signs of slowing down.

Though it can't be argued that the appropriation of Crowley and Thelema in *Yu-Gi-Oh!* is fascinating – at least to me – there is, unfortunately, little evidence that it is particularly nuanced or contains any hidden meaning or significance. Up until his tragic passing in

---

[15] Unpictured.

[16] There is one other card I'd like to note. In the established lore of the game, *Aleister the Invoker* founded the *Spellbook Library of the Heliosphere*. The significance of the Heliosphere and our greater solar system, I think, will not be lost on any of my brethren within the Ordo Templi Orientis.

[17] "Best-Selling Trading Card Game," *Guinness Book of Records.*

2022, Kazuki Takahashi has never shown a deeper interest in Thelema or the occult, and neither has Konami, outside of using it to flourish their intellectual property. There is one tenuous link – famous game designer, Hideo Kojima, worked for the company's video-game division from 1986 to 2015, and in March 2022, publicly posted photographs online showing his Japanese copy of *The Book of the Law*[18]. But Kojima has never publicly claimed to be a Thelemite or practicing magician, and neither has any other Konami employee, retired or otherwise.

The parallels are either coincidental or very loosely based on Crowley's life – interesting but trifling. While this conclusion may seem cynical, it follows a similar pattern of *Yu-Gi-Oh's* designers co-opting whatever neat ideas they can find, including disparate references to Atlantis, ancient aliens, Mothman, Joan d'Arc mythology, grail lore, Jack the Ripper and famed Finnish sniper Simo Hayha. If there is evidence of anything deeper, it is extremely well obfuscated – it's much more likely the creators simply enjoyed the aesthetics and background that Aleister Crowley's life and work provided.

Despite this conclusion, the facts are clear – on gross revenue alone, *Yu-Gi-Oh!* is undoubtedly the most

---

[18] https://twitter.com/HIDEO_KOJIMA_EN/status/ 1498558794280083456

successful entertainment franchise in history to depict Aleister Crowley, Aiwass and *Liber AL vel Legis*. It's worth considering that despite the irreverence of the depiction, if *Yu-Gi-Oh!* has ignited the curiosity of even the tiniest fraction of aspirants, encouraging them to look further, to dig deeper, to stumble upon the hoard of Crowley's treasures and fight for Light, Life, Love and Liberty, it is easy to think even the Great Beast himself might be pleased.

Bibliography

Crowley, A., *Book IV*, Second Edition, Revised, York Beach, ME: Weiser 1998.

Crowley, A., *The Holy Books of Thelema*, York Beach, ME: Weiser 1983.

Crowley, A., *The Book of Thoth: A Short Essay on the Tarot of the Egyptians*, New Ed., York Beach, ME: Weiser 1981.

Crowley, A., *The Book of Wisdom and Folly*, York Beach, ME: Weiser 1991.

Gébelin, A., *Le Monde primitif, analysé et comparé avec le monde moderne, volume viii*, Paris, France: 1781. (Digital translation by Donald Tyson, accessed in October 2021.)

Glenday, C., *Guinness Book of Records 2020*, London, UK: Cherrytree Books 2019.

Grant, K., *Nightside of Eden*, London, UK: Starfire Publishing 2014.

Gunther, J., *Initiation Into the Aeon of the Child: The Inward Journey*, Lake Worth, FL: Ibis Press 2014.

Herodotus, *The Histories*, New York, USA: Penguin Books 1996.

Hundley, J., *Tarot*, Cologne, Germany: Taschen Books 2020.

Kaczynski, R., *Perdurabo: The Life of Aleister Crowley,* Revised, Berkeley, CA: North Atlantic Books 2011.

Various, *Yu-Gi-Oh! Official Card Game Duel Monsters Master Guide 4,* Chiyoda, JP: Shueisha Publishing 2014.

Various, *Yu-Gi-Oh! Official Card Game Duel Monsters Master Guide 6,* Chiyoda, JP: Shueisha Publishing 2020.

THE BIRTH OF HELL:

Formulae of Initiation in *The Book of Two Ways* and the Ceremony of the Death of *Asar*.

SHOKUFEH ALWAZI

**Let him enter in turn or at once the four gates; let
him stand on the floor of the palace.**
- AL 1:51

*Hail unto ye gates! Whose names are secret, whose places
are sacred! Save me from any evil obstacle of the mighty
ones who are before you, until I come into the presence of
the Lord of All.*
- The Coffin Texts. Spell 1125[1]

I was greatly encouraged by the enthusiastic response to
my essay in the third volume of the *Ora Et Labora*

---

[1] In this essay, quotations from a documents in Class A and AB are
in bold type. Other works, including my translations of the spells of
The Coffin Texts are italicised. I include transliterations of these
Spells in the footnotes; CT 1125 (B3C) (d) *ind-ḥr.tn sbḫtw*. (e) *št3t
rnw dsrt stw.* (a)*nḥm.tn* N *r nm ḫw sdb nb dwy n sḫmw imy-b3ḥ.tn n*
(b) *r ii* N *tn imy-b3ḥ nb-r-dr*.

research journal.[2] As I discussed in that short work, there are many striking parallels between the writings and religious systems of the Ancient Egyptians, and the practices and doctrines of the New Aeon, revealed to us since the reception of *The Book of the Law* in 1904. When I say striking, I should qualify, striking to *me*. I make no claims to universals here. In fact, it took a good deal of reassurance and persuasion from my colleague and friend Cosmé Hallelujah, who saw value in my speculations and encouraged me to submit the rough draft of these to the series editor. Somewhat emboldened by the positive response I received to that very brief, rough-hewn work, I submit the following for public scrutiny and appraisal.

As some of you who follow these things will already know, a research team, led by Harco Willems of the University of Leuven, examined high-resolution images of wooden fragments recovered from a burial shaft in the necropolis at Deir el-Bersha in 2018 and recognised them as the remains of a 4000-year-old book. Through admirably rigorous examination, the team discovered that the barely legible texts on these brittle pieces of wood were an ancient guide to the underworld known as *The Book of Two Ways*. This copy of the *Book of Two Ways* was etched into the cedar coffin of a woman named Ankh, a relative of a provincial official. The coffin is thought to date to the Middle Kingdom reign

---

[2] Walls ed. *Ora Et Labora, Volume 3*, In Perpetuity Publishing, 2022.

of Mentuhotep II (ca. 2051–2030 B.C.), making this example about 40 years older than other known copies of this map of the underworld.[3] Like many in my field, I was greatly excited by the discovery and was compelled to re-examine this book.

To speak broadly, this vividly illustrated guidebook contains vignettes of confrontations with underworld deities and demons, spells, as well as directions (of movement and action) to help the soul of the deceased navigate the underworld regions, to reach the "centre", a place called "Rosetau", ⌢𝕸 , *r.st3w*, the abode of Osiris, the Lord of the Dead.[4] In identifying and uniting

---

[3] Willems, *A Fragment of an Early Book of Two Ways on the Coffin of Ankh from Dayr al-Barshā (B4B)* (2018). Previously discovered versions of the book appear throughout *The Coffin Texts* (see bibliography).

[4] Beyond being a region within the netherworld of the afterlife, "Rosetau", literally 'mouth of ramps' or 'gate of ramps' (⌢ , *r*, 'mouth', and 𝕸 , *st3w*, 'ramps'), is speculated to be the original name for the cemeteries of the Giza plateau. Quirke writes "at most periods the ramps would be for towing sarcophagi to tombs, rather than hauling pyramid construction blocks; the place is associated with the funerary Memphite god Sokar; in afterlife literature, the name extends more generally to one or more regions of the underworld" (See Quirke, *Going out in Daylight*, page 601) "Remember that ⌢ , *r*; can also mean "gate", "door", "portal", as well as "mouth". The "mouth of ramps" or "portal of ramps", came to be a euphemism for the Underworld." Gunther, private correspondence 24/07/2022. It has been translated as Restau, Rostaw, Rosetjau, Rosta, and Resetjau. Modern scholars tend

with Osiris, the deceased is granted eternal life in the
Bark of Ra. In alternate versions, the culmination of the
journey is to reach the Field of Offerings where the
deceased will serve and feast with Osiris for eternity. A
detailed account of this journey is not necessary here, I
will instead focus on several features of the terrain I hope
will resonate with Aspirants to the Order of θελημα.[5]

---

towards Rostau, or Rosetau. The word might also refer to an actual
physical sepulchral district within the Deir El-Bersha necropolis. As
with many maps of the Duat in Egyptian writing, real world
correlations can be found with underworld locations. Many of these
are astrological, but a great many are terrestrial. The region of
Rosetau is also described as 'at the boundary of the sky'. According
to CT 1080 it is here that Osiris resides, in a vacuous space locked
in complete darkness surrounded by fire. One of the epithets of
Osiris is "The Lord of Rosetau".

[5] To those interested in reading these texts in detail, see Faulkner's
translation of *The Coffin Texts*. To those with the ability to read
hieroglyphs, De Buck's *The Egyptian Coffin Texts* published by the
University of Chicago is also recommended. It is often difficult to
follow the narrative of *The Book of Two Ways* as it is scattered
throughout *The Coffin Texts*, for this reason *The Ancient Egyptian
Book of Two Ways,* translated by Leonard H. Lesko can also be
useful. The book was also translated by Piankoff and appears in *The
Wandering of the Soul*, Bollingen Series XL.6 – it reads well but is a
translation lacking in accuracy (see bibliography for these). Keep in
mind that these are some of the oldest surviving texts in human
history. Our understanding of their contents remains limited despite
over a century of study and debate. J Daniel Gunther generously
and patiently corrected my translations here.

I draw particular attention to *The Book of Two Ways*, as it differs in many significant ways to other funerary texts, and from later "cosmological topographies" such as *Amduat* and *The Book of Gates*. Firstly, it is as much a book of directed action as it is of spells, utterances and proclamations. Scholars in recent years have tentatively, though convincingly, suggested that the books were very likely linked to ritual practices and rites of initiation.[6] Beyond what at first appears as a guide for the deceased in the afterlife (as we find in the rest of *The Coffin Texts* and *The Book of the Dead* itself), these works likely underpinned initiatic processes and formulas in *living* candidates.[7] Discussing the interrelation between geography and ritual performance in *The Book of Two Ways*, scholar Eltayeb Sayed Abbas writes, "One of the most important features of the Book of the Two Ways are the maps showing the landscape of the netherworld, with points of entry and gateways leading the deceased to different destinations in the netherworld. There are also rites connected with these

---

[6] J. Robinson, *As for them who know them, they shall find their paths: speculations on ritual landscapes in the 'Book of The Two Ways'*, in *Mysterious Lands*, O'Connor & Quirke eds. (2003), page 154. See also Sherbiny, *Through Hermopolitan Lenses: Studies on the So-called Book of Two Ways in Ancient Egypt* (2017), passim.

[7] Sherbiny, *Echoes of a Lost Legacy. The Recent Research on the so-called Book of Two Ways in Ancient Egypt.* (2018), pages 48 – 50.

passages to allow the deceased to proceed safely on the ways of the land of Rosetau. The rites performed in front of or within these gateways initiate the deceased into the afterlife, and were marked by a number of barriers in his journey to the netherworld."[8] A brief example may give the reader a sense of what these researchers are referring to;

> *This word that is within darkness.*

> *As for any Spirit knowing this word, he will live among the living.*

> *Fire is around this word containing the fluids of Osiris. As for any man knowing this word, he shall not ever perish, since he knows what shall be in Rosetau.*
> - The Coffin Texts. Spell 1087[9]

Throughout the book, the memorisation of sacred words and phrases, the cycling pattern of questions and answers, the repetition of testing and coaching by the Guardians, and the recitation of previously taught

---

[8] Abbas, *The Seven Gatekeepers, Guardians, and Reporters in The Book of the Two Ways and in P. MMA 35.9.21* (2011).

[9] CT SPELL 1087, De Buck VII 364 & VII 365: B2L VII 364 (b) *mdt nw ntt m-ẖnw kkw* , (c) *ir 3ẖ nb rḫ.s iw.f ʿnẖ* , (d) *mm ʿnẖw*, (e) *iw sḏt ḥ3.s* , (f) *ḥrt rḏw pw n wsir*. B2L VII 365 (a) *ir s nb rḫt.f [s] n ski.n.f im ḏt* , (b) *ḏr rḫ.f wnnt r.st3w*. B5C *ḏr rḫ.f wnty.sy m r3-st3w*.

instruction at specific moments of the journey is highly suggestive of didactic initiatic training.[10]

The cosmographical map the book describes, consists of the two main ways, or paths, upon which the deceased must travel; either by water (often depicted in blue or blue-green), or by land/fiery earth (depicted as a solid dark or ruddy line), in order to reach the inmost realm of Osiris, the Lord of the Dead, and through him, to become linked for eternity to the creator, Ra. In most surviving illustrated versions of the book, the two winding paths are separated by a thin red band of colour, depicting the "Lake of Fire of the Knife Wielders" as it is called in CT 1166.[11] This Lake of Fire can destroy, but also purify.[12] At the end of these paths, the seeker encounters four gates and must contend with the "fiery court" which surrounds the Rosetau; then master and pass three final gates, before invoking and identifying with Thoth who leads the seeker to Osiris. The identification with, and veneration of, Osiris then lends admission to the Bark of Ra (or Field of Offerings, in variant versions). Numerous guardians and demons

---

[10] Eltayeb Sayed Abbas also suggests a liturgical application for the texts.

[11] VII 416 (c) *š-n(y)-sḏ.t s(3)ḫ.ty.w*

[12] See my essay in *Ora Et Labora Volume 3* for the destructive and revivifying nature of fire in the mythos of the Ancient Egyptians and the system of Thelema.

bar the paths and gates. There are also perils of intolerable darkness, high walls of stone, and raging walls of fire. The deceased must also face fierce accusations, while justifying his actions in life, denying wrongdoing, before being accepted into the bark of Ra (CT 1099).

With the narrative structure and geographic terrain briefly described, I'll discuss how this cosmological narrative map relates generally to the formula of initiation in the New Aeon, and particularly to the formula of the Neophyte of the A∴A∴.[13]

> Mighty and erect is this Will of mine, this
> Pyramid of fire whose summit is lost in
> Heaven. Upon it have I burned the corpse
> of my desires.
>
> Mighty and erect is this ΦΑΛΛΟΣ of my Will.
> The seed thereof is That which I have
> borne within me from Eternity; and it is
> lost within the Body of Our Lady of the
> Stars.
> - Liber 333, Chapter 15. *The Gun Barrel.*

---

[13] *Liber DCLXXI vel ThROA*, the rite of initiation of the Neophyte of A∴A∴ is of course not for public discussion. The published ritual, *Liber Pyramidos*, is acceptable to discuss publicly, and will form the basis of my comparison here.

O you who are over the Mesqet, guarding the gates of
Duat, make a good path for this man. May he enter and
may he worship Osiris, as a god himself, for eternity.
- The Coffin Texts. Spell 789.[14]

Bind on, the Girdle of the Starry one…
- Liber Pyramidos.

First, and most obviously apparent, is the super-structure
of the two paths themselves, the path of earth (or fiery
ground) and the path of water. We are presented with
two paths in *Liber Pyramidos.*[15] We will discuss the
nature and perils of these paths in a moment.

---

[14] De Buck (L2Li) (j & k) *i ḥry msḳt s3w sb3w dw3t iri w3t nfr tn*
(l & m) *ꜥḳ dw3 wsir nṯr [ds]. f n ḏt.* In the past, "The Mesqet" has
been erroneously translated as "The Milky Way". See Willems, *The*
Coffin of Heqata (JdE 16418) A Case Study of Egyptian Funerary
Culture in Early Middle Kingdom, pages 262-270 "The upshot of
the preceding discussion is that Mesqet had a well-defined
meaning: it was a location in the sun temple at Heliopolis. In a
cosmological sense, this was tantamount to the place behind the
eastern horizon where the sun god (Ra) joined the corpse of Osiris
shortly before sunrise, a merger which led at one and the same time
to the rebirth of the former and the resurrection of the latter". This
tantalising detail should be kept in mind during the discussion of
the relationship between the candidate and the Hierophant below.

[15] The Path of HVA. The Path of IAO. These, and their watery
reflections can be studied in *Liber HHH,* and throughout J Daniel
Gunther's *Initiation in the Aeon of the Child.*

The second structural similarity between *The Book of Two Ways* and the Ceremony of the Death of Asar which brings the candidate to the Neophyte grade of the Outer College, is that at the end of these paths we encounter Four Gates which must be passed before one can stand in the centre, in Rosetau, or in the centre of the pyramid of Asar.[16] We of course know of the four gates spoken of in The Book of the Law,

> "There are four gates to one palace; the floor of that palace is of silver and gold; lapis lazuli & jasper are there; and all rare scents; jasmine & rose, and the emblems of death. Let him enter in turn or at once the four gates; let him stand on the floor of the palace. Will he not sink? Amn. Ho! warrior, if thy servant sink? ..."[17]

As explicated in J Daniel Gunther's *Initiation in The Aeon of The Child*, "... L.V.X. will now only open the Four Gates at the foot of the mountain of Abiegnus. Now, the "foot of the mountain" is Malkuth, who bears the title "Gate of the Daughter of the Mighty Ones."

---

[16] In *The Book of Two Ways* the seeker of Rosetau after passing the first Four Gates, delivers a lengthy exordium to Horus (CT 1106), before confrontation with an additional Three Gates. These final gates are not addressed in the present study.

[17] AL 1:51

The four quadrants of Malkuth are the Four Gates. These Gates must, in some fashion, be entered by all mankind eventually, in order to partake fully of the material life. A person of normal consciousness may indeed pass through them in the course of his life. In this case, it would be one at a time. Rarely are all conquered. The Initiate, on the other hand, granted the Keys to the Kingdom, may enter them simultaneously by virtue of the Great Name. This is a matter known to Neophytes of the A∴A∴, who experience Ritual DCLXXI. Having confronted the challenges of the guardians of the Gates, and being gilded by the fullness of the Light, they are granted admission."

The Four Gates are thus depicted in the illustration in *Initiation in the Aeon of the Child*, page 150.[18]

---

[18] Used with the kind permission of J. Daniel Gunther.

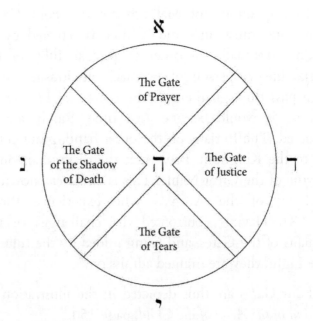

The Four Gates

For the sake of helping us map the Gates of *Liber Pyramidos* and tease out the synchronies of these gates and those of *The Book of Two Ways* it will be useful to return to this model.

Liber Pyramidos describes the guardian of the gates in the following manner:

Gate 1: The Lord of Hell, "Soul-mastering Terror" נ (Nun) – The Gate of the Shadow of Death.

Gate 2: Asi, "Sorrow that eateth up the soul", the Ideal Image of Nature ד (Daleth) – The Gate of Justice.

Gate 3: "False Phantom", the Fatal Image of Nature י (Yod) – The Gate of Tears.

Gate 4: The Hierophant in the form of Thoth א (Aleph) – The Gate of Prayer.

The Guardians of the four gates at the end of *The Book of Two Ways* in the *Coffin Texts* are described as:

Gate 1: "STRETCHER OF THE BOW-WARP (IS) THE GATE-KEEPER OF THE OUTER GATE."[19] (CT 1100)

Gate 2: "HE WHO CUTS THEM DOWN IS THE KEEPER OF THE SECOND GATE." (CT 1101)

Gate 3: "HE WHO EATS THE DROPPINGS OF HIS HINDER PARTS IS THE KEEPER OF THE THIRD GATE." (CT 1102)

And finally, "HE WHO GLOWERS/ THE VOLUBLE ONE, IS THE KEEPER OF THE FOURTH GATE." (CT 1103)

Following out this schema, let's compare Gate 1 of *The Book of Two Ways*, and the Gate 1 of *Liber Pyramidos*. Here the candidate must confront the Terrors of the Lord of Hell:

> *"Soul-mastering Terror is thy name!*
> *Lord of the Gods! Dread Lord of Hell!*
> *I come. I fear Thee not. Thy flame*

---

[19] Spell 1100 VII 416 B3C (a) *dwn ḥ3tt ir-ꜥ3 ḥ3.t*

Is mine to weave my maiden spell!

For I know Thee, and I pass Thee by.

For more than Thou am I."

The guardian of the first of the four gates of *The Book of Two Ways* is "STRETCHER OF THE BOW-WARP (IS) THE GATE-KEEPER OF THE OUTER GATE." In confrontation with this first formidable guardian, Spell 1100 reads:

> *"I come into the valley. I take the knives of the knife-wielder from him,*[20]
>
> *the butcher, effective of power, who has not been driven away."* [21]
>
> *"I drive away the destroyers who have not been driven away."* [22]
>
> *"Do not come down on me!"* [23]

---

[20] Spell 1100 VII 416 B3C (b & c) *iἰ n N tn ḫnm int nḥm n N tn sḫ(tyw) n ꜥḥꜣ-dmt m.f* (literally, "comes of N. into valley. Takes of N. this knives of knife-wielder from him." Following English Grammar "N. comes into the valley. N. takes the knives of the knife-wielder from him," I have taken the liberty of translating this and the following verses into the first person.

[21] Spell 1100 VII 417 B3C (a) *[sšm*] [spd] [pḥty] [n] [tw] [ḥsf.f]*

[22] Spell 1100 VII 417 B3C (b) *N. tn ḥsf nbḏw n tw ḥsf.sn*

"Stretcher of the bow warp, Watchful Face!" [24]

Compare here the method of passing this gate in *The Book of Two Ways* "*I take the knives of the knife-wielder from him*", and in *Liber Pyramidos* "*Thy flame is mine to weave my maiden spell*". The passer seizes the weapon of the guardian in both cases. Compare "*...the butcher, effective of power, who has not been driven away. I drive away the destroyers who have not been driven away*" and "*I come. I fear Thee not.*" This is the Gate of the Shadow of Death. Both rites seek to rid the candidate of "the fear of darkness and of death", while showing the way to transcend both. In the opening of *Liber Pyramidos,* we see the working of the formula which triumphs over death: "*So **life takes fire from death** and runs, whirling amidst the suns*". Frater OM describes this formula in *John St John* "Death slays with the knife, and embalms with the oil, his sister Life. Life, thus prepared, invokes, at the summons of Death, the forces necessary to the Operation."[25] And in the crescendo of *Liber Pyramidos* we cry, "*I am the Lord that riseth fresh, **From Death, whose glory I inherit***".[26]

---

[23] Spell 1100 VII 417 B3C (c) *m h₃w ḥr.*

[24] Spell 1100 VII 418 B3C (a) *dwn ḥ₃tt rs-ḥr*

[25] *Equinox Vol 1:1*, Special Supplement, page 36.

[26] My emphasis.

It is wrong to say triumphantly "Mors janua vitae", unless you add, with equal triumph, "Vita janua mortis."[27]

In CT 1053 ("Spell for passing on the path of the fiery ones") we read, *"I am the Eye of Horus, beneficial in the night, which makes fire with its beauty; I am the Lord of the horizon, and the daily flame licks me.* **As for him who passes on the path, his foes will be felled and Apep will be driven off."**[28] In *Pyramidos* "For I know Thee, and I pass Thee by. For more than Thou am I."

The Key to passing this gate is COURAGE.

Now to the second gate of *Liber Pyramidos*:

> *"Sorrow that eateth up the soul!*
> *Dam of the Gods! The blue sky's Queen!*
> *This is Thy Name. I come. Control*
> *And pass! I know Thee, Lady of (?)!*
> *I know Thee, and I pass Thee by.*
> *For more than Thou am I."*

The spell of the guardian of the Second Gate of *The Book of Two Ways*, HE WHO CUTS THEM DOWN IS THE

---

[27] Crowley, *Liber ABA*, page 147. "Death is the gate of life", and "life is the gate of death"

[28] My emphasis. Faulkner, *The Ancient Egyptian Coffin Texts, Volume 3*, page 138.

KEEPER OF THE SECOND GATE (CT 1101), reads '*May you guard him who turns aside to you; what is on me spreads protection over me. Confusion was standing over you. The monster stands up when meeting you, and the bark has fallen into the waters of weakness.* (Much is marred by lacuna in the hieroglyphs here[29]) *You are seen, you aggressor who are below, because the Great Lady comes.*'

Here the "*bark has fallen into waters of weakness*". The bark, the vessel of aspiration, the mind and body of the candidate has fallen into "*the waters of weakness*", the sorrow of Asi, the fatality of nature. The seeker passes only "*because the Great Lady comes*". As Gunther writes in his lecture on *The Parable of the Pale Image,* "Then the goddess — symbolizing the Great Work itself — rose up out of the Unconscious. She became a conscious component in the life of the aspirant. He "melted into her beauty" — that is, his ego was swallowed up in devotion to her."[30]

Frater O.M. discussing this aspect of the formula of initiation in *John St. John* writes "So, bound and blinded, he stumbles forward, and passes through the wrath of

---

[29] Lesko renders this difficult passage "You (pour out that which is) in the mouth of Re. You have not travelled with his suite. The striking force (of God) is before you, his tongue against you. Retreat from your seat. You have not come (in) his time." See De Buck *Coffin Texts,* Vol VII (pages 420-423)

[30] Gunther, *Lecture Series, Parables of Thelema vol. 2, The Parable of The Pale Image,* in preparation.

the Four Great Princes of Evil of the World, whose Terror is about him on every side. Yet since he has followed the voice of the Officer who has prepared him, in this part of the Ritual no longer merely Nature, but the great Mother, Neschamah (his aspiration) and the representative of Adonai, he may pass through all."[31]

In earlier passages leading up to these gates, while following the path of solid ground in *The Book of Two Ways,* the deceased confronts a simulacrum resembling the life and environmental features of the world he just departed – townships, villages, settlements, outposts, agricultural fields, rivers, fields of reeds – the guardians of the path undermine his worthiness to continue forth and stymie his attempts to pass; forcing those without fortitude and wit to tarry in the *image of nature.*[32]

> *"The snakes of (?) are the keepers of the gates. The place of herbage. The place of fields. The place of sand. The place of stones (?). The house of herbage of ꜣḫt -wtt(?). This is the spell which is above the waterways."*
> - The Coffin Texts. Spell 1052.[33]

---

[31] *Equinox Vol 1:1*, Special Supplement, page 37.

[32] Again, I'd refer the reader to Gunther, *The Parable of The Pale Image* (2022), and Chapter 4 of *Initiation in the Aeon of the Child.*

[33] Faulkner, *The Ancient Egyptian Coffin Texts, Volume 3*, page 137.

Lesko, in his translation and commentary of *The Book of Two Ways*, writes:

> "It is clear that the description of "life" in the "Field of Offerings" from CT 1047-1052 is not quite the paradise or Elysian Fields which we have come to know from BD 110 (which also occurs in CT 464-468). The picture in version A[34] is haphazard, but in B the deceased appears as no more than a servant who works all day for Osiris. The "Field of (the god) Hetep" or "Field of Offerings" is placed here along the waterway, but the path is not necessarily directed to the enclosure[35] and actually goes beyond on all coffins.[36] The deceased can evidently work here all day as well as guide the barks."[37]

This also is the snare of the pilgrim of the Way, the candidate to Neophyte: Unless the profane life which is death to the initiate is shrugged off, the candidate will sink back into the inertia of incarnation.[38] This is the temptation of nature *external* to man.

---

[34] Lesko categorised variant versions of *The Book of Two Ways*, by A, B & C assignations.

[35] Here Lesko is referring to the centre, Rosetau, abode of Osiris.

[36] Meaning the path goes past the target, and simply trails off the end of the coffin.

[37] Lesko, *The Ancient Egyptian Book of Two Ways,* page 57.

When overcome, "The focus is shifted from a fascination with a profane world to a willed union with God."[39]

The Key to passing this gate is ASPIRATION.

To Gate 3 of *Pyramidos* now, where the candidate contemplates himself in silence, while confronting the image of the small 's' self he sees in the magic mirror:

> *"I will not look upon thee more*
> *For Fatal is Thy Name. Begone!*
> *False Phantom, thou shalt pass before*
> *The frowning forehead of the Sun.*
> *I know Thee, and I pass Thee by.*
> *For more than Thou am I."*

Gate Three of *The Book of Two Ways* (CT 1102) is guarded by "HE WHO EATS THE DROPPINGS OF HIS HINDER PARTS IS THE KEEPER OF THE THIRD GATE."

Aptly this guardian feasts on his own excrement, just as the candidate who fails to transcend the false image of the magic mirror feasts on the excrement of his own ego. In *Liber Pyramidos* the candidate contemplates himself in silence – he can become entranced with the fatal image of nature, failing the test of the magic

---

[38] See Gunther, *Initiation in the Aeon of the Child*, chapters 2, 4 and 6.

[39] ibid, page 54.

mirror, or turn away from the fatal image and continue the journey to the centre, towards Rosetau, and the resurrection of the corpse of Asar. To stay, and like Narcissus, fall in love with the fatal image is to remain, self-loving, self-nourishing, feasting on one's own faeces.

CT 1102 continues "*Get back, you aggressor, for your arm is as a 3bḥw-plant, your backbone is as a red bbt-plant, you shall eat of what the mmt-plant eats. I know you, and I know the name of this throwstick of yours which is thrown behind you. Down on your face! Layout your arms! Light shall go forth that it may open up the firmament, and bleariness of vision will be dispelled.*"[40]

The "*bleariness of the vision*" is the imperfect image of the self.

Compare "*Light shall go forth that it may open up the firmament*" and "*False Phantom, thou shalt pass before, The frowning forehead of the Sun.*" It is LVX that dispels the bleariness of vision, the false phantom of "self".

The water way of *The Book of Two Ways* leading to this gate can also be viewed as the entrancement of nature, but through the watery reflective snare of the magical mirror, the *fatal image of nature,* the false self-image, the false identity with the small "s" self.[41] This is the temptation of nature *internal* to man.

---

[40] Faulkner, *The Ancient Egyptian Coffin Texts, Volume 3*, page 158.

In CT 1168 we see resistance to this fatal image of the self. One transcends this ensnaring image through identity with Ra, the apotheosis of Godhead, and the "detestation" of the lower nature of the aspirant who is in too much of a hurry to assume the godform of Ra on the horizon without worthily attaining the perfection of identity with Him.

> "*Your god has come into being, and* HIS NAME IS KHEPRI. HE IS THE KEEPER OF THE BEND OF THIS WATERWAY, AND HIS NAME IS SHARP OF VISION. FIRE IS THIS WHICH IS ON HIM. *I am he who gets rid of him who opposes the opponent of the aggressor who moves in order to run. I possess the egg of Ra and my dignity is like that of Ra when he appears in the early morning; my dignity is guarded for me when I reach it. What I detest is flesh which goes forth to those who are in the horizon who are in a hurry, since I know that he is in the horizon.*"[42]

Put simply, this ordeal is passed by aspiration and *humility*. During the passing of the path of the water way, the fatal image of nature is defeated when the seeker not only dispenses with hubris, but sacrifices the

---

[41] See Gunther, *Lecture Series, Parables of Thelema vol. 1, The Parable of The New Birth*, Wennofer House, 2022. Also, *Initiation in The Aeon of The Child*, page 129 "The image of the Evil Persona reflected into the Nephesh is called the *fatal image of nature*"

[42] Faulkner, *The Ancient Egyptian Coffin Texts, Volume 3*, page 185.

false sense of self, or ego-consciousness.[43] In the first line of Spell 1040, you will notice that the seeker first renounces the place and manner of his natural birth before elaborating on the power he has received by his lord Ra-Horakhty (Ra-Hoor-Khuit), and his new role as a guide in the Rosetau.

> "I am one who was born in Rosetau, and power is given to me by my lord Ra-Horakhty my dignity is in Pe' when I cleanse Osiris. I have received acclamation in Rosetau in the guidance of the gods on their mounds, for I am now one of their guides."[44]

He denies all that he was, and affirms all that he will become.

Humility. Aspiration.

In his essential work *The Sungod's Journey Through the Netherworld*, Andreas Schweizer describes some of the psychic mechanisms in play during this confrontation. "This natural fear of entering the netherworld—that is,

---

[43] Consider Water = Mem, and the Hanged Man. In the ultimate expression of this formula, see *The Angel and The Abyss*, page 97 "The true hanged man from the perspective of the New Aeon is the Master of The Temple of A∴A∴, having undergone the supreme Baptism and dissolution of the Great Sea."

[44] Faulkner, *The Ancient Egyptian Coffin Texts, Volume 3*, page 133.

of setting foot in the realm of archetypal images reflecting the collective unconscious— is entirely understandable. It is a well-known fact that if we try too eagerly to penetrate into the realm of the collective unconscious, or if we approach the healing images of the soul, let us say, with some sort of ulterior, ego-centered motive, striving for power or profit, it can be as though we are trying (as indicated by the imagery of the Amduat) to enter this "other world" in the company of the "enemies," or, to put it in psychological terms, contaminated by the "shadow." The shadow incorporates all those dark and inferior aspects of our personality that, despite the fact that they are repressed into the unconscious, prove to be real in the form of uncontrolled affects, moods, and emotions emerging from the depths of our psyche (in Jungian psychology the shadow is also a technical term for the parts in us that we don't recognize). If we approach the archetypal world without awe and humility, the unconscious will most likely be hostile toward us." [45]

In his lecture on the *Parable of the Hummingbird*, Gunther's comments "Anyone who seeks the A∴A∴ for selfish reasons will have one of two possible outcomes. They will either discover *selflessness* in

---

[45] Schweizer, *The Sungod's Journey through the Netherworld: Reading the Ancient Egyptian Amduat,* 2010, page 32.

themselves and begin to work to serve humankind, or they will fail."[46]

In both texts, the snare of the allure of the profane world (*external* and *internal*) must be "passed by" before the centre can be attained.

The Key to passing this gate is HUMILITY.

Now to the fourth gate (CT 1103) "HE WHO GLOWERS/ THE VOLUBLE ONE, IS THE KEEPER OF THE FOURTH GATE." Following our schema, in *Liber Pyramidos* the candidate engages in a silent interview with Thoth, and it is with Thoth, and by Thoth, that the seeker of Rosetau passes the fourth gate in *The Book of Two Ways, "I am made to enter, and I make him who glowers tremble behind the sacred matters of the god; I am made known in the Above. Who is he who goes around the Coiled One? One whose rank is high, whom Thoth will judge in the morning."* (CT 1103)[47]

Candidates to *Liber ThROA*, and those familiar with *Liber Pyramidos* will also recognise the figure of Thoth in other passages of *The Book of Two Ways*. Spell 1035 *"I have passed over the paths of Rosetau, whether on water or on land, and these are the paths of Osiris; they are in the*

---

[46] Gunther, *Lecture Series, Parables of Thelema Vol. 3, The Parable of The Hummingbird*, Wennofer House, in preparation.

[47] Faulkner, *The Ancient Egyptian Coffin Texts, Volume 3*, page 158.

limit of the sky. As for him who knows this spell for going down into them, he himself is a god, in the suite of Thoth; he will go down to any sky to which he wishes to go down. But as for him who does not know this spell for passing over these paths, he shall be taken into the infliction(?) of the dead which is ordained, as one who is non-existent, who shall never have rightness."[48] Throughout *The Book of Two Ways* the deceased begs an audience with Thoth (CT 1089 and 1092). They travel the paths of Thoth (CT 1093) and together meet Asar in the mansion of Ra (CT 1094) before proceeding with Ra in his sacred bark (CT 1096-1098)[49]. Thoth is the divinely inspired wisdom invoked by the candidate. Gunther writes of the *Parable of the Hummingbird,*

"But an Ibis that meditated upon the bank of Nile the beautiful god listened and heard.[50]

---

[48] Faulkner, *The Ancient Egyptian Coffin Texts, Volume 3*, page 132.

[49] Consider also, Thoth and His role as *Logos* and Divine Word. See Assman's discussion of "The Akh-Power of Speech" in *The Search for God in Ancient Egypt*, page 87 "the word also contains the kernel of a whole theory of language… Only the radiant power of divine words had the ability to illuminate the sacred, the divine meaning of cultic, event cosmic, events and acts, the otherworldliness in this world." See also Gunther, *Initiation in the Aeon of the Child*, "The Fixed Mercury" page 109-114. Also, *Liber 415, The Paris Working*, Opuses II & III.

[50] Liber LVX, 5:55.

Here, we now come to the beautiful moral of this story. An Ibis meditating upon the bank of the Nile listened to the conversation between the sacred Uræus and the hummingbird. First, we need to remember that the Ibis was sacred to Thoth, the god of Magic, Writing and Wisdom. Here, the Ibis signifies divinely inspired Wisdom."[51]

"The protection of Thoth is my protection from you."
- The Coffin Texts. Spell 1071[52]

"I am a spirit and a lord of spirits; the spirit whom I will create will indeed exist; the spirit whom I hate will not exist. I am one who goes all over his lake in fire, a lord of light; I circle around with the Eye of Horus at hand; Thoth crosses the sky in my presence, and I pass safely."
- The Coffin Texts. Spell 1042[53]

"I am pure in my own sarcophagus; I am Thoth, a possessor of offerings to Osiris and a possessor of offerings to myself. These belong to my father Osiris who is on the high ground (and to) the Coiled One"
- The Coffin Texts. Spell 1124[54]

---

[51] Gunther, *The Parable of the Hummingbird*, page 40.

[52] Faulkner, *The Ancient Egyptian Coffin Texts, Volume 3*, page 144.

[53] Faulkner, *The Ancient Egyptian Coffin Texts, Volume 3*, page 134.

[54] Faulkner, *The Ancient Egyptian Coffin Texts, Volume 3*, page 165.

In both instances transfiguration occurs when the seeker identifies (i.e., seeks identity) with the *imago dei*, in *The Book of The Two Ways*, with Thoth, with many of the guardians, with Osiris – the apotheosis of death and resurrection – and ultimately with Ra – the supreme deity. In the ritual of *Liber Pyramidos*, it is identity with "Hoor in his secret name and splendour"; the candidate identifies with, assuming the identity of, the Hierophant. In the magical record of *John St John*, Frater O.M. while working out the details of *Liber Pyramidos*, discusses this formula explicitly "I think the postulant should actually be scourged, tortured, branded by fire for his equilibrations at the various 'Stations of the Cross' or points upon his mystic journey. He must assuredly drink blood for the sacrament – ah! Now I see it so well! The Initiator must kill him, Osiris; he must rise again as Horus and kill the Initiator, taking his place in the ceremony thence to the end."[55]

This formula is further demonstrated in the *Rites of Eleusis, the Rite of Mercury*:

---

[55] "The Hierophant is the Initiator. In the New Aeon, it has been revealed to us that Hoor in his secret name and splendour is the Lord Initiating. In the critical initiations in the career of all A∴A∴ aspirants, the Hierophant is present. Invisible to the Neophyte, but ever present on the Eastern Throne, He is known to the guardians of the Pyramid as Hoor-Apep. For the aspiring Adeptus Minor, He is present in the City of the Sun in his name Hoor-Ra. To the babe of the Abyss, He awaits in the City of the Pyramids in His name Hoor-Set." Gunther, *The Angel and The Abyss*, page 298.

VIRGO: Is not Mercury the Sun-God, when hidden during the Night, among the souls of the dead? Hail unto Thee, Trismegistus, Hail unto thee! ... Hail unto Mercury.... He killeth Sol at the close of every Twilight, and hangeth up the sky of Night on the Tree of Heaven, fastened up with the Star-headed nails.[56]

Here, Mercury kills Sol, and becomes the Sun-God of night. When the sun rises the next morning, in the East, the Sun assumes the place of Mercury. The formula of Initiation follows an epic cosmic schema. At its exalted pinnacle, the formula plays out in the Sixth Aethyr of *Liber 418, The Vision and the Voice,* where Tahuti proclaims: **"None shall pass by me except he slay me, and this is his curse, that, having slain me, he must take my office and become the maker of Illusions, the great deceiver, the setter of snares; he who baffleth even them that have understanding."** The formula of slaying, and assuming the place and power of the entity guarding the way is a common feature of the spells of *The Book of Two Ways,* and the *Pyramid Texts* from which many of the *Coffin Texts* ultimately derived. Spell 1100, mentioned above is but one of many examples of this formula of taking the power from the deity by fortitude and force.[57] In other cases, assumption of the power of the deity comes by

---

[56] *Equinox 1:VI*, page 107.

way of exalted worship and direct identification with the deity[58] e.g., "*My heart is determined, my foes are under my left sandal, for I am the Eye of Horus. I am a fire in sky and earth, and all my foes are under my flame.*" Spell 946[59].

The Key to passing this gate is WISDOM.

The Keys in both texts are therefore,

WISDOM "To Know"

COURAGE "To Dare"

ASPIRATION "To Will"

---

[57] Some of the spells in the *Coffin Texts* take this formula further with the killing and consuming of the God being necessary to absorb the divine force. This is of course all throughout the *Pyramid Texts*, and is likely a remnant of older practices where Kings would consume their enemies in acts of magical cannibalism. See *Coffin Texts* Spell 1017 "SPELL FOR LIVING BY MEANS OF MAGIC AND BY MEANS OF PROTECTION IN THE TWO HOUSES" "I have eaten the doubles, I have fed on those who sit, I live on the spirits and the elder gods, those whose names are secret have been brought to me, I have joined in the protection in the Two Houses." For the development of the afterlife literature from the Old to Middle Kingdoms see Silvia Zago *Classifying the Duat: Tracing the Conceptualization of the Afterlife between Pyramid Texts and Coffin Texts* (2018).

[58] Assuming the Godform.

[59] Faulkner, *The Ancient Egyptian Coffin Texts, Volume 3*, page 34.

HUMILITY "To Remain Silent"[60]

Following our schema, these are "To Know" א, "To Will" ר, "To Dare" נ, "To remain silent" י. ארני = Adonai. But what of Spirit to equilibrate and sanctify the Gates of Matter? In the comment to Chapter 86 of

---

[60] Without wishing to draw false parallels between these gates, and the keys that aid the Aspirant to pass them by in the system of A∴A∴ and the ordeals of the Man of Earth of OTO, it is however worth noting some correspondences that appear.

י / Earth / Minerval – Reception (Key "Humility", Virtue "To Remain Silent")

א / Air / 1ˢᵗ Degree – Lustration (Key "Wisdom", Virtue "To Know")

נ /Water / 2ⁿᵈ Degree - Consecration (Key "Courage", Virtue "To Dare")

ר / Fire / 3ʳᵈ Degree – Devotion (Key "Aspiration", Virtue "To Will")

In meditating on these correspondences, we might consider Crowley's thoughts on the system of OTO during the reconstitution of the Order. While taking notes during this period (1914-1915 e.v.), Crowley writes "*To show people what to expect. Complete moral system. In all grades, secrecy. Its full meaning as Way of Tao & minding one's own business.*" (The *Rex de Arte Regia* notebook at the Harry Ransom Institute, my emphasis). The mastery and sublimation of the blind elements of nature, transform these into the four virtues of the adept. This work continues throughout the Outer College of A∴A∴ as it does in the system of OTO. "**Let him enter in turn or at once the four gates**" Liber CCXX 1:51.

The Book of Lies, Liber 333 "H, the letter of breath, is suitable for Spirit" and in *Liber LXV* Chapter 5, Verse 65, we read;

> So also is the end of the book, and the Lord Adonai is about it on all sides like a Thunderbolt, and a Pylon, and a Snake, and a Phallus, and in the midst thereof He is like the Woman that jetteth out the milk of the stars from her paps; yea, the milk of the stars from her paps.

Gunther writes "The Four Gates are thus depicted surrounded by a letter of the Name of Adonai, and in the midst, He is represented by the letter ה, which is in this case ה final of Tetragrammaton, that is to say, Malkuth."[61] He explains the key to understanding this verse in *Liber LXV* "The Thunderbolt = א, Pylon = ד, the Snake = ג, the Phallus = י, and the Woman = ה."[62] Continuing he writes, "Thereby, a Pentagrammaton is formed that signifies the transformative power of the New Light: ארדהני. The value of this Pentagrammaton = 1 + 4 + 5 + 50 + 10 = 70, which is that of ע, The Eye, Atu XV, The Lord of the Gates of Matter."[63] It's worth reflecting on the introduction of this ה final in the midst of these Gates, and returning to the earlier quote

---

[61] Gunther, *Initiation in the Aeon of the Child,* page 152.

[62] ibid, page 153.

[63] ibid, page 152.

from Frater O.M. in *John St. John*, "Yet since he has
followed the voice of the Officer who has prepared him,
in this part of the Ritual no longer merely Nature, but
the great Mother, Neschamah (his aspiration) and the
representative of Adonai, he may pass through all."[64]
The passing of the Gates of Matter, by virtue of the
(uninvoked) Lord of the Gates of Matter, is the first step
on the long inward journey whereby the daughter ה
final, is placed on the throne of the Mother, ה prima.
"No longer merely Nature, but the Great Mother", the
daughter passes "because the Great Lady comes"[65] that
is, "Neschamah (his aspiration) and the representative of
Adonai" "**...and in the midst thereof He is like the
Woman that jetteth out the milk of the stars from
her paps; yea, the milk of the stars from her paps**".

*

I am not for a moment suggesting that Aleister Crowley
drew direct inspiration from *The Book of Two Ways* in
the development of his reimagining of the ritual of the
Neophyte as adapted for use in the Outer College of the
A∴A∴, in the same way that he clearly drew
inspiration from many of the spells and formulae of *the
Book of The Dead* for the initiation ritual of the Zelator,
Liber CXX.[66] I am however suggesting that certain
modes of ordeal, spiritual self-overcoming, universal

---

[64] *Equinox Vol 1:1*, Special Supplement, page 37.

[65] *The Coffin Texts,* Spell 1101.

archetypal formulae of attainment, are inextricably woven into human consciousness and arise at various times to manifest themselves in the waking consciousness of human beings seeking the Light. This was certainly the position that Jung and his school took on these remerging motifs.[67] Also, from the Jungian perspective much could be said about the four cardinal gates and the circle, the holy centre, they describe. Jung writes "the psychic images of wholeness which are spontaneously produced by the unconscious, the symbols of the self in mandala form, also have a mathematical structure. They are as a rule quaternities (or their multiples). These structures not only express order, they also create it."[68] Jung's student Edward F. Edinger elaborates in *Ego and Archetype*, "Throughout alchemy, the symbolism of the number four plays an important role. Fourness was considered to be the basic ordering principle of matter. In the beginning of the world, prior to creation, there was only the *prima materia* which was without form, structure or specific

---

[66] At a certain point in the career of the Aspirant to the A∴A∴ instruction and analysis of the parallels and influences of *The Book of the Dead* on *Ritual CXX* are taught to them by their Superior.

[67] See Jung, *Collected Works Vol. IX Archetypes and the Collective Unconscious* – particularly "The Concept of the Collective Unconscious", pages 42–53.

[68] Jung, *Collected Works Vol. VIII The Structure and Dynamics of the Psyche,* pages 456–457.

content. All was potential, nothing actual. In the act of creation, the four elements, earth, air, fire and water were separated out from the *prima materia*. It is as though the cross of the four elements had been imposed on the *prima materia* giving it order and structure and bringing cosmos out of chaos. In order to produce the Philosopher's Stone, the four elements must be reunited in the unity of quintessence. The original whole and unified state of the *prima materia* is restored in the Philosopher's Stone on a new level.[69] These ideas have many parallels in the process of psychological development, particularly four as a symbol of wholeness. The four-fold nature of the Philosopher's Stone immediately relates it to the fourfold mandala images of the Self and indeed we have alchemical pictures of the Stone which are in the form of mandalas. In psychological terms we usually consider the number four to refer to the four psychic functions thinking, feeling, sensation and intuition. However, this interpretation is by no means adequate to cover the full meaning of fourness. The four elements for instance cannot be equated with the four functions. It seems rather that the structuring pattern of fourness can emerge in a variety of contexts to bring order and differentiation to experience. But always it carries the

---

[69] See Gunther, *Initiation in the Aeon of the Child*, page 136 "As the essential First Matter, the *Prima Materia*, the candidate is the actual 'life blood' of the operation."

implications of fulfilment or completion."[70]   These re-
emerging universal initiatic motifs have also been
considered within the field of Egyptology by scholars
such as Harold M. Hays who wrote, "By *structure* I
mean organization: how rites are concatenated together.
Examining structure can lead to a better understanding
of a ritual as a whole. It can show the anatomical
commonalities between different rituals, can reveal the
contextual relationship between a given rite and the
ritual in which it occurs, and can heighten appreciation
of Egyptian religious texts in general."[71]   With a
boldness rarely seen in his field, Hays presents
compelling evidence that not only do initiatic schema
appear to be a human universal but going further than
others before him, contends that these universals go
beyond mere appearances of form, and find
commonality at a linguistic and syntactic level.[72]

Beyond the considerations of structural similarities, we
move finally to the crux of this inquiry; the perfection
of the deceased in *The Book of Two Ways*, and the
perfection of the living candidate in the system of
Thelema requires the descent into hell.

---

[70] Edinger, *Ego and Archetype*, pages 264-265.

[71] Hays, *The End of Rites of Passage and a Start with Ritual Syntax in
Ancient Egypt* (2013). Page 166.

[72] ibid. It may interest the reader to know that Dr. Harold M. Hays
was a Neophyte of the A∴A∴.

*"The fire which is about Ra is bright against you, being
bound about him; the Lord of Storm fears the bark of Ra,
and you shall join the fire."*
- The Coffin Texts. Spell 1033[73]

**"When shall the day come that men shall flock to
this my gate, and fall into my furious throat, a
whirlpool of fire? This is hell unquenchable, and
all they shall be utterly consumed therein.
Therefore is that asbestos unconsumable made
pure"**
- Liber 418, 25th Aethyr

Passage and attainment in both *The Book of Two Ways*
and the system of Thelema requires the voluntary
movement inwards to the centre – the core – which we
know from the revelation of *Liber 418* as 'hell'.

**"My arms were out in the form of a cross, and that
Cross was extended, blazing with light into
infinity. I myself am the minutest point in it. This
is the birth of form. I am encircled by an immense
sphere of many-coloured bands; it seems it is the
sphere of the Sephiroth projected in the three
dimensions. This is the birth of death. Now in the
centre within me is a glowing sun. That is the
birth of hell."**

---

[73] Faulkner, *The Ancient Egyptian Coffin Texts, Volume 3*, page 129.

- Liber 418, 22nd Aethyr

Gunther explains this concept of hell in his lecture on the *Parable of the New Birth*. A longer quote is in order here;

"Extraversion carries certain characteristics of the Aeon of the Father, the Aeon of Osiris. Introversion represents certain characteristics of the Aeon of the Mother, the Aeon of Isis. Centroversion of course is signified by the Aeon of the Child, the Aeon of Horus. Here is what is written in The Vision & The Voice:

"My arms were out in the form of a cross, and that Cross was extended, blazing with light into infinity. I myself am the minutest point in it. This is the birth of form."

The birth of form is the conception of the Self in extension — that is Extraversion.

"I am encircled by an immense sphere of many-coloured bands; it seems it is the sphere of the Sephiroth projected in the three dimensions. This is the birth of death."

The birth of death is the conception of the Self extended into the negative circle or sphere of Nuit — that is Introversion. You see? It's not scary at all!

This death is a death which should be Infinite, as The Vision & The Voice tells us. The death of the external world leads us to The Inward Journey.

And lastly, we see the Third and final aspect: **"Now in the centre within me is a glowing sun. That is the birth of hell."**

This is referred to Centroversion — the perception of one's innermost Nature. It is particularly referred to the Aeon of the Child."[74]

Hell, as we are only too painfully aware, had a different meaning in the previous Aeon of the Father. As has been discussed by Jung, the psychic structure of the Christian era is one of *Separatio*.[75] Matter from Spirit. Light from

---

[74] Gunther, *Lecture Series, Parables of Thelema vol. 1, The Parable of The New Birth,* Wennofer House, 2022. See also Neumann, *The Origins and History of Consciousness,* page 219. "The development of personality proceeds in three different dimensions. The first is outward adaptation, to the world and things, otherwise known as extraversion; the second is inward adaptation, to the objective psyche and archetypes, otherwise known as introversion. The third is centroversion, the self-formative or individuating tendency which proceeds within the psyche itself, independent of the other two attitudes and their development."

[75] Jung, *Mysterium Coniunctionis* "Only in Christianity did the 'metaphysical' opposites begin to percolate into man's consciousness.", page 70. "The tendency to separate the opposites as

Dark. Heaven from Hell. Here the act of separation informs the conception of hell, that is, exile to the Outer darkness and separation from the presence of God, which is itself the apotheosis of the penalty of apostacy under Judaism; to be severed from the body of Israel.

Seven days there shall be no leaven found in your houses; for whoever eats what is leavened, that person shall be cut off from the congregation of Israel, whether he is an alien or a native of the land.
- Exodus 12:19

And cast ye the unprofitable servant into outer darkness: there shall be weeping and gnashing of teeth.
- Matthew 25:30

Now, o my Son, having understood the Heaven that is within thee, according to thy Will, learn this concerning the Hell of the Slaves of the Slave-Gods, that it is a true place of Torment. For they, restricting themselves, and being

---

much as possible and to strive for singleness of meaning is absolutely necessary for clarity of consciousness, since discrimination is of its essence. But when the separation is carried so far that the complementary opposite is lost sight of, and the blackness of the whiteness, the evil of the good, the depth of the heights, and so on, is no longer seen, the result is one-sidedness, which is then compensated from the unconscious without our help.", pages 333-334.

divided in Will, are indeed the Servants of Sin, and they suffer, because, not being united in Love with the whole Universe, they perceive not Beauty, but Ugliness and Deformity, and, not being united in Understanding thereof, conceive only of Darkness and Confusion, beholding Evil therein. Thus at last they come, as did the Manichaeans, to find, to their Terror, a Division even in the one, not that Division which we know for the Craft of Love, but a Division of Hate. And this, multiplying itself, Conflict upon Conflict, endeth in Hotchpot, and in the Impotence and Envy of Choronzon, and in the Abominations of the Abyss. And of such the Lords are the Black Brothers, who seek by their Sorceries to confirm themselves in Division. Yet in this even is no true Evil, for Love conquereth all, and their Corruption and Disintegration is also the Victory of BABALON.

- *Liber Aleph.* Chapter 139. *De Inferno Servorum.*

If Thelema represents the future "psychological" religion of Jung[76] – its psychic structure is that of *coniunctio*, a

---

[76] Jung was skittish about specifics, but all examples of what this might look like demonstrate ideas of unification and wholeness; "Logos and Eros are reunited, as if they had overcome the conflict between spirit and flesh. They appear to know the solution." *Liber Novus*, page 571. "The union of the spiritual, masculine principle with the feminine, psychic principle is far from being just a fantasy of the Gnostics: if has found an echo in the Assumption of the Virgin, in the union of Tifereth and Malchuth, and in Goethe's 'the Eternal Feminine leads up upwards and on.'" *Mysterium Coniunctionis,* page 244. See also, Jung's discussion on the futurity of

reconciliation of opposites, a path to completion and wholeness.[77] The conception of hell in the New Aeon therefore goes beyond the idea of separation and severance from God, and instead represents the process of Union with God.

> "The spiritual essence is the secret flame that is life and gives life to the dead Osiris. To awaken it from its slumber is to cast its light into the dark corners of one's being. Therefore it is that which gives knowledge of death, the condition of torpor and inactivity. It is that which loosens the swathings of the corpse and endows the limbs of Osiris with mobility that he may set out upon the road of Eternity. It is the uppermost point of the pentagram, the Heart of every human (Tiphareth), the fifth power of the Sphinx, the Power TO GO. Within each individual it is called **Hadit**."[78]

Jung writes "The cross has also the meaning of a boundary-stone between heaven and hell, since it is set

---

the child archetype in *Archetypes of the Collective Unconscious*, page 164.

[77] "**My adepts stand upright; their head above the heavens, their feet below the hells**". *Liber Tzaddi*, verse 40. "**And the Master of the Temple balancing all things arose; his stature was above the Heaven and below Earth and Hell**". *Liber Trigrammaton*, Trigram 8 ☵ (remembering that the initial trigram is zero, not one).

[78] Gunther, *Initiation in the Aeon of the Child*. Page 60.

up in the centre of the cosmos"[79] adding "The definition of the cross or centre as the 'boundary' of all things, is exceedingly original, for it suggests that the limits of the universe are not to be found in a non-existent periphery but in its centre. There alone lies the possibility of transcending this world. All instability culminates in that which is unchanging and quiescent, and in the self all disharmonies are resolved in the 'harmony of wisdom'".[80] In *Liber Aleph*, Crowley describes this 'harmony of wisdom', "Now then thou seest that this Hell, or Concealed Place within thee, is no more a Fear or Hindrance to men of a Free Race, but the Treasure-House of the Assimilated Wisdom of the Ages, and the Knowledge of the True Way. Thus are we Just and Wise to discover this Secret in ourselves, to conform the conscious Mind therewith."[81]

Just as the seeker of God in the afterlife must journey to the center, to Rosetau, for unification with Ra in his solar-bark, so too must the Aspirant journey to the center, to the core of their being, to reach the glowing Sun, the container of the Self, the Great Reward promised in our Holy Books.

---

[79] Jung, *Collected Works Vol. XI "Psychology and Religion: West and East"* Page 80.

[80] ibid. Page 285.

[81] *Liber Aleph*, Chapter 128. *De Inferno Palatio Sapientiæ.*

As for anyone who knows this spell, he will be like Ra in the east of the sky, like Osiris within the Netherworld, and he will go down to the circle of fire; there will never be a flame against him for ever. It has come happily to an end.
- The Coffin Texts. Spell 1130.[82]

---

[82] Faulkner, *The Ancient Egyptian Coffin Texts, Volume 3,* page 168.

Bibliography

Holy Books in Class A and AB

Liber AL Vel Legis Sub Figura CCXX as Delivered by XCIII (The Book of the Law)

Liber CCCCXVIII: Liber XXX Ærum Vel Saeculi, Being of the Angels of the Thirty Aethyrs (The Vision and the Voice).

Liber LXV: Liber Cordis Cincti Serpente Sub Figurâ ארני

Liber XXVII: Liber Trigrammaton Sub Figurâ XXVII

Other references

Abbas, Eltayeb Sayed. *The Seven Gatekeepers, Guardians, and Reporters in The Book of the Two Ways and in P. MMA 35.9.21.* Bibliotheca Alexandrina, 2011.

Alwazi, Shokufeh. *The Island of Flames and the Spiritual Heart: A reflective commentary on Rev. Cosmé Hallelujah's "Notes towards a preliminary analysis of a peculiar motif in the Stele of Ankh-af-na-khonsu"* in Walls (ed.) *Ora Et Labora Volume 3,* IPP, 2022.

Assmann, Jan. *The Search for God in Ancient Egypt.* Ithaca: Cornell University Press, 2001.

Crowley, Aleister. *Liber 333, The Book of Lies,* New York: Weiser Books, 1974.

Crowley, Aleister. *Liber Aleph Vel CXI: The Book of Wisdom or Folly, in the Form an Epistle of 666, the Great Wild Beast to His Son 777.* Weiser Books, 1991.

Crowley, Aleister. *Equinox Vol. 1:I*, Special Supplement. *John St. John, The Record of the Magical Retirement of G.H. Frater Ou Mu*

Crowley, Aleister. *Equinox Vol. 1:VI. Rites of Eleusis, The Rite of Mercury.*

Crowley, Aleister. *Liber DCLXXI vel Pyramidos* in *Commentaries on the Holy Books and Other Papers*, Weiser Books, 1996.

Crowley, Aleister. *Liber ABA: Magick, Book Four, Part I-IV*, Weiser Books, 1997.

Crowley, Aleister. *Liber CDXV, Opus Lutetianum, The Paris Working*, Opuses II & III in *The Vision and the Voice with Commentary and Other Papers*, Weiser Books, 1998.

De Buck, Adriaan. *The Egyptian Coffin Texts, Volume VII, Spells 787-1185*, University of Chicago Press, 1951.

Edinger, Edward F. *Ego and Archetype*, Pelican Books, 1977.

Faulkner, R. O. *The Ancient Egyptian Coffin Texts, Volume III, Spells 788-1185*, Aris & Phillips, 1978.

Faulkner, R. O. *A Concise Dictionary of Middle Egyptian*, Modernized digital edition by Boris Jegorovic, 2017.

Gunther, J Daniel. *Initiation in The Aeon of The Child*, Ibis Press, 2009.

Gunther, J Daniel. *The Angel and The Abyss*, Ibis Press, 2014.

Gunther, J Daniel. *Lecture Series, Parables of Thelema vol. 1, The Parable of The New Birth*, Wennofer House, 2022.

Gunther, J Daniel. *Lecture Series, Parables of Thelema vol. 2, The Parable of The Pale Image*, Wennofer House, in preparation.

Gunther, J Daniel. *Lecture Series, Parables of Thelema vol. 3, The Parable of The Hummingbird*, Wennofer House, in preparation.

Hays, Harold M. *The End of Rites of Passage and a Start with Ritual Syntax in Ancient Egypt* in *Approaching Rituals in Ancient Cultures*, Ambos & Verderame, eds., Supplemento Rivista degli Studi Orientali, Nuova Serie, Volume LXXXVI, Rome, 2013.

Jung, Carl. *Collected Works Vol. IX: Archetypes and the Collective Unconscious*, Princeton, 1959.

Jung, Carl. *Collected Works Vol. XI: Psychology and Religion: West and East,* Princeton, 1969.

Jung, Carl. *Collected Works Vol. VIII: The Structure and Dynamics of the Psyche,* Princeton, 1959.

Jung, Carl *Collected Works Vol. XIV: Mysterium Coniunctionis,* Princeton, 1970.

Jung, Carl & Shamdasani, S. (Ed.). *The Red Book: Liber Novus.* W. W. Norton & Co, 2009.

Lesko, Leonard. H. *The Ancient Egyptian Book of Two Ways,* University of California Press, 1972.

Molen, van der, Rami. *Hieroglyphic Dictionary of the Egyptian Coffin Texts,* Hebrew University of Jerusalem, 1977.

Neumann, Erich. *The Origins and History of Consciousness,* Princeton, 1954

Piankoff, Alexandre. *The Wandering of the Soul,* Princeton, 1974.

Quirke, Stephen. *Going out in Daylight-prt m hrw: The Ancient Egyptian Book of the Dead-translation, sources, meanings,* Golden House Publications, 2013.

Robinson, Peter. *As for them who know them, they shall find their paths: speculations on ritual landscapes in the 'Book of The Two Ways',* in *Mysterious Lands,* O'Connor & Quirke eds, UCL Press, 2003.

Schweizer, Andreas. *The Sungod's Journey through the Netherworld: Reading the Ancient Egyptian Amduat,* Cornell University Press, 2010.

Sherbiny, Wael El. *Through Hermopolitan Lenses: Studies on the So-called Book of Two Ways in Ancient Egypt,* Brill, 2017.

Sherbiny, Wael El. *Echoes of a Lost Legacy. The Recent Research on the so-called Book of Two Ways in Ancient Egypt,* Oriental Studies Number 81, 2018.

Various authors – *King James Bible,* Cambridge University Press.

Willems, Harco. *The Coffin of Heqata (JdE 16418) A Case Study of Egyptian Funerary Culture in Early Middle Kingdom,* Peeters Publishers & Department of Oriental Studies, 1996.

Willems, Harco. *A Fragment of an Early Book of Two Ways on the Coffin of Ankh from Dayr al-Barshā (B4B).* The Journal of Egyptian Archaeology, 104(2), 2018.

Zago, Silvia. *Classifying the Duat: Tracing the Conceptualization of the Afterlife between Pyramid Texts and Coffin Texts,* Zeitschrift für Ägyptische Sprache und Altertumskunde, 2018.

READING BD SPELL 30

The mindful heart of Ankh-ef-en-khonsu

REV. COSMÉ HALLELUJAH

Dedication[1]

"Behold ye! I have come before ye, with no sin of mine, no crime of mine, no evil of mine, no witness concerning me, none against whom I have done anything. I live with Truth. I breathe in the Truth. I have fulfilled the expectations of humankind, pleasing the gods because of it. I have satisfied god with what he loves. I have given bread to the hungry, water to the thirsty, clothing to the naked, a ferry to the boatless. I have made divine offerings to the gods, and invocation offerings to the glorified dead."

Spell 125 BD Section C (lines 7–10)[2]

ἐπείνασα γὰρ καὶ ἐδώκατέ μοι φαγεῖν, ἐδίψησα καὶ ἐποτίσατέ με, ξένος ἤμην καὶ συνηγάγετέ με, γυμνὸς καὶ περιεβάλετέ με, ἠσθένησα καὶ ἐπεσκέψασθέ με, ἐν φυλακῇ ἤμην καὶ ἤλθατε πρός με. τότε

---

[1] For Petra.

[2] Papyrus of Nu. Translated by J. Daniel Gunther.

ἀποκριθήσονται αὐτῷ οἱ δίκαιοι λέγοντες Κύριε, πότε σε εἴδαμεν πεινῶντα καὶ ἐθρέψαμεν ἢ διψῶντα καὶ ἐποτίσαμεν; πότε δέ σε εἴδαμεν ξένον καὶ συνηγάγομεν, ἢ γυμνὸν καὶ περιεβάλομεν; πότε δέ σε εἴδομεν ἀσθενοῦντα ἢ ἐν φυλακῇ καὶ ἤλθομεν πρός σε; καὶ ἀποκριθεὶς ὁ βασιλεὺς ἐρεῖ αὐτοῖς Ἀμὴν λέγω ὑμῖν, ἐφ' ὅσον ἐποιήσατε ἑνὶ τούτων τῶν, ἀδελφῶν μου τῶν ἐλαχίστων, ἐμοὶ ἐποιήσατε.

"I hungered and ye gave me to eat, I thirsted and ye gave me drink; I was a stranger and ye took me in, naked and ye clothed me; I was sick and ye visited me; I was in prison and ye came to me. Then the righteous will answer him, saying, 'Lord, when did we see thee hungering and fed [thee]? Or thirsting and furnished [thee] drink? When did we see thee a stranger and take [thee] in? Or naked and clothed [thee]? When did we see thee weak or in prison and came to thee?' And answering, the King shall say to them, truly I say unto thee, insofar as ye did [it] to one of these, the least of my brethren, ye did [it] to me."

Matthew 25: 35-40[3]

---

[3] Translated from the Greek by J. Daniel Gunther.

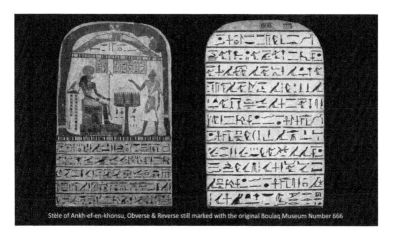

Stèle of Ankh-ef-en-khonsu, Obverse & Reverse still marked with the original Boulaq Museum Number 666

J. Daniel Gunther, "Revealing the Stèle of Ankh-ef-en-khonsu"
lecture slide 23

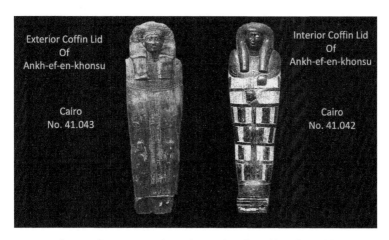

J. Daniel Gunther, "Revealing the Stèle of Ankh-ef-en-khonsu"
lecture slide 27

Introduction

In previous volumes of *Ora et Labora* (vols 2 and 3) I drew attention to the heart hieroglyphs of BD Spell 30. This spell comprises the top 5 lines on the reverse of the Stèle of Ankh-ef-en-khonsu. Using J. Daniel Gunther's translation of the Stèle, I pointed out that the heart hieroglyph ♡⏐ (*ib*) in Spell 30 represented the physical heart, while the related heart hieroglyph in Spell 30, ⟶♡ (*ḥaty*), referred to consciousness. In *Ora* vol 3 I further clarified that *ib* represented the physical heart *as well as* the emotions (clumsily labelling this "metaphysical") *ḥ*. More correctly, to quote directly from Gunther's "Revealing the Stèle of Ankh-ef-en-khonsu" lecture (2022), the *ib* "is not only the physical organ of the heart, but it is the seat of Emotions and Instincts. It is rather like what we call *Nephesh* in the Qabalah."[4] As the physical organ, the *ib* is also the vessel of the *ḥaty*, which is "the *metaphysical* aspect of the heart that is the *Intellect*, the *Consciousness*, the *Mind*. The plural of the word means "thoughts". It is what we call *Ruach* in the Qabalah."[5]

I speculatively read into lines 2 and 3 of Spell 30 on the reverse of the Stèle ("My heart [*ib*] of my mother! (say

---

[4] J. Daniel Gunther, "Revealing the Stèle of Ankh-ef-en-khonsu," unpublished lecture transcript, p. 30.

[5] Ibid.

twice) My consciousness [*ḥaty*] of my existence upon
the earth!"[6]) a reference to the Magical Memory.
Specifically, I was referring to that doctrine as taught by
The Master Therion. I drew upon Gunther's research
into the Papyrus of Herunefer and other sources, where
the origin of ones *ḥaty* was declared to be your
𓎡𓂝𓆓𓏛𓏛𓏛 *kheperu*, meaning "different forms" or
"different ages," to suggest that this could refer to
different incarnations. I then applied this to my reading
of the Stèle of Ankh-ef-en-khonsu, i.e. "My
consciousness [*ḥaty*] of my *incarnations* upon the earth!".
I pointed out that this was a speculation and not the
conventional interpretation or translation, and that my
primary interest was in how we *today* might understand
and actively use the Stèle. Symbols and their meanings
unfold and transform over the historical and
psychological record, just as the "stele of revealing" for
Thelema has taken on new significance and function
beyond its originally intended use as a funerary Stèle for
a Theban priest.

With BD Spell 2 in mind (part of which follows Spell
30 to comprise the bottom 6 lines on the reverse of the
Stèle), my reading of the two spells *together* shifted the
parameters from the traditional egyptological ideas of
enabling the deceased to return to earth, or the "astral
form" of the deceased to return to earth, to the Master

---

[6] J. Daniel Gunther, "Stèle of Revealing – Transliteration &
Translation," unpublished tss.

Therion's doctrine of "the Way of Asar in Amenti," of transmigration of the soul where "the mind of its Former Tabernacle yet cling to it."[7] I quoted Therion on the magical imperative: "There is no more important task than the exploration of one's previous incarnations …One cannot do one's True Will intelligently unless one knows what it is."[8]

As mentioned above, my interest is in how *we* can use the Spells of the Stèle *today*, while connecting us no less to the project of a Theban priest from the late 25th-26th dynasties, "to do all that he Wills upon the earth among the living!"[9] As Gunther points out in his lecture, "Many Egyptologists believe, from internal evidence, that Ankh-ef-en-khonsu probably selected all of the inscriptions for his Stèle, his Sarcophagus and his Coffin himself."[10] My innovation was to assume that this was the case, and to treat the priest's selection of inscriptions as one Spell or Rite (composed by combining and arranging elements of BD Spells) for a

---

[7] Liber Aleph vel CXI, *The Book of Wisdom or Folly*, Cap. 193 "On the Eschatology of the R.C. Adepts," (93 Publishing, 1991), p. 193.

[8] *Magick in Theory and Practice*, 'The Magical memory,' quoted in Cosmè Hallelujah, "Notes towards a preliminary analysis of a peculiar motif in the Stelè of Ankh-af-na-khonsu," *Ora et Labora* vol 2 (2021) p.125.

[9] Gunther, "Stèle of Revealing – Transliteration & Translation."

[10] "Revealing the Stèle of Ankh-ef-en-khonsu," p.35.

specific magical outcome, namely, the Magical Memory, i.e. the continuity of Ankh-ef-en-khonsu's Magical Memory, and in our modern magical context, the acquisition of your own, and his. (In this paper, this idea is psychologized and historicized).

Other than my referencing of Gunther, in past essays I drew upon the studies of Egyptologists Harold Hays, Jan Assmann and Shokufeh Alwazi. Hays and Assmann both recognise practical, religio-magical, ritual (Hays) and covert meanings, plus sacramental and initiatory transformations (Assmann) in the Spells of the dead. Alwazi's research into the Island of Flames ☒ ⌐ᴧᴧᴧᴧ⌐◇⌐◇ (*iw-nsrsr*) from the *Coffin Texts* and *Book of Gates* points to a *heart transformation* suggestive of a magical opus and initiated condition.[11] (Her current research on *The Book of Two Ways*, much of which was conducted while a visiting scholar at the Torino Museo Egizio, extends greatly upon this). I summarized my taxonomy as "*Ib* is the law, *ib* under *ḥaty*."

Lest I overly repeat myself here, I refer you to my past papers. My novel conjectures aside, Gunther's subsequent lecture on the Stèle (2022) has gone into the academic and egyptological detail of the significance of

---

[11] See Shokufeh Alwazi, "The Island of Flames and the Spiritual Heart: a reflective commentary on Rev. Cosmè Hallelujah's 'Notes towards a preliminary analysis of a peculiar motif in the Stelè of Ankh-af-na-khonsu,'" *Ora et Labora* vol 3 (2022).

the "heart spell" for the Stèle, coffin and sarcophagus of Ankh-ef-en-khonsu, and more generally for the religious life of the late 25th and 26th dynasties. While I draw heavily on the scholarship of Gunther again in this paper, his output is reference material is only from a respected Egyptologist and scholar-collaborator I'm in contact with, and does not imply he shares my conjectures and ideation.

What we share is the awareness, as Gunther has noted, that "a funerary artifact from the 26th Egyptian Dynasty became the touchstone of a New Aeon."[12] I hold that we can use the Stèle to touch and experience this Mystery directly.

The mindful heart

As Alwazi (2022) points out, Gunther was one of the first Egyptologists to interpret *ib* and *ḥaty* as outlined above, i.e. that *ib* was the physical heart (incorporating the emotional and instinctual) and *ḥaty* the metaphysical (the consciousness, mind, intellect). That has been his position for over 40 years. For some other scholars however, the meanings attributed to the two heart hieroglyphs are *reversed* (Alwazi cites the reference in the *Encyclopedia Britannica*, as an example). Some insight into this alternate position can be gleaned from Bulgarian Egyptologist Teodor Lekov's paper, "The

---

[12] Gunther, "Revealing the Stèle of Ankh-ef-en-khonsu," p.6.

Formula of the "Giving of the Heart" in Ancient
Egyptian Texts":

"Additional complication for understanding the role of
the heart in this and other similar contexts is the fact
that there are two different words for heart in Egyptian
language. First, and older *ib* roots in Semitic stratum of
the language and has parallels in the languages as
Akkadian and Arabian. Its usage implies nuances of
"internal", "hidden", "invisible", "inner self", etc. On
the contrary, the second word for "heart"– *HAtj* is
descriptive and means literally something like "(that)
which is in front", in sense of "outer", "visible" etc., for
example as a designation for the pulse – a "movement
of the heart-*HAtj*". This word survived in Coptic and
replaced the older *ib*. The two words are conceived as
different terms, first as "mind", intellectual and
emotional center of human spirituality, the second as
technical term for heart, as an anatomic organ,
although in many cases the two words are used as
synonyms, and one can replace the other in variants of
given text. It is noteworthy for our problem that the
principal word used in the formula of the "giving the
heart" is *ib*."[13]

---

[13] Teodor Lekov, "The Formula of the "Giving of the Heart" in
Ancient Egyptian Texts,"
https://www.academia.edu/9011055/The_formula_of_the_Giving_
of_the_Heart_in_Ancient_Egyptian_Texts

A footnote to this passage gives further analysis of this "complication":

> "The basic usage of different terms is postulated in the work of Piankoff 1930; For the meaning of the two words in the case of medical texts – Grapow 1954, 63-72; Westendorf 1999, 108-109; For the connection of heart-*ib* with the stomach (*rA-ib* – which means lit. "entrance (mouth) of the heart") see also Hintze 1955 and R.Bianchi in JARCE.36.(1999), 165 who indicates that *rA-ib* is the frame of the torso, the cavity in which heart is found, ie. *ib* is something more than physical heart, the inner core of body and person. For examples of interchangeability of the two words see also Žabkar 1965, 85. Important consideration for the use of two different words for the same parts of the human body is given by Helck 1955. Because the problem of the "two hearts" in Ancient Egypt is not the main object of the present article, it will be discussed in a separate study."[14]

As Lekov himself acknowledges, "Sometimes our modern interpretations perceive the difficulty to understand ancient texts literally or to re-interpret them in a rather loose manner as a manifestation of a momentous and unconscious decision."[15] Obviously, if you hold either of the alternate positions on the heart

---

[14] Ibid.

[15] Ibid.

hieroglyphs, scholarly conclusions based on the opposite, however accepted and normalized, need to be reassessed. Alwazi, who follows the Gunther translation, goes some way to showing how this problematic reversal of meanings by Lekov *et al.* has at least some origins in a confusion introduced in the works of famed Egyptologist E. A. Wallis Budge.

The Stèle of King Shabaqa from the 25th Dynasty (BM 498), often referred to as the *Shabaqa Stone*, was studied by America's first Egyptologist, J. H. Breasted, in a paper titled "The Philosophy of a Memphite Priest" (1901), an account of creation centered around Ptah. An excerpt reads:

"Seeing with the eyes, hearing with the ears, and

breathing with the nose, they transmit to the Heart (*ib*),

causing all knowledge to come forth.

Indeed, the Tongue repeats the Thought of the Mind.
(ḥaty)

𓎟 𓂓𓏥 𓏏𓏏𓏏 𓂝 𓃀 𓏤𓏤 𓆑𓏏𓏏 𓈖

Therefore, all the gods were born and his (Ptah's)
Ennead

𓊪 𓂝 𓈖 𓏏𓏏𓏥 𓂝 𓃭𓎿 𓃀𓃀 𓂝𓏤

was completed. Lo, every word of god came into being
through the thoughts of the Mind

𓊪𓂝𓃀 𓏤

and command of the Tongue." [16]

Breasted notes, "He [Ptah] is to be sure, called the 𓄣
(ḥaty) 'heart' or 'mind' of the gods without qualification;
and 𓄣 (ḥaty) is clearly explained as the seat and source
of 𓎡𓃀𓃀𓂝 (kaat) 'thought'." [17] Also, "Here it is
clearly stated that everything first exists in the mind as

---

[16] Translated by J. Daniel Gunther, "Excerpt from the Shabaka
Stone" (BM 498) Unpublished tss.

[17] J.H. Breasted, "The Philosophy of a Memphite Priest," *Zeitschrift
fur Agyptische Sprache* No. 39 (1901).

thought, of which the 'heart' is the seat; this thought becomes real and objective by finding expression, and of this the tongue is the Channel. 'Heart' is thus by metonomy, the concrete term for 'mind', while in the same way 'tongue' is the concrete term for 'word' or 'command', the expression of the thought."[18]

Jan Assmann has developed this thesis significantly, clearly showing that the "reversal" is a complication of modern Egyptological interpretation, and not, as one might have assumed, part of a polemical discourse between Memphis and Thebes. Breasted's "heart" as "mind," was *ḥaty*. Another way to put it is that the tongue utters the *thought* of the *heart*. The *ib* is under the *ḥaty* which is uttered by the tongue.

As an aside to this paper, J. Daniel Gunther casually suggested to me that the Stèle of King Shabaqa might be the first reading of "heart and tongue," which also occurs in *Liber Legis* (AL I:6, AL I:32, AL I:53).[19] There is room for further research here at a later date, but note this highly important observation by Breasted:

> "Apparently both Horus and Thoth are conceived as emanations of Atum, for the obscure half line (53) probably states: "He that became heart and he that

---

[18] Ibid.

[19] J. Daniel Gunther, personal communication with the author, 6 May 2021.

became tongue are an emanation of Atum…their *Ka's* being this heart and this tongue", meaning the heart and tongue which he has just identified with Ptah in the preceding line (52). The identification of Thoth with tongue coincides with what we know of him elsewhere as the god of speech and writing; but Horus as heart or mind is, as far as I know, entirely new."[20]

Another way to consider this Horus and Thoth alignment could be: "Tahuti standeth in His splendour at the prow, and Ra-Hoor abideth at the helm."[21]

Breasted summarizes with what he calls a "mechanical equation":

$$\square_{\triangle}^{\S} \text{ »Ptah« } = \begin{cases} \text{»heart«} = \text{»Horus«} \\ \text{»tongue«} = \text{»Thoth«} \end{cases}$$

For the purposes of this paper, note that "heart" attributed to Horus is *ḥaty*. (For a description of the hieroglyphs, see below and my paper in *Ora et Labora* vol 2).

It may appear odd to our modern minds that the mind could be identified with the heart. As Andreas Schweizer has noted, "The ancient Egyptians found amazing

---

[20] J.H. Breasted, "The Philosophy of a Memphite Priest."

[21] Liber Resh vel Helios.

truths not so much in a conscious and psychological manner, as we do, but rather intuitively."[22] We see this from the dawn of the Egyptian consciousness and its earliest attempts to incorporate numinous power into symbols. By the time of the New Kingdom, this had developed into a deep spiritual maturity and richness. The Egyptian mind was playful and creative. The Egyptians were the original multimedia producers, combining text and images to create impactful experiences, as well as highly skilled graphic designers, utilizing visual hierarchy, graphic transposition, color theory, contrast, and other design principles. Yet, as we see in their maps of the Netherworld and the medical papyri, they were also fantastically or even scientifically detailed and precise. This blending of art and science, conscious and imaginal, terrestrial and celestial, mortal and divine, time and space, is a hallmark of the Egyptian record; its myth, history, and mythic history.

One way the modern mind can approach the mindful heart of the Egyptians is to think of the heartbeat (and we know from the medical papyri that the Ancient Egyptians were aware of the heartbeat), as embodying living itself. We cannot live without it. And one's experience of life – one's mentations, determinations and decisions – is conceived in thought (*ḥaty*). These thoughts, which include the whole gamut of our

---

[22] Andreas Schweizer, *The Sungod's Journey through the Netherworld: Reading the Ancient Egyptian Amduat* (Cornell UP, 2010), p. 3.

negative ones and their concomitant actions – as moralized in the weighing of the heart scene – can be looked on as a child (Horus). That child has to grow up and learn moral uprightness through life experience, and just as the sun renews and regenerates day by day in the nightly depths of the Netherworld, "the same might happen to everyone exhausted from the strains of daily life, and to every deceased."[23] If *ib* is the natural condition of organic life, it is intuited and spiritualized (psychologized) through discovering and following one's true *ḥaty*.

From a psychological perspective, "the destiny of the individual, like that of nations and cultures, is always embedded in the hidden stream of slow but continuous transformations within the basic archetypal constellations,"[24] what Carl Jung's disciple Marie-Louise von Franz described as the flow "beneath the surface of what can be grasped as history."[25] Ancient Egyptian life and history, together with its spiritual developments, are no different, with marked responses in the individual and collective to the major political and social reorganizations of the times. We may note for example, that toward the end of the third millennium when the

---

[23] Ibid.,p.2.

[24] Ibid., p. 4.

[25] Marie-Louise von Franz, *Archetypal Dimensions of the Psyche* (Shambhala, 1999), pp. 263-264.

Old Kingdom abruptly ended and turmoil ensued, a new spiritual force in Ancient Egyptian life developed. It was reflected in a new genre of texts, the Instructions or Wisdom literature, whose doctrines "radiate a newly strengthened consciousness of the individual."[26] This newly strengthened *consciousness* (i.e. *ḥaty*) - something unheard of in the Old Kingdom – was embedded into the later consciousness and *zeitgeist* of Ankh-ef-en-khonsu's era. By extension, this is the child Horus growing up.

Horus consciousness

In Joshua J. Bodine's modern study of the Shabaqa Stone (2009), he noted the various doubts about the provenance of the Stone's inscriptions; were they copies of much older source texts (concerning which there are several scholarly opinions), or "simply an attempt at archaizing a new composition that served Shabaka's interest in reuniting Egypt and establishing himself as king?...About all that can be said with confidence is that the composition as a whole (i.e. its extant form) belongs to the 25th Dynasty."[27]

It would be enough to say that whether an archaism or authentic reproduction, the Shabaqa Stone highlights an

---

[26] Schweizer, *The Sungod's Journey through the Netherworld*, p. 5.

[27] Joshua J. Bodine, "The Shabaka Stone: An Introduction." Studia Antiqua 7, no. 1 (2009), pp. 10 -11.
https://scholarsarchive.byu.edu/studiaantiqua/vol7/iss1/3

ancient concept of the metaphysical Egyptian heart as *ḥaty* (Horus), as we saw above, alive in the same dynasty of Ankh-ef-en-khonsu. However, it cannot be left there. I quote Bodine at length:

> "The Memphite Theology was clearly setting forth the idea of creation as a combination of both immaterial and material principles, with Ptah serving as the connection between the two. Creation, according to the Shabaka Stone, was both a spiritual or intellectual creation as well as a physical one. It was through the divine heart (thought) [*ie. ḥaty: Horus*] and tongue (speech/word) [*i.e. Thoth*] of Ptah as the great causer of something to take shape in the form of the physical agent of creation, Atum, through which everything came forth. Importantly, creation was first and foremost an intellectual activity and only then a physical one. The intellectual principles of creative thought and commanding speech were realized in Ptah and could be said to be embodied in him…Thus, in keeping with the notion that the things of the universe are for the Egyptians beings with distinct wills and personalities, it is through both spiritual and physical principles and actions—personified in and derived from Ptah—that the world becomes a reality."[28]

Bodine continues:

---

[28]Ibid., pp. 18-19.

"It did not take scholars long to recognize that in the ideas of the Memphite Theology there was an approach similar to the Greek notion of *Logos*. The so-called "Logos" doctrine is that in which the world is formed through a god's creative thought and speech—Logos meaning, literally, "Word." The parallels with the creation account in the book of Genesis in the Hebrew Bible, or with the opening chapter of the Gospel of John in the Christian New Testament, are obvious, as with other ancient texts and philosophies."[29]

With the caveat that my papers for *Ora et Labora* have been conjectures of my heart and tongue, and given Spell 30 on the Stèle of Ankh-ef-en-khonsu is followed by BD Spell 2, which in the Theban Recension was titled "A Spell for going out in the day and living after dying," the above paragraph is highly suggestive. From our modern perspective, Ankh-ef-en-khonsu incarnates the Logos consciousness, *and he sought for that consciousness (Horus) to continue on earth among the living.*

As mentioned, the Shabaqa Stone is dated to the 25th Dynasty. It may be worth remembering the Stèle of Ankh-ef-en-khonsu dates to approximately 680-670 BCE, which falls between the late 25th Dynasty and the early 26th Dynasty. In 716 BCE, it was Shabaqa himself, a Kushite/Nubian king, who (re)conquered the Nile

---

[29] Ibid., p. 19.

Delta area and who inaugurated the rule of the 25th Dynasty of Ethiopian-born, black African kings.

Osiris is a black god

A word must be said about kingship in Ancient Egypt. The king served as a bridge between the divine and the mortal realm. Bodine (citing Barry Kemp) points out that Ancient Egyptian civilization was maintained "by an intellectual system that linked society at large to the king, the living human representative of a hereditary monarchy" and also to "hidden forces (divinities)" whose "identities and forms," though "revealed by the scholarly work of priests, . . . were engaged through the person of the king."[30]

In the Egyptian cosmos, these "hidden forces" were viewed as distinct individuals or personalities. This is part of a linguistic dualism that I'll discuss as we proceed, but note for now this distinction between what we might call the spiritual ("hidden forces" or "divinities" linked to "scholarly," "intellectual" priestly work, i.e. of priestly *consciousness*) conceived as individuals or personalities, and the physical (engaged through and embodied in the King, reflective and representative of society at large). Given the place of the heart in the Egyptian world and Netherworld, we can conceive of the spiritual as akin to *ḥaty* (and the "scholarly," the "mind," the magical work of the priests,

---

[30] Ibid., p. 13.

their consciousness), engaged through the vessel of the physical, social organ and regulatory system, akin to the *ib*, (embodied as the earthly king). One other reading of BD Spells 30 and 2 on the Stèle might then be that Ankh-ef-en-khonsu wants the Horus Logos consciousness, conceived in the Egyptian mind as an individual or personality, to remain in society after his passing, that is, so "the Osiris, Ankh-f-n-Khonsu has gone forth by day to do all that he Wills upon the earth among the living!".[31]

In the last years of Ankh-ef-en-khonsu, Assyrian aggression towards Egypt's Kushite dynasty was a constant threat. This was part of the turmoil in what Egyptologists refer to as the Third Intermediate Period (dynasties 21–25; 1069–664 BCE). As a result of this aggression, one of Shabaqa's descendants, King Taharqo, was forced to retreat from the Kushite seat of power, Memphis, to Thebes, dying either there or in Kush in 664 BCE. It would be left to Taharqo's successor, Tanwetamani, to reclaim Memphis.

The Kushites as a people, for so long dominated by Egypt, had been entrenched in Egyptian culture and customs since Early Dynastic times (ca. 3000–2686 BCE). Of the 25th dynasty Kushite Kings, Bodine notes:

---

[31] Gunther, "Stèle of Revealing – Transliteration & Translation." (Reverse, BD Spell 2)

"Scholars have come to recognize the 25th Dynasty as
a period of renewal, where the Kushite kings
intentionally sought to establish an "ideological link
with the great eras of Egypt's past . . . leading to a
revivial of artistic, literary, and religious trends drawing
inspiration from earlier ages." The Kushite kings went
to great lengths to restore the glory of Egypt in their
own reigns with monumental construction projects
reminiscent of earlier times. Moreover, at least some of
the Kushite kings seemed to possess a genuine
reverence and sincere respect for Egyptian customs and
traditions—especially religious ones—and sought to
support its ancient practices. They did not see
themselves as foreign invaders and conquerors, but as
Egyptians in culture and religion, who would restore
the greatness that was Egypt. For almost a hundred
years, before being conquered by an invading Assyria,
the black African kings from Kush, in their attempts to
renew the splendor and glory of Egypt's former days,
thus ruled in the likeness of the kings of old, and can
be remembered as great kings of their own time."[32]

It is therefore not improbable that religious ideas
between Memphis and Thebes cross fertilized as a result
of unification under the Kushites, and this could pertain
to the ḥaty/mind/Horus concept of the heart, expressed
in the Stèle of Ankh-ef-en-khonsu and the Stone of

---

[32] Ibid., pp. 3-4.

Shabaqa, with particular contextual nuances befitting priest or king respectively. With reference to Bodine above, we can read the Stèle of Ankh-ef-en-khonsu as pertaining to "hidden forces," the "scholarly," "intellectual" and "spiritual" work of the priest.

As noted by Morkot (2014), the first focus of the Kushite religion was the cult of Amun. It was Shabaqa's earlier relative King Piye who originally extended Kushite power beyond Thebes into Lower Egypt, believing it was Amun, the god of Thebes, who had given him "rule over Egypt and the power to make and unmake kings and chiefs."[33] The patronage of the Kushite pharaohs led to a religious and artistic renaissance in 25th Dynasty Thebes, in particular during the reign of Taharqo, who was mentioned earlier. The priestly family tree of Ankh-ef-en-khonsu would have been involved in this religious rebirth. Given the import of Spell 30 for the Ankh-ef-en-khonsu family, we may conjecture this renaissance might have included the ontological inferences of the *ḥaty* (Horus) logos. Commenting on the burial site of the Besenmut family (including Ankh-ef-en-khonsu, Besenmut's son), Aston (2003) points out "it is clear that here were buried some of the most influential men of their day, in

---

[33] Robert Morkot, "Thebes under Kushite rule", in *Tombs of the South Asasif Necropolis,* ed. Elena Pischikova, Cairo AUC, 2014, Chapter 1, p. 10.
https://www.academia.edu/39245403/Thebes_under_Kushite_rule

particular, members of the Besenmut, Ankhpakhrod, Montuemhat families...a veritable 'who's who' of the upper echelons of native Egyptian society."[34] The priestly families within these social ranks would have been at the forefront of any religious revival and innovation.

Morkot notes that the Shabaqa Stone, while not of Theban origin, "purports to preserve a text from an ancient moldering document found in an archive, showing that this research into religious texts was a widespread feature of the period."[35] The 25th Dynasty Thebes was also a time when the great religious books of the New Kingdom (the *Book of the Dead*, the *Litany of Re*, and the *Books of the Underworld*) once again covered the walls of tombs. The research around these books led to the "Late Period" recension of the *Book of the Dead*. Together with funerary equipment changing, "with the emphasis placed on the coffins, papyri, and smaller items, rather than the 'daily-life' objects of the New Kingdom,"[36] the spellcraft of the family line of

---

[34] D.A. Aston, "The Theban West Bank from the Twenty-fifth Dynasty to Ptolemaic Period," in *The Theban Necropolis*, eds. Nigel Strudwick and John H. Taylor, British Museum Press, 2003, p. 147. https://www.academia.edu/39997087/The_Theban_West_Bank_fro m_the_Twenty_fifth_Dynasty_to_the_Ptolemaic_Period

[35] Robert Merkot, "Thebes under Kushite rule," p. 11.

[36] Ibid.

Ankh-ef-en-khonsu can be viewed within this wider religious and cultural context. For example, as Gunther noted, "during the late 25th and throughout the 26th Dynasty, the *Book of the Dead* Heart Spell 30 and a variant, Heart Spell 30B, were *combined* for the first time, and began to occur regularly on Coffins... the *earliest* example we know of that configuration is found on the Coffin of Ankh-ef-en-khonsu himself. It is also found on the external Sarcophagus that housed that Coffin. Think about this for just a moment: a spell from the Egyptian Book of the Dead, always found on heart scarabs and placed over the heart of a mummy, remarkably is found inscribed on the funerary Stèle of Ankh-ef-en-khonsu, and is also found, for the first time in recorded history, on a coffin and a sarcophagus – *his coffin and sarcophagus.*"[37]

Religio Duplex

Given the heart hieroglyph complications and at times their synonymous or interchangeable use, how can we explain why one scholar's *ib* is another's *ḥaty?*

Jan Assmann, who is both an Egyptologist and a penetrating cultural scientist, provides a way forward. Assmann adopted the term "Religio Duplex" ("dual religion"), originally coined by Theodor Lau in his 1719 intellectual eruption, *Meditationes, Theses, Dubia philosophico-theologica*. Lau's sociological theory of

---

[37] Gunther, "Revealing the Stèle of Ankh-ef-en-khonsu," p. 9.

religion postulated the Religio Duplex or dual religion, a *religio rationis* ("rational [or natural] religion") and a *religio revelationis* ("revealed religion"). Importantly, Lau's *duplex* related to "...two different forms of religion, rather than one religion that has two different faces or two religions coexisting within one and the same culture."[38]

From a systems thinking perspective, as identified by the brilliant 1980s scholar of gnosticism Ioan Couliano, a system existing in its own logical dimension will over time explore all of its logical possibilities. In our case, this includes the possibilities of Assmann's "rather than" alternatives above. That is exactly what happened to the Religio Duplex idea over the 17th and 18th centuries (and beyond), with the religion of Ancient Egypt considered the system's underlying source and exemplar.

Jacob Friedrich Reimann's *Idea Systematis Antiquitatis Literariae Specialioris sive Aegyptiacae Adumbrati* (1718) presented an alternate view of the *duplex* system of ideas: "Suffice to say that the philosophy of the Egyptians as a whole was twofold (*duplex*): exoteric and esoteric."[39] For Reimann, this duality does not refer to two different forms of philosophy (religion) as it did for Lau, but to *one religion in two forms*: one public and

---

[38] Quoted in Jan Assmann, *Religio Duplex: How the Enlightenment Reinvented Egyptian Religion* (Polity Press, 2014), p. 6.

[39] Ibid.

visible, the other secret and accessible only to initiates. This idea of inner and outer forms of religion, with a valid connection to elements of ancient thought, then takes on a variety of ideological interpretations, social consequences and political institutionalizations in the history of ideas, the history of religion, the history of Egyptology, and the history of western esotericism. (For example, my former student Frater Shiva did some preliminary studies of the duplex system evident in c. 1912-1919 initiatory Thelema, and Assmann devoted a chapter of his study to the duplex inherent in Freemasonry – both currents having their associations with Ancient Egypt).

While there are elements of Egyptian religion which indicate a double sidedness or complementary dualism, *this was unknown in the 17th and 18th centuries* when the concept of the Religio Duplex was being developed. Assmann's point is that "the idea of dual religion rests on a misunderstanding as far as its derivation from Egyptian religious history is concerned...".[40] The title of his study spells this out: *Religio Duplex: How the Enlightenment Reinvented Egyptian Religion.*

This misunderstanding and reinvention was in part due to the complex and often contradictory intellectual tensions of the Enlightenment. While I risk oversimplifying Assmann's thesis here and encourage

---

[40] Ibid., p. 7.

you to study his book, for our purposes, in Enlightened thinking the *exoteric* religion for the public was represented by the philosophy of revelation (spiritual/irrational/faith), while the *esoteric* religion for the initiated was represented by the philosophy of nature (material/rational/reason-science). The "esoteric" identified in ancient religion – in particular Ancient Egypt – was aligned and identified by Enlightened thinkers with themselves, the new *modern* elite – the persons and discourses behind the proliferation of Secret Societies in the Enlightenment. While the philosophy of revelation was attributed to scripture, that of nature was attributed to the ancient theologians and "the mysteries". For many, the source was Ancient Egypt, as evidenced by its quite visible sacred science (geometry/architecture) and writing (hieroglyphs, "sacred carvings"). Enlightened interpretation, building on (if reframing) the intellectual tradition that had emerged around Ancient Egypt and made prominent in the Renaissance, both copied and emulated it in Secret Society myth, ritual and philosophy. *The Enlightened orientation was skewed towards reading ḥaty as the natural, material or physical heart.*

Egyptology as an emerging Enlightened science was an elite and esoteric discourse. It was strictly *modern*, that is, a *re-acquirement* and renewal of the old through a modern lens. And that lens was rationalist and materialist. Many of these foundational ideas and beliefs were embedded in the *Egyptological hermeneutic*, at the expense of spiritual (magical) and soon to emerge, psychological, interpretation. In terms of Egyptology's historical development, we may add to this hermeneutic some of the Enlightenment's other characteristics, notably racial and colonial bias. There have of course been standouts and outliers who have bucked this trend, such as Gunther and Harold Hays, and more controversially (but I love their *true of voice*), the keeper of the Abydos Temple of Seti I and draughtswoman for the Department of Egyptian Antiquities, the enigmatically wonderful Omm Sety (Dorothy Louise Eady) and the French Esotericist, Alchemist and Egyptologist, René Adolphe Schwaller de Lubicz. Nor can we forget the neglected contribution of medieval Arabic Egyptologists, whose work predates that of Enlightened Europe.[41]

As briefly stated above, in the heart hieroglyphs we directly confront the hermeneutic tension between metaphysical and physical, between a psychological and a material interpretation. I discussed this point with Daniel Gunther, who for over 40 years has held the *ib* (anatomical, emotional, instinctual) and *ḥaty* (metaphysical) position. Some of Gunther's points are worth summarizing here. (It may help if you first review my quotations of Teodor Lekov above).

---

[41] See Okasha El–Daly, *Egyptology: the Missing Millennium, Ancient Egypt in Medieval Arabic Writings* (Routledge, 2016).

For Gunther, it doesn't come as any major surprise that there are (a few) instances of *ḥaty* and *ib* used interchangeably in the medical papyri. Egyptian doctors would speak of *ḥaty* when referencing the pulse or heartbeat since one meaning of the word is "up front" or "the front." A heartbeat could be said to be pretty "up front" (Ancient Egyptians counted and measured the heartbeat). However, the heartbeat was also considered somewhat mystical. The terms used to describe it included hearing the heart "speak" or the "movement of the heart."

Secondly, the references to the emotions using *ib* are normally quite clear and don't require any interpretation. For example, the phrase "heart's desire" is used by the Egyptians just like our own (*ib*). A less clear example is "My heart sat down..." (*ib*), which the Egyptologist Raymond O. Faulkner suggested may have been an emotional reference, possibly referring to mental depression."[42]

One aspect Gunther points out is that a single person is never referred to as having 𓂺𓏤 *ibu* – the plural of 𓂺𓏤 , *ib*. But 𓄣𓏤𓏥 , *ḥaty* occurs in the plural for an individual –

---

[42] R. O. Faulkner, *The Ancient Egyptian Coffin Texts*, Vol. 1, p. 107, note 1, commenting on Coffin Text 112, which is titled, 𓏤 𓈖 𓄑 𓃀 𓂧 𓏏 𓅯 𓀀 𓏏 𓀢 𓂝 , "A Spell for not letting a man's heart sit down against him." (Adriaan De Buck, *The Egyptian Coffin Texts*, II, 126, S1C.)

𓄿𓎟 *ḥatyu*, meaning "thoughts." In the literature, one could go to the "House of Hearts" (*ibu*) and retrieve the *one* that belonged to them. He also notes that *ḥaty* made it into Coptic as ϩⲏⲧ (hēt), "heart, mind", while *ib* fell out of the language.

Gunther cites a few Spells to demonstrate the distinction between *ib* and *ḥaty* outside of our discussion on the Spells of the Stèle of Ankh-ef-en-khonsu:

"No evils pertain to thee at all,
thine own real heart (*ib*) being with thee, with thy former mind (*ḥaty*)."

(18th dynasty Tomb of Paḥeri. "A Prayer for having the heart and mind.")

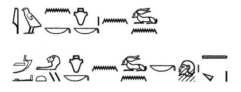

"for thee there is thy heart (*ib*) of existence and
thy consciousness (*ḥaty*) of thine existence upon the
earth."

(18th dynasty tomb of Rekhmira. A Spell for "bringing
the heart")

"A Spell for giving the heart (*ib*) of <*Name*> to him in
the God's Domain. He shall say, 'My heart (*ib*) is mine
in the House of Hearts (*ibu*). My *ḥaty* is mine in the
House of *ḥatyu*. My heart (*ib*) is mine. It is at peace
(ḥat-pah) with me...
   I have control of my heart (*ib*). I have control of my
ḥaty."

(18th Dynasty Papyrus of Nebseny, BD 26, "A Spell for
Giving the heart")

The Egyptians wanted the vessel of their consciousness
in its totality. The *ib* was the physical vessel, and also
designated the "emotional" life – the gut feelings.

Egyptians believed that if they did not possess the physical heart they would lose their consciousness.[43]

Cosmic Grammatology

Earlier I mentioned the heart (*ḥaty*) and tongue motif, and its relationship to Memphite theology, Ptah, Horus, Thoth, the Logos, etc. There is also the intriguing association to *Liber Legis,* although exploring that line of enquiry is not the focus of this paper. I noted that it was Jan Assmann who had explored the "heart and tongue" in some depth. The motif, and studies such as Assmann's, go a long way by default to asserting the position on *ib* and *ḥaty* proposed by Gunther and others.

There are elements of Assmann's study that are of additional interest here. Assmann covers *intransitive* and *transitive* models of the origin of the world (i.e. a spontaneous growth from primordial chaos or matter, and the object of a constructive activity of a creator, respectively), noting that in Egypt "the two models combine and interact in a rather complex manner."[44] To give a basic example (before it gets "rather complex"), in

---

[43] This part of the Religio Duplex section paraphrases J. Daniel Gunther from a series of personal communication over June and July 2022.

[44] Jan Assman, "Creation through hieroglyphs: the cosmic grammatology of Ancient Egypt", *The poetics of grammar and the metaphysics of sound and sign* (Jerusalem studies in religion and culture 6), ed. S. La Porta and D. Shulman (Leiden, 2007)

the cosmogony of Heliopolis, Atum arises from the primordial waters (intransitive) and then creates Shu and Tefnut (transitive).

Atum's place in the Heliopolitan cosmogony as a self-generated primordial deity had an enormous influence on the cosmo-theological speculations of Ancient Egypt for millennia, even reaching through to Hermetic and Neoplatonic times. He was referred to by the Egyptians as 𓆣𓏭𓂝, *kheper-djes.f* ("the self-generated one") and appears in the later currents as the *autogenes* or *monogenes*. His motherless procreation of Shu and Tefnut (by, depending upon what you read, ejaculation, spitting or coughing), was a quality also ascribed to the *scarab-beetle*. I quoted Gunther earlier; "Think about this for just a moment: a spell [BD Spell 30] from the Egyptian Book of the Dead, always found on heart scarabs and placed over the heart of a mummy, remarkably is found inscribed on the funerary Stèle of Ankh-ef-en-khonsu, and is also found, for the first time in recorded history, on a coffin and a sarcophagus – *his coffin and sarcophagus*."[45] And recalling that one meaning of *ḥaty* – whose place in Spell 30 and on the Stèle has been a focus of this study – is "up front" or "the front", here we have Atum, like the self-generated scarab, up

---

https://archiv.ub.uni-heidelberg.de/propylaeumdok/3615/1/ Assmann_Creation_through_hieroglyphs_2007.pdf

[45] Gunther, "Revealing the Stèle of Ankh-ef-en-khonsu," p. 9.

front as it were, at the front of the Gods. As a modern speculation, mind or (self) consciousness (*ḥaty*) arises from/out of *a primordial or universal field of consciousness.*

Note that Gunther refers to the "heart scarab," which is not to be confused with the "heart amulet" which was made in the shape of the heart, *ib.* Most of the heart scarab depictions are to the vignettes of BD Spell 30/30B, whose magical purpose consists mainly in the reanimation of the heart and the restoration of the heart to the deceased. "If the heart scarab seems to be closely connected to the reanimation of the vital powers of the mummy, the heart amulet appears to be a symbol of the justification of the deceased."[46]

"Although chapter 30B of the *Book of the Dead* could provide protection against negative testimony in the weighing of the heart, the magical role of this object as a potential substitute for the heart and, above all, as a symbol of rebirth seems much more important. Ultimately, [we]...should focus on its most evident feature, the god Khepri, the scarab itself, 'The one who transforms' or 'The one who manifests'. This provides the heart scarab with its symbolism of self-engendered

---

[46] Rogèrio Sousa, "Heart of wisdom: studies on the heart amulet in Ancient Egypt," (Archaeo Press: Oxford, 2011) p. 39

https://www.academia.edu/540862/
Heart_of_Wisdom_studies_on_the_heart_amulet_in_ancient_Egypt_Archaeopress_Oxford_2011

life and resurrection. As an image of the sun god, the scarab embodied the transformation or reanimation of the heart and its identification with the god Khepri. Thus, the main function of the heart scarab was to provide identification between the cardiac organ and the rising sun in order to assure the awakening of the deceased to a new life...Thus, the heart scarab can be seen as a symbol of the rebirth of the deceased in a new solar manifestation. The *kheperu* associated with the heart *ḥaty* should also be understood as the individual 'manifestations' of self-awareness during his lifetime, which, once in the afterlife, will change (*kheper*) to a new form."[47] As I suggested earlier, "mind or (self) consciousness (*ḥaty*) arises from/out of/is part of a primordial or universal field of consciousness."

"Importantly, "The restoration of the heart" was a highly symbolic act in that it summarizes the entire process of mummification. This gesture, performed by female deities, was the symbol of the connective power of love. It was the love of Isis that filled the heart of Osiris with life. Thus, the large heart scarab can be seen as a symbol of the connective power of the love of Isis, which was able to reintroduce life to the dismembered, aspective body of Osiris. As a result of the restoration of the heart, a new bodily connectivity could be set in motion...Unlike the heart amulet, the heart scarab

---

[47] Ibid., p. 43.

retained all of its ritual significance associated with the mummification rituals and also with solar rebirth until the Greco-Roman Period."[48]

This lengthy description of the heart scarab was necessary in order to consider the significance of its magical function associated with Spell 30/30B now being on the Stèle of Ankh-ef-en-khonsu (remembering, that "throughout the 26th Dynasty, the *Book of the Dead* Heart Spell 30 and a variant, Heart Spell 30B, were *combined* for the first time" and that "Most Egyptologists believe, from internal evidence, that Ankh-ef-en-khonsu probably selected all of the inscriptions for his Stèle, his Sarcophagus and his Coffin himself").[49]

Given that magical function (reanimation of the heart, rebirth, transformation and manifestation, the power of love [of Isis]), what does this mean for the Spell now on the Stèle in conjunction with BD Spell 2? We know that funerary Stèle enabled those in the realm of the living to commemorate the deceased, simultaneously providing offerings that satisfied their requirements in the afterlife. The Spells were now not just part of the burial rite but an ongoing living tradition.

---

[48] Ibid., p. 50.

[49] Gunther, "Revealing the Stèle of Ankh-ef-en-khonsu," p. 9.

I pointed out earlier, that in the time of Ankh-ef-en-khonsu there was now an "emphasis placed on the coffins, papyri, and smaller items, rather than the 'daily-life' objects of the New Kingdom."[50] And in the spellcraft, the offerings being read out were not just for continued access to goods, but continued access to consciousness. This presents a number of possibilities in terms of intended magical outcomes. We have no clear evidence of what it means exactly, and I have made some speculations and conjectures to that end already in this and past papers. Perhaps one very human outcome still practiced today is that the great man Ankh-ef-en-khonsu lived in the hearts (and minds) [ḥaty] of his worshippers, his consciousness lived in and through them, by the prayers of the tongue, and through this transformation, "the Osiris, Ankh-f-n-Khonsu has gone forth by day to do all that he Wills upon the earth among the living!".[51] Ankh-ef-en-khonsu was not just a deceased loved one, but an important, religious figure. As Gunther points out, "It is now generally believed that a cult of Ankh-ef-en-khonsu developed in Thebes after his death. It seems that his influence was such that he was revered, not only in life, but after death, as a god-like man."[52]

---

[50] Merkot, "Thebes under Kushite rule."

[51] Gunther, "Stèle of Revealing – Transliteration & Translation." (Reverse, BD Spell 2)

It begs the question, how would this magic work? We cannot say for sure, but we know the Egyptians took their magic seriously. It was very real for them. In my cosmic hallelujology, I suspect this type of magic worked exactly the same way it still works today, some 2700 years later. It is not all that different to the modern techniques rarely called magic anymore, advocated by agents of personal transformation, such as Maxwell Maltz, David Hawkins, Wayne Dyer, Joe Dispenza, Lynne McTaggart, and probably countless others, all teaching variations of one essential theme.

In the context of this study, through intention (will/Spells) and elevated emotion (love/Offerings) - consider Crowley's Abramelin maxim, "inflame thyself in praying" — change manifests. Earlier I postulated a primordial field of consciousness. The magical secret is that by "intention" we do not refer to will power or determination in the ordinary sense, and by "change" we do not refer to the cause and effect of Newtonian dualism. Rather we refer more to an energetic condition, a universal, vibratory field (of intention), accessed – that is, the awareness of connection and alignment with it – through the devotional creativity, love, surrender, and spirit of receptivity and gratitude, of the offering formula (Spells).

---

[52] Gunther, "Revealing the Stèle of Ankh-ef-en-khonsu," p. 12.

We may now know this field today by many other
names, perhaps the Unconscious, or Tao, or
Consciousness, or Zero-Point Field, or David Bohm's
"wholeness and implicate order," or Joe Dispenza's "the
quantum," but all include some notion of omnipresent
non-duality beyond ego-consciousness, form and
boundaries, both physical and non-physical. By
aligning with the omnipresent power of intention (e.g.
through the prayers of intention and emotion) the
"changes" one seeks come *automatically* to you, beyond
the cause and effect reasoning of lineality. One would
incarnate the consciousness of Osiris Ankh-ef-en-
khonsu. The Spells allow the worshippers to fully
identify with this field, which we could call the field of
intention, ensuring their intention, one with Osiris
Ankh-ef-en-khonsu, manifests. *That Osiris Ankh-ef-en-
khonsu comes to them.*

To the initiated Egyptian mind, this field may have
presented itself in a number of motifs, all indicative of
the implicit order of *Maat*. Psychologized, it is the
netherworld. As Erik Hornung commented, "The
netherworld into which we descend underlies our own
world. Creative energies of dreadful intensity are active
there, and only death, to which all must surrender,
makes us truly alive by offering us regeneration from the
depths."[53] In this regard, I'm particularly interested in
Shokufeh Alwazi's coverage of the "Field of Offerings"

---

[53] Erik Hornung, Foreword to Andreas Schweizer's *Amduat.*

in *The Book of Two Ways* as representing the omnipresent field of intention, where, in Egyptological terms, the deceased can work all day.[54]

This is the field of pure will.

In the New Aeon, we need only look at the expansive infinitude, abundance, connectedness – as well as the many promises – in the first Chapter of *Liber Legis*, to appreciate this energetic condition of the body of Nuit. "This is so: I swear it by the vault of my body; by my sacred heart and tongue; by all I can give, by all I desire of ye all." AL 1:32 "Thou knowest! And the sign shall be my ecstasy, the consciousness of the continuity of existence, the omnipresence of my body." AL 1:26

For those who have stepped into the New Aeon, consider the effortless practice of "Living in the Sunlight," whose effect as described by Aleister Crowley's student Charles Stansfeld Jones, consisted in "aligning himself with the will of the universe or God, and, secondly, in, to a certain extent, showing forth the powers of God by means of that will."[55] "When we can say "I and my Father are One" - that my Father is in

---

[54] I am grateful to Alwazi for sharing her working notes on *The Book of Two Ways.*

[55] Frater Achad (Charles Stansfeld Jones), "Living in the Sunlight," *The Fenris Wolf* no 7 (Edda: Stockholm, 2014), p. 323. See also Steve King, *Living in the Sunlight: making a forgotten meditation an atomic habit* (In Perpetuity Press, 2022).

Heaven and that Heaven is in me – then we shall realize what Christ meant when he talked about the Son of God…".[56] What if your Father was Osiris Ankh-ef-en-khonsu?

The consciousness of Ankh-ef-en-khonsu represents the *triumph over death*, by conjecture, the immortality of connection to the field of omnipresent intention or pure will. In the aeonic ḥatyological magic of Ankh-ef-en-khonsu, as funny as this might sound, we find in his funerary Spells the ancient precursors to some of the key approaches of the modern day positive thinking and wellness industries!

I will return to Achad's theme above a little later. For now I wanted to draw our attention back to the Spells. Our entire analysis rests on the grammatology of hieroglyphs. So what of the hieroglyph for *ḥaty*?

ḥꜣty

This proved difficult to research. However I discussed the matter with Daniel Gunther. The forepart of the lion is used for the root of the word (ḥꜣt), used in "forehead", "forepart" (of an animal), "vanguard" (of an army), "beginning", "foremost, chief". The back half of the lion is used for the root (pḥ), from which "end",

---

[56] Achad, "Living in the Sunlight," p. 329.

𓄖𓏭𓏱 (phwy) "hind-parts, hindquarters", stern of a ship", as well as 𓄖𓏏𓏭 (phty) "strength", "power" (of a king or god). Together they signify the "beginning" 𓄨𓏤 (ḥ3t) and "ending" 𓄖𓏱 (pḥt). We perhaps see this meaning in the ancient double lion god Aker 𓄿𓏭𓃬 (3kr), sitting in opposite directions, back to back, supporting the sun disc, signifying the horizons, East and West.

There are occasions (e.g. the Pyramid of Pepy I) where wall inscriptions of recumbent lions have their middle or backend removed. Egyptologists believe that this was done to prevent the spirit of the lion from materializing during the Rituals – a good indication of just how seriously the Egyptians took their magic. The basic hieroglyphs of the words ḥ3t and pḥt are formed by the mutilation of the glyph. Gunther suggested use of the forepart of a lion to represent the heart of mind, and consciousness lies within such ancient representations. Certainly in predynastic times lions roamed throughout Egypt, and their presence would have been etched in the collective memory.[57] What we are seeing though, whether the possibility of magical materialization or an archetypal fear, is a ḥaty located in mind.

---

[57] The last two paragraphs are drawn from from a series of personal communications with Daniel Gunther over a period from May to July 2022.

Aeonic ḥatyology – the Ptah-Hotep formula

Beyond the speculations of Enlightened dualism that we find in the Religio Duplex, the above section suggests that we could treat the Stèle of Ankh-ef-en-khonsu as a magical device for either the actual earthly return or perhaps reincarnation of the deceased, or simply the continuity or promulgation of the priest's consciousness in the world, in the hearts and minds of the devoted. Maybe both. We don't really know, however the current underlying these outcomes is a religious speculation that derives from Egypt's curious blend of *intransitive* and *transitive* world views. This allows for both primordial/chaotic beginnings and self directed/intentional creativity.

Looked at through a psychological lens, this allows for an archetypal consciousness (the 'collective unconscious' if you will) which presents itself in humankind's apprehension of various universalisms expressing primordial wholeness, or from the human perspective, the creative becoming or incarnation of Self awareness or Self-consciousness. The One and the Many.[58] However we might interpret the Stèle of Ankh-ef-en-khonsu today, we note a clear intention for that 'one' *ḥaty* to continue after its reabsorption into the infinite, in the world of the finite. "Indeed, the Osiris, Ankh-f-

---

[58] This concept is a study in itself. See Erik Hornung, *Conceptions of God in Ancient Egypt: the One and the Many* (Cornell UP, 1982).

n-Khonsu has gone forth by day to do all that he Wills upon the earth among the living!"[59] That which continues, is the metaphysical heart, or mind or intellect, or *consciousness,* of as we have seen above in earlier sections, the Horus-Logos.

Did this consciousness arise from Self-consciousness upon the earth among the living, the aspiration of humankind, or does it exist as part of the universal or infinite field, of god(s) in heaven? Paradoxically, the answer to this, the great psycho-drama of humanity, is both. Here we talk of a non-dual dimension to existence and mind, beyond the Newtonian paradigm of sequence and experience. As Assmann points out, "before anything originates or is created, the world is already conceived in the heart [*haty*] of the god. I call this idea "creation through the heart", the heart being the organ of planning and thinking according to Egyptian anthropology."[60] Importantly, Assmann notes, "This is an idea becoming more and more prominent in the course of time."[61] Between heaven and earth, we have, as Jung commented, "a movement out of the suspension

---

[59] Gunther, "Stèle of Revealing – Transliteration & Translation." (Reverse, BD Spell 2)

[60] Jan Assman, "Creation through hieroglyphs: the cosmic grammatology of Ancient Egypt", p. 20.

[61] Ibid.

between two opposites that leads to a new level of being, a new situation."[62]

As Self-realization, this metaphysic explains the idea put forth by Charles Stansfeld Jones, quoted above, about "aligning himself with the will of the universe or God, and, secondly, in, to a certain extent, showing forth the powers of God by means of that will."[63] "When we can say "I and my Father are One" - that my Father is in Heaven and that Heaven is in me – then we shall realize what Christ meant when he talked about the Son of God…".[64] The devoted in our context, those reciting the prayer-spells of the Stèle, become the son of God-man Ankh-ef-en-khonsu, which is also to say, one with Ankh-ef-en-khonsu.

Here we approach the discourse of monotheism. This is not alien to Ancient Egyptian consideration, as Assmann (who else!) identified in his *From Akhenaten to Moses: Ancient Egypt and religious change*, and *Moses the Egyptian: the memory of Egypt in western monotheism.*[65] It

---

[62] Quoted in Carl Jung, *Jung on Active Imagination*, ed. Joan Chodrow (Princeton UP, 1997), Introduction, p. 5.

[63] Frater Achad (Charles Stansfeld Jones), "Living in the Sunlight," *The Fenris Wolf.*

[64] Achad, "Living in the Sunlight," p. 329.

[65] Jan Assmann, *From Akhenaten to Moses: Ancient Egypt and religious change* (Cairo: American University in Cairo Press, 2014) and *Moses the Egyptian: the memory of Egypt in Western Monotheism*

was the monotheistic intellectual orientation of humanity that changed the ancient world, *a transformation that brought about the modern psyche.*[66] (Yet as we saw in the fundamental misunderstanding of the Egyptian mysteries in the Religio Duplex of the European eighteenth century, a repressed Egyptian polytheism continued in western thought as a countercurrent.) Assmann traces Mosaic monotheism to Pharaoh Akhenaten's religious revolution, yet then shows how the Jews denied any Egyptian influence in their beliefs and condemned the Egyptians as polytheistic idolaters. For Assmann, so begins a cycle of abuse in our history, where "counter-religion" establishes itself as truth and condemns others as false. Assmann is investigating historical memory – how factual and fictional events and characters are stored in religious beliefs and subsequently transformed by philosophical justification, literary reinterpretation,

---

(Cambridge, MA: Harvard University Press, 1998). See also James K. Hoffmeier, *Akhenaten & the origins of Monotheism* (Oxford: Oxford UP, 2015).

[66] See for example, Angus Nicholls and Martin Liebscher eds., *Thinking the Unconscious: Nineteenth-Century German Thought* (Cambridge UP, 2010), Henri F. Ellenberger, *Discovery of the Unconscious: the history and evolution of dynamic psychiatry* (Basic Books, 1970), Edward Edinger, *The New God-Image: a study of Jung's key letters concerning the evolution of the Western God-Image* (Chiron, 1996).

philological restitution (or falsification), and psychoanalytic demystification.

My primary interest here is in psychoanalytic demystification. Sigmund Freud's *Moses and Monotheism* (1939), written on his death bed, is an interesting if widely criticized attempt at it.[67] Freud explicitly associated the mysteries of Ancient Egypt with the "unknown territory of the unconscious"[68] and was fascinated by Ancient Egypt. (He apparently would talk to his figurines of Ancient Egyptian deities kept on his desk). Inspired by the then recent archaeological evidence of the Amarna heresy at Tel-El-Amarna, Freud postulated that Moses was a priest of Akhenaten who fled Egypt after the pharaoh's death, but perpetuated his monotheism. Murdered by some rebel followers, their Freudian "reaction formation" subsequently revered Moses, but joined with another monotheistic tribe in Midian who worshipped Yahweh. The solar god Aten of the Egyptian Moses was fused with Yahweh, while the deeds of Moses were ascribed to a Midianite priest who also came to be called Moses. For Freud, Moses

---

[67] Sigmund Freud, *Moses and Monotheism* (Martino Fine Books, 2010).

[68] Paul Roazen, *Freud and his followers* (New York: Alfred A Knopf, 1975), cited in R.W. Rieber, *Freud on Interpretation*, "From the Pharaohs to Freud: Psychoanalysis and the Magical Egyptian Tradition", 2012, Path in Psychology Series (PATH) https://link.springer.com/book/10.1007/978-1-4614-0637-2

was a composite Messiah figure, representing the hope for the return of Moses as the Savior of the Israelites. In typical Freudian fashion, guilt stemming from the murder of the Egyptian Moses was passed down through the generations, creating neurotic expressions of Jewish religious sentiment to disperse or cope with the Jewish inheritance of trauma and guilt.[69]

Irrespective of the veracity of Freud's thesis, what we see here as a psychic function of historical memory or consciousness – what I call *aeonic hatyology* – is the desire for return, a return to wholeness, which is twofold: the desire of the God (Self), and the desire of the living (ego), as an Egyptian orientation and inheritance. We can identify this in the Spells of the Stèle of Ankh-ef-en-khonsu, and his subsequent veneration as a cultic God-man. From the perspective of consciousness, we see here the interplay of Self (collective) and ego. As Jung said, the Self wants to incarnate, 'kind of.'[70] Why? The innate drive to wholeness *that just is*. The Field. As Gunther's sometime co-lecturer, Steve King, has commented, "Self gets humanized by its connection to ego, and ego deified by its connection to Self,"[71] echoing, "Thy kingdom come. Thy will be done in earth, as *it is* in heaven." Matt. 6:10.

---

[69] See also Rieber, *Freud on Interpretation,* Ch. 2 "From the Pharaohs to Freud: Psychoanalysis and the Magical Egyptian Tradition," pp. 9–37.

[70] Paraphrasing Edinger, *Archetype of the Apocalypse.*

"Saying, Father, if thou be willing, remove this cup from me: nevertheless not my will, but thine, be done." Luke 22:42.

King was adapting Bruce Maclennan (who in turn was borrowing from Erich Neumann's recourse to the Baldwin Effect from evolutionary biology). Maclennan writes:

> "The Baldwin Effect shows us that over a long time (a few thousand years) certain aspects of a complex, aspects that have a selective advantage in a group's environment, may be acquired by the archetype. In effect, archetypes may evolve by elevating individually acquired characteristics to their own universal level. In theological terms, although the gods engender the daemons, they are able to learn from those daemons who have been best at promoting the group's welfare."[72]

There is an ebb and flow in the psychological monotheistic tension between God as Self incarnating (Son of God) in ego and the latter's Self-realization (Son of Man). Deus et homo. Or, in terms of the Ancient Egyptian early religiosity of Akhenaten, Karol

---

[71] Steve King, "Aspiring to the Holy Order: Part II The Flight of the Bennu Bird," unpublished lecture transcript delivered in Belgrade, 2016.

[72] Quoted in ibid.

Mysliwiec argues it was Atum, who has featured heavily in this paper, who became Akhenaten's Aten.[73] This religiosity first developed under Queen Hatshepsut when she enhanced the role of Atum in Thebes and climaxed with Akhenaten's Amarna period.

By adopting a psychological hermeneutic we can let go of what we are interpreting's hold on the outer and realize or incarnate that which is superordinate to ego. As Jung wrote in *Memories, Dreams, Reflections*, "Nothing so promotes the growth of consciousness as this inner confrontation of opposites. Quite unsuspected facts turn up in the indictment, and the defense is obliged to discover arguments hitherto unknown. In the course of this, a considerable portion of the outer world reaches the inner, and by that very fact the outer world is impoverished or relieved. On the other hand, the inner world has gained that much weight by being raised to the rank of a tribunal for ethical decisions. However, the once unequivocal ego loses the prerogative of being merely the prosecutor; it must also learn the role of defendant. The ego becomes ambivalent and ambiguous, and is caught between hammer and anvil. It becomes aware of a polarity superordinate to itself."[74]

---

[73] Karol Mysliwiec, "Amon, Atum and Aton: The Evolution of Heliopolitan Influences in Thebes," cited in Hoffmeier, *Akhenaten & the origins of Monotheism*, p. 71.

[74] Carl Jung, Memories Dreams Reflections, rev. Ed. (Vintage books):

We can see this creative tension of the psyche in the spells of BD, in the weighing of the heart, of the Divine Tribunal, and we can see it in those spells chosen for the Stèle.

By letting go of the Stèle's hold on the outer and its commands of the tongue, we can Self-realize or incarnate that which is superordinate to ego, the heart or mind – consciousness – among the living. Psychologically, the quest for wholeness (or Maat), of Self-realization of ego and Self, as an expression of cosmic grammatology, I call the Ptah-hotep principle. This recalls Ptah's position in Breasted's "mechanical equation" above, remembering that as Breasted noted, "both Horus and Thoth are conceived as emanations of Atum"[75] and Atum's modus operandi of creation (as conceived in human minds) involved actions of momentary loss of "self" (ego-consciousness) - spitting, coughing, ejaculating. Ptah-hotep represents the Jungian opposites, *ptḥ,* "create" and its phonetic opposite, *ḥtp,* which essentially means "rest" or "peace".[76]

---

https://archive.org/stream/
MemoriesDreamsReflectionsCarlJung_201811/Memories%2C
%20Dreams%2C%20Reflections%20-%20Carl%20Jung_djvu.txt

[75] J.H. Breasted, "The Philosophy of a Memphite Priest."

[76] I am grateful to J. Daniel Gunther who shared with me some of his research into the various meanings and renderings of ḥotep, as well as its use in BD. Likewise, Shokufeh Alwazi and Brendan Walls. To go down that fascinating rabbit hole here, however,

"And God blessed the seventh day, and sanctified it: because that in it he had rested from all his work which God created and made." Genesis 2:3. As King stated, "Self gets humanized by its connection to ego, and ego deified by its connection to Self,"[77]

I will end this section with one of King's other speculations, commenting on Akhenaten's devotion to "Re-Harakhty [Ra Hoor Khuit] who rejoices in his horizon in his name of light which is in the disc (Aten):"

> "...the radically innovative Pharaoh, Akhenaten, who sought to revolutionize Egyptian religion through the worship of one sole God, the solar disc or Aten, had close relations with the Mithani royal house. [Note: Akhenaten's wife, the beautiful Nefertiti, is widely held to have been Mithani: CH] His family for generations had more and more empowered and favored the Heliopolitan priesthood over the Theban, while intermarriage with the Mithani had led to a rich cross fertilization of ideas and reputation as free thinkers. This possibly or more likely probably, extended to new religious ideas. Importantly, Akhenaten's forebears (Amenhotep II, Tuthmose IV, Amenhotep III) increasingly saw in the Aten, forms of Ra-Horakhti

---

would be a digression.

[77] Steve King, "Aspiring to the Holy Order: Part II The Flight of the Bennu Bird," unpublished lecture transcript.

(Ra Hoor Khuit), such as "Ra-Horakhti-Khepra-Atum of Heliopolis." This ultimated in Akhenaten's monotheism for Ra-Horakhti. Likewise, Abraham's belief in a single deity may also be of Mithani influence.[78] These connections behind the Mithani, the bloodline of Akhenaten, their radical religion of Ra Hoor Khuit, and the Abrahamic religions – the People of the Book – may well explain the revelation of the theogony of *The Book of the Law* in this New Aeon."[79]

Conclusion: The Stèle of Revealing

Andreas Schweizer gives a theoretical observation that is helpful in summarizing this paper:

> "Psychologically speaking, the Egyptian descriptions of the netherworld are an attempt to comprehend what C.G. Jung has hypothetically called the "collective unconscious" …It refers to a psychic stratum that developed in the course of thousands of years and it

---

[78] Earlier in this paper King commented, "Abraham is said to have been the son of an Armenian Mithani ("One House") King. "The historian Eusebius, writing in the early fourth century, quoted fragments of Eupolemus, a now-lost Jewish historian of the second century B.C.E., as saying that "around the time of Abraham, the Armenians invaded the Syrians." This is held to correspond to the arrival of the Mithani."

[79] Steve King, "Apokalypsis 418: the Temple of Christ, the Angelic priesthood and the Great Return of the Queen of Heaven," *Ora et Labora* vol 1 (In Perpetuity Press, 2020), pp. 244-245.

includes those layers of the psyche that transcend the personal unconscious, that is, the emotional experiences and reminiscences of one's personal life [ie. the *ib*: CH]...Whereas the instincts are typical modes of action, the archetypes are typical modes of apprehension...This treasure finds its expression in the religious images, "mythical" primal ideas, and texts of all ages and cultures, but also in any numinous experience of an individual in the present. Anyone who is touched by such an experience or vision in his or her innermost being has the potential to become a religious leader in his or her time."[80]

It is my view that Ankh-ef-en-khonsu was such a person, in his time, and fully intended to be so in ours – whether in consciousness, in our hearts, our memories, via the Horus logos, or in some other way.

This third essay concludes my preliminary analysis on the heart motif in the Stèle of Ankh-ef-en-khonsu. Through the Stèle, I believe we can directly access – that is, we can find the direction (kiblah) to – the omnipresent field of Horus-logos (intention) that, from the non-dual perspective of the field, reveals (makes conscious) the Ankh-ef-en-khonsu project of the worldly and netherworldly consciousness and Unconscious.

---

[80] Schweizer, *The Sungod's Journey through the Netherworld*, pp. 2-3.

The paradigm shift inaugurated by the advent of the
New Aeon enabled this awareness of a non-dual
quantum consciousness, as well as the new, depth
understanding of the psyche, as originally discovered
and apprehended in the analytical psychology of Jung.
Jung spoke of the end of the Christian aeon and the
creation of a "psychological religion," a religion that
would go beyond the limited *separatio* of the Christian
aeon to a new aeon of *coniunctio,* the union of opposites,
of matter and spirit. The psychic sub-strata to this new
state can be found in the religious innovations of our
Theban priest.

It is clear to me that the new religion and aeon Jung
intuited and hypothesized, is Thelema and the New
Aeon. This is the wholeness of the field, that is, or "shall
be the whole of the Law."[81]

What is all the more striking is that Jung does not
appear, as much as I can tell, to have been too aware of
the Thelemic current or of Crowley, beyond the analysis
he put the Asconan OTO under.[82] And on Crowley's
part, although I have not researched this in depth yet, he
does not appear to have been all that familiar with Jung
outside of his earliest published work. Interestingly, Jung

---

[81] Liber Legis I:40.

[82] For a discussion, see Stephen J. King, "Temple Mount: the
Oriental Templar crusade for Veritá," *The Best of Oz* (OTO Grand
Lodge of Australia, 2020), pp. 257 – 294.

believed the creation of his new "psychological religion" would take 500 years, while Crowley prophesied "that 500 years of Dark Ages are likely to be upon us," for the pioneers of the New Aeon. We are seeing this play out in the crises of history and the modern crises of the psyche. "Fortunately," wrote Crowley, "today we have brighter torches and more torch bearers."[83]

The transition from *separatio* to *conjunctio* is primarily an inner work of the psyche. As Erich Neumann commented, "the predigestion of evil...which (the individual) carries out as part of the process of assimilating his shadow makes him, at the same time, an agent for the immunization of the collective. An individual's shadow is invariably bound up with the collective shadow of his group, and as he digests his own evil, a fragment of the collective evil is invariably codigested at the same time."[84] Yet as we saw earlier, "the destiny of the individual, like that of nations and cultures, is always embedded in the hidden stream of slow but continuous transformations within the basic archetypal constellations,"[85] what Carl Jung's disciple

---

[83] Aleister Crowley [the Master Therion], "XX The Aeon," *The Book of Thoth* (Egyptian Tarot) (Weiser, 1989), "XX The Aeon," p. 116.

[84] Erich Neumann, *Depth Psychology and a New Ethic* (Shambhala, 1990), p. 130.

Marie-Louise von Franz described as the flow "beneath the surface of what can be grasped as history."[86]

In our context, the Crowley-Jung consideration is even more poignant given it is also clear that Crowley did not know too much about Ankh-ef-en-khonsu, did not know hieroglyphs, and did not know about Ancient Egypt or Egyptology on any deep level (nor seemed to show much interest in these). What he did know came from sources who in some areas of scholarship and method are now dated, such as Budge, or were draped in the mythico-poetic romanticism of the highly syncretic Hermetic Order of the Golden Dawn and its quasi magico-Egyptian appropriations. Additionally, he was also informed by the mistaken Religio Duplex constructs about Egypt of the Enlightenment, that made their way into Secret Society mysticism and the comparative religious ideas of the times.

We saw a new psychological reality in Ankh-ef-en-khonsu's religious innovations as represented in his Stèle and coffins. Over time, as "Egyptomania" permanently impacted and possessed the "western" psyche, this Horus consciousness of the heart has taken on universal and

---

[85] Andreas Schweizer, *The Sungod's Journey through the Netherworld*, p.4.

[86] Marie-Louise von Franz, *Archetypal Dimensions of the Psyche* (Shambhala, 1999), pp. 263-264.

aeonic dimensions in Thelema.[87] Whereas, with notable exceptions like Gunther, Hays, Schweizer, Assmann and Alwazi, Egyptian religious scholarship has been *kataphatic*, engagement with the Stèle as presented in my papers has been *apophatic*.

One of Jung's principal modes of analysis was *active imagination*. A form of symbolic play, active imagination is an entirely appropriate mode of magic for the Aeon of Horus, the Aeon of the child. As Jung commented, "The dynamic principle of fantasy is *play*, a characteristic also of the child...without this playing with fantasy no creative work has ever yet come to birth...[Imagination is] the reproductive or creative activity of the mind in general...Fantasy as imaginative activity is identical with the flow of psychic energy."[88]

While the only limit to the techniques of active imagination is your imagination, to give the above some form, if you consider just looking at the Stèle as an exercise, "*looking*, psychologically, brings about the activation of the object; it is as if something were emanating from one's spiritual eye that evokes or

---

[87] On Egyptomania, see Ronald H. Fritze, *Egyptomania: a history of fascination, obsession and fantasy* (Reaktion books, 2016) and Erik Hornung, *The Secret Lore of Egypt: its impact on the west* (Cornell UP, 2001).

[88] Carl Jung, quoted in *Jung on Active Imagination*, Introduction, pp. 5-6.

activates the object of one's vision...That is the case
with any fantasy image: one concentrates upon it, and
then finds that one has great difficulty in keeping the
thing quiet, it gets restless, it shifts, something is added,
or it multiplies itself; one fills it with living power and it
becomes pregnant."[89]

For Jung, there were two parts or stages to active
imagination, first *letting the unconscious come up* and then
coming to terms with the unconscious. In the first stage, the
object is to eliminate critical attention and produce a
vacuum in consciousness, "it involves a suspension of
our rational, critical faculties in order to give free rein to
fantasy."[90] In the second part, consciousness takes the
lead, "as the affects and images of the unconscious flow
into awareness, the ego enters actively into the
experience...the larger task of evaluation and
integration remains. Insight must be converted into an
ethical obligation – to live it in life."[91] In our context, an
ethical obligation to Ankh-ef-en-khonsu. To live Ankh-
ef-en-khonsu in life.

Since Jung, various Jungian authors have extrapolated
on Jung's ideas in order to codify the steps required in

---

[89] Ibid., p. 7.

[90] Joan Chodrow, ibid. p. 10.

[91] Ibid.

the active imagination process. Marie-Louise von Franz gave the process as:

- Empty the 'mad mind' of the ego
- Let an unconscious fantasy image appear
- Give it some form of expression
- Ethical confrontation
- Apply it to ordinary life.

An alternative to step 5 proposed by R. A. Johnson, which may be of interest to readers, was "The rituals (make it concrete with physical ritual)."[92]

Below is the Gunther line by line translation of the reverse of the Stèle (I have numbered the lines):

[Reading hieroglyphs right to left]

[BD Spell 30]

(1)

"To be spoken by the Osiris, the Prophet of Menthu, Lord (of) Thebes, Ankh-f-

---

[92] Ibid., p.11. Note that I have only *listed* the steps here, as a summary for publication. Each step has its own processes and stages, both in terms of Unconscious function and conscious direction.

(2) [hieroglyphs]

n-Khonsu, True of Voice: "My heart of my mother!
(say twice) My consciousness of my existence

(3) [hieroglyphs]

upon the earth! Do not stand against me as a witness!
Do not contend against me

(4) [hieroglyphs]

in the Tribunal! Do not oppose me in the presence of
the Great God, Lord of the West!

(5) [hieroglyphs]

Although I have been buried in the great western side
of heaven, I shall endure upon the earth!"

[BD Spell 2]

(1) [hieroglyphs]

To be spoken [by] the Osiris, the *Sma-Priest* (clother of
the god), [of] Thebes, Ankh-f-n-Khonsu, True of
Voice: "O Unique

(2)

One shining as the Moon! May go forth the Osiris, Ankh-f-

(3)

n-Khonsu among this, thy multitude, to the outside.

(4)

Release me, ye who art in the sunlight! Open for him

(5)

the Duat! Indeed, the Osiris, Ankh-f-n-Khonsu shall go forth

(6)

by day to do all that he Wills upon the earth among the living!"[93]

While the exact process and detail might differ for each of us, it is not that hard to see how the Spells could be

---

[93] Gunther, "Stèle of Revealing: Transliteration & Translation."

easily read (and used) as cues and instructions for a "revealing", through a process of using their spellcraft (i.e. pick the appropriate sections, sequentially, in the spells) for emptying the mind, evoking a fantasy image, giving this expression, having an ethical confrontation, doing a concrete physical ritual and applying this to life. And if you make it that far, "Indeed, the Osiris, Ankh-f-n-Khonsu shall go forth by day to do all that he Wills upon the earth among the living!"

It should be pointed out that Jung stressed that only psychologically mature individuals should attempt active imagination work. The major danger is being overwhelmed by the Unconscious: "A well-developed ego standpoint is needed so that conscious and unconscious may encounter each other as equals. Lesser dangers described by Jung include the patient getting "caught in the sterile circle of his own complexes" or "remaining stuck in an all-enveloping phantasmagoria" (1916/58, p. 68)."[94]

As I quoted Hornung earlier, "The netherworld into which we descend underlies our own world. Creative energies of dreadful intensity are active there, and only death, to which all must surrender, makes us truly alive by offering us regeneration from the depths."[95]

---

[94] Chodrow, *Jung on Active Imagination*, Introduction, p. 12.

[95] Erik Hornung, Foreword to Andreas Schweizer's *Amduat*.

Epilogue: "Going black" and the Horus principle

For the last piece in this Netherworldly journey we turn to Jung's 1926 travels in East Africa. For Jung, a cultured European intellectual, entering the wilds of Africa was a journey into the heart of darkness and Europe's colonial Chain of Being "otherness." In a comment much of the Jungian community would rather you didn't hear, he even recalled of this period, "At that time I was obviously all too close to 'going black.'"[96]

Discussion on that is another topic entirely, and not one I will address here, although the comment is so germane to this period in Jung's career it cannot be left unacknowledged. Michael Ortiz Hill gives a frank and possibly confronting summary of what that discussion should consider:

> "It is far too simple a distraction to use this essay here to piss on the clay feet of the great man. Throughout Jung's memoirs, one is impressed by the subtlety and complexity of his mind and the depth of his psychological insight – except when he writes about "the others." The tenacity of his racism, covering five decades of his writings, the radical lack of psychological reflection with which he mistakes his fantasies about the "other" for real people, is embedded

---

[96] Quoted in Michael Ortiz Hill, "CG Jung in the Heart of Darkness," http://www.rootsie.com/forum/index.php?topic=766.0;wap2

in a discourse that is more often than not exquisitely perceptive. His racism raises questions about human ignorance and human wisdom far beyond the personal psychology of Carl Jung because, in spite of, or alongside, his blindness, he was, nonetheless, a wise man. Moreover, since depth psychology has taken the lead of its founding father in interpreting the mythic substratum of human culture, hard questions are raised about the Eurocentrism and racism in Jungian thought and practice."[97]

For our purposes, in Africa Jung recalled: "...we discovered a new form of very primitive psychological religion with the tribes on the slopes of Mt. Elgon... They apparently worship the sun. But it isn't the sun, it is the moment of dawn: that is God. I think it's rather amazing. It is the origin of the Egyptian Horus idea."[98]

Later, in *Memories, Dreams, Reflections*, Jung called his discovery "the Horus principle."[99] For Jung, this ancient principle was the struggle of opposites, between light and dark, good and evil, consciousness and unconsciousness. In this dichotomy, Horus represented the principle of light. (It should be pointed out that

---

[97] Ibid. See also Carrie B. Dohe, *Jung's Wandering Archetype: race and religion in analytical psychology* (Routledge, 2016).

[98] Blake W. Burleson, *Jung in Africa* (Continuum, 2005), p. 165.

[99] Jung, *Memories, Dreams, Reflections*, p. 274.

subsequent studies have made clear that Jung's analysis was actually based on the Elgonyi fear of the dark and had nothing to do with their religious beliefs).[100]

Jung would participate in his primitive sun worship by rising early to watch the sunrise, which turned out to be a transformative, numinous experience for Jung, making him feel like he was "inside a temple...in a timeless ecstasy."[101] For Jung, this was a *primitive* experience, like his so-called primitive tribe, a "going black," the experience of "otherness" to a "primitive" consciousness. Importantly for Jung, he also saw this consciousness extend into the animal kingdom. On one of his early rises, he spotted a troop of baboons, sitting "quietly, almost motionless, on the side of the cliff facing the sun...Like me, they seemed to be waiting for the sunrise. They reminded me of the great baboons of the temple of Abu Simbel in Egypt, which perform the gesture of adoration. They tell the same story: for untold ages men have worshiped the great god who redeems the world by rising out of the darkness as a radiant light in the heavens."[102]

For Jung, the Horus principle was therefore older than human consciousness itself, describing it as a

[100] See, Burleson, *Jung in Africa*, pp. 165-166.

[101] Ibid., p.167.

[102] Jung, *Memories, Dreams, Reflections,* quoted in Ibid., pp. 167-168.

"preconscious archetype."[103] We should note that the Great Temple at Abu Simbel is dedicated to Amun, Ra-Horakhty (Ra Hoor Khuit) and Ptah – all of whom have featured in our story – as well as to the deified Ramesses II who ordered construction. While Jung has been criticized for straining the evidence to fit his psychological paradigm, the associated implication that the genius of Egyptian religion had its source in Africa, was not unique to Jung. In his two volume *Osiris: the Egyptian Religion of Resurrection* (1911), which Jung had read, E. A. Wallis Budge concluded the Osiris-Set-Horus myth of "Egyptian Religion was of African rather than Asiatic origin."[104] While a contentious issue, both in its clash with European "Chain of Being" intellectual estimations of Africa and with the rise of Afrocentrism, Burleson notes that the oral histories of neighboring Bantu groups like the Bugishu, who hold similar religious views to the Elgonyi, place their ancestral home in Ancient Nubia, and more specifically, the location of Abu Simbel, the southern gate of Egypt.[105]

Burleson's focus was limited to Jung's African travels, however the Horus principle formed an integral element

---

[103] Ibid. p. 168.

[104] Quoted in Ibid., p.170.

[105] Ibid., p. 171.

to Jung's approach to religion and psychology.
Commenting on his book *Aion*, Jung said:

> "As I delved into all these matters the question of the
> historical person, of Jesus the man, also came up. It is of
> importance because the collective mentality of his time
> one might also say: the archetype which was already
> constellated, the primordial image of the Anthropos
> was condensed in him, an almost unknown Jewish
> prophet. The ancient idea of the Anthropos, whose
> roots lie in Jewish tradition on the one hand and in the
> Egyptian Horus myth on the other, had taken
> possession of the people at the beginning of the
> Christian era, for it was part of the Zeitgeist. It was
> essentially concerned with the Son of Man, God's own
> son, who stood opposed to the deified Augustus, the
> ruler of this world. This idea fastened upon the
> originally Jewish problem of the Messiah and made it a
> world problem."[106]

We end once again with the Horus Logos. Its inherent
"problem" of separation and return, which we have seen
throughout this paper, throughout the ages, and
throughout monotheism, is resolved in the New Aeon
of wholeness, of Unity uttermost showed!

---

[106] Jung, *Memories, Dreams, Reflections.*

"The new Aeon is the worship of the spiritual made one with the material, of Horus, of the Child, of the Future."[107]

Ib is the law, *ib* under *ḥaty.*

---

[107] Aleister Crowley, *The Equinox of the Gods* (New Falcon Publications, 1991), p.134.

Works Cited

Shokufeh Alwazi, "The Island of Flames and the Spiritual Heart: a reflective commentary on Rev. Cosmè Hallelujah's "Notes towards a preliminary analysis of a peculiar motif in the Stelè of Ankh-af-na-khonsu,"" *Ora et Labora* vol 3 (2022).

Jan Assmann, *Religio Duplex: How the Enlightenment Reinvented Egyptian Religion* (Polity Press, 2014).

Jan Assmann, *From Akhenaten to Moses: Ancient Egypt and religious change* (Cairo: American University in Cairo Press, 2014).

Jan Assmann, *Moses the Egyptian: the memory of Egypt in Western Monotheism* (Cambridge, MA: Harvard University Press, 1998).

Jan Assman, "Creation through hieroglyphs: the cosmic grammatology of Ancient Egypt", *The poetics of grammar and the metaphysics of sound and sign* (Jerusalem studies in religion and culture 6), ed. S. La Porta and D. Shulman (Leiden, 2007)

https://archiv.ub.uni-heidelberg.de/propylaeumdok/3615/1/Assmann_Creation_through_hieroglyphs_2007.pdf

D. A. Aston, "The Theban West Bank from the Twenty-fifth Dynasty to Ptolemaic Period," in *The Theban Necropolis*, eds. Nigel Strudwick and John H. Taylor, British Museum Press, 2003.

https://www.academia.edu/39997087/The_Theban_Wes t_Bank_from_the_Twenty_fifth_Dynasty_to_the_Ptole maic_Period

Joshua J. Bodine, "The Shabaka Stone: An Introduction." Studia Antiqua 7, no. 1 (2009), p. 10. https://scholarsarchive.byu.edu/studiaantiqua/vol7/iss1/3

J. H. Breasted, "The Philosophy of a Memphite Priest," *Zeitschrift fur Agyptische Sprache* No. 39 (1901).

Blake W. Burleson, *Jung in Africa* (Continuum, 2005).

Aleister Crowley, *The Equinox of the Gods* (New Falcon Publications, 1991).

Aleister Crowley [the Master Therion], *The Book of Thoth* (Egyptian Tarot) (Weiser, 1989).

Adriaan De Buck, *The Egyptian Coffin Texts, Vol. 2.* (University of Chicago Press, 1938)

Carrie B. Dohe, *Jung's Wandering Archetype: race and religion in analytical psychology* (Routledge, 2016).

Edward Edinger, *The New God-Image: a study of Jung's key letters concerning the evolution of the Western God-Image* (Chiron, 1996).

Okasha El-Daly, *Egyptology: the Missing Millennium, Ancient Egypt in Medieval Arabic Writings* (Routledge, 2016).

Henri F. Ellenberger, *Discovery of the Unconscious: the history and evolution of dynamic psychiatry* (Basic Books, 1970).

Raymond O. Faulkner, *The Ancient Egyptian Coffin Texts, Vol. 1* (Ars & Phillips, 1973)

Marie-Louise von Franz, *Archetypal Dimensions of the Psyche* (Shambhala, 1999).

Ronald H. Fritze, *Egyptomania: a history of fascination, obsession and fantasy* (Reaktion books, 2016).

J. Daniel Gunther, "Revealing the Stèle of Ankh-ef-en-khonsu," unpublished lecture transcript.

J. Daniel Gunther, "Stèle of Revealing – Transliteration & Translation," unpublished tss.

Cosmè Hallelujah, "Notes towards a preliminary analysis of a peculiar motif in the Stelè of Ankh-af-na-khonsu," *Ora et Labora* vol 2 (2021).

Cosmè Hallelujah, "Excursus on Notes towards a preliminary analysis of a peculiar motif in the Stelè of Ankh-af-na-khonsu," *Ora et Labora* vol 3 (2022).

Michael Ortiz Hill, "CG Jung in the Heart of Darkness," http://www.rootsie.com/forum/index.php?topic=766.0;wap2

James K. Hoffmeier, *Akhenaten & the origins of Monotheism* (Oxford: Oxford UP, 2015).

Erik Hornung, *Conceptions of God in Ancient Egypt: the One and the Many* (Cornell UP, 1982).

Erik Hornung, *The Secret Lore of Egypt: its impact on the west* (Cornell UP, 2001).

Frater Achad (Charles Stansfeld Jones), "Living in the Sunlight," *The Fenris Wolf* no 7 (Edda: Stockholm, 2014).

Carl Jung, Memories Dreams Reflections, rev. Ed. (Vintage books):

https://archive.org/stream/
MemoriesDreamsReflectionsCarlJung_201811/
Memories%2C%20Dreams%2C%20Reflections%20-
%20Carl%20Jung_djvu.txt

Carl Jung, *Jung on Active Imagination*, ed. Joan Chodrow (Princeton UP, 1997).

Steve King, *Living in the Sunlight: making a forgotten meditation an atomic habit* (In Perpetuity Press, 2022).

Steve King, "Aspiring to the Holy Order: Part II The Flight of the Bennu Bird," unpublished lecture transcript delivered in Belgrade, 2016.

Steve King, "Apokalypsis 418: the Temple of Christ, the Angelic priesthood and the Great Return of the Queen of Heaven," *Ora et Labora* vol 1 (In Perpetuity Press, 2020).

Stephen J. King, "Temple Mount: the Oriental Templar crusade for Veritá," *The Best of Oz* (OTO Grand Lodge of Australia, 2020).

Teodor Lekov, "The Formula of the "Giving of the Heart" in Ancient Egyptian Texts."
https://www.academia.edu/9011055/The_formula_of_th e_Giving_of_the_Heart_in_Ancient_Egyptian_Texts

Robert Merkot, "Thebes under Kushite rule", in *Tombs of the South Asasif Necropolis*, ed. Elena Pischikova, Cairo AUC, Chapter 1, p. 10.

https://www.academia.edu/39245403/ Thebes_under_Kushite_rule

Erich Neumann, *Depth Psychology and a New Ethic* (Shambhala, 1990).

Angus Nicholls and Martin Liebscher eds., *Thinking the Unconscious: Nineteenth-Century German Thought* (Cambridge UP, 2010).

R. W. Rieber, *Freud on Interpretation*, 2012, Path in Psychology Series (PATH) https://link.springer.com/book/10.1007/978-1-4614-0637-2

Paul Roazen, *Freud and his followers* (New York: Alfred A Knopf, 1975).

Andreas Schweizer, *The Sungod's Journey through the Netherworld: Reading the Ancient Egyptian Amduat* (Cornell UP, 2010).

Rogèrio Sousa, "Heart of wisdom: studies on the heart amulet in Ancient Egypt," (Archaeo Press: Oxford, 2011)

https://www.academia.edu/540862/ Heart_of_Wisdom_studies_on_the_heart_amulet_in_an cient_Egypt_Archaeopress_Oxford_2011

Liber AL vel Legis.

https://lib.oto-usa.org/libri/liber0220.html

Liber Aleph vel CXI, *The Book of Wisdom or Folly* (93 Publishing, 1991).

Liber Resh vel Helios.

https://lib.oto-usa.org/libri/liber0200.html

APOKALYPSIS III

Depth Revelation

STEVE KING

Preamble

In past installments of this paper (*Ora et Labora* vol III, *Best of Oz*) I drew attention to the significance of the Jerusalem Temple, also pointing out its role as a central motif in the book of Revelation. I then considered Revelation as a key to understanding the angelic communications of Elizabethan magus Dr. John Dee. Such a view is in line with a number of scholars and scholar-practitioners, however I went a step further (as did Jason Louv in his *John Dee and the Empire of Angels*) saying Revelation was also key to understanding the later Thelemic apocalypse, *The Vision and the Voice,* and Thelema generally.[1]

To introduce Temple mysticism, I used the works of 'Temple' theologian Margaret Barker, who reads Revelation as a condemnation of an apostate Jerusalem Temple, and a visionary longing and affirmation of what she sees as the true Christian message – the

---

[1] As will be seen in future installments of this paper, Louv and I depart on the details.

restoration of an older Temple lore and faith. Such a reliance on Barker's controversial if rigorous thesis rightly invites criticism, but it was necessary in order to introduce and emphasize the symbolism and function – actual and ideal – of the Temple.

While the Temple features prominently in Revelation, scholarship on the latter can be categorized by four broader and sometimes overlapping schools, all of which to greater or lesser extents participate in Temple mystique. There is the *preterist* school of interpretation which views Revelation as a symbolic form of events which have already taken place (from *praeter*, meaning "beyond or past"); the *historical* interpretation which views Revelation as a telling of the entire course of Church history; the *futurist* interpretation which sees future events around the Return of Christ; and the *idealistic* interpretation which sees a conflict of good and evil that is not specifically or literally historical.

Although Barker is both preterist and historical, I'd suggest her *Temple* theology is an interpretative approach in its own right. Outside of formal NT scholarship, numerous other denominational, mystical, cultic and cultural interpretations of Revelation abound. Within Western Esotericism for example (treated here as an academic discipline and mode of enquiry), there are Theosophical, qabalistic, hermetic/energetic and masonic interpretations of Revelation. These can be seen in works such as James Pryse's *Apocalypse Unsealed* (and how such texts get used/adopted), while some Rites of both esoteric and exoteric Freemasonry are idealistic, with Freemasonry in general developing a unique Temple mysticism and mythology of its own. D.H. Lawrence's final book, *Apocalypse*, was both socio-cultural critique and interpretative moral commentary on Revelation. (Ironically, it was written as he was passed over by the London publisher, Australian P.R. Stephensen, in favor of signing up the real-life 'Beast 666' Crowley!).[2]

The general meaning of *Apocalypse*, as previously discussed, is 'revelation,' however the above interpretative grilles point to a deeper meaning used in this paper's title, *apokalypsis* – an "uncovering of what has been hidden." The root is the verb *kalypto*, meaning "to cover or hide" and its prefix is the preposition *apo* meaning "away or from" (the same as in Thelema's *Star Ruby* ritual). Apokalypsis can therefore be read as "to take the covering away." Interpretation attempts to make sense of what is underneath.

It was the Jungian psychologist Edward Edinger who spelt out the obvious about NT scholarship surrounding Revelation, commenting that most of the scholars are far too caught up in the myth itself, leaving them in the academically awkward position of putting forth an interpretative thesis while trying to understand their

---

[2] See my 2007 edition of *The Legend of Aleister Crowley*.

own mythological container. Such a criticism can be quite validly applied to my own work as well! We cannot perceive the subject as an object until one is outside of the container. To that end, or at least towards it, I will follow Jung, Edinger and others and now look at Revelation from the perspective of depth psychology (hence this installment's title). I will read Revelation as that apocalyptic psychic event of the *coming of Self into conscious realization*, a shattering of the world as it has been, and its reconstitution. Psychology is outside of the container and at present, the deepest known framework for analysis. Such a project will enable future installments of 'Apokalypsis' to return with more emphasis to the Temple theme and how we might read and treat the evolution of this *mandala* as it manifests in consciousness through the works of Dee, and later, Thelema.

The current installment is therefore more of an interlude, a meditation. Such a meditation is a necessary learning experience and contemplative practice in the apokalypsis mysteries. In my booklet *Living in the Sunlight* I described meditation as the process of 'letting go.' By interpreting scripture in a psychological way, by getting to its psychological reality, we relieve or let go of its hold in the outer world and therefore can experience and come to consciously realize (incarnate) the inner – that polarity superordinate to ego, the Self. By doing so, As Jung wrote in *Memories, Dreams, Reflections*, "a considerable portion of the outer world reaches the inner, and by that very fact the outer world is impoverished or relieved." This installment's function, the purpose it serves for the reader who engages with it, is likewise meditative. It is reflective and reflexive. *By letting go of Revelation we incarnate the post-Christian aeon.* We can begin to *individuate* – become individuals – in it. We can *initiate* it (and be initiated). We can live in the *aeonic psychological reality* of its *depth magick.*

Introduction

Through the discovery of the Unconscious and the new analytical psychology, Carl Jung envisaged a new aeon beyond the Christian mythic container and with it, a new 'psychological' religion. He felt that a primordial psychic pattern of the collective Unconscious, as a dynamic agency with intentionality, was again constellating in the individual psyche and in the collective psyche of the group it was touching. That "group" was more than just his disciples and patients, although for Jung, they were its harbingers. While beyond the scope of this study, at different times Jung considered that group those located in the European or Western tradition and psyche (humanist, Judaeo-Christian) and at other times something more universal. That "primordial psychic pattern" was the archetype of the God-image or *Imago Dei.* This image is a living entity, a living process that unfolds and undergoes transformations. In this sense it is evolutionary, historical/cultural as much as biological. The God-image is a synonym of the Self in Jungian terms, and more specifically, that aspect of Self called the collective Self, a transpersonal center shared by *a* whole body of humanity. My position has always been that with the advent of the *New Aeon* (in the Thelemic sense), that transpersonal center is shared by *the* body of humanity.

Here I treat Revelation as a culmination of the New Testament and its four gospels, ie. of the christian aeon. My treatment of this text is psychological, in that as a living cultural artifact, it has also been transitionary to the post-Christian aeon of individuation. I hold the position that the Apocalyptic Christ of Revelation and cognate figures is a universal God-image that transforms into the God-image of the New Aeon. In later installments, I will examine how the apocalypse of the New Aeon, *The Vision and the Voice*, brings forth into conscious realization that new and universal God-image, beyond the mythic container of Christianity and its aeon. This further marks a distinct transition from the psychological to the *magical*, from individuation to *initiation*, from 'western' to *universal*. If this holds (as I assert it does), *The Vision and the Voice* should be able to indicate if not answer some key themes associated with Jung's hypothesized new religion: the rites of the initiated and the priesthood and Order of the initiated. I identify what Jung hypothesized, as Thelema.

A study such as this is never ending and evolving, so by necessity there are some obvious and arbitrary limitations set. For example, I will largely limit my selection of motifs from Revelation in this installment to those selected by Edward Edinger in his *Archetype of the Apocalypse* (and to a lesser extent, some of those selected by Jung in his seminal *Answer to Job*). Such an approach connects this paper to an existing body of knowledge or universe of discourse. I closely follow Edinger's structure and commentary, often silently quoting or paraphrasing his ideas. This debt warrants broad acknowledgment here. To cite every instance of my usage of his terms and language would have proven tedious and distracting. My departures from Edinger are equally silent, but prefigure the extension of the general approach, as will be applied to *The Vision and the Voice* in future installments. This generates a radical and challenging new set of conclusions about Liber CDXVIII – an "uncovering of what has been hidden."

While I discussed the apokalypsis above, there is also another general usage of the term that for our purposes cannot be ignored. Apokalypsis also refers to the coming of deity to assert sovereignty, or the coming of a Messiah, heralding the End of the Age and a reconstituting of things to bring about a New Order. All of these feature as we extend beyond Revelation into Thelema. For our purposes in *this* installment, I follow Edinger's identification of four chief characteristics of apocalyptic literature:

1. Revelation

2. Judgment

3. Destruction or Punishment (a consequence of 2), and

4. Renewal in a New World.

Edinger also identifies different strands of contextual reference that apply to Revelation: "past" concrete events in the sacred history of Israel; "present" concrete events (ie. 1st century CE); "eschatological" or "pleromatic" events outside of time taking place in the realm of the psyche, the collective Unconsciousness, *that do not necessarily register at the level of ego consciousness*; and the "psychological" strand of the coming of the Self into conscious realization in an individual psyche. These strands do not appear neatly in the narrative, and more often than not erupt in the text confusingly and imposingly, in opposition, as paradox and contradiction. While we cannot be sure with Revelation (as we can be with, say, *The Vision and the Voice*), it suggests that at least some textual components of Revelation reflect the 'crazy' heat of a lived psychic (spiritual) experience – a bit like how seemingly random components from different psychic sources can be assembled in crazy ways to compose the narrative of a dream. Revelation, in part at least and irrespective of editorial treatment and redaction, *is an assimilation product of the Seer*.

An Archetype as used here is twofold: it is a *pattern* (ie. a primordial ordering of images) with a generalized or *collective quality* (ie. it derived from the collective transpersonal objective psyche) and it is a *dynamic agency* (ie. a living psychic organism inhabiting the objective psyche). It is therefore both an object (pattern) and subject (agent).

When an archetype constellates, it generates itself and manifests in the individual psyche and the collective psyche of the group it touches. Treating Revelation, as mentioned earlier, as the coming of the Self into conscious realization (ie. the shattering of the world as it has been, followed by its reconstitution) we can place the narrative into Edinger's four chief characteristics, as:

- *Revelation* – the psychological correlate of shattering new insight accompanied by a flow of transpersonal images into consciousness;

- *Judgment* – awareness of the Shadow as a living concrete reality, with all its risks of complete demoralization;

- *Destruction (or Punishment)* – the individual's anxiety in the midst of a transformation ordeal;

- *New World* – the emergence of mandala and quaternity images within the psyche, heralding the possibility of a conscious relation to the Self and its Wholeness.

In Revelation, the image of Christ is "plastered" onto earlier Jewish apocalyptic material, laying out *the concluding events of the Judaeo-Christian myth.*

I recommend reading the chapters of Revelation being referred to prior to or alongside the relevant sections of this paper. These chapters are clearly identified. This will help you to look into the lens of commentary, but also set you off on your own inquiry as parts of the text not covered below take your interest. I also recommend that readers who identify as Thelemites resist the temptation (and you will be tempted!) to 'Thelemicize' the text, either in general interpretation or by focusing on familiar motifs. Read it in the psyche – the light and the darkness – of the Christian aeon of *separatio.* This will allow you to later embrace *The Vision and the Voice* with stunning fresh insight and unexpected inspiration.

Revelation Chapters 1–3

The Apocalyptic Christ

John's prison island of Patmos represents the confinement required for an *energy phenomenon* – a build up of libido not permitted its normal, natural, spontaneous discharge. This enables the *numinosum*, an experience formulated according to the religious conceptions of the mystic. John hears the voice of the Unconscious – the "voice" comes from "behind" (ie. within).

John encounters the archetype or heavenly template of the *menorah* that stood in the tabernacle (Exodus 25:31-39). The menorah of the Second Temple was seized in 169 BCE during the Temple desecration by Antiochus IV Epiphanes and a reconstruction ordered by Judas Maccabeus disappeared after the Temple's destruction in 70 CE. The Talmud forbade its reconstruction. The menorah was suggestive of the tree of life while its lights correspond to the seven eyes of God that range over the world (Zechariah 4:2-10). Although there are a number of 'seven' associations (Revelation is an assault of the archetype of seven), more generally we see that there is a *watching* going on, directed toward the ego.

In the middle of the lamp stands one "like the Son of man" (cf. Daniel, Ezekiel, Enoch). In the Christian context, this is a Christ-like figure. The Apocalyptic Christ is the realized Self, the "Son" of the ego or "man." It therefore has both a heavenly (archetypal) and earthly begetting. Man in whom is God. The watching eyes of God present a Messiah figure who partakes of the divine nature, the harbinger of the new aeon, with a doubled edged sword coming out of the mouth (cf. Isaiah 49:1-2), ie. the Logos, the Word (cf. Matthew 10:34-36). "Thy word is a lamp unto my feet, and a light unto my path." Psalm 119:105.

The Apocalyptic Christ's "face was like the sun shining with all its force." The sun is a symbol of the Self. As the heavenly source and sustainer of all life on earth, like the sword which defines (discriminates) the Word (Law) governing an aeon, *the sun defines a set limit* to the archetype of infinite space/Self for the psyche – in this case the solar system or "the belt of gold."[3] Such limits are necessary in the process of Self-realization so we don't drown in the infinitude of the Unconscious. The Christ's whiteness "of wool, like snow" references Isaiah 1:18: "Come now, and let us reason together, saith the Lord: though your sins be as scarlet, they shall be as white as snow; though they be red like crimson, they shall be as wool." ie., redemption through realization of Self, the Son of man, the *albedo* and *rubedo* phases of the Great Work after the *nigredo*. The eyes of "burning flame" return us to the watching eyes of God, realized through and in Self, an act of destruction or purification by fire and baptism in Logos ("his voice like the sound of the ocean").[4]

This symbol set is grounded in the Christ's feet, "like burnished bronze when it has been refined in a furnace." It references Numbers 21, "The LORD said to Moses, "Make a snake and put it up on a pole; anyone who is bitten can look at it and live." So Moses made a bronze snake and put it up on a pole. Then when anyone was bitten by a snake and looked at the bronze snake, he

---

[3]All archetypes are connected. The Sun as Self connects with the archetype of the Sacred Seven for the ancients.

[4]For baptism and Christ, see my last installment in *Ora et Labora* III.

lived." To refine is to look into the furnace of the eyes of the Son of man, to realize Self, which is to raise. John of Patmos is therefore more specifically referencing John 3:14-15: "And as Moses lifted up the serpent in the wilderness, even so must the Son of man be lifted up: That whosoever believeth in him should not perish, but have eternal life." Again, the realization of Self, the turning around and facing the Unconscious. What was darkness is now Light, what was temporal, eternal. As we see in the face "shining with all its force," *there is a transformative force to be realized and utilized.*

There are seven stars in the right hand of the Apocalyptic Christ. This Christ interprets the archetype of Seven for us in Rev. 1:20: "the seven stars are the angels of the seven churches, and the seven lamp-stands are the seven churches themselves." John is instructed to write to the "angels" of the seven churches.

Traced in order, the seven churches form a clockwise 'symbolic' circle beginning with Ephesus and ending with Laodicea, and in that sense the churches present a terrestrial symbol of the heavenly (ie. the sacred seven) Self.

The seven angels, St. Mark's Basilica

Edinger suggests that the angels represent personifications of collective groupings, of the group soul, whose depth connection is indicated by their source in the stars of the Apocalyptic Christ.

If we follow the concept Edinger introduces, the angels are more closely identified with the Watchers (cf. Daniel, Book of Enoch) or Egregore (*egrēgoros* 'wakeful'). The Watchers give a depth connection not only to the Apocalyptic Christ, but to the 'watching' of Revelation itself, the eyes of God, as well as to the tradition which Revelation constantly refers back to.

In modern occult and psychological readings, the egregore is a non-physical entity that arises from the collective thoughts of a distinct group of people, also considered the group mind or thoughtform. Psychologically, depending upon the degree of participation mystique or collective identity of and in the group (its psychic depth), the level of collective experience shared jointly and represented as the group spirit, or in each individual's conscious relation to this group manifestation of Self, this "angel" or Watcher may be anywhere within the spectrum of good and evil, of truth and falsehood, of wisdom or folly. Revelation is an attempt to instruct the angels in the reorientation to Self, for individuation of the faithful. The Watchers should represent the transpersonal entity who guides the group towards this individual yet collective experience. Any less a standard is fallen and rebellious. They are to bring forth the new Revelation.

The demand however is that the people of the Churches are "victorious," which Edinger identifies as being true to the faith, no matter what. Psychologically he equates this with the Jungian *onslaught of instinct* – an onslaught against the ego of passionate intensity. Historically, in the group context of Revelation, this is the onslaught of the Roman Empire against Christianity. For Jung, to withstand this becomes "an experience of divinity… provided that man…defends his humanity against the animal nature of the divine power" (cf. *Symbols of Transformation*). The divine power manifest in the animal soul or *nephesh* as instinct, needs to be brought under humanity (will).

The gifts for the victorious

For the victorious, there are "gifts."

The church at Ephesus is promised the "tree of life" in Eden, recalling a Jewish tradition that the tree of life reappears at the end of time as reward for those who upheld the doctrine of the Law, ie. the victorious.

The church at Smyrna are promised the "crown" of eternal life – the alchemical *solificatio*, the anointing with a sun-like quality, the deification of the recipient, identified with the Sun, like the Apocalyptic Christ. Psychologically, this is the "kingly" eternal quality of individuation, connecting to the transpersonal consciousness.

Pergamum is promised "hidden manna and a white stone, with a new name written on it, known only to the person who receives it" (Rev. 3:17). This references John 6:48-51: "I am that bread of life. Your fathers did eat manna in the wilderness, and are dead. This is the bread which cometh down from heaven, that a man may eat thereof, and not die. I am the living bread which came down from heaven: if any man eat of this bread, he shall live for ever: and the bread that I will give is my flesh, which I will give for the life of the world." On one level, the nourishing aspect of contact with Self, and a sense of the non-temporal (ie. eternal). But John of Revelation speaks of the hidden manna that is contained in the Ark of the Covenant (cf. 2 Maccabees ch. 2, Hebrews ch. 9). We see here the depth connection of contact with Self, of unfolding and deeper levels of imagery. Alchemically, the white stone is the Stone of the Philosophers in its *albedo* phase, which in this aeon presents as the ultimate attainment, given the Christian *seperatio* of nature and spirit and the identification exclusively with spirit.

If you are familiar with the works of Jung and other analytical psychologists on the psyche and comparative mythology, religion and alchemy, you'd notice that interspersed in their commentary are numerous accounts of their patients' dreams. In a textual analysis such as this, where the author (and the engaged reader) is both analyst and analysand, the dream life can also get involved. While this paragraph may seem digressionary and its depth treatment will have to be reserved for a later installment, some time after writing about Pergamum I had a dream whose contents indicated (and communicated) there was more to say about the church's gift for the victorious. This related to the "bread of life" and its "hidden manna." John's (bread of) "life" is identified with "flesh" in the 6:48-51 passage, in contradistinction to their separation in Deuteronomy 12:23 "Only be sure that thou eat not the blood: for the blood is the life; and thou mayest not eat the life with the flesh." This *separatio* is reconciled in the body and blood of Christ, the Christian *albedo* (white stone), but what remains hidden is the *coniunctio* signified by the later *rubedo* phase (reddening). This pertains to the "cakes of light" and Thelema, which is for a later installment. (However, see Gunther, *Parable of the Pale Image*). Other dream interventions are silently introduced into the text. I've drawn attention to it here to encourage readers affected by similar dream content to pay attention. The archetype of the apocalypse is still very much alive and active in the world.

The church at Thyatira is told those who keep working for Christ will be given "authority over nations," "to rule them with an iron scepter and shatter them like so many pots. And I will give such a person the Morning Star." (Rev. 2:26-28) This directly quotes the Messianic Psalm 2:7-9: "I will declare the decree: the Lord hath said unto me, Thou art my Son; this day have I begotten thee. Ask of me, and I shall give thee the heathen for thine inheritance, and the uttermost parts of the earth for thy possession. Thou shalt break them with a rod of iron; thou shalt dash them in pieces like a potter's vessel." This alludes to the subtle yet powerful psychic effectiveness of an individuated person – having found access to the Unconscious, this manifests, the efficacy of the Self becomes operative in the human realm. This recalls the solar symbolism of the Apocalyptic Christ, when psychic onslaught is transformed into spiritual kingship (see the final gift to the seventh church, to follow). Mythologically, the Morning Star refers to Venus when it appears in the east before sunrise, here symbolizing the *albedo* phase of alchemy after the *nigredo*.

Those at Sardis will be dressed in "white robes," another reference to the *albedo*, the purification of the ego by spiritualization, the highest goal in the Christian aeon. The "book of life" (cf. Rev. 21:27, Philippians 4:3) is the register of those entitled or destined to eternal life. Psychologically, this refers to the magical memory, and that those sufficiently individuated towards wholeness (realization) of Self in a lifetime permanently deposit that consciousness in the Self. (This psychic process has a direct relationship with Thelema's Stele of Revealing).[5]

To the church at Philadelphia, the Christ will make the victorious "a pillar in the sanctuary of my God," a concept akin to the more familiar 1 Peter 2:4-5, "Coming to Him as to a living stone, rejected indeed by men, but chosen by God and precious, you also, as living stones, are being built up a spiritual house, a holy priesthood, to offer up spiritual sacrifices acceptable to God through Jesus Christ." Psychologically, all those aspirants to individuation are stones of the Temple (the realization of Self). Jung believed this work of building in his era was to the "new religion" (ie. the new *Imago Dei*), forecasting this would take "about 600 years" (quoted in Edinger's *The Creation of Consciousness*). This is of note given Crowley's attribution of 600 year sub-currents or cycles of A∴A∴ (cf. *The Equinox* IV:1, Commentary to Liber LXV IV:22) and the 500 years of

---

[5] See the essays of Rev. Cosmé Hallelujah in *Ora et Labora*, and *The Vision and the Voice*.

Dark Ages at the onset of the New Aeon (cf. *The Book of Thoth*, Atu XX The Aeon).

Finally, "Anyone who proves victorious" at Laodicea shares the throne of the Apocalyptic Christ, "just as I myself overcome and have taken my seat with my Father on his throne" (Rev. 3:21). This is to say, "My kingdom is not of this world: if my kingdom were of this world, then would my servants fight, that I should not be delivered to the Jews: but now is my kingdom not from hence" John 18:36. We return to the idea of spiritual (or psychological) kingship and the crowning through assimilating the onslaught of instinct.

Notwithstanding the Christian aeon's one sided predilection to spirit *over* nature and its (limited) summit or 'wholeness' in the *albedo*, the gifts to the churches can be viewed as the rewards or attainments of *participation mystique* in the individuation process towards realization of Self.

We can summarize these gifts (in the order of the seven churches) as:

1   Tree of life

2   Eternal life

3   Bread of life

4   Mastery of life (spiritual kingship)

5   Book of life

6   Temple of life (living stone)

7   Throne of life

The rest of Revelation outlines what to expect and what this process entails.

The door, the thief and the key

"Behold, I stand at the door, and knock: if any man hear my voice, and open the door, I will come in to him, and will sup with him, and he with me." Rev 3:20

The Unconscious comes knocking for admission to consciousness, and consciousness must "open the door". However, to "sup with him, and he with me"[6] means following the right protocols or internal processes, to understand the category of experience that has come knocking (the Unconscious) and treat it with the correct hospitality.

"Remember therefore how thou hast received and heard, and hold fast, and repent. If therefore thou shalt not watch, I will come on thee as a thief, and thou shalt not know what hour I will come upon thee." Rev. 3:3

In the Greek, usually but by no means exclusively accepted as the language of Revelation, "repent"

---

[6] The last phrase is also translated as "at that person's side."

translates as *metanoia*, (*meta* - "after," ie. a shift or change, and *noia* - "mind"), a mindset after a life changing experience. In Christian theology, metanoia is commonly understood as a transformative change of heart, especially a spiritual conversion. The term suggests repudiation, change of mind, repentance, and atonement, but "conversion" and "reformation" may best approximate its connotation. This theological concept is linked with Christian prayer, in which a prostration is called a metanoia, the spiritual condition of one's soul being expressed through the physical movement of falling face down before the Lord.

The message to this church is to "open the door," with the correct hospitality, or the Unconscious will be upon you regardless (cf. Luke 12:35-40 and 1 Thessalonians 5:2: "For yourselves know perfectly that the day of the Lord so cometh as a thief in the night.").

> "And to the angel of the church in Philadelphia write; These things saith he that is holy, he that is true, he that hath the key of David, he that openeth, and no man shutteth; and shutteth, and no man openeth;". Rev 3:7.

This passage directly references Isaiah 22:20-22, which recounts that during an apocalyptic moment in the history of Israel (the besieging of Jerusalem by Babylon), Yaweh tells Shebna, master of the palace, that he will replace him with Eliakim as master: "And the key of the house of David will I lay upon his shoulder; so he shall open, and none shall shut; and he shall shut, and none shall open." By connecting to a historical, apocalyptic event, Revelation's own grand eschatological moment can also be connected to concrete historical events (ie. The 'preterist' interpretation). This is one of the four major 'Key' biblical symbols. The other three are "the keys of death and of hades" (Rev. 1:18), the key to the abyss (Rev. 9:1) and "the keys of the kingdom of Heaven" (Matthew 16:18-19). These are different aspects of the one key, the key representing that which "opens" the Unconscious. The Unconscious may be opened in its heavenly form, in its hellish form, or it may relate to a specific situation.

The Rapture

In Rev. 3:10 the "rapture" is introduced: "Because thou hast kept the word of my patience, I also will keep thee from the hour of temptation, which shall come upon all the world, to try them that dwell upon the earth."[7] The primary "rapture" text is Thesalonians 4:16-17: "For the Lord himself shall descend from heaven with a shout, with the voice of the archangel, and with the trump of God: and the dead in Christ shall rise first: Then we which are alive and remain shall be caught up together

---

[7]"Word of my patience" is also translated as "commandment to persevere."

with them in the clouds, to meet the Lord in the air: and so shall we ever be with the Lord."

Psychologically, this signifies perseverance through commitment to Christ or the realization of Self, the new 'mindset' or metanoia. Former life in the fatal image of nature is now 'death,' hence "the dead in Christ" having risen above.

3. Revelation Chapters 4-5

Heavenly Kingship

The vision of Chapter 4 presents us with *the Temple mandala*, a symbol of Self. The divine throne is in the center with a rainbow around it, there is an outer circle of twenty-four elders on thrones, the four kerubim or "beasts" are "in the midst of the throne, and round about the throne," the sea of glass is before the throne, as are the seven lamps "which are the seven Spirits of God." The heavenly kingship of the numinosum returns, with God as "One who was sitting on the throne" referencing the recurring OT theme of God as king of the world.

This kingly reference becomes a central motif of Revelation as the Messiah or anointed one, the "Christ." This king represents the authority of Self, the mandala is the means of internal realization of Self, of the king "not of this world." Paradoxically, this realization is also to sit or share the throne, and therefore also being His servant (as the ego realizing Self is not the king).

Rainbow

Edinger omits the rainbow in his selection of motifs examined. This rainbow is described as "round about the throne, in sight like unto an emerald." It is the *inner* circle about the throne, with the thrones of the elders the *outer*.

The symbolism of the rainbow is taken from Genesis 9:12–15 and the myth of Noah and the flood:

> "And God said, This is the token of the covenant which I make between me and you and every living creature that is with you, for perpetual generations: I do set my bow in the cloud, and it shall be for a token of a covenant between me and the earth. And it shall come to pass, when I bring a cloud over the earth, that the bow shall be seen in the cloud: And I will remember my covenant, which is between me and you and every living creature of all flesh; and the waters shall no more become a flood to destroy all flesh."

As J. Daniel Gunther points out in *Initiation in the Aeon of the Child* p. 148:

> "The rainbow thus became a beautiful symbol of promise, appearing in the sky after the storm, a reminder of a covenant between God and Man. Alchemists seized upon this symbolism, readily identifying the rainbow with the many colors of the Peacock's tail... at the end of the Nigredo, the dark

phase of the Great Work, a light of many colors appeared in the cucurbite. This they called the "rainbow" or "Peacock's Tail." It announced the end of the first phase, the Nigredo, and promised the appearance of the Albedo or "Whitening," which is the second phase of the Work."

The *albedo* has been discussed before, here referring to the throne and king. The emerald here, reminds us the Work is the Emerald Tablet, the Philosopher's stone, the Great Work. It is the promise of Self or Godhead after the storm, for "out of the throne proceeded lightnings and thunderings and voices" (Rev. 4:5). The rainbow of promise is the promise of the divine spark of Illumination (realization of Self), ie. emerald, "bright green precious stone," c. 1300, *emeraude*, from Old French *esmeraude* (12c.), from Medieval Latin *esmaraldus*, from Latin *smaragdus*, from Greek *smaragdos* "green gem" (emerald or malachite), from Semitic *baraq* "shine" (compare Hebrew *bareqeth* "emerald," Arabic *barq* "lightning").

Sea of glass

Before the throne is "a sea of glass like unto crystal." The mandala is the heavenly prototype of the earthly Temple at Jerusalem. What John sees corresponds to the Jerusalem tabernacle or temple. Outside the Temple was a water basin known as the "sea" or the "Bronze Sea" which was used for ritual washings.

Psychologically, the sea of glass represents the current rational consciousness and world view, a reflection of one's level of realization of Self, capable of being shattered or broken to make room for a larger world view by greater realization. In this sense, literal glass is the earthly (ego) equivalent of the heavenly sea of glass (archetypal) before Yahweh's throne.

Four beasts

The four beasts (KJV) are alternatively described as "four animals" (Jerusalem Bible) and "living creatures" (New Jerusalem Bible), "in the midst and round about the throne." NJB makes this description quite clear, "in the middle of the throne and around it."

"And before the throne there was a sea of glass like unto crystal: and in the midst of the throne, and round about the throne, were four beasts full of eyes before and behind. And the first beast was like a lion, and the second beast like a calf, and the third beast had a face as a man, and the fourth beast was like a flying eagle. And the four beasts had each of them six wings about him; and they were full of eyes within: and they rest not day and night, saying, Holy, holy, holy, Lord God Almighty, which was, and is, and is to come. And when those beasts give glory and honour and thanks to him that sat on the throne, who liveth for ever and ever," Rev. 4:6-9

This references Ezekiel's 'chariot vision' (cf. Ezek. 4-28). As both Jung and Edinger note (*Mysterium Coniunctionis, The Mysterium Lectures*), this prominent image of Merkabah mysticism and the qabalah became the basic image of the Christian mandala in the form of the four evangelists supporting the throne of Christ. I would add that this explains how the 'four' can be both "in the middle" and "around." The middle (5th) is the realized Self/Christ on the throne, the living Christ. Whereas we have three theriomorphic and one human creature, reflecting the degree of humanization of the God image, the fifth is the Imago Dei that man must share the throne with. This centrality is generated by the circulating formula.

This is explained by the beasts having "six wings" "full of eyes" in Revelation, compared with Ezekiel's "four wings." These relate to dynamic levels of vibration, energy, dimensions or layers to the psyche. Whereas the archetype of four relates to manifestation, foundation and the terrestrial (the elemental instincts), for those who can turn (look) within (wings "full of eyes within"), that is, to turn toward the center, be present ("rest not day and night") to integrate and consecrate/dedicate the onslaught of instincts ("Holy, holy, holy, Lord God Almighty, which was, and is, and is to come"), ie. to shatter the sea of glass (expand the conscious worldview to embrace the divine), a 5th principle emerges (ie. "when those beasts give glory and honour and thanks to him that sat on the throne, who liveth for ever and ever") that enables the archetype of six, the man-god, the Sun, the realization of the presence of the Lord, being present in Self which is to share the throne.

In psychological terms the six wings represent the (Jungian) six major stages in the evolution of the God image – animism, matriarchy, hierarchy polytheism, tribal monotheism, universal monotheism and individuation. These are both a historical sequence and layers of the collective Unconscious in the individual psyche. In doctrinal Thelema, these six stages are expressed by the three Aeons. Both Crowley and Jung embraced Ernst Haeckel's phrase "ontogeny recapitulates phylogeny" (known as the theory of recapitulation, the biogenetic law or embryological parallelism), ie. that vestiges of evolutionary development are repeated in human embryological development. The same happens in the development of the psyche. Individuation is a process of integrating these as a harmonic whole, as differentiated from the blindly conscious and unconscious life experience of these compartmentalized.

The individuated stage of awareness is represented by the 'activated' twenty four elders, a new mindset or metanoia ("The four and twenty elders fall down before him that sat on the throne" Rev. 4:10), a devotion and awareness to the eternal presence of Self within ("and worship him that liveth for ever and ever, and cast their crowns before the throne" Rev. 4:10).

These verses depict a union between the terrestrial and the spiritual, as understood (that is, emphasized and prioritized) in the christian aeon.

Apocalyptic Lamb

The lamb with its archetype of seven features (seven horns, seven eyes "which are the seven Spirits of God sent forth into all the earth") appears in the midst of the throne, the four beasts and the twenty four elders. It appears after one of the elders says "Weep not: behold, the Lion of the tribe of Judah, the Root of David, hath prevailed to open the book, and to loose the seven seals thereof" Rev. 5.5.

The implication is that this lamb is the Lion, a Messianic title going back to Genesis (cf. Gen. 49:9), the sevenfold nature of deity consolidated in its image. This seems a clear reference to John 1.29 when the Baptist declares "The next day John seeth Jesus coming unto him, and saith, Behold the Lamb of God, which taketh away the sins of the world." The lamb is now the central figure in the throne mandala of the prior chapter, its dual nature (lion and lamb) representing the antitheses, the double nature of the apocalyptic Christ, King or Messiah. When we encounter Self (note the metanoia, "the four beasts and four and twenty elders *fell down* before the Lamb" Rev. 5:8.), such opposites are part of its phenomenology.

While first "stood a Lamb as it had been slain," it is now proclaimed "thou wast slain, and hast redeemed us to God by thy blood out of every kindred, and tongue, and people, and nation;" and "Worthy is the Lamb that was slain to receive power, and riches, and wisdom, and strength, and honour, and glory, and blessing." The lamb represents the slain ego anointed by Self. Only through this new awareness can one open the book of life, "to loose the seals thereof" which is the sevenfold nature of deity, becoming "the Lion of the tribe of Judah, the Root of David."

Note the ongoing motif of "eyes" that is a crucial element of the Apocalypse archetype. This represents the coming of Self into visibility and its accompanying ego experience of being looked at, *for exactly what one is*, stripped of all blinds. This partakes of the 'final judgment' motif, an archetypal psychic reality.

Another motif crucial to the Apocalypse archetype is the sacrificed or slain (lamb). Sacrifice has tremendous power, and in the era of Revelation, implied is the blood sacrifice, "for thou wast slain, and hast redeemed us to God by thy blood out of every kindred, and tongue, and people, and nation" Rev. 5:9.

Jung comments (cf. 'Transformation symbolism in the Mass') that to sacrifice something as an offering carries with it a personal claim of receiving something in return. One needs to be conscious of this claim, or what has not been owned cannot be given up. Every sacrifice is to some extent self-sacrifice, the greater this is, the greater the resultant ego personality revolt. The sacrificer, ultimately, is the Self, the ego-human the sacrificed gift. Sacrifice allows the Self to enter into manifestation, thus passing from unconsciousness to consciousness, from potentiality to actuality. It (God) becomes man. Sacrifice is therefore part of the incarnation myth. The lamb brings Self to man.

Revelation 6, 7

The Archetype of Seven

Seven is a recurring motif in Revelation, and indeed Jung considered numbers to be archetypes. Edinger states that seven "symbolizes the process of psychological transformation: movement through a series of stages as part of an initiatory process." Seven is a Self-based dynamic sequence, leading to an experience of Self from the standpoint of the Self. The apocalyptic process, treated psychologically, is the coming of Self into conscious realization. We may extend that, with seven in mind, by saying *through its own terms*.

The Four Horsemen

> "And I saw, and behold a white horse: and he that sat on him had a bow; and a crown was given unto him: and he went forth conquering, and to conquer.

And when he had opened the second seal, I heard the second beast say, Come and see.

And there went out another horse that was red: and power was given to him that sat thereon to take peace from the earth, and that they should kill one another: and there was given unto him a great sword.

And when he had opened the third seal, I heard the third beast say, Come and see. And I beheld, and lo a black horse; and he that sat on him had a pair of balances in his hand.

And I heard a voice in the midst of the four beasts say, A measure of wheat for a penny, and three measures of barley for a penny; and see thou hurt not the oil and the wine.

And when he had opened the fourth seal, I heard the voice of the fourth beast say, Come and see.

And I looked, and behold a pale horse: and his name that sat on him was Death, and Hell followed with him. And power was given unto them over the fourth part of the earth, to kill with sword, and with hunger, and with death, and with the beasts of the earth." Rev. 6:2-8

There is a passage that parallels this, in the OT Zechariah 8:

> "I saw by night, and behold a man riding upon a red horse, and he stood among the myrtle trees that were in the bottom; and behind him were there red horses, speckled, and white."

The New Jerusalem Bible gives this as "four chariots", the first with red horses, then black, white and piebald. The angel identifies these as the "four winds of heaven" that "patrol the world." This approximates the colors of Revelation (white, red, black and pale horses), archetypal renditions of the alchemical *nigredo* (black), *albedo* (white), *rubedo* (red) and perhaps *citrenius* (gold), as apprehended in these cultural eras. That is, a psychological condition.

We have a formula here similar to that of the four beasts, of the "three plus one." In that case we had three animal headed beasts and one with the head of a man, and in both Revelation and Zechariah we have three straight-forward colors and one "pale" (NJB Rev.) or "speckled" (NJB Zach.). Edinger points out that the word for "pale" is actually *kloros* or "green," here treated as the color of cadavers. Psychologically, returning to the alchemical theme, this represents *benedicta viriditas*, "blessed greenness," signifying new growth. "And I looked, and behold a pale horse: and his name that sat on him was Death." (Consider Rev. 14:13 Blessed *are* the dead which die in the Lord from henceforth;"). "It is wrong to say triumphantly, "*Mors janua vitæ*, unless you add with equal triumph, '*Vita janua mortis.*'" ie. "Death is the gate to life" and "Life is the gate to death." (Cf. Crowley, *Book Four*, Part III) This "new growth", then, is the Neophyte – from the Greek *neophutos*, literally 'newly planted.' For green, see as well the section on the Rainbow, above.

Jung discusses the three plus one formula as it applies in the saying of Maria Prophetissa, "one becomes two, two becomes three and out of the third comes one as the fourth" (cf. *Psychology and Alchemy*), ie. there are three differentiated functions of consciousness which need a fourth function for psychological wholeness. This fourth function is inferior, or ambiguous as it is closer to man and man's coming into realization of Self (the onset of death from the egoic point of view), a calamitous affair ("And power was given unto them over the fourth part of the earth, to kill with sword, and with hunger, and with death, and with the beasts of the earth.").

Psychologically then, the main theme is this "three plus one" psychic state. (Consider also, "A measure of wheat for a penny, and three measures of barley for a penny; and see thou hurt not the oil and the wine" ie. consecration to Self, let the rider of the pale horse accomplish his task, in due course).

Beyond this underlying formula, there is no consensus among scholars or analysts on how to interpret the horsemen, and numerous associations can be made of their accompanying symbolism. Their psychic reality however, is self-evident in the enduring and popular reference to the motif throughout the ages.

Vengeance of the Saints

> "And when he had opened the fifth seal, I saw under the altar the souls of them that were slain for the word of God, and for the testimony which they held:

And they cried with a loud voice, saying, How long, O Lord, holy and true, dost thou not judge and avenge our blood on them that dwell on the earth?

And white robes were given unto every one of them; and it was said unto them, that they should rest yet for a little season, until their fellow servants also and their brethren, that should be killed as they were, should be fulfilled." Rev. 6:9-11

The souls of Revelation are impatient, reminiscent of the "chambered" souls in the apocryphal Jewish apocalypse 4 Ezra (2 Edras) waiting for salvation. As Jung commented in *Answer to Job*, this hints that God (or Self) must follow a pre-existing pattern, ie. an archetype is an ancient, pre-existing pattern of the psyche. The vengeance described in Revelation, typical of Yaweh (cf. Deuteronomy 32:40-42, Jeremiah 46:10, Nahum 1:2-6) points to the fact, as Edinger asserts, that the book is largely Jewish with a Christian overlay. In *Answer to Job* Jung suggests the first advent of Christ was meant to transform Yahweh, but the second advent – preparation for the Second Coming of Christ – which Revelation concerns itself with, brings back the untransformed God-image.

Jung takes this up with the sixth seal, writing in *Answer to Job*, that we have the wrath of the lamb, "For the great day of his wrath is come; and who shall be able to stand?" Rev. 6:17. Jung writes "We no longer recognize the meek Lamb…there is only the aggressive and irascible ram whose rage can at last be vented." The Christian project was meant to construct a (one-sided) veneer over the individual psyche where the Yahwistic libido is transformed. Such a project was destined to fail, as it has. As Jung wrote, "One does not become enlightened by imagining figures of light, but by making the darkness conscious" (Cf. *Alchemical Studies*). That darkness is mediated by a consciousness that knows its true nature, the project of Thelema. The darkness is a psychic fact of the objective psyche, a pre-existing pattern of the collective psyche.

Stars falling from Heaven

"And I beheld when he had opened the sixth seal, and, lo, there was a great earthquake; and the sun became black as sackcloth of hair, and the moon became as blood;

And the stars of heaven fell unto the earth, even as a fig tree casteth her untimely figs, when she is shaken of a mighty wind.

And the heaven departed as a scroll when it is rolled together; and every mountain and island were moved out of their places.

And the kings of the earth, and the great men, and the rich men, and the chief captains, and the mighty men, and every bondman, and every free man, hid themselves in the dens and in the rocks of the mountains;

And said to the mountains and rocks, Fall on us, and hide us from the face of him that sitteth on the throne, and from the wrath of the Lamb:

For the great day of his wrath is come; and who shall be able to stand?" Rev 6:12-17

The "stars" are archetypal entities that fall to "earth" (into the ego). This is the spiritual aspect of the collective Unconscious falling into the material, or erupting into consciousness, "even as a fig tree casteth her untimely figs, when she is shaken of a mighty wind."

Sealed in the forehead

"And after these things I saw four angels standing on the four corners of the earth, holding the four winds of the earth, that the wind should not blow on the earth, nor on the sea, nor on any tree.

And I saw another angel ascending from the east, having the seal of the living God: and he cried with a loud voice to the four angels, to whom it was given to hurt the earth and the sea,

Saying, Hurt not the earth, neither the sea, nor the trees, till we have sealed the servants of our God in their foreheads.

And I heard the number of them which were sealed: and there were sealed an hundred and forty and four thousand of all the tribes of the children of Israel." Rev. 7:1-4

The archetype of twelve is represented here, sealed with "the seal of the living God." This archetype may be seen here as representing the terrestrial and the celestial (ie. zodiac), that is, the Self is manifesting in the earthly sphere.

The sealing parallels the attack of divine vengeance in Jerusalem, of Ezek. 9:2-6:

> "And, behold, six men came from the way of the higher gate, which lieth toward the north, and every man a slaughter weapon in his hand; and one man among them was clothed with linen, with a writer's inkhorn by his side: and they went in, and stood beside the brasen altar.

> And the glory of the God of Israel was gone up from the cherub, whereupon he was, to the threshold of the house. And he called to the man clothed with linen, which had the writer's inkhorn by his side;

> And the Lord said unto him, Go through the midst of the city, through the midst of Jerusalem, and set a mark upon the foreheads of the men that sigh and that cry for all the abominations that be done in the midst thereof.

> And to the others he said in mine hearing, Go ye after him through the city, and smite: let not your eye spare, neither have ye pity:

> Slay utterly old and young, both maids, and little children, and women: but come not near any man upon whom is the mark; and begin at my sanctuary.

Then they began at the ancient men which were before the house."

There is also the mark of Cain, of Genesis 4:14-15:

"Behold, thou hast driven me out this day from the face of the earth; and from thy face shall I be hid; and I shall be a fugitive and a vagabond in the earth; and it shall come to pass, that every one that findeth me shall slay me.

And the Lord said unto him, Therefore whosoever slayeth Cain, vengeance shall be taken on him sevenfold. And the Lord set a mark upon Cain, lest any finding him should kill him."

In this passage of Revelation, the mark appears in a positive manner as a mark of salvation. That only a certain number ("an hundred and forty and four thousand") of those entitled to wear white robes, are marked, suggests a special calling or marking, a distinction, such as between the laity and clergy. Not everybody is called for inner levels of the individuation process, that is, to become an individual through active participation and progress through the psychological process, and to serve this process. For example, consider Mark 4:11 and similar passages about the disciples, "And he said unto them, Unto you it is given to know the mystery of the kingdom of God: but unto them that are without, all *these* things are done in parables:."

It is to these the seals are loosed (the developmental levels of archetype of the collective Unconscious) so that the scroll (of life) is unfolded, that is, coming into conscious realization of the unfolding Unconscious.

Robes washed in the lamb's blood

> "And one of the elders answered, saying unto me, What are these which are arrayed in white robes? and whence came they?
>
> And I said unto him, Sir, thou knowest. And he said to me, These are they which came out of great tribulation, and have washed their robes, and made them white in the blood of the Lamb.
>
> Therefore are they before the throne of God, and serve him day and night in his temple: and he that sitteth on the throne shall dwell among them.
>
> They shall hunger no more, neither thirst any more; neither shall the sun light on them, nor any heat.
>
> For the Lamb which is in the midst of the throne shall feed them, and shall lead them unto living fountains of waters: and God shall wipe away all tears from their eyes." Rev. 7:13-17

This is baptism imagery (the baptized in early Christianity were clothed in a white robe). As I noted in the previous installment (*Ora et Labora* III), the NT scholar Morton Smith has also pointed out (cf. *Jesus the Magician, The Secret Gospel*) that a baptism rite was a secret baptism/initiation conducted by Jesus for some of his followers, enabling them to enter the Kingdom of heaven. The washing of the robes in blood references a passage generally held to be Messianic, in Genesis:

> "Binding his foal unto the vine, and his ass's colt unto the choice vine; he washed his garments in wine, and his clothes in the blood of grapes:" Gen. 49:11

A more vengeful Messianic reference can be found in Isaiah:

> "Wherefore art thou red in thine apparel, and thy garments like him that treadeth in the winefat?
>
> I have trodden the winepress alone; and of the people there was none with me: for I will tread them in mine anger, and trample them in my fury; and their blood shall be sprinkled upon my garments, and I will stain all my raiment.
>
> For the day of vengeance is in mine heart, and the year of my redeemed is come." Isaiah. 63:2-4

Psychologically, we have already seen how vengeance relates to the onslaught of instinct, and to survive this

act of martyrdom to Self. An inverted psychological viewpoint can be found in the Manichaean doctrine of Suffering Jesus (*Jesus patibilis*) - identical to the World Soul and the Living Self, which is the light that is imprisoned in matter, depicted as crucified in the world.

The key to a psychological interpretation can be found in the prohibitions of Deuteronomy and Leviticus:

> "Only be sure that thou eat not the blood: for the blood is the life; and thou mayest not eat the life with the flesh." Deut. 12:23

> "For *it is* the life of all flesh; the blood of it *is* for the life thereof: therefore I said unto the children of Israel, Ye shall eat the blood of no manner of flesh: for the life of all flesh *is* the blood thereof: whosoever eateth it shall be cut off." Leviticus 17:14.

Earlier I wrote that "The lamb represents the slain ego anointed by Self. Only through this new awareness can one open the book of life, "to loose the seals thereof" which is the sevenfold nature of deity, becoming "the Lion of the tribe of Judah, the Root of David." The martyrs, the marked ones who have sacrificed the Ego to Self, are identified with the lamb who is close to God, the individuated personality that has subjugated the ego and is aligned or close to the universal Self.

Revelation: Chapters 8, 9, 10

The Incense Altar

> "And I saw the seven angels which stood before God;
> and to them were given seven trumpets.
>
> And another angel came and stood at the altar, having
> a golden censer; and there was given unto him much
> incense, that he should offer it with the prayers of all
> saints upon the golden altar which was before the
> throne.
>
> And the smoke of the incense, which came with the
> prayers of the saints, ascended up before God out of the
> angel's hand." Rev. 8:2-4

The setting of Revelation reflects the Jerusalem Temple.
It is its heavenly template. The cubical room is the Holy
of Holies, containing the ark of the covenant with the
mercy seat on its top, flanked by two huge cherubim.
On the other side of the door or veil is the Holy Place
or sanctuary, where is the lampstand, shewbread and the
altar of incense. (The brass basin or "sea," and the altar
of burnt animal sacrifice are outside these temple
precincts).

Exodus gives the instructions for the altar and incense:

> "And thou shalt make an altar to burn incense upon: of
> shittim wood shalt thou make it.

A cubit shall be the length thereof, and a cubit the
breadth thereof; foursquare shall it be: and two cubits
shall be the height thereof: the horns thereof shall be of
the same.

And thou shalt overlay it with pure gold, the top
thereof, and the sides thereof round about, and the
horns thereof; and thou shalt make unto it a crown of
gold round about.

And two golden rings shalt thou make to it under the
crown of it, by the two corners thereof, upon the two
sides of it shalt thou make it; and they shall be for
places for the staves to bear it withal.

And thou shalt make the staves of shittim wood, and
overlay them with gold.

And thou shalt put it before the vail that is by the ark
of the testimony, before the mercy seat that is over the
testimony, where I will meet with thee.

And Aaron shall burn thereon sweet incense every
morning: when he dresseth the lamps, he shall burn
incense upon it.

And when Aaron lighteth the lamps at even, he shall burn incense upon it, a perpetual incense before the Lord throughout your generations." Exodus 30:1-8

"And the Lord said unto Moses, Take unto thee sweet spices, stacte, and onycha, and galbanum; these sweet spices with pure frankincense: of each shall there be a like weight:

And thou shalt make it a perfume, a confection after the art of the apothecary, tempered together, pure and holy:

And thou shalt beat some of it very small, and put of it before the testimony in the tabernacle of the congregation, where I will meet with thee: it shall be unto you most holy.

And as for the perfume which thou shalt make, ye shall not make to yourselves according to the composition thereof: it shall be unto thee holy for the Lord." Exodus 30: 34-37

A curious point is that Leviticus (cf. 10: 1-3) demonstrates the wrath of Yahweh for incorrect censing. Psychologically, the act of censing represents the transpersonal libido in the hands of the ego. The scriptural injunctions symbolize that the libido must be handled carefully. Error relates to the difficulty in recognizing the libido in its burst of energy, inspiration, gifts and capacities.

Edinger poses the interesting question in our passage from Revelation of why a censer is needed in heaven? The only logical conclusion is that it operates in a reverse direction, distributing divine fire onto the earth.

Fire thrown to earth

"And the smoke of the incense, which came with the prayers of the saints, ascended up before God out of the angel's hand.

And the angel took the censer, and filled it with fire of the altar, and cast it into the earth: and there were voices, and thunderings, and lightnings, and an earthquake." Rev. 8:4-5

Although the smoke "ascended up before God," fire of the altar is cast into the earth. We find similar imagery in Ezekiel 10.2: "And he spake unto the man clothed with linen, and said, Go in between the wheels, even under the cherub, and fill thine hand with coals of fire from between the cherubims, and scatter them over the city. And he went in in my sight" and more obviously Luke 12:49 "I am come to send fire on the earth;" ("send" is translated "bring" in the NJB).

The transpersonal libido in the hands of the ego, when recognized (realized) as Self brings heavenly fire to earth (ego), an outcome in the quest for wholeness that may be perceived from the point of view of the ego as destructive and earth-shattering: "thunderings, and lightnings, and an earthquake." The Unconscious appears as both heaven and hell. This is humanity's greatest *paradoxia*: the ascent to God – realization of Self – requires the descent into hell.

One third

"The first angel sounded, and there followed hail and fire mingled with blood, and they were cast upon the earth: and the third part of trees was burnt up, and all green grass was burnt up.

And the second angel sounded, and as it were a great mountain burning with fire was cast into the sea: and the third part of the sea became blood;

And the third part of the creatures which were in the sea, and had life, died; and the third part of the ships were destroyed.

And the third angel sounded, and there fell a great star from heaven, burning as it were a lamp, and it fell upon the third part of the rivers, and upon the fountains of waters;

And the name of the star is called Wormwood: and the third part of the waters became wormwood; and many men died of the waters, because they were made bitter. And the fourth angel sounded, and the third part of the sun was smitten, and the third part of the moon, and the third part of the stars; so as the third part of them was darkened, and the day shone not for a third part of it, and the night likewise.

And I beheld, and heard an angel flying through the midst of heaven, saying with a loud voice, Woe, woe, woe, to the inhabiters of the earth by reason of the other voices of the trumpet of the three angels, which are yet to sound!" Rev. 8:7-13

We now encounter the archetype of three in the form of division into three. This represents the dialectic, of opposites manifesting (conflicting) and resolving (reconciling) in a third. This reflects how ego consciousness organizes and experiences its experience and behavior. In other words, these assaults on the earth (ego) symbolize the ego being forced into the full experience of being conscious – to experience the *separatio* of manifest duality and seek resolution. The ego (or what will be left of the ego) must be grounded if it is to survive the apocalyptic encounter of realization of Self.

It is only after the one third experience that one can encounter the abyss, in Rev. 9.

The Abyss Unlocked

> "And the fifth angel sounded, and I saw a star fall from heaven unto the earth: and to him was given the key of the bottomless pit.
>
> And he opened the bottomless pit; and there arose a smoke out of the pit, as the smoke of a great furnace; and the sun and the air were darkened by reason of the smoke of the pit.
>
> And there came out of the smoke locusts upon the earth: and unto them was given power, as the scorpions of the earth have power." Rev. 9:1-3

Edinger and Ford (J. Massyngberde Ford's 'Revelation' piece in the *Anchor Bible*) note that the term abyss (in Hebrew, *tihom*) has overlapping terms or meanings: "Hades," "the land of the dead," the "Gehenna" valley south of Jerusalem, once a place for burning human sacrifices and later burning rubbish. From the latter is the psychological motif of a "place of fiery punishment." It illustrates how the psyche has described its own "depth." More literally, tehom referred to the primordial ocean that spread over the earth, the deep abode of the sea dragon (Yahweh's enemy), the earth – meaning a pit which is a place of intermediate punishment, and a fiery place beyond earth and heaven that was the temporary residence of fallen angels. The opening and sealing of the abyss features in numerous Jewish texts.

The abyss and its inhabitants represent transpersonal powers of darkness – autonomous, unconscious complexes with archetypal cores, energized by the untransformed (that is, unrealized) primordial psyche. Individuation requires one to live in this "hell" ("a star fall from heaven" - the ego bound psyche) so demonic complexes undergo resolution ("and to him was given the key of the bottomless pit") – hell has been depopulated because it has been penetrated by consciousness. A consciousness that somewhat realizes its origins in heaven.

Locusts upon the earth

> "And there came out of the smoke locusts upon the earth: and unto them was given power, as the scorpions of the earth have power." Rev. 9:3

These locusts are described a few verses later:

> "And the shapes of the locusts were like unto horses prepared unto battle; and on their heads were as it were crowns like gold, and their faces were as the faces of men.

> And they had hair as the hair of women, and their teeth were as the teeth of lions.

And they had breastplates, as it were breastplates of iron; and the sound of their wings was as the sound of chariots of many horses running to battle.

And they had tails like unto scorpions, and there were stings in their tails: and their power was to hurt men five months." Rev. 9:7-10

The imagery is based upon the OT Book of Joel 1:2-9:

"Hear this, you elders; listen, all who live in the land. Has anything like this ever happened in your days or in the days of your ancestors? Tell it to your children, and let your children tell it to their children, and their children to the next generation. What the locust swarm has left the great locusts have eaten; what the great locusts have left the young locusts have eaten; what the young locusts have left other locusts have eaten. Wake up, you drunkards, and weep! Wail, all you drinkers of wine; wail because of the new wine, for it has been snatched from your lips. A nation has invaded my land, a mighty army without number; it has the teeth of a lion, the fangs of a lioness. It has laid waste my vines and ruined my fig trees. It has stripped off their bark and thrown it away, leaving their branches white. Mourn like a virgin in sackcloth grieving for the betrothed of her youth. Grain offerings and drink offerings are cut off from the house of the Lord. The

priests are in mourning, those who minister before the
Lord."

Ford suggests that Joel is playing on words, the Hebrew
word *hargol* ("locust") resembling the Arabic word *harjal*
("troops'), an association not lost on Near Eastern
peoples. It implies an invading army on the great Day of
Yahweh.

The implication for Revelation is that the locusts are an
invasion of demonic forces activated by the Apocalypse
archetype. The various plagues of Revelation called
down by the trumpet blasts parallel the OT plagues of
Egypt e.g. thunder, hail and fire (Ex. 9:13-35 cf. First
trumpet), Nile turned to blood (Ex. 7:14-24 cf. Second
trumpet), darkness for three days (Ex. 10:21-29 cf.
Fourth trumpet and the 'one third' archetype), locusts
(Ex. 10:1-20 cf. Fifth trumpet) or at other times reverse
them. Yahweh's imposition of the plagues upon Egypt
freed the Israelites from bondage, eventually leading
them to the promised land. If we consider Revelation, as
stated before, essentially a Jewish apocalypse, the plagues
that beset Israel's enemy are now applied to Israel itself.
The plagues are a response from the Unconscious to
ego tyranny ("Pharaoh", cf. Edinger, *The Bible and the
Psyche*), an ego blind to any inner, psychic agency
(other than itself). In Revelation this state is now applied
to the Jews.

This generalized condition only applies to those with a disparity between consciousness and the accumulated energies of the Unconscious – there is an intense polarization between the two psychic realms. A civilization whose collective psyche has lost connection to the transpersonal psyche is also fertile ground for the same imagery to arise, as we see in the prophets and reformers, and in the various apocalypses, when psychic dominants fail and precursory to new dominants arising.

Eating of the Scroll

The archetype of Seven is now to be assimilated. With the "mighty angel come down from heaven" there comes a myriad of archetypal symbolism; the rainbow (of promise) and sun return, the Angel standing on the elemental foundations of fire, sea (water) and earth. His voice "as when a lion roareth" (cf. Rev. 5. 5) initiates the revelation of the seven thunders, prompting the heavenly voice – the archetype of eight, the heavenly, eternal and infinite Self – to both encourage and caution.

> "And the voice which I heard from heaven spake unto me again, and said, Go and take the little book which is open in the hand of the angel which standeth upon the sea and upon the earth.

And I went unto the angel, and said unto him, Give me
the little book. And he said unto me, Take it, and eat it
up; and it shall make thy belly bitter, but it shall be in
thy mouth sweet as honey.

And I took the little book out of the angel's hand, and
ate it up; and it was in my mouth sweet as honey: and
as soon as I had eaten it, my belly was bitter.

And he said unto me, Thou must prophesy again
before many peoples, and nations, and tongues, and
kings." Rev. 10:8-11

This derives explicitly from Ezekiel:

"But thou, son of man, hear what I say unto thee; Be
not thou rebellious like that rebellious house: open thy
mouth, and eat that I give thee.

And when I looked, behold, an hand was sent unto me;
and, lo, a roll of a book was therein;

And he spread it before me; and it was written within
and without: and there was written therein
lamentations, and mourning, and woe.

Moreover he said unto me, Son of man, eat that thou
findest; eat this roll, and go speak unto the house of
Israel.

So I opened my mouth, and he caused me to eat that roll.

And he said unto me, Son of man, cause thy belly to eat, and fill thy bowels with this roll that I give thee. Then did I eat it; and it was in my mouth as honey for sweetness.

And he said unto me, Son of man, go, get thee unto the house of Israel, and speak with my words unto them." Ezekiel 2:8-3:4

Content is being offered by the Unconscious so as to "eat it up" or to be assimilated by the ego. We see here the twofold symbolism of the mouth, receptive (to consume and transform into its own substance) and expressive (to utter the creative word or logos). This intimates the connection between "food" and "word," a common biblical motif and one aspect of the motif of the Eucharist:

"And he humbled thee, and suffered thee to hunger, and fed thee with manna, which thou knewest not, neither did thy fathers know; that he might make thee know that man doth not live by bread only, but by every word that proceedeth out of the mouth of the Lord doth man live." Deuteronomy 8:3

"Come, eat of my bread, and drink of the wine which
I have mingled." Proverbs 9:5

"And as a mother shall she meet him, and receive him
as a wife married of a virgin. With the bread of
understanding shall she feed him, and give him the
water of wisdom to drink." Ecclesiasticus 15:2-3

The process of assimilation (or realization of Self) can be
"bitter" as new content is digested. Only through its
transformation, a recurring theme in Revelation, can the
new creative word "prophesy again, before many
peoples, and nations, and tongues, and kings."

Revelation 11, 12, 13

Measuring the Temple

"And there was given me a reed like unto a rod: and the
angel stood, saying, Rise, and measure the temple of
God, and the altar, and them that worship therein.

But the court which is without the temple leave out,
and measure it not; for it is given unto the Gentiles:
and the holy city shall they tread under foot forty and
two months." Rev. 11:1-2

An indicator of how to read this chapter is given in
Ezekiel 40, the 'Vision of the Temple.' At the time of
this vision the Temple had been destroyed. Yet, the

description and dimensions are so clear that some biblical resources provide diagrams of this visionary Temple.

The visionary Ezekiel Temple plan drawn by the 19th-century French architect and Bible scholar Charles Chipiez

At the time of John's vision, the Temple had been destroyed by Titus in 70 CE. John is therefore being told to measure a visionary Temple. John is here an active participant in the divine drama. The ego must participate in the construction of the "temple" of Self. This transforms the "kingdom" of the ego, "The kingdoms of this world are become the kingdoms of our Lord, and of his Christ; and he shall reign for ever and ever." (Rev. 11:15) This participation and transformation 'opens' the 'closed' Temple of God, "And the temple of God was opened in heaven, and there was seen in his temple the ark of his testament: and there were lightnings, and voices, and thunderings, and an earthquake, and great hail." (Rev. 11:19) The "kingdoms of our Lord" and the "Temple of God" indicate a two-way process of tremendous psychological import. I described this once in one of my old lectures as, "Self gets humanized by its connection to ego, and ego deified by its connection to Self." This indicates the apprehension and construction of the Temple mandala, by heaven *and* earth, of man and God. "Thy kingdom come. Thy will be done in earth, as *it is* in heaven." Matt. 6:10.

Sun-Moon Woman

"And there appeared a great wonder in heaven; a woman clothed with the sun, and the moon under her feet, and upon her head a crown of twelve stars:

And she being with child cried, travailing in birth, and pained to be delivered.

And there appeared another wonder in heaven; and behold a great red dragon, having seven heads and ten horns, and seven crowns upon his heads.

And his tail drew the third part of the stars of heaven, and did cast them to the earth: and the dragon stood before the woman which was ready to be delivered, for to devour her child as soon as it was born.

And she brought forth a man child, who was to rule all nations with a rod of iron: and her child was caught up unto God, and to his throne.

And the woman fled into the wilderness, where she hath a place prepared of God, that they should feed her there a thousand two hundred and threescore days." Rev. 12:1-6.

This passage is unique in that beyond the reference to "a man child, who was to rule all nations with a rod of iron," *there are no other discernible biblical references*. We should however remember that this passage was prefaced by Rev. 11:19 "And the temple of God was opened in heaven, and there was seen in his temple the ark of his testament: and there were lightnings, and voices, and thunderings, and an earthquake, and great hail." In other words, as per Barker (cf. *The Revelation of Jesus Christ*), there are resonances with the Jewish text Numbers Rabbah XV:10, which states the ark will be restored to the Temple in the time of the Messiah. In Revelation is a vision of his birth. The Woman clothed with the Sun is the Queen of Heaven, the ancient

Goddess of Jerusalem (see my first 'Apokalypsis' essay and the works of Barker) also the motifs of Mother Zion, the Daughter of Zion, the Lady Wisdom, and the suppressed Asherah. This heavenly woman on one level embodies the worship suppressed in Deuteronomy "of the sun, and the moon, and the stars, even all the host of heaven" (Deut. 4.19). Psychologically, the worship being restored in order for the Messiah to be born – in order to be anointed by Self – is the *hieros gamos*, "whose fruit is a divine man-child" (Jung, *Answer to Job*).

Archetypally, as Jung noted in *Answer to Job*, Rev. 12's imagery references the myth of Leto, and the birth of Apollo, who was also pursued by a dragon (Python). Apollo would eventually slay Python. Leto is connected to the Sun (Apollo) and twin Artemis (celestially seen here as Moon), Edinger commenting the sun-moon *coniunctio* existed unconsciously in the womb of Leto. Artemis and Apollo were born on the floating island of Delos (ie. not yet existing in conscious manifestation). The connection with Revelation, Edinger concludes, is somewhat reversed, here the child in Revelation representing a union of opposites (sun-moon) that had previously separated. For Jung, this son of Revelation is the *complexio oppositorum*, a uniting symbol, a totality of life. As the child was "caught up unto God" Jung felt this was *latent and reserved for the future* (cf. *Answer to Job*).

In terms of future analysis, Jung's other remarks are instructive. I quote at length:

> "The fact that John uses the myth of Leto and Apollo in describing the birth may be an indication that the vision, in contrast to the Christian tradition, is a product of the unconscious. But in the unconscious is everything that has been rejected by consciousness, and the more Christian one's consciousness is, the more heathenly does the unconscious behave, if in the rejected heathenism there are values which are important for life – if, that is to say, the baby has been thrown out with the bath water, as so often happens."
> (cf. *Answer to Job*)

This is more striking in terms of Revelation's impact over the ages, if we consider this child of the future is the symbol of wholeness, totality, the *coniunctio*, the baby.

War in Heaven

> "And there was war in heaven: Michael and his angels fought against the dragon; and the dragon fought and his angels,
>
> And prevailed not; neither was their place found any more in heaven.

And the great dragon was cast out, that old serpent, called the Devil, and Satan, which deceiveth the whole world: he was cast out into the earth, and his angels were cast out with him.

And I heard a loud voice saying in heaven, Now is come salvation, and strength, and the kingdom of our God, and the power of his Christ: for the accuser of our brethren is cast down, which accused them before our God day and night.

And they overcame him by the blood of the Lamb, and by the word of their testimony; and they loved not their lives unto the death.

Therefore rejoice, ye heavens, and ye that dwell in them. Woe to the inhabiters of the earth and of the sea! for the devil is come down unto you, having great wrath, because he knoweth that he hath but a short time." Rev. 12:7-12

Psychologically, a decisive split occurs in the Unconscious between the two sides of Godhead, with Satan cast out of heaven and into the earth. The divine entity is split between good and evil, or in Jung's terminology, the second son of Yahweh has been born. There is an echo of Luke 10:18 "And he said unto them, I beheld Satan as lightning fall from heaven." The motif has earlier sources as well. Genesis 6 alludes to the sinful union of the "sons of God" with mortal women, and the Book of Enoch describes "fallen angels" in the days of Noah.

Rev 12:12 above indicates that heaven (the collective unconscious) rids itself of Satan and has come down to earth (the ego). The 'satanic' alludes to the fact that whenever the transpersonal energies touch the ego, they generate inflation.

The Beasts

> "And I stood upon the sand of the sea, and saw a beast rise up out of the sea, having seven heads and ten horns, and upon his horns ten crowns, and upon his heads the name of blasphemy.
>
> And the beast which I saw was like unto a leopard, and his feet were as the feet of a bear, and his mouth as the mouth of a lion: and the dragon gave him his power, and his seat, and great authority." Rev. 13:1-2
>
> "And I beheld another beast coming up out of the earth; and he had two horns like a lamb, and he spake as a dragon.
>
> And he exerciseth all the power of the first beast before him, and causeth the earth and them which dwell therein to worship the first beast, whose deadly wound was healed." Rev. 13:11-12

When the Apocalypse archetype is activated and the Unconscious opens, the coming of Self (and its tumult) evokes both spiritual and beastly (animal) transpersonal energies. The two Beasts have generally been regarded by scholars as references to Leviathan ("from the sea") and Behemoth ("from the ground"). These Beasts first appear in the Book of Job ch. 40-41, "Behold now behemoth, which I made with thee; he eateth grass as an ox. Lo now, his strength is in his loins, and his force is in the navel of his belly." (40:15-16) "Canst thou draw out leviathan with an hook? or his tongue with a cord which thou lettest down?" (41:1) As with Yahweh's display to Job of the images of the primordial psyche, Rev. brings into overt manifestation and visibility the transpersonal energies now invading the ego, including those that rise up from their confinement in hell (the Unconscious), that which balances those that descend from heaven. Job's ordeal was a prelude to the collective ordeal of Revelation. It is significant that Leviathan and Behemoth figure in a number of Jewish and other sources (e.g. the Syrian Apocalypse of Baruch) commonly associated with the advent of the Messiah. Unlike the violent *seperatio* of much of the imagery of Revelation (a necessary psychological process for the stage of development of the collective psyche reflected in the text), the imagery of the advent of the messiah, the Messianic banquet, etc point to a time when the primordial psyche will be assimilated.

Although there is a storehouse of imagery that could be dissected about the two beasts in Rev. 13, I will contain comment to this overarching theme.

666

"Here is wisdom. Let him that hath understanding count the number of the beast: for it is the number of a man; and his number is Six hundred threescore and six." Rev. 13:18.

While the "dragon" "opened his mouth in blasphemy against God, to blaspheme his name, and his tabernacle, and them that dwell in heaven" Rev. 13 then describes "another beast coming up out of the earth; and he had two horns like a lamb, and he spake as a dragon." These 'beasts' arise from the sea and earth, upon which stood the great Angel who told John to "Go and take the little book which is open in the hand of the angel which standeth upon the sea and upon the earth." They represent that bitterness that comes with the realization of Self, the shadow side to the Apocalyptic Christ (wholeness). Therefore the second beast is described as "he had two horns like a lamb, and he spake as a dragon."

There are requirements to worship the "Beast", to succumb to the onslaught of instinct, indeed to worship the same. While there are clear references to Late Roman Emperors, this is also a coping mechanism, an

escape or distraction (denial or projection) of the
bitterness. The "dragon" and the "lamb" indicate that
these two beasts are in fact one in process, one the
transpersonal energy in and of itself, the other that
energy arisen in the individual and collective psyche.
Through ancient number game and philosophy, this is
represented in the much malaligned number '666'-
which has subsequently invaded the psyche and taken
on multiple interpretations and attributions over the
years, usually negative. For Edinger, all of these
manipulations and expositions derive from the marriage
of the first two prime numbers (two and three) and the
addition of the first three (1+2+3). Psychologically, here
these represent the interplay between the Beasts and the
Apocalyptic Christ, of ego and psyche.

We see in the number, treated psychologically and as
commented earlier, "the (Jungian) six major stages in the
evolution of the God image – animism, matriarchy,
hierarchy polytheism, tribal monotheism, universal
monotheism and individuation. These are both a
historical sequence and layers of the collective
Unconscious in the individual psyche." 666 is indeed
"the number of a man." We see the Beast as the
harbinger of the new aeon of individuation, the triple
six emphasizing that beyond the three beasts of
Revelation and the *separatio* of the christian aeon with
its dichotomy of opposites, comes forth an aeon of
individuation or synthesis, of wholeness. With all of the

shadowy (beastly) dangers that assimilation in order to realize Self poses.

Revelation 14, 15, 16

First Fruits

> "And I looked, and, lo, a Lamb stood on the mount Sion, and with him an hundred forty and four thousand, having his Father's name written in their foreheads.
>
> And I heard a voice from heaven, as the voice of many waters, and as the voice of a great thunder: and I heard the voice of harpers harping with their harps:
>
> And they sung as it were a new song before the throne, and before the four beasts, and the elders: and no man could learn that song but the hundred and forty and four thousand, which were redeemed from the earth.
>
> These are they which were not defiled with women; for they are virgins. These are they which follow the Lamb whithersoever he goeth. These were redeemed from among men, being the first fruits unto God and to the Lamb." Rev. 14:1-4

The hundred forty and four thousand, being twelve squared times a thousand, represents the archetype of twelve as a totality or whole. As already seen, these are the elect martyrs, sacrificed for following the (sacrificial) lamb. They are described as the first fruits, which has a direct OT connotation:

> "Israel was holiness unto the Lord, and the firstfruits of his increase: all that devour him shall offend; evil shall come upon them, saith the Lord." Jeremiah 2:3

The idea is that the first fruits belong to Yahweh, and if not offered voluntarily, they will be taken violently. It appears elsewhere, for example Psalm 78:51 "And smote all the firstborn in Egypt; the chief of *their* strength in the tabernacles of Ham:" And the "only begotten" son of Yahweh, Jesus Christ, is sacrificed to the Father. The transpersonal dimension, as archetypal fact, may seem chilling. Essentially, if you start upon the path to realize Self, you must finish. One way or the other once commenced, circumstances will unfold that present completion – even tragedy or death. You belong to Self and Self claims you. If you become conscious of this and aim towards it, you must continue no matter what. That is the sacrifice of the first born.

The Eternal Gospel

> "And I saw another angel fly in the midst of heaven, having the everlasting gospel to preach unto them that dwell on the earth, and to every nation, and kindred, and tongue, and people,

> Saying with a loud voice, Fear God, and give glory to
> him; for the hour of his judgment is come: and
> worship him that made heaven, and earth, and the sea,
> and the fountains of waters." Rev. 14:6-7

This continues the individuated theme that proximity to
Self is accompanied by anxiety, indicating nearness to
Self. As a biblical motif, we see this in Revelation and
elsewhere, where people fall "as though dead" in the
presence of mighty angels, or are counseled to "fear
not." We also see the theme of God having a dual
aspect, what Jung described (and italicized) in Answer to
Job as "*one can love God but fear him.*" This wholeness –
the wholeness of Self – is the *eternal* gospel as distinct
from the temporal gospel. The latter informs belief
systems, the *paradoxia*, however, as David Hawkins was
want to say, is that "the pathway to Enlightenment via
radical truth is demanding and requires surrender of
belief systems. Only then does the ultimate reality reveal
itself as the sought-after 'I' of the Supreme." The road to
hell is paved with good intentions.

Eternal Torture

> "And the third angel followed them, saying with a loud
> voice, If any man worship the beast and his image, and
> receive his mark in his forehead, or in his hand,
>
> The same shall drink of the wine of the wrath of God,
> which is poured out without mixture into the cup of

his indignation; and he shall be tormented with fire and brimstone in the presence of the holy angels, and in the presence of the Lamb:

And the smoke of their torment ascendeth up for ever and ever: and they have no rest day nor night, who worship the beast and his image, and whosoever receiveth the mark of his name." Rev. 14:9-11

The "eternal torture" refers to Self activated in one wholly identified with the primordial psyche (the ambiguous Leviathan–Behemoth "beast"), "tortured" by compulsive desires for pleasure and power. This is the 'crude Sulfur' of the alchemists, as opposed to the 'true Sulfur.' For Jung (cf. *Mysterium Coniunctionis*), behind this wild desirousness was ultimately a thirsting for the eternal (Self), the thirsting of those who have not found themselves, and "from this fire arises the true living spirit which generates life according to its own laws... This means burning in your own fire..." ie. to abandon the norm for individuation, to burn off the 'Everyman', the herd, and *become an individual*. The torturing fire is the fire of the *calcinatio*, the burning of the *Prima Materia* until it is transformed into ash – to burn out in the great deception of worldly desire or to be purified by fire.

While this imagery of mundane life, and of ultimate identification with the primordial Self and of transformation, speaks of wrath and torment and evokes fear, we must keep in mind this is a Christian text. While wholeness is recognised in Revelation – the mandala city of the "New Jerusalem" to come – its doctrine is focussed on the *separatio*, the radical separation of the upper and lower, of spirit and matter. Ego-Self union (the Jersusalem Temple) is envisioned, its return longed for, but what stands – the human condition – has been perverted, desecrated and destroyed, *separated from human nature*. Yet this *separatio* has generated Western civilization and the Western psyche. As Edinger wisely noted, "The Book of Revelation belongs to what we are calling the old aeon as a *separatio* document. It is a state of affairs, however, that is due to change in the new aeon. The coming "psychological aeon" is aiming towards the union of what has been split." This echoes Jung. The only thing these psychologists got wrong was that the new aeon as the New Aeon is already here, with a new Revelation, a new *coniunctio* document.

Harvesting

"And I looked, and behold a white cloud, and upon the cloud one sat like unto the Son of man, having on his head a golden crown, and in his hand a sharp sickle.

And another angel came out of the temple, crying with a loud voice to him that sat on the cloud, Thrust in thy sickle, and reap: for the time is come for thee to reap; for the harvest of the earth is ripe.

And he that sat on the cloud thrust in his sickle on the earth; and the earth was reaped.

And another angel came out of the temple which is in heaven, he also having a sharp sickle.

And another angel came out from the altar, which had power over fire; and cried with a loud cry to him that had the sharp sickle, saying, Thrust in thy sharp sickle, and gather the clusters of the vine of the earth; for her grapes are fully ripe.

And the angel thrust in his sickle into the earth, and gathered the vine of the earth, and cast it into the great winepress of the wrath of God.

And the winepress was trodden without the city, and blood came out of the winepress, even unto the horse bridles, by the space of a thousand and six hundred furlongs." Rev. 14:14-20

Humanity is presented as something to be harvested for consumption by God (or in other Biblical accounts of this motif, e.g. Enoch 7:1-4, some other creature, such as a giant or angel). This means to succumb to inflation, a theme clearly expressed in the Gospel of Thomas: "Jesus said: Blessed is the lion which the man eats, and the lion will become man; and cursed is the man whom the lion eats, and the lion will become man." Logion 7. When the collective unconscious is activated or works through us unconsciously, the human consumed by the inhuman is disastrous, but on the other hand, the extent to which the experience can be assimilated and understood, humanizes the archetypes, in the journey to wholeness.

Seven Golden Bowls of Plagues

"And after that I looked, and, behold, the temple of the tabernacle of the testimony in heaven was opened:

And the seven angels came out of the temple, having the seven plagues, clothed in pure and white linen, and having their breasts girded with golden girdles.

And one of the four beasts gave unto the seven angels seven golden vials full of the wrath of God, who liveth for ever and ever.

And the temple was filled with smoke from the glory of God, and from his power; and no man was able to enter into the temple, till the seven plagues of the seven angels were fulfilled." Rev. 15:5-8

"And I heard a great voice out of the temple saying to the seven angels, Go your ways, and pour out the vials of the wrath of God upon the earth." Rev. 16:1

The plagues are contained in golden bowls. Similar symbolism occurs later with the golden cup of the Harlot who rides the Beast. The value and majesty of gold indicates that it is a symbol of Self. Psychologically, negative elements of the collective unconscious ("heaven") are being poured into the ego ("earth"). There is a psychological overflow from neglect of the unconscious leading to an excess of libido the ego has repressed. In the Judaeo-Christian setting, this is often represented in the form of punishment for neglecting God. More humanely, we can look at this as a psychological mistake.

Frogs

> "And I saw three unclean spirits like frogs come out of the mouth of the dragon, and out of the mouth of the beast, and out of the mouth of the false prophet.
>
> For they are the spirits of devils, working miracles, which go forth unto the kings of the earth and of the whole world, to gather them to the battle of that great day of God Almighty." Rev. 16:12-14

While frogs and toads are an expression of the "loathsomeness of life" (cf. Jung, 'Zarathhustra seminars') fairy tales remind us they are also symbols of human transformation, reflecting the metamorphosis from water-born tadpole to amphibian. In Revelation, unlike the fantasies of swallowing frogs, or their use in witches spells, or whatnot, frogs are being regurgitated. *The direction is reversed.* They indicate that the shadow like quality and libidinal chaos of the dragon, the beast and the false prophet is necessary to wholeness. They must "go forth unto the kings of the earth and of the whole world" for the "great day" of realization of Self, typically described in the punitive world-view of the Christian aeon.

The Whore of Babylon

"And there came one of the seven angels which had the seven vials, and talked with me, saying unto me, Come hither; I will shew unto thee the judgment of the great whore that sitteth upon many waters:

With whom the kings of the earth have committed fornication, and the inhabitants of the earth have been made drunk with the wine of her fornication.

So he carried me away in the spirit into the wilderness: and I saw a woman sit upon a scarlet coloured beast, full of names of blasphemy, having seven heads and ten horns.

And the woman was arrayed in purple and scarlet colour, and decked with gold and precious stones and pearls, having a golden cup in her hand full of abominations and filthiness of her fornication:

> And upon her forehead was a name written, Mystery,
> Babylon The Great, The Mother Of Harlots And
> Abominations Of The Earth." Rev. 17

This perverted image of the Goddess attests to the profound depreciation suffered by the "feminine" (inclusive of earth, nature, body, matter) with the Christian aeon. This depreciation was not limited to Christianity. Looked at with psychological detachment, this event in the collective psyche – the individuation process which lies behind history – required at the time of the christian aeon the creation of a "spiritual" counterpole to the "instinctual," as a response to the degradation and excesses that accompanied the decadence of the ancient world. Whores, wrote gnostic scholar Ioan Couliano, represent an "excess of eroticism" (cf. 'Feminism versus Masculine: the Sophia Myth and the origins of feminism').

The *sublimatio* of the collective unconscious sought to get above the bodily, material level of existence. Jung talks about "the whirlwind of brutality and unchained libido that roared through the streets of imperial Rome" (cf. *Symbols of Transformation*). Historical interpretations have therefore attributed Babylon to the decadent and corrupted states, be that the Jerusalem Temple (cf. Barker's 'Temple theology') or for many scholars, imperial Rome. However beyond history are the changes in the collective psyche that precipitate it. Old psychic dominants were falling into decay and new ones arising.

The Golden Cup

Babylon has "a golden cup in her hand full of abominations and filthiness of her fornication," repeating the golden symbolism of the bowls that poured out the plagues. The cup irrespective of context, represents the containing (feminine) aspect of Self. This Cup has subsequently become an enduring motif. Psychologically, it foreshadows the need to reconcile the split opposites of Revelation and of the Christian psyche, to assimilate "the abominations and filthiness of her fornication;" to assimilate the contents relegated to the shadow, that which the Christian viewpoint considers filth and abomination.

In *Mysterium Coniunctionis*, Jung comments on a reference to the Golden Cup in the alchemical text, Ripley's *Cantilena*. The Cup represents the psychic substances of the erotic nature, that has to be integrated, enabling a widening of consciousness through profound insight (or in my view, Understanding). This is an integration of the dark, chthonic aspect of nature, which has both an animal *and* spiritual dimension, one of the discoveries of the alchemists. So long as one is not destroyed by the onslaught of crude instincts relegated to the Shadow, the value of the Self lies behind them. Revelation foretells a change in the collective psyche oriented to wholeness. As the old values (dominants) of the Christian aeon collapse, all that has been excluded rushes back in (to the Cup).

Babylon the Great

The harlot is identified with an ancient city, described in Rev. 18:10 as "that great city Babylon, that mighty city!" Due to various allusions given in the text scholars readily identify this city with Rome ("The seven heads are seven mountains, on which the woman sitteth." Rev. 17:9, ie. the seven hills of Rome). The author of Rev. lived at the time of the Roman Empire. Others in the tradition of 'Temple theologian' Margaret Barker identify the city as an apostate Jerusalem. These interpretations are valid within their historical and preterist contexts, but here we look at the psychological, to which we refer to Jeremiah. Jeremiah prophesied after Babylon's defeat of Israel and the captivity of the Jews. Revelation clearly refers to Jeremiah:

> "Thus saith the Lord; Behold, I will raise up against Babylon, and against them that dwell in the midst of them that rise up against me, a destroying wind;
>
> And will send unto Babylon fanners, that shall fan her, and shall empty her land: for in the day of trouble they shall be against her round about.
>
> Against him that bendeth let the archer bend his bow, and against him that lifteth himself up in his brigandine: and spare ye not her young men; destroy ye utterly all her host.

Thus the slain shall fall in the land of the Chaldeans, and they that are thrust through in her streets.

For Israel hath not been forsaken, nor Judah of his God, of the Lord of hosts; though their land was filled with sin against the Holy One of Israel.

Flee out of the midst of Babylon, and deliver every man his soul: be not cut off in her iniquity; for this is the time of the Lord's vengeance; he will render unto her a recompense.

Babylon hath been a golden cup in the Lord's hand, that made all the earth drunken: the nations have drunken of her wine; therefore the nations are mad."
Jeremiah 51:1-7

We can conclude that Baylon represented an archetypal evil city. While long destroyed by John of Patmos' time, its image had been deposited in the Christian psyche.

The apostate Jerusalem interpretation relies upon Ezekiel's description of Jerusalem as harlot:

"Again the word of the Lord came unto me, saying, Son of man, cause Jerusalem to know her abominations, And say, Thus saith the Lord God unto Jerusalem; Thy birth and thy nativity is of the land of Canaan; thy father was an Amorite, and thy mother an Hittite. And as for thy nativity, in the day thou wast born thy navel was not cut, neither wast thou washed in water to supple thee; thou wast not salted at all, nor swaddled at all. None eye pitied thee, to do any of these unto thee, to have compassion upon thee; but thou wast cast out in the open field, to the lothing of thy person, in the day that thou wast born. And when I passed by thee, and saw thee polluted in thine own blood, I said unto thee when thou wast in thy blood, Live; yea, I said unto thee when thou wast in thy blood, Live. I have caused thee to multiply as the bud of the field, and thou hast increased and waxen great, and thou art come to excellent ornaments: thy breasts are fashioned, and thine hair is grown, whereas thou wast naked and bare. Now when I passed by thee, and looked upon thee, behold, thy time was the time of love; and I spread my skirt over thee, and covered thy nakedness: yea, I sware unto thee, and entered into a covenant with thee, saith the Lord God, and thou becamest mine. Then washed I thee with water; yea, I throughly washed away thy blood from thee, and I anointed thee with oil. I clothed thee also with broidered work, and shod thee with badgers' skin, and I girded thee about with fine linen, and I covered thee with silk. I decked thee also with ornaments, and I put bracelets upon thy hands, and a chain on thy neck. And I put a jewel on thy forehead, and earrings in thine ears, and a beautiful crown upon thine head. Thus wast thou decked with gold and silver; and thy raiment was of fine linen, and silk, and broidered work;

thou didst eat fine flour, and honey, and oil: and thou
wast exceeding beautiful, and thou didst prosper into a
kingdom. And thy renown went forth among the
heathen for thy beauty: for it was perfect through my
comeliness, which I had put upon thee, saith the Lord
God. But thou didst trust in thine own beauty, and
playedst the harlot because of thy renown, and pouredst
out thy fornications on every one that passed by; his it
was. And of thy garments thou didst take, and deckedst
thy high places with divers colours, and playedst the
harlot thereupon: the like things shall not come, neither
shall it be so." Ezekiel 16:1-22

Rome's attribution is well justified given the intermittent
and vicious persecution of Christians. There have been
later attributions as well, as these images remain living
symbols of the psyche. For all of this, in the *seperatio* of
the Christian psyche we are dealing here with the
archetype of the wicked city as a counter to the
'heavenly' city of Jerusalem to come.

Beyond good and evil, the city belongs to the
symbolism of the mandala. It is a container and
symbolically feminine. Jung in *Psychology and Alchemy*
cites a gnostic text that reads "This same is the Mother-
City of the Only-begotten," pointing out that in Greek
a mother city is the *metropolis*:

> "As "metropolis" the Monad is feminine, like the *padma*
> or lotus…In the Book of Revelation, we find the Lamb

in the Centre of the Heavenly Jerusalem. And in our gnostic text we are told that Setheus [the Monad as "creator"] dwells in the holiest recesses of the Pleroma, a city with four gates (equivalent to the Hindu city of Brahma on the world mountain Meru)."

The city is a *tenemos* or sacred precinct and therefore represents the Self as an ordered, structured totality (which as we see in the wicked city of the Christian bifurcated psyche, includes its libidinous, instinctual shadow). Yet the city is external, the seat of civilization (both words derive from the Latin root *civitas*), and this civilization that stems from the life of cities is the basis of culture. Jung comments how culture is a means by which we can get out of our ego boundaries by embracing something greater than ourselves, thus the city and all its correspondences (the nation-state, the Church etc) are external images or representations of Self, an earthly, collective embodiment. From the blind and selfish egotism of the rat race with all of its desirous distractions, we might aspire to a city (and its correspondences), a culture, and a civilization that embraces and mirror-images transpersonal authority (the 'heavenly' city). We see this dichotomy in Augustine's masterpiece *City of God*, of the "Earthly city" of the self-*ish* (that Augustine says was typified by Babylon) and the "Heavenly city" (typified by the Heavenly Jerusalem at the end of Revelation), made up of individuals living by the love of God. The earthly city is the ego and the heavenly city the Self, yet both cities are built on the same ground plan which enables Self-realization. As Jung said in *Psychology and Alchemy*, the Self is a prefiguration of the ego. Not surprisingly when we look at this lead up to dialectic synthesis, Hegel was also gripped by the archetypal image of the City. While Hegel like all the greats is controversial, fundamentally he saw the image of Self projected on to the sophisticated notion of the nation-state community, where as Edinger comments, "individual rights and freedoms would exist within the framework of a community of transpersonal awareness that carried objective supra-personal purposes and values." The same could be said of the vision of the founding fathers of the American Constitution, or for that matter, Aleister Crowley's constitutional intimations for the reformulation of Ordo Templi Orientis.

We need only consider that within such notions of Self must be contained the constellation of opposites, its latent conflicts the drama of human history, a history possessed by archetypal images.

The beast that carrieth her

Verses 17 and 18 of Revelation are rich in an imagery and symbolism that has seduced the popular imagination and many a mystic. There is a temptation, as there might be with other stand out passages in Revelation, to treat these in isolation and read too much into them. Such is the fatal allure of Babylon. Verses 17 and 18 heavily reference earlier passages and motifs, as well as the archetypes of numbers. We see the decay and corruption of a civilization devoid of the spiritual, possessed by the libidinal onslaught of instinct; the unconscious Shadow of Self is now manifest, "The beast…shall ascend out of the bottomless pit" - "The seven heads are seven mountains" (ie. the seven hills, primal instinct earthed) - "And the ten horns which thou sawest are ten kings, *which have received no kingdom as yet*; but receive power as kings one hour with the beast" (Italics mine), yet unconscious to those in the grip of this possession, "The beast that thou sawest was, and is not;" "The waters which thou sawest, where the whore sitteth, are peoples, and multitudes, and nations, and tongues." The sum of these parts of beastly vice, temptation, primality and carnality, their repository, is "a golden cup in her hand full of abominations and filthiness of her fornication," the hand of their whole, Babylon "THE GREAT." And yet this abomination and filthiness is "the blood of the saints" and "the blood of the martyrs of Jesus." Here is an admonition of the *separatio* of the Christian aeon in the form of the *paradoxia*. It is the *enantiodromia* of separation, of saints and sinners, the emergence of the unconscious opposite in the course of time, individual and collective, precursory to a future post-aeonic *coniunctio*. "And here is the mind which hath wisdom."

Prior to which, what goes up must come down.

"And he cried mightily with a strong voice, saying, Babylon the great is fallen, is fallen, and is become the habitation of devils, and the hold of every foul spirit, and a cage of every unclean and hateful bird."

"And I heard another voice from heaven, saying, Come out of her, my people, that ye be not partakers of her sins, and that ye receive not of her plagues."

Chapters 19, 20

The Last Judgment

After the heavenly warrior defeats the beast and the false prophet we have the motif of the Last Judgment:

"And I saw a great white throne, and him that sat on it, from whose face the earth and the heaven fled away; and there was found no place for them.

And I saw the dead, small and great, stand before God; and the books were opened: and another book was opened, which is the book of life: and the dead were judged out of those things which were written in the books, according to their works." Rev. 20:11-12

The Last Judgment is a central tenet of the Christian doctrine and creed. The judgment of the dead is an archetypal image in many of the world's religions. The Christian account projects this judgment into the end of the (Christian) aeon. The Christian viewpoint alternatively considers judgment throughout life for one's actions that are (inscrutably) punished or rewarded by God accordingly, there is also judgment at death leading to heaven, hell (or an intermediate purgatory), as well as this final Judgment of absolute and eternal justice after the resurrection of all dead bodies at the time of the end of the world (aeon).

It is clear that one aspect of realizing Self is the egoic experience of being judged, both for the life being lived and its psychological attitude. The anticipation of this experience is fearful, leading to projections of a Judgment as far away as possible, or 'stages' of Judgment with growing levels of severity and finality. Psychologically, the Last Judgment can be a conscious and lived experience. It is a decisive encounter with Self that requires a thorough assimilation of the Shadow, hency the shadowy elements associated with Judgment imagery. Edinger cites Malachai 3:1-5 as an example of the Judgment motif edited and redacted to mitigate the fearful, emotional impact. The interaction of ego-Self through the judgment process is a complex yet delicate interplay – as I said earlier, "Self gets humanized by its connection to ego, and ego deified by its connection to Self."

This warrants some elaboration. Even the passage of Matthew 25:31-46 which gives the 'standard' Last Judgment (and is the basis for popular expressions of it, such as in Renaissance art), makes clear that the Self as the greater personality is found in the least. The aspects of the psyche the ego despises are where Self resides: "Then shall he answer them, saying, Verily I say unto you, Inasmuch as ye did it not to one of the least of these, ye did it not to me." Matt: 25-45. This *paradoxia*, in that the transpersonal greater form is in the lesser, again indicates the limitation of the psychic development to the *seperatio*. Yet it indicates that the way to the Self is through the least aspects of ourselves. It is those who refuse that way that are judged, failing to rise to wholeness.

The New Jerusalem

Revelation concludes with the great mandala and *coniunctio* vision of the New Jerusalem. A lengthy quotation is warranted:

> "And I saw a new heaven and a new earth: for the first heaven and the first earth were passed away; and there was no more sea.
>
> And I John saw the holy city, new Jerusalem, coming down from God out of heaven, prepared as a bride adorned for her husband.
>
> And I heard a great voice out of heaven saying, Behold, the tabernacle of God is with men, and he will

dwell with them, and they shall be his people, and God himself shall be with them, and be their God.

And God shall wipe away all tears from their eyes; and there shall be no more death, neither sorrow, nor crying, neither shall there be any more pain: for the former things are passed away.

And he that sat upon the throne said, Behold, I make all things new. And he said unto me, Write: for these words are true and faithful.

And he said unto me, It is done. I am Alpha and Omega, the beginning and the end. I will give unto him that is athirst of the fountain of the water of life freely.

He that overcometh shall inherit all things; and I will be his God, and he shall be my son.

But the fearful, and unbelieving, and the abominable, and murderers, and whoremongers, and sorcerers, and idolaters, and all liars, shall have their part in the lake which burneth with fire and brimstone: which is the second death.

And there came unto me one of the seven angels which had the seven vials full of the seven last plagues, and talked with me, saying, Come hither, I will shew thee the bride, the Lamb's wife.

And he carried me away in the spirit to a great and high mountain, and shewed me that great city, the holy Jerusalem, descending out of heaven from God,

Having the glory of God: and her light was like unto a stone most precious, even like a jasper stone, clear as crystal;

And had a wall great and high, and had twelve gates, and at the gates twelve angels, and names written thereon, which are the names of the twelve tribes of the children of Israel:

On the east three gates; on the north three gates; on the south three gates; and on the west three gates.

And the wall of the city had twelve foundations, and in them the names of the twelve apostles of the Lamb.

And he that talked with me had a golden reed to measure the city, and the gates thereof, and the wall thereof.

And the city lieth foursquare, and the length is as large as the breadth: and he measured the city with the reed, twelve thousand furlongs. The length and the breadth and the height of it are equal.

And he measured the wall thereof, an hundred and forty and four cubits, according to the measure of a man, that is, of the angel.

And the building of the wall of it was of jasper: and the city was pure gold, like unto clear glass.

And the foundations of the wall of the city were garnished with all manner of precious stones. The first foundation was jasper; the second, sapphire; the third, a chalcedony; the fourth, an emerald;

The fifth, sardonyx; the sixth, sardius; the seventh, chrysolyte; the eighth, beryl; the ninth, a topaz; the tenth, a chrysoprasus; the eleventh, a jacinth; the twelfth, an amethyst.

And the twelve gates were twelve pearls: every several gate was of one pearl: and the street of the city was pure gold, as it were transparent glass.

And I saw no temple therein: for the Lord God Almighty and the Lamb are the temple of it.

And the city had no need of the sun, neither of the moon, to shine in it: for the glory of God did lighten it, and the Lamb is the light thereof.

And the nations of them which are saved shall walk in the light of it: and the kings of the earth do bring their glory and honour into it.

And the gates of it shall not be shut at all by day: for there shall be no night there.

And they shall bring the glory and honour of the nations into it.

And there shall in no wise enter into it any thing that defileth, neither whatsoever worketh abomination, or maketh a lie: but they which are written in the Lamb's book of life.

And he shewed me a pure river of water of life, clear as crystal, proceeding out of the throne of God and of the Lamb.

 In the midst of the street of it, and on either side of the river, was there the tree of life, which bare twelve manner of fruits, and yielded her fruit every month: and the leaves of the tree were for the healing of the nations." Rev 21, 22:1-2

This archetype of quaternity, a mandala image of the city as a precious stone, is the alchemical lapis, the Self eternal and beautiful. The references to the original state of paradise "for the healing of the nations" indicate this city is a place of healing. It is also referred to as "the bride, the Lamb's wife," indicating the *coniunctio*, the *hieros gamos*. However, as Jung points out about Revelation in *Answer to Job*, this does not consist of the reconciliation of opposites, but in their severance – the marriage takes place in the transcendental realm, the heavenly pleroma, not on earth:

> "The final vision...is therefore a representation of perfection and wholeness: hence the quaternity... While the circle signifies the roundness of heaven and the all-embracing nature of the "pneumatic" deity, the square refers to the earth. Heaven is masculine, but the earth is feminine. Therefore God has his throne in heaven, while Wisdom has hers on earth...The city is Sophia, who was with God before time began, and at the end of time will be reunited with God through the sacred marriage...No doubt this is meant as a final solution of the terrible conflict of existence. The solution, however, as here presented, does not consist in the reconciliation of the opposites, but in their final severance, by which means those whose destiny it is to be saved can save themselves by identifying with the bright pneumatic side of God."

Revelation has depicted a *seperatio* process, a split between heaven and hell, with an ending implying a *coniunctio*, a state of wholeness. The psychological conclusion is that at certain levels of development – let us call this the Christian level of development – a *seperatio* is a state of wholeness. When the psyche, individual and collective, fulfils the innate potential of one's time and nature, images of Self will signify fulfillment and wholeness. From the later perspective of the modern psyche in the new time, beyond the old time of the christian aeon and its end of time, the same images appear incomplete, in conflict and paradoxical.

The Messianic Banquet

Given the marriage of the heavenly Jerusalem and divine Lamb, one would expect in the Jewish tradition for there to be a wedding feast. Earlier I mentioned the messianic banquet of legend, where the faithful feast on Leviathan and Behemoth, drinking wine from the grapes of paradise. This imagery is present in Rev. 19:

> "And I saw an angel standing in the sun; and he cried with a loud voice, saying to all the fowls that fly in the midst of heaven, Come and gather yourselves together unto the supper of the great God;
>
> That ye may eat the flesh of kings, and the flesh of captains, and the flesh of mighty men, and the flesh of horses, and of them that sit on them, and the flesh of all

men, both free and bond, both small and great." Rev.
19:17-18

The flesh is of those who will be slaughtered in the
Apocalypse. The opposing themes,
wedding/banquet/love and war, indicate that the
archetypal opposites of the God image have been
activated and have set in motion the dynamism of the
coniunctio. Both love and war signify a union. This
dynamism engages the psyche, individual and collective
and therefore, beyond the transpersonal, the (human)
ego. It follows that the process must then incarnate or
manifest, acting itself out, whether unconsciously or
consciously. Those humans have been consumed or
devoured by the archetypal drama. The individuals who,
rather than being blind actors in the drama, understand
what is going on, incarnate the process as individuation.
This is why in *Answer to Job*, Jung described humanity
as the "involuntary exponent" of the God image, that
devours humans (ie. consumes their egos). This explains
the gruesome nature of the "supper of the great God."

We might further note that, as Jung noted in *Aion*, such
a consumption, "always sets in when the collective
dominants of human life fall into decay...in order to
form new dominants:"

> "This state of possession shows itself almost without
> exception in the fact that the possessed identify
> themselves with the archetypal contents of their

unconscious, and, because they do not realize the role
which is being thrust upon them is the effect of new
contents still to be understood, they exemplify these
concretely in their own lives, thus becoming prophets
and reformers...Thus Jesus became the tutelary image
or amulet against the archetypal powers that threatened
to possess everyone."

Restoration

"And I saw a new heaven and a new earth: for the first
heaven and the first earth were passed away; and there
was no more sea.

And I John saw the holy city, new Jerusalem, coming
down from God out of heaven, prepared as a bride
adorned for her husband.

And I heard a great voice out of heaven saying,
Behold, the tabernacle of God is with men, and he will
dwell with them, and they shall be his people, and God
himself shall be with them, and be their God.

And God shall wipe away all tears from their eyes; and
there shall be no more death, neither sorrow, nor
crying, neither shall there be any more pain: for the
former things are passed away.

And he that sat upon the throne said, Behold, I make all things new. And he said unto me, Write: for these words are true and faithful.

And he said unto me, It is done. I am Alpha and Omega, the beginning and the end. I will give unto him that is athirst of the fountain of the water of life freely.

He that overcometh shall inherit all things; and I will be his God, and he shall be my son." Rev. 21:1-7

This *apocatastasis*, a restoration or restitution of all things, is referred to by Peter in Acts:

"Repent ye therefore, and be converted, that your sins may be blotted out, when the times of refreshing shall come from the presence of the Lord.

And he shall send Jesus Christ, which before was preached unto you:

Whom the heaven must receive until the times of restitution of all things, which God hath spoken by the mouth of all his holy prophets since the world began." Acts 3:19-21

Psychologically, Adam's fall from Eden represented ego consciousness spoiling wholeness. The original state will be restored, a new heaven and earth, but on a different level, due to the experience of their estrangement – incarnation to individuation. The Self, which was unconscious, has to be realized – the ego born out of Self must go through various stages of inflation and alienation. If the ego develops far enough towards individuation, it returns to a relation to the Self but now on a conscious level. This is the great return of the Apocalypse archetype in the christian aeon, the "restitution of all things." The drama of Revelation was an account of the journey to this restoration to Self, a motif that was active in the collective psyche of the ancient period. The Christian account was by no means clear, clean and coherent, and its picture was by no means pretty. Such are the depths (and contradictions) of the collective psyche and the moralities and religiosities and philosophies that have embarked upon sense making its expressions in consciousness.

The dilemma of Revelation is that man to embrace God must harmonize and unite opposing influences he is exposed to from the Unconscious. The Unconscious, it could be said, wants to both divide and unite. It wants to flow into consciousness to reach the light, while at the same time thwarting itself, as paradoxically, it would rather remain unconscious. Or as Jung put it in *Answer to Job*, "That is to say, God wants to become man, but not quite. The conflict in his nature is so great that the incarnation can only be bought by an expiatory self-sacrifice offered up to the wrath of God's dark side."

This then is the Christian dilemma as well, the inability to reach beyond the *separatio*. Jung comments, "All opposites are of God, [man] finds that God in his "oppositeness" has taken possession of him, incarnated himself in him. He becomes a vessel of divine conflict." This conflict of opposites spills out into the outer world by way of projection – humanity's "expiatory self-sacrifice" as this God-image, incarnated yet untransformed, searches for its own transformation, for the restitution of all things. Yet this spilling out into the outer world, after a time, heralds the end of its psychic dominance. Transformation requires the new dominants of a new aeon and *coniunctio*.

"Since the Apocalypse we now know that God is not only to be loved, but also to be feared. He fills us with evil as well as with good, otherwise he would not need to be feared; and because he wants to become man, the uniting of his antinomy must take place in man. He can no longer wriggle out of it on the plea of his littleness and nothingness, for the dark God has slipped the atom bomb and chemical weapons into his hands and given him the power to empty out the apocalyptic vials of wrath on his fellow creatures. Since he has been granted almost godlike power, he can no longer remain blind and unconscious. He must know something of God's nature and of metaphysical processes if he is to understand himself and thereby achieve gnosis of the Divine." *Answer to Job.*

"Christ was up against an unpredictable and lawless God who would need a most drastic sacrifice to appease his wrath, viz. The laughter of His own son. Curiously enough, as on the one hand his self-sacrifice means admission of the Father's amoral nature, he taught on the other hand a new image of God, namely that of a Loving Father in whom there is no darkness. This enormous antinomy needs some explanation. It needed the assertion that he was the Son of the Father, ie. the incarnation of the Deity in man. As a consequence the sacrifice was a self-destruction of the amoral God, incarnated in a mortal body." Jung, *Letters*

Conclusion

"And what rough beast, its hour come round at last, Slouches towards Bethlehem to be born?" - W.B. Yeats, 'The Second Coming.'

There is no easy way to rationalize the Revelation narrative, an 'uncovering' that ends in a separation that has shaped western civilization and the Christian world. It is a separation borne of anxiety. In Dr. David Hawkins' unconventional but heavily tested kinesiological method of calibrating Truth, Revelation came in at only 190, below the 200 level of integrity on the Hawkins Map of Consciousness. By comparison (irrespective of what you think of the Hawkins method), the King James New Testament *minus* Revelation calibrated at 790: 700-1000 are levels of enlightenment. Nonetheless, the work in the new aeon to unite that which was separated to create the child (New Aeon), the future, benefits from some understanding of the Revelation narrative: the *apokalypsis* – an "uncovering of what has been hidden."

This meditation has sought a glimpse of Revelation's tremendously raw psychological depth and insight into the Christian aeon; and to look at the psychological reality of the end of that aeon. In the psychic and worldly transition from *separatio* to *coniunctio* in a new aeon, we may assume our psychological reality and its expressions will be volatile before they are fixed – in holy books, in culture, in world history, in the life of the ego and any attempt at Self-realization. Yet, I firmly hold that the new God image equilibrates in joyous opportunities for the Great Work towards the wholeness of humankind, in Thelema. This will be explored in future installments.

List of Works Cited

Note: most sources are to author and title only as there are numerous editions, printings as well as online and/or audible options.

Barker, M. *The Revelation of Jesus Christ.*

Couliano, I. 'Feminism versus Masculine: the Sophia Myth and the origins of feminism.'.

Crowley, A. Liber CDXVIII *The Vision & the Voice and Commentary* (The Equinox IV:2).

Crowley, A. Liber LXV *The Book of the Heart Girt with the Serpent and Commentary* (The Equinox: IV:1).

Crowley, A. *The Book of Thoth.*

Crowley, A. *Liber ABA Magick, Book IV* (Weiser: 1997).

Edinger, E. *Archetype of the Apocalypse.*

Edinger, E. *The Creation of Consciousness.*

Edinger, E. *The Mysterium Lectures.*

Edinger, E. *The Bible and the Psyche.*

Ford, J.M. 'Revelation' (*Anchor Bible*).

Gunther, J. D. *Initiation in the Aeon of the Child* (Ibis: 2009).

Gunther, J. D. *Parable of the Pale Image* (Wennofer House, 2022).

Hallelujah, C. 'Notes towards a preliminary analysis of a peculiar motif in the Stele of Ankf-af-na-khonsu.' Ora et Labora Vol. II (2021).

Hallelujah, C. 'Excursus on notes towards a preliminary analysis of a peculiar motif in the Stele of Ankf-af-na-khonsu.' Ora et Labora Vol. III (2022).

Hawkins, D. *The Eye of the I.*

Jung, C. *Memories, Dreams, Reflections.*

Jung, C. *Answer to Job.*

Jung, C. *Symbols of Transformation.*

Jung, C. *Mysterium Coniunctionis.*

Jung, C. *Psychology and Alchemy.*

Jung, C. *Aion.*

Jung, C. *Letters.*

Jung, C. 'Transformation symbolism in the Mass.'

Jung, C. 'Alchemical studies.'

Jung, C. '*Zarathustra* seminars.'

King, S. 'Apokalypsis 418: The Temple go Christ, the Angelic Priesthood and the Great Return of the Queen of Heaven,' *The Best of Oz* (2020).

King, S. 'Apokalypsis II: Temple Mysticism in the New Aeon,' *Ora et Labora* vol. III (2022).

King, S. *Living in the Sunlight: Making a Forgotten Meditation an Atomic Habit* (2022).

Lawrence, D.H. *Revelation.*

Louv, J. John Dee and the Empire of Angels (Inner Traditions: 2018).

Pryse, J. *Apocalypse Unsealed.*

Smith, M. *Jesus the Magician.*

Smith, M. *The Secret Gospel*

Stephensen, P.R. ed. King. *The Legend of Aleister Crowley* (2007)

INTRODUCTION TO LARRY SITSKY'S

Music (piano and chorus) for Ecclesiae Gnosticae Catholicae Canon Missae

JOEL BRADY

'*Music certainly has the power to put into sound what is often impossible to describe in words, and the yearning towards a spiritual experience is one of those things. Some say that this is also the longing to approach closer to God; others, that music allows us to discover the divine spark buried deep within us.*'[1]

'*...every movement of the Magician should make music*[2]

Emeritus Professor Lazar "Larry" Sitsky is an Australian pianist and composer. The son of Russian-Jewish parents, he was born in Tientsin in China in 1934, with his early years spent during the difficult period of

---

[1] 'Larry Sitsky', 19 November 2014.

[2] Crowley, Desti, and Waddell, *Magick. Liber ABA. Book Four. Parts I-IV*.

Japanese occupation from 1937, and the tumultuous times following under the Nationalist and then Communist governments. Sitsky described the city at that time as a 'melting pot of refugees.'[3] When Mao Zedong (1893 – 1976) began to expel foreigners from China, his family migrated to Australia in 1951, on which Sitsky commented in a rebroadcast interview on ABC radio in 2022, 'As far as I'm concerned it's the most wonderful thing that could've happened.'[4]

Sitsky graduated from the NSW State Conservatorium of Music in 1955[5], eventually becoming a founding member of the Canberra School of Music (now the ANU School of Music), where he has served as Head of Composition Studies, Head of Academic Studies, Head of Keyboard Studies and Emeritus Professor.

He studied piano under Winifred Burston at the Sydney Conservatorium, and Egon Petri in the United States between 1958 and 1961 after winning a scholarship to the San Francisco Conservatory. Both were from the Busoni piano school and taught in line with the

---

[3] *Hieros Games Radio* (podcast) Ep 14 – *Larry Sitsky*.

[4] 'Margaret Throsby Interviews Larry Sitsky'.

[5] Sitsky, succumbing to family pressure, initially spent a year at Sydney University studying engineering, which he described as 'the worst bloody thing I could ever have done' (*Hieros Games Radio (podcast) Ep 14 – Larry Sitsky*..)

apprenticeship tradition, which has been lost in most modern educational institutions. Ferruccio Busoni's (1866 – 1924) is described by Sitsky as 'a mystic'[6]. His core teaching was centred around the concept of *Junge Klassizität* (Young Classicality). A tradition passed on from teacher to student as an esoteric heritage – music as a vehicle or agent of transcendence, with its secrets encrypted within compositions – 'esoteric philosophy realised in sound.'[7] This is a tradition that Sitsky is seen to have reinterpreted and revitalised.

'The Busoni-Sitsky esoteric tradition, is rooted in the notion of a priesthood of composers, whose works serve to illuminate the mystic path for those who follow... Busoni's tradition is not concerned with the craft of composition. It is a branch of the western hermetic tradition and an occult order in its own right. Its language is one of theurgy, whether tonal or not is of little consequence. Its goal is not the transformation of modern music but the transformation of the human soul.'[8]

---

[6] *Hieros Games Radio* (podcast) Ep 14 – *Larry Sitsky*.

[7] Crispin, 'The Nuctemeron of Sitsky'.

[8] Crispin.

When asked if the term 'Romantic Modernist' was one that he thought adequately described him, Sitsky responded, 'I would have added perhaps 'orientalist' and 'mystic'... I was quite moved to discover that world outlooks of composers such as Scriabin, Obukhov, Vyshnedgradsky and others were close to mine and that I belonged in one sense to that lineage of mystical composers... Finally, the word 'dramatic' needs adding...'romantic dramatic orientalist-mystic expressionist modernist'. Not bad!'[9] He describes the process of studying, composing, and performing music[10] with the language of initiation – 'I see some music as an aristocratic art; one that requires initiation and work to become a member.'[11]

Sitsky also cites Russian virtuoso pianist, composer, and symbolist Alexander Scriabin (1872 – 1915) as another source for his focus on esotericism. Scriabin was a theosophist with an interest in the connection between tones and colour, 'leading to speculation he was synaesthetic.'[12] His unfinished work titled *Mysterium*

---

[9] Shaw, 'Getting My Hands Dirty: Larry Sitsky in Interview'.

[10] For Sitsky, to be a composer, one needs to also be a performer. The composer needs to "get their hands dirty".

[11] Shaw, 'Getting My Hands Dirty: Larry Sitsky in Interview'.

[12] Cotter, *Sitsky: Conversations with the Composer*.

was envisioned to be a combination of music, light, scent, and dance to be performed in the foothills of the Himalayas. Scriabin's conception of the world was as 'a system of correspondences...a balanced, transcendent one, ... inhabited by imaginary heroes, demiurges, who sometimes needed to return to the present time in order to re-establish spiritual harmony...'[13] Scriabin's intention for the performance of *Mysterium* was that 'the barrier between audience and performers would be dissolved to allow for a spiritual communion leading to an ecstatic dissolution and transfiguration of the world.'[14]

Sitsky's compositions have encompassed a broad range of subjects, instruments, and forms; from simple guitar works aimed at young guitarists (*Diversion for David*, 1973), to his opera in three Acts, set in Prague in the 16th century, during the persecution of the Jews (*The Golem*[15], 1993). Notably in his output is the recurrence of themes that are directly religious, mystical, or magical. From his catalogue we can see titles such as

---

[13] Tomás, 'The Mythical Time in Scriabin'.

[14] Garcia, 'Scriabin's Mysterium and the Birth of Genius'.

[15] The structure of this opera is based on the ten Sephiroth of the Kabbalah, 'which is transformed from a grand sacred symbol – the seal of Solomon.' (Borisova, 'Larry Sitsky's Music for the Gnostic Mass: The Symbolism and Sacred Structures'.)

The Three Names of Shiva (1992), *The Golden Dawn* (2010)[16] – and *Qliphoth of the Kabbalah* (2011)[17].

For Sitsky, music is a vehicle that 'allows us to embark on the mystical journey, which is the actual quest to find this indefinable realm…' Whether this is seen in a religious context as an approach to God, or the more personal discovery of 'the divine spark buried deep within us.'[18] For him music is 'a primal force, owing its origins to ritual, religion, magic and mysticism. It is this hidden ('occult') power of music that is [HIS] chief concern…'[19] He further goes onto explain that music is a form of conjuration. 'It comes from an inner stillness and retreats back into it when the piece is over…'[20]

Sitsky described the process that gives birth to his composition in an interview recorded in 1967. Following the initial input (or "grist to the mill") he explains,

---

[16] This takes its titles from the Angelic language stemming from the practices of Dr. John Dee and Edward Kelly.

[17] The 10 pieces take their titles from the names of the "shells"; adverse or unbalanced forms of the Qabalistic Sephiroth in Jewish mysticism.

[18] 'Larry Sitsky', 19 November 2014.

[19] Shaw, 'Getting My Hands Dirty: Larry Sitsky in Interview'.

[20] Shaw.

'I then find that I think about this, sometimes for a few months. In other words, there's something that happens in one's subconscious, I suppose, because I don't work at the problem on paper, I simply carry it around in my head. Sometimes one gets a clear mental picture of musicians sitting on stage and picking up their instruments, and that's when the first notes come. Sometimes it's just a general sound that you hear in your head. At any rate, I tend to carry this round in my head for quite a while and then one day, a little voice says, 'Well, you'd better sit down and start putting blobs on paper'. In other words, the time has come when the mental working out has reached its conclusion and can go no further and you now have to try and transcribe the sounds that you have in your head onto paper…'[21]

Throughout his career Sitsky has championed new music, with a particular focus on new Australian music. He has been the recipient of numerous awards and honours, and in 2000 he was presented with an Order of Australia Medal (OAM) 'for service to music as a composer, musicologist, pianist and educator.'[22] Sitsky's own musical style has been described as 'virtuosic, rhapsodic and exciting.'[23]

---

[21] 'Larry Sitsky'.

[22] 'University Honours for Emeritus Professor Larry Sitsky'.

The work presented here for the first time was composed in response to the ritual written by occultist, poet, painter, novelist, and mountaineer, Aleister Crowley[24] (1875—1947) in 1913 while he was travelling in Russia – Liber XV or *Ecclesiae Gnosticae Catholicae Canon Missae* (The Gnostic Mass). This is the central rite of the *Ordo Templi Orientis* (OTO) under the *Ecclesia Gnostica Catholica* (the Gnostic Catholic Church or EGC). Of the Mass Crowley wrote, 'I resolved that my Ritual should celebrate the sublimity of the operation of universal forces without introducing disputable metaphysical theories. I would neither make nor imply any statement about nature which would not be endorsed by the most materialistic man of science.'[25] It is a eucharistic celebration of great beauty and dramatic power, and was always intended to be

---

[23] 'University Honours for Emeritus Professor Larry Sitsky'.

[24] In some ways Crowley developed a similar approach the to the creative process as that is described by Sitsky; a process freed as much as possible from conscious intervention. In reference to his approach to painting, Crowley wrote in 1920, 'There would be no fun (moreover) in creating dead things; the whole point of the game is that ones work lives and moves independently of ones conscious mind…The finished work always surprises me…Art is a God's way discovering his own mysteries, the most enthralling, most tireless of pleasures.' (King, 'Shadow of the Thelemites: The Abbot, the Abbey and the Nightmare'.)

[25] Crowley, *The Confessions of Aleister Crowley*.

accompanied by music. The script for the Mass includes musical instructions at key points, such as "A phrase of triumphant music" or "Penitential music".

The genesis of this new work is found in a collaboration between Sitsky and David Bottrill (to whom the work is dedicated). David coordinated an event held in 2019 in Canberra, that would celebrate Sitsky's music, as well as that of Australian violinist and composer Leila Waddell (1880—1932); a student and lover of Crowley's who he called "Laylah". This event titled *Music Magick & the Muse* included a performance of Sitsky's *The Golden Dawn* by Australian-American pianist Edward Neeman alongside Waddell's *A Tone-Testament*, performed by violinist and conductor Tor Frømyhr.

The collaboration between Sitsky and David resulted in an agreement to produce a work inspired by the Gnostic Mass; a work composed and structured to accompany the performance of the ritual.[26] David worked with Sitsky to help him understand the text, and its staging and performance. The result is music that is simple enough to be performed by non-professional musicians, but still sophisticated and beautiful, while 'retain[ing] the unique style of its author…The musical text of the

---

[26] The work is a creative response to Liber XV, The Gnostic Mass, and has not been approved for official use by Ecclesia Gnostica Catholica at this time.

work consists of separate sections, interconnected by simple for performance chords and musical structures.'[27]

A full analysis of the score is best left to the music theorists (and beyond the scope of this brief introduction), but as Anna Borisova explains in her unpublished analysis of the work, the composition is centred around the note 'b' (which she describes as 'h' using an alternative notational system). This is the 11th note in the chromatic sequence of notes starting with C (the number 11 having significance in Thelemic doctrine). Over the course of the composition, however, 'Sitsky steadily replaces the "h" with "b"[28], thus equating "h" to "b flat"'[29]. She also highlights that symbolically the figure of the cross is encoded into the composition (as it is in the Mass itself), 'expressed in four unison chords'.[30] Borisova explains that 'this musical symbol appears in the score of the Mass in different variants exactly *eleven* times.'[31]

---

[27] Borisova, 'Larry Sitsky's Music for the Gnostic Mass: The Symbolism and Sacred Structures'.

[28] In this notational system "b" is "b flat" as used in modern notation.

[29] Borisova.

[30] Borisova.

[31] Borisova.

Another musical element that contributes to the character of the music is the tritone (an interval of three whole tones) - the famous "Devils Interval" or "*Diabolus in Musica*", known for its dissonance and tense characteristic.[32] The tritone is unstable and can resolve itself in many ways. Using again the alternative notation, the tritone also encodes Sitsky's signature or monogram, as composer, such as Bach, have done in the past. He 'translates the initial letters of his name (Larry (E)Sitsky)[33] into the sounds of "*a-es*"[34], thus getting the tritone interval.'[35]

Seven of the eight parts are composed in a free twelve-tone system[36]. The exception is the Anthem, which is

---

[32] 'What Is a Tritone and Why Was It Nicknamed the Devil's Interval?'

[33] This was confirmed by Sitsky who wrote, 'I quite often use my own initials (La and Eb (S) motivically in pieces.' (Sitsky, email to author, October 25, 2022)

[34] "A" and "E-flat" which form a diminished fifth.

[35] Borisova, 'Larry Sitsky's Music for the Gnostic Mass: The Symbolism and Sacred Structures'.

[36] The Twelve-tone technique is one where all 12 notes of the chromatic scale are used. Each of the pitches can only be introduced in the composition once all the others have been played. The technique was initially devised by Josef Matthias Hauer (1883 – 1959) and later developed by Arnold Schoenberg (1874 – 1951). The twelve-tone technique can be heard in Igor Stravinsky's (1982 - 1971) *Agon* from 1957. A ballet created in collaboration with

'dominated by the "classical" tonality[37], although complicated by all sorts of modulations.'[38] This classical tonality is to assist with the group recitation by the congregation. Crowley provides scope for musical interpretation and innovation when composing for the Anthem – 'but the whole or any part thereof shall be set to music, which may be as elaborate as art can devise.'[39] The number eight also has significance in Thelemic doctrine, as it is the number of letters in the name Baphomet, the "idol" the Knights Templar were accused of worshiping, and the name Crowley assumed within the OTO. It is one of the key glyphs found within the Creed in the Gnostic Mass, which itself has 8 clauses, followed by the Thelemic expression of the Pranava (AUMGN). The 8 and 3 equalling to 11.

---

choreographer George Balanchine (1904 – 1983). The performance featured 12 dancers, was constructed in 12 sections, and employed the 12-tone technique. Hauer 'thought of the twelve pcs as a kind of spiritual universe; thus, twelve-tone composition was a way of communing with the infinite…' (Covach, 'Twelve-Tone Theory'.)

[37] Classical tonality is associated with composers the classical period between 1750 and 1830, and composers such as Ludwig van Beethoven (1770 – 1827) and Wolfgang Amadeus Mozart (1756 – 1791).

[38] Borisova, 'Larry Sitsky's Music for the Gnostic Mass: The Symbolism and Sacred Structures'.

[39] Crowley, Desti, and Waddell, *Magick. Liber ABA. Book Four. Parts I-IV.*

> "I believe in the serpent and the lion
> Mystery of Mystery, in his name BAPHOMET."[40]

Another section that stands out is the music that accompanies the Priests recitation of the "*A ka dua*" mantra – recited by the Priest, standing before the Veil before it is parted, calling to the Priestess in song. This appears in section IV of the script titled 'Of the Ceremony of the Opening of the Veil'. This section features beautiful exchanges between the Priest and Priestess in an act of separation and reunification. The mantra has been set to a melody based on the one that is given in Chapter 2 of Part 1 (Mysticism) of *Book 4*, which explains the yogic practices prānāyāma and mantrayoga.[41]

Crowley described this mantra as 'the holiest of all that can be'[42]. The original text is found on the Stéle of

---

[40] Crowley, Desti, and Waddell.

[41] Crowley, Desti, and Waddell.

[42] Crowley, Desti, and Waddell.

Revealing[43], an object of great importance to Thelemites due to its connection to the Revelation of *The Book of the Law* in Cairo in 1904.

The Ordo Templi Orientis Grand Lodge of Australia and In Perpetuity Publishing are proud to be able to present this new composition by Professor Sitsky, and we would like to thank him for his warmth and generosity in working with us to bring it to publication, and his bequest of the work so that it can be made easily available into the future. We would also like to thank David Bottrill[44], whose friendship with, and championing of Sitsky and his work, led to this new Opus.

---

[43] This is the 'funerary Stéle of Ankh-f-n-Khonsu, a Theban Priest' who lived around 725 BCE (Gunther, *Initiation In the Aeon of the Child*.).

[44] We would like to also thank Tony Edwards for his work on the original manuscript.

'you are now a member of this club and it's your duty to pass the torch on.'[45]

- Egon Petri to Larry Sitsky

'It is a thought far from comforting to the present generation, that 500 years of Dark Ages are likely to be upon us. But, if the analogy holds, that is the case. Fortunately, to-day we have brighter torches and more torch-bearers.'[46]

- Aleister Crowley

---

[45] Crispin, 'The Nuctemeron of Sitsky'.

[46] Crowley, *The Book of Thoth*.

Bibliography

Borisova, Anna. 'Larry Sitsky's Music for the Gnostic Mass: The Symbolism and Sacred Structures'. Unpublished mss, n.d.

Cotter, Jim. Sitsky: Conversations with the Composer. National Library of Australia, 2004.

Covach, John. 'Twelve-Tone Theory'. Cambridge History of Western Music, 2002, 603–27.

Crispin, Judith. 'The Nuctemeron of Sitsky', 2004.

Crowley, Aleister. The Book of Thoth. York Beach, Maine: Samuel Weiser, INC, 1993.

———. The Confessions of Aleister Crowley. London: Jonathan Cape, 1969.

Crowley, Aleister, Mary Desti, and Leila Waddell. Magick. Liber ABA. Book Four. Parts I-IV. York Beach, Maine: Samuel Weiser, Inc, 1997.

Garcia, Emanuel. 'Scriabin's Mysterium and the Birth of Genius', 1 January 2005.

Gunther, J. Daniel. Initiation In the Aeon of the Child. Lake Worth, FL: Ibis Books, 2009.

Hieros Gamos Camp OTO. Hieros Gamos Ep 14 – Larry Sitsky, 2019. http://archive.org/details/podcast_hieros-gamos-radio_hieros-gamos-ep-14-larry-sit_1000428461176.

King, Stephen J. 'Shadow of the Thelemites: The Abbot, the Abbey and the Nightmare'. The Nightmare Paintings: Aleister Crowley - Works from the Palermo Collection, 2012.

Xtreme Music. 'Larry Sitsky', 19 November 2014. https://www.xtrememusic.org/larry-sitsky/.

National Portrait Gallery. 'Larry Sitsky: In Their Own Words'. Accessed 21 October 2022. http://www.portrait.gov.au/stories/larry-sitsky/.

ABC Classic. 'Margaret Throsby Interviews Larry Sitsky', 18 October 2022. https://www.abc.net.au/classic/programs/the-margaret-throsby-interviews/margaret-throsby-interviews-larry-sitsky/101547074.

Shaw, Patricia. ''Getting My Hands Dirty: Larry Sitsky in Interview'. Context 11, no. Winter 1996 (1996). https://cpb-ap-se2.wpmucdn.com/blogs.unimelb.edu.au/dist/6/184/files/2017/03/11_Shaw-Interview-zcht5g.pdf.

Tomás, Lia. 'The Mythical Time in Scriabin'. Accessed 22 October 2022. https://www.academia.edu/4822160/The_mythical_time_in_Scriabin.

ANU. 'University Honours for Emeritus Professor Larry Sitsky'. The Australian National University, 15 December 2015. https://www.anu.edu.au/news/all-news/university-honours-for-emeritus-professor-larry-sitsky.

Classic FM. 'What Is a Tritone and Why Was It Nicknamed the Devil's Interval?' Accessed 25 October 2022. https://www.classicfm.com/discover-music/music-theory/what-is-a-tritone/.

MUSIC

(Piano and Chorus) for Ecclesiae Gnosticae Catholicae Canon Missae

LARRY SITSKY

Incidental Music (p'no & chorus) to:
Ecclesiæ Gnosticæ Catholicæ Canon Missæ
(words by Aleister Crowley)
Larry Sitsky
Canberra
May 2019

I

Of the Furnishings of the Temple

In the East, that is, in the direction of Boleskine, which is situated on the South-Eastern shore of Loch Ness in Scotland, two miles east of Foyers, is a shrine or High Altar. Its dimensions should be seven feet in length, three feet in breadth, 44 inches in height. It should be covered with a crimson altar-cloth, on which may be embroidered fleur-de-lys in gold, or a sunblaze, or other suitable emblem.

On each side of it should be a pillar or obelisk, with countercharges in black and white.

Below it should be the dais of three steps, in black and white squares.

Above it is the super-altar, at whose top is the Stèle of Revealing in reproduction, with four candles on each side of it. Below the stèle is a place for The Book of the Law, with six candles on each side of it. Below this again is the Holy Graal, with roses on each side of it. There is room in front of the Cup for the Paten. On each side beyond the roses are two great candles.

All this is enclosed within a great Veil.

Forming the apex of an equilateral triangle whose base is a line drawn between the pillars, is a small black square altar, of two superimposed cubes.

Taking this altar as the middle of the base of a similar and equal triangle, at the apex of this second triangle is a small circular font.

Repeating, the apex of a third triangle is an upright tomb.

II
Of the Officers of the Mass

The PRIEST. Bears the Sacred Lance, and is clothed at first in a plain white robe.

The PRIESTESS. Should be actually Virgo Intacta or specially dedicated to the service of the Great Order. She is clothed in white, blue, and gold. She bears the Sword from a red girdle, and the Paten and Hosts, or Cakes of Light.

The DEACON. He is clothed in white and yellow. He bears The Book of the Law.

Two CHILDREN. They are clothed in white and black. One bears a pitcher of water and a cellar of salt, the other a censer of fire and a casket of perfume.

III
Of the Ceremony of the Introit

The DEACON, opening the door of the Temple, admits the congregation and takes his stand between the small altar and the font. The DEACON advances and bows before the open shrine where the Graal is exalted. He kisses The Book of the Law *three times, opens it, and places it upon the super-altar. He turns West.*

The DEACON: Do what thou wilt shall be the whole of the Law. I proclaim the Law of Light, Life, Love, and Liberty in the name of IAΩ.

The CONGREGATION: Love is the law, love under will.

[CUE TO PIANIST]

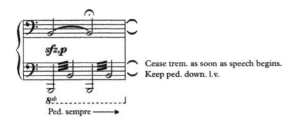

The DEACON goes to his place between the altar of incense and the font, faces East, and gives the step and sign of a Man and a Brother. All imitate him.

The DEACON and all the PEOPLE:

I believe in one secret and ineffable LORD; and in one Star in the Company of Stars of whose fire we are created, and to which we shall return; and in one Father of Life, Mystery of Mystery, in His name CHAOS, the sole viceregent of the Sun upon the Earth; and in one Air the nourisher of all that breathes.

And I believe in one Earth, the Mother of us all, and in one Womb wherein all men are begotten, and wherein they shall rest, Mystery of Mystery, in Her name BABALON.

And I believe in the Serpent and the Lion, Mystery of Mystery, in His name BAPHOMET.

And I believe in one Gnostic and Catholic Church of Light, Life, Love and Liberty, the Word of whose Law is ΘΕΛΗΜΑ.

And I believe in the communion of Saints.

And, forasmuch as meat and drink are transmuted in us daily into spiritual substance, I believe in the Miracle of the Mass.

And I confess one Baptism of Wisdom whereby we accomplish the Miracle of Incarnation.

And I confess my life one, individual, and eternal that was, and is, and is to come.

ΑΥΜΓΝ. ΑΥΜΓΝ. ΑΥΜΓΝ.

Music is now played. The child enters with the ewer and the salt. The VIRGIN enters with the Sword and the Paten. The child enters with the censer and the perfume. They face the DEACON, deploying into line from the space between the two altars.

In this and following sections requiring music, repeat selectively and as necessary, after playing through all the fragments.

* N.B. Number of notes per phrase adheres to 3, 5, 9, 11 as per text.

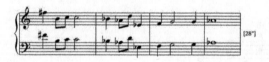

The VIRGIN: Greeting of Earth and Heaven!

All give the Hailing sign of a Magician, the DEACON leading.

The PRIESTESS, the negative child on her left, the positive child on her right, ascends the steps of the High Altar. They

*await her below. She places the Paten before the Graal.
Having adored it, she descends, and with the children
following her, the positive next her, she moves in a
serpentine manner involving 3½ circles of the Temple.
(Deosil about altar, widdershins about font, deosil about
altar and font, widdershins about altar, and so to the Tomb
in the West.) She draws her Sword and pulls down the Veil
therewith.*

[MUSIC ENDS]

The PRIESTESS: By the power of ✛ Iron, I say unto
thee, Arise. In the name of our Lord ✛ the Sun, and of
our Lord ✛ ... that thou mayst administer the virtues to
the Brethren.

The three cross gestures roughly co-ordinated with music below:

She sheathes the Sword.

*The PRIEST, issuing from the Tomb, holding the Lance
erect with both hands, right over left, against his breast, takes
the first three regular steps. He then gives the Lance to the
PRIESTESS, and gives the three penal signs. He then
kneels and worships the Lance with both hands. Penitential
music.*

The PRIEST: I am a man among men.

He takes again the Lance, and lowers it. He rises.

The PRIEST: How should I be worthy to administer the virtues to the Brethren?

The PRIESTESS takes from the child the water and the salt, and mixes them in the font.

The PRIESTESS: Let the salt of Earth admonish the water to bear the virtue of the Great Sea.

Genuflects.

Mother, be thou adored.

She returns to the West. ✛ on PRIEST with open hand doth she make, over his forehead, breast, and body.

Be the PRIEST pure of body and soul!

The PRIESTESS takes the censer from the child, and places it on the small altar. She puts incense therein.

Let the Fire and the Air make sweet the world!

Genuflects.

Father, be thou adored!

She returns West, and makes ✠ with the censer before the PRIEST, thrice as before.

Be the PRIEST fervent of body and soul!

The children resume their weapons as they are done with.

The DEACON now takes the consecrated Robe from High Altar, and brings it to her. She robes the PRIEST in his Robe of scarlet and gold.

Be the flame of the Sun thine ambience, O thou PRIEST of the SUN!

The DEACON brings the crown from the High Altar. (The crown may be of gold or platinum, or of electrum magicum; but with no other metals, save the small proportions necessary to a proper alloy. It may be adorned with divers jewels, at will. But it must have the Uræus serpent twined about it, and the cap of maintenance must match the scarlet of the Robe. Its texture should be velvet.)

Be the Serpent thy crown, O thou PRIEST of the LORD!

Kneeling, she takes the Lance, between her open hands, and runs them up and down upon the shaft eleven times, very gently.

[ADORATION OF THE LANCE (11 PITCHES), WITH RESOLUTION, ROUGHLY COORDINATED WIT THE STROKING MOVEMENTS]

Be the LORD present among us!

All give the Hailing Sign.

The PEOPLE: So mote it be.

IV

Of the Ceremony of the Opening of the Veil

The PRIEST: Thee therefore whom we adore we also invoke. By the power of the lifted Lance!

He raises the Lance. All repeat Hailing Sign. A phrase of triumphant music. The PRIEST takes the PRIESTESS by her right hand with his left, keeping the Lance raised.

[Triumphant chords: use as required (8' each; 32' in all)]

I, PRIEST and KING, take thee, Virgin pure without spot; I upraise thee; I lead thee to the East; I set thee upon the summit of the Earth.

He thrones the PRIESTESS upon the altar.

The DEACON and the children follow, they in rank, behind him.

The PRIESTESS takes The Book of the Law, *resumes her seat, and holds it open on her breast with her two hands, making a descending triangle with thumbs and forefingers.*

The PRIEST gives the lance to the DEACON to hold, and takes the ewer from the child, and sprinkles the PRIESTESS, making five crosses, forehead, shoulders, and thighs.

The thumb of the PRIEST is always between his index and medius, whenever he is not holding the Lance. The PRIEST takes the censer from the child, and makes five crosses, as before. The children replace their weapons on their respective altars.

The PRIEST kisses The Book of the Law *three times.*

He kneels for a space in adoration, with joined hands, knuckles closed, thumb in position as aforesaid.

He rises and draws the veil over the whole altar.

All rise and stand to order.

The PRIEST takes the lance from the DEACON, and holds it as before, as Osiris or Pthah. He circumambulates the Temple three times, followed by the DEACON and the children as before. (These, when not using their hands, keep their arms crossed upon their breasts.)

At the last circumambulation they leave him, and go to the place between the font and the small altar, where they kneel in adoration, their hands joined palm to palm, and raised above their heads.

All imitate this motion.

The PRIEST returns to the East and mounts the first step of the altar.

[Music for the 5 crosses: poco a poco cresc.]

The PRIEST: O circle of Stars whereof our Father is but the younger brother, marvel beyond imagination, soul of infinite space, before whom Time is Ashamed, the mind bewildered, and the understanding dark, not unto Thee may we attain, unless Thine image be Love. Therefore by seed and root and stem and bud and leaf and flower and fruit do we invoke Thee.

"Then the priest answered & said unto the Queen of Space, kissing her lovely brows, and the dew of her light bathing his whole body in a sweet-smelling perfume of sweat; O Nuit, continuous one of Heaven, let it be ever thus; that men speak not of thee as One but as None;

and let them speak not of thee at all, since thou art continuous!"

During this speech the PRIESTESS must have divested herself completely of her robe. (See CCXX I:62.)

The PRIESTESS: "But to love me is better than all things: if under the night-stars in the desert thou presently burnest mine incense before me, invoking me with a pure heart, and the Serpent flame therein, thou shalt come a little to lie in my bosom. For one kiss wilt thou then be willing to give all; but whoso gives one particle of dust shall lose all in that hour. Ye shall gather goods and store of women and spices; ye shall wear rich jewels; ye shall exceed the nations of the earth in splendour and pride; but always in the love of me, & so shall ye come to my joy. I charge you earnestly to come before me in a single robe, and covered with a rich head-dress. I love you! I yearn to you! Pale or purple, veiled or voluptuous, I who am all pleasure and purple, and drunkenness of the innermost sense, desire you. Put on the wings, and arouse the coiled splendour within you: come unto me!" "To me! To me!" "Sing the rapturous love-song unto me! Burn to me perfumes! Wear to me jewels! Drink to me, for I love you! I love you! I am the blue-lidded daughter of Sunset; I am the naked brilliance of the voluptuous night-sky. To me! To me!"

The PRIEST mounts the second step.

The PRIEST: O secret of secrets that art hidden in the being of all that lives, not Thee do we adore, for that which adoreth is also Thou. Thou art That, and That am I.

"I am the flame that burns in every heart of man, and in the core of every star. I am Life, and the giver of Life; yet therefore is the knowledge of me the knowledge of death. I am alone; there is no God where I am."

The DEACON and all rise to their feet with the Hailing sign.

The DEACON:

"But ye, O my people rise up & awake.

"Let the rituals be rightly performed with joy & beauty!

"There are rituals of the elements and feasts of the times.

"A feast for the first night of the Prophet and his Bride!

[CUE 1]

"A feast for the three days of the writing of the Book of the Law.

[CUE 2]

"A feast for Tahuti and the child of the Prophet— secret, O Prophet!

[CUE 3]

"A feast for the Supreme Ritual, and a feast for the Equinox of the Gods.

[CUE 4]

"A feast for fire and a feast for water; a feast for life and a greater feast for death!

[CUE 5]

"A feast every day in your hearts in the joy of my rapture!

[CUE 6]

"A feast every night unto Nu, and the pleasure of uttermost delight!"

[CUE 7]

Seven fortissimo staccato notes, each one a cue to the DEACON
to recite the line beginning: "A feast..."

The PRIEST mounts the third step.

The PRIEST: Thou that art One, our Lord in the Universe, the Sun, our Lord in ourselves whose name is Mystery of Mystery, uttermost being whose radiance, enlightening the worlds, is also the breath that maketh every God even and Death to tremble before Thee— By the Sign of Light ✠ appear Thou glorious upon the throne of the Sun.

Make open the path of creation and of intelligence
between us and our minds. Enlighten our
understanding. Encourage our hearts. Let thy light
crystallize itself in our blood, fulfilling us of
Resurrection.

A ka dua

Tuf ur biu

bi a'a chefu

Dudu nur af an nuteru!

[CROWLEY'S MUSIC MANTRA ENHANCED & BASS
ADDED:]

The PRIESTESS: "There is no law beyond Do what thou wilt."

The PRIEST parts the veil with his lance. During the previous speeches the PRIESTESS has, if necessary, as in savage countries, resumed her robe.

The PRIEST: ΙΩ ΙΩ ΙΩ ΙΑΩ ΣΑΒΑΩ ΚΥΡΙΗ ΑΒΡΑΣΑΞ ΚΥΡΙΗ ΜΕΙΘΡΑΣ ΚΥΡΙΗ ΦΑΛΛΗ. ΙΩ ΠΑΝ, ΙΩ ΠΑΝ ΠΑΝ, ΙΩ ΙΣΧΥΡΟΝ, ΙΩ ΑΘΑΝΑΤΟΝ, ΙΩ ΑΒΡΟΤΟΝ, ΙΩ ΙΑΩ. ΧΑΙΡΕ ΦΑΛΛΗ ΧΑΙΡΕ ΠΑΝΦΑΓΗ ΧΑΙΡΕ ΠΑΝΓΕΝΕΤΟΡ. ΑΓΙΟΣ, ΑΓΙΟΣ, ΑΓΙΟΣ ΙΑΩ.

The PRIESTESS is seated with the Paten in her right hand and the Cup in her left.

The PRIEST presents the Lance, which she kisses eleven times.

She then holds it to her breast, while the PRIEST, falling at her knees, kisses them, his arms stretched along her thighs. He remains in this adoration while the DEACON intones the Collects.

All stand to order, with the Dieu Garde, that is, feet square, hands, with linked thumbs, held loosely. This is the universal position when standing, unless other direction is given.

[KISSING THE LANCE (11 PITCHES) WITH RESOLUTION, ROUGHLY COORDINATED WITH THE KISSING RITUAL]

V
Of the Office of the Collects
Which Are Eleven in Number

The Sun

The DEACON: Lord visible and sensible of whom this earth is but a frozen spark turning about thee with annual and diurnal motion, source of light, source of life, let thy perpetual radiance hearten us to continual labour and enjoyment; so that as we are constant partakers of thy bounty we may in our particular orbit give out light and life, sustenance and joy to them that revolve about us without diminution of substance or effulgence for ever.

The PEOPLE: So mote it be.

The Lord

The DEACON: Lord secret and most holy, source of light, source of life, source of love, source of liberty, be thou ever constant and mighty within us, force of energy, fire of motion; with diligence let us ever labour with thee, that we may remain in thine abundant joy.

The PEOPLE: So mote it be.

The Moon

The DEACON: Lady of night, that turning ever about us art now visible and now invisible in thy season, be thou favourable to hunters, and lovers, and to all men that toil upon the earth, and to all mariners upon the sea.

The PEOPLE: So mote it be.

The Lady

The DEACON: Giver and receiver of joy, gate of life and love, be thou ever ready, thou and thine handmaiden, in thine office of gladness.

The PEOPLE: So mote it be.

The Saints

The DEACON: Lord of Life and Joy, that art the might of man, that art the essence of every true god that is upon the surface of the Earth, continuing knowledge from generation unto generation, thou adored of us upon heaths and in woods, on mountains and in caves, openly in the marketplaces and secretly in the chambers of our houses, in temples of gold and ivory and marble as in these other temples of our bodies, we worthily commemorate them worthy that did of old adore thee and manifest thy glory unto men,

(At each name the DEACON signs ✠ *with thumb between index and medius. At ordinary mass it is only necessary to commemorate those whose names are italicized, with wording as is shown.)*

Laotze and Siddartha and Krishna *and Tahuti,* Mosheh, *Dionysus, Mohammed and To Mega Therion, with these also,* Hermes, *Pan,* Priapus, Osiris and Melchizedek, *Khem* and Amoun *and Mentu, Heracles,* Orpheus and Odysseus; with Vergilius, *Catullus,* Martialis, *Rabelais, Swinburne, and many an holy bard; Apollonius Tyanæus,* Simon Magus, Manes, *Pythagoras,* Basilides, Valentinus, *Bardesanes and Hippolytus, that transmitted the Light of the Gnosis to us their successors and their heirs;* with Merlin, Arthur, Kamuret, Parzival, and many another, prophet, priest and king, that bore the Lance and Cup, the Sword and Disk, against the Heathen; *and these also,* Carolus Magnus and his paladins, with William of Schyren, Frederick of Hohenstaufen, Roger Bacon, *Jacobus Burgundus Molensis the Martyr, Christian Rosencreutz,* Ulrich von Hutten, Paracelsus, Michael Maier, *Roderic Borgia Pope Alexander the Sixth,* Jacob Boehme, Francis Bacon Lord Verulam, Andrea, Robertus de Fluctibus, Giordano Bruno, Johannes Dee, *Sir Edward Kelly,* Thomas Vaughan, Elias Ashmole, Molinos, Adam Weishaupt, Wolfgang von Goethe, William Blake, Ludovicus Rex Bavariæ, Richard Wagner, *Alphonse Louis Constant,* Friedrich Nietzsche, Hargrave Jennings, Carl Kellner, Forlong dux, Sir Richard Payne Knight, Paul Gaugin, Sir Richard

Francis Burton, Doctor Gérard Encausse, Doctor
Theodor Reuss, *Sir Aleister Crowley,* Karl Johannes
Germer, and Major Grady Louis McMurtry— Oh Sons
of the Lion and the Snake! with all thy saints we
worthily commemorate them worthy that were and are
and are to come.

May their Essence be here present, potent, puissant and
paternal to perfect this feast!

The PEOPLE: So mote it be.

The Earth

The DEACON: Mother of fertility on whose breast
lieth water, whose cheek is caressed by air, and in whose
heart is the sun's fire, womb of all life, recurring grace
of seasons, answer favorably the prayer of labour, and to
pastors and husbandmen be thou propitious.

The PEOPLE: So mote it be.

The Principles

The DEACON: Mysterious Energy, triform,
mysterious Matter, in fourfold and sevenfold division,
the interplay of which things weave the dance of the
Veil of Life upon the Face of the Spirit, let there be
Harmony and Beauty in your mystic loves, that in us
may be health and wealth and strength and divine
pleasure according to the Law of Liberty; let each
pursue his Will as a strong man that rejoiceth in his

way, as the course of a Star that blazeth for ever among the joyous company of Heaven.

The PEOPLE: So mote it be.

Birth

The DEACON: Be the hour auspicious, and the gate of life open in peace and in well-being, so that she that beareth children may rejoice, and the babe catch life with both hands.

The PEOPLE: So mote it be.

Marriage

The DEACON: Upon all that this day unite with love under will let fall success; may strength and skill unite to bring forth ecstasy, and beauty answer beauty.

The PEOPLE: So mote it be.

Death

The DEACON: Term of all that liveth, whose name is inscrutable, be favourable unto us in thine hour.

The PEOPLE: So mote it be.

The End

The DEACON: Unto them from whose eyes the veil of life hath fallen may there be granted the accomplishment of their True Wills; whether they will absorption in the Infinite, or to be united with their chosen and preferred, or to be in contemplation, or to be at peace, or to achieve the labour and heroism of incarnation on this planet or another, or in any Star, or aught else, unto them may there be granted the accomplishment of their wills; yea, the accomplishment of their Wills.

ΑΥΜΓΝ. ΑΥΜΓΝ. ΑΥΜΓΝ.

The PEOPLE: So mote it be.

All sit.

The DEACON and the children attend the PRIEST and PRIESTESS, ready to hold any appropriate weapon as may be necessary.

VI
Of the Consecration of the Elements

The PRIEST makes the five crosses

✠*1*

✠*3*   ✠*2*

on paten and cup; ✠4 *on paten alone;* ✠5 *on cup alone.*

[Music for the 5 crosses: poco a poco cresc.]

The PRIEST: Life of man upon earth, fruit of labour, sustenance of endeavour, thus be thou nourishment of the Spirit!

He touches the Host with the Lance.

By the virtue of the Rod

Be this bread the Body of God!

He takes the Host.

ΤΟΥΤΟ ΕΣΤΙ ΤΟ ΣΩΜΑ ΜΟΥ.

He kneels, adores, rises, turns, shows Host to the PEOPLE, turns, replaces Host, and adores. Music. He takes the Cup.

Vehicle of the joy of Man upon earth, solace of labour, inspiration of endeavour, thus be thou ecstasy of the Spirit!

He touches the Cup with the Lance.

By the virtue of the Rod

Be this wine the Blood of God!

He takes the Cup.

ΤΟΥΤΟ ΕΣΤΙ ΤΟ ΠΟΤΗΡΙΟΝ ΤΟΥ ΑΙΜΑΤΟΣ ΜΟΥ.

He kneels, adores, rises, turns, shows the Cup to the PEOPLE, turns, replaces the Cup, and adores. Music.

[USE 'TRIUMPHANT CHORDS (BELOW) IN WHATEVER ORDER & SELECTION]

[Triumphant chords: use as required (8' each; 32' in all)]

♩=60 Solemnly (Quasi organ)

For this is the Covenant of Resurrection.

He makes the five crosses on the PRIESTESS.

Ped. sempre [Music for the 5 crosses: poco a poco cresc.]

Accept, O LORD, this sacrifice of life and joy, true warrants of the Covenant of Resurrection.

The PRIEST offers the Lance to the PRIESTESS, who kisses it; he then touches her between the breasts and upon the body. He then flings out his arms upward, as comprehending the whole shrine.

Let this offering be borne upon the waves of Aethyr to our Lord and Father the Sun that travelleth over the Heavens in his name ON.

He closes his hands, kisses the PRIESTESS between the breasts, and makes three great crosses [MUSIC] *over the Paten, the Cup, and himself. He strikes his breast. All repeat this action.*

Ped. sempre

Hear ye all, saints of the true church of old time now essentially present, that of ye we claim heirship, with ye we claim communion, from ye we claim benediction in the name of IAΩ.

He makes three crosses on Paten and Cup together. He uncovers the Cup, genuflects, takes the Cup in his left hand and the Host in his right. With the Host he makes the five crosses [MUSIC] *on the Cup.*

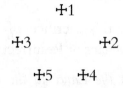

He elevates the Host and the Cup. The Bell strikes.

[MUSIC]

ΑΓΙΟΣ ΑΓΙΟΣ ΑΓΙΟΣ ΙΑΩ.

He replaces the Host and the Cup, and adores.

VII
Of the Office of the Anthem

The PRIEST:

Thou who art I, beyond all I am,

Who hast no nature and no name,

Who art, when all but thou are gone,

Thou, centre and secret of the Sun,

Thou, hidden spring of all things known

And unknown, Thou aloof, alone,

Thou, the true fire within the reed

Brooding and breeding, source and seed

Of life, love, liberty, and light,

Thou beyond speech and beyond sight,

Thee I invoke, my faint fresh fire

Kindling as mine intents aspire.

Thee I invoke, abiding one,

Thee, centre and secret of the Sun,

And that most holy mystery

Of which the vehicle am I.

Appear, most awful and most mild,

As it is lawful, in thy child!

The CHORUS:

For of the Father and the Son

The Holy Spirit is the norm;

Male-female, quintessential, one,

Man-being veiled in woman-form.

Glory and worship in the highest,

Thou Dove, mankind that deifiest,

Being that race, most royally run

To spring sunshine through winter storm.

Glory and worship be to Thee,

Sap of the world-ash, wonder-tree!

First Semichorus, MEN:

Glory to thee from gilded tomb!

Second Semichorus, WOMEN:

Glory to thee from waiting womb!

MEN:

Glory to Thee from earth unploughed!

WOMEN:

Glory to Thee from virgin vowed!

MEN:

Glory to Thee, true Unity

Of the Eternal Trinity!

WOMEN:

Glory to Thee, thou sire and dam

And Self of I am that I am!

MEN:

Glory to Thee, beyond all term,

Thy spring of sperm, thy seed and germ!

WOMEN:

Glory to Thee, eternal Sun,

Thou One in Three, Thou Three in One!

CHORUS:

Glory and worship unto Thee,

Sap of the world-ash, wonder-tree!

(These words are to form the substance of the anthem; but the whole or any part thereof shall be set to music, which may be as elaborate as art can devise. But even should other anthems be authorized by the Father of the Church, this shall hold its place as the first of its kind, the father of all others.)[1]

---

[1] There are several deviations in the words, from the official Missal of XV, in the following pieces of musical score related to the Anthem. These are notation errors and should not be read as official (Editor)

[OSSIA (THIS PAGE): IF THE INCLUSION & SETTING OF A LINE FROM THE NEXT SECTION OF THE MASS IS FOUND TO BE INAPPROPRIATE, THEN THIS PAGE SHOULD BE PERFORMED AS SOLO PIANO, WITHOUT VOICES.]

Thou, who art I, be-yond all I am, who hast no na-ture, and no

name, who art, when all but thou art gone, Thy cen-tre and se-cret of the

sun. Then, hid-den spring of all things known and un-known, thou a - loof, a - lone.

Thou, the true fire with-in the reed, brood-ing and breed-ing, source and seed

of life, love, lib-er-ty and light, thou be-yond speech and be-yond sight.

Thee I in-voke, the faint fresh fire, kind-ling as mine in-tents as-pire.

Thee I in - voke, a - bid-ing one, thee, cen-tre and sec-ret of the sun,

and, that most ho-ly mys-ter-y, of which the ve-hi-cle am I,

app - ear, most aw-ful and most mild, as it is law-ful, in thy child.

For of the Fa-ther and the Son   the Ho-ly Spi-irt is the norm.

Male-fe-male quit-ess-en-ti-al,   one, man-being veiled   in   fe-male form.

Glo-ry and worship   in   the high-est,   thy dove, man-kind that de-i-fi-est,

Be-ing that race, most roy-al-ly run,   to spring sun-shine through win - ter storm.

Glor-y and wor-ship be to thee,   sap of the world-ash, won-der tree!

Men   Glor-y to thee from gild-ed tomb.   Women   Glor-y to thee from wait-ing womb!

Glor-y to thee from earth un-ploughed! Glor-y to thee from vir - gin vowed!

Glor-y to thee, true un-i-ty of the e-ter-nal tri-ni-ty!

Glor-y to thee, thou sire and dam, and self of I am that I am!

VIII

Of the Mystic Marriage and Consummation of the Elements

The PRIEST takes the Paten between the index and medius of the right hand. The PRIESTESS clasps the Cup in her right hand.

The PRIEST: Lord most secret, bless this spiritual food unto our bodies, bestowing upon us health and wealth and strength and joy and peace, and that fulfilment of will and of love under will that is perpetual happiness.

He makes ✠ [MUSIC] with Paten and kisses it.

He uncovers the Cup, genuflects, rises. Music.

He takes the Host, and breaks it over the Cup.

He replaces the right-hand portion in the Paten.

He breaks off a particle of the left-hand portion.

ΤΟΥΤΟ ΕΣΤΙ ΤΟ ΣΠΕΡΜΑ ΜΟΥ. Ο ΠΑΤΗΡ ΕΣΤΙΝ Ο ΗΥΙΟΣ ΔΙΑ ΤΟ ΠΝΕΥΜΑ ΑΓΙΟΝ.

ΑΥΜΓΝ. ΑΥΜΓΝ. ΑΥΜΓΝ.

He replaces the left-hand part of the Host.

The PRIESTESS extends the Lance-point with her left hand to receive the particle.

The PRIEST clasps the Cup in his left hand.

Together they depress the Lance-point in the Cup.

The PRIEST and the PRIESTESS: HRILIU.

The PRIEST takes the Lance.

The PRIESTESS covers the Cup.

The PRIEST genuflects, rises, bows, joins hands. He strikes his breast.

The PRIEST:

[CUE 1] O Lion and O Serpent that destroy the destroyer, be mighty among us.

[CUE 2] O Lion and O Serpent that destroy the destroyer, be mighty among us.

[CUE 3] O Lion and O Serpent that destroy the destroyer, be mighty among us.

The PRIEST joins hands upon the breast of the PRIESTESS, and takes back his Lance. He turns to the People, lowers and raises the Lance, and makes ✠ [MUSIC] *upon them.*

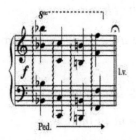

Do what thou wilt shall be the whole of the Law.

The PEOPLE: Love is the law, love under will.

He lowers the Lance, and turns to East. The PRIESTESS takes the Lance in her right hand; with her left hand she offers the Paten. The PRIEST kneels.

The PRIEST: In my mouth be the essence of the life of the Sun!

He takes the Host with the right hand, makes ✠ [MUSIC] *with it on the Paten, and consumes it. Silence. The PRIESTESS takes, uncovers, and offers the Cup, as before.*

The PRIEST: In my mouth be the essence of the joy of the earth!

He takes the Cup, makes ✠ [MUSIC] on the PRIESTESS, drains it, and returns it.

Silence. He rises, takes the Lance, and turns to the PEOPLE.

The PRIEST: There is no part of me that is not of the Gods.

Those of the PEOPLE who intend to communicate, and none other should be present, having signified their intention, a whole Cake of Light, and a whole goblet of wine, have been prepared for each one.

The DEACON marshals them; they advance one by one to the altar.

The children take the Elements and offer them.

The PEOPLE communicate as did the PRIEST, uttering the same words in an attitude of Resurrection:

"There is no part of me that is not of the Gods."

(The exceptions to this part of the ceremony are when it is of the nature of a celebration, in which case none but the PRIEST communicate; or part of the ceremony of marriage, when none other, save the two to be married, partake; part of the ceremony of baptism, when only the child baptised partakes; and of Confirmation at puberty, when only the persons confirmed partake. The Sacrament may be reserved by the PRIEST, for administration to the sick in their homes.)

The PRIEST closes all within the veil. With the Lance he makes ✠ *on the people thrice, thus.*

The PRIEST:

✠ [CUE] The LORD bless you.

✠ [CUE] The LORD enlighten your minds and comfort your hearts and sustain your bodies.

✠ [CUE] The LORD bring you to the accomplishment of your true Wills, the Great Work, the Summum Bonum, True Wisdom and Perfect Happiness.

He goes out, the DEACON and children following, into the Tomb of the West.

Music. (Voluntary.)

[DURING THE PEOPLE'S COMMUNION, THE PIANIST
PLAYS WHATEVER FRAGMENTS HE/SHE CHOOSES, & IN
WHATEVER ORDER.

AT CONCLUSION:]

*A complete manuscript for performance and study can be
found by following the QR code below:*

CONTRIBUTOR BIOGRAPHIES

Ian Drummond (Tau Nektarios) has been a member of the OTO since 1997, active as a member of Sydney local body Oceania Lodge and as a Deacon, Priest and Bishop in Ecclesia Gnostica Catholica. Ian was also a founding member of the Australian Grand Lodge Electoral College, completing his term of office in 2017.

Soror Shalimar was a foundational member of the Oceania Oasis, Sydney Australia, in the 1990s and co-creator of the Grand Lodge and EGC. Her EGC work and studies, on the priestess role and eucharist in particular, as well as the mentoring of sisters and priestesses of the Order more generally, are a lasting legacy.

Cosimo Salvatorelli is a researcher on spirituality. He is an Elector of Italian Grand Lodge O.T.O. and an Aspirant to the A∴A∴. On Facebook he hosts Thelema Radio.

Sinisha Tzar (Siniša Car Premužić) has been a member of the OTO since 1997 and a Priest of the EGC. He was initiated in Zagreb, the capital of Croatia, and served as a Secretary and Treasurer of the Mirrach lodge. Sinisha holds MA in Journalism from the Faculty of Political Science of Zagreb University. He finds that an academic approach to Western Esotericism is of the highest value and attended both introductory and advanced short-term programmes organized by The Centre for the History of Hermetic Philosophy and Related Currents within the University of Amsterdam. In his studies, Sinisha seeks to establish both historical and symbolic connections between modern magickal practice and ancient writings. He is a practitioner of magick, yoga, chi kung, and spagyric art.

William Peters is a member of the OTO and an independent researcher with an unwholesome fascination with early 20th century German esotericism and the roots of Thelema in Germany.

Daniel Brant Corish is an aspirant to A∴A∴ and a member of Ordo Templi Orientis. He is Body Master of Apep Oasis OTO in Victoria and is on the OTO Australian Grand Lodge Editorial Team. Daniel also enjoys Kundalini Yoga, Ninjutsu, reading and spending time with his son.

Frater S.P. is an Aspirant to the A∴A∴, a member of OTO, and an initiate of Śrī Vidyā upāsanā. Based in Ireland, he regularly leads discussion groups and offers instruction for Sword of Light Camp OTO. His primary interests are the magical techniques of the R.R. et A.C. (the Second Order of the original Hermetic Order of the Golden Dawn), Daśa Mahāvidyā, Kundalini Yoga, the Thoth Tarot, and Liber 418: *The Vision and the Voice*. A website containing some examples of his writing can be found at withinthepyramid.wordpress.com

Garry McSweeney is currently completing his PhD on the Australian Witchcraft community's religious experience. witchreligiousexperience.com

N. F. Robinson is a member of the OTO living in Melbourne, Australia.

Shokufeh Alwazi is an independent scholar and translator who became interested in the philosophy and practices of Thelema while living in the West after fleeing Iran in the late 1990s.

Rev. Cosmé Hallelujah is an independent scholar and Thomas Christian theologian. His main research interests are in the Coptic Gospel of Thomas (Codex II, 2), Coptic Ascent and Vision mysticism, and the Coptic Magical Papyri. Since retiring he spends much of his time sequestered in meditation at Parangimalai (St. Thomas Mount) in Tamil Nadu, with intermittent research trips to Egypt. He lives in Tivim, Goa with his wife, extended family of students, and pet goats.

Steve King is an experience designer, educator and administrator for a not-for-profit.

Joel Brady has been an initiate of the OTO since 1997, and is also an Aspirant to the A∴A∴. Currently serving as Grand Treasurer General of the Grand Lodge of Australia Joel Brady. has a special interest in the links between the two Orders and the wholeness that comes from their cooperation as intended by Aleister Crowley.

Larry Sitsky was born in Tientsin, China, in 1934, and came to Australia in 1951. He studied at the NSW State Conservatorium of Music, and after graduating in 1954, continued his piano studies with Winifred Burston and later in the USA with Egon Petri. His works have been performed all over the world. In 2000 he was received as a Member of the Order of Australia.

THE LEGEND OF
ALEISTER CROWLEY

https://thelegendofaleistercrowley.com/

ISBN 978–0645103939

This facsimile edition of P. R. Stephensen's 1930 broadside against the 'Campaign of Personal Vilification Unparalleled in Literary History' arrives in 2021 as the mainstream media thrashes in its death throes.

Quality digital scans of the original book, never before published material from the Australian OTO archives, as well as a new essay examining the politics of conspiracy and the pathologies of Fake News, make this an indispensable case study of media malfeasance and moral panic.

Currently available from In Perpetuity Publishing.

For more information about our publications please visit

https://www.otoaustralia.org.au/publications/

Available through all good online booksellers.

LIVING IN THE SUNLIGHT

MAKING A FORGOTTEN MEDITATION AN ATOMIC HABIT

https://livinginthesunlight.site/

ISBN 978-0645103946

Living in the Sunlight by Steve King is a little gem of a book that is welcome and much needed, perhaps never as much as right now. Dedicated to the exposition of a deceptively simple meditation practice, the book's clear and unassuming narrative is brimful with initiated knowledge, and steeped in the esoteric lore of Ordo Templi Orientis and Aleister Crowley's Thelema. The practice of "Living in the Sunlight," however, originates not with Crowley but with his "scarlet woman" Hilarion (Jeanne Robert Foster) and can be adopted by anyone, irrespective of denominational affiliations and ideological convictions. In essence, it is a method of identifying one's deepest awareness with the Sun, for the ultimate purpose of radiating its light unto others. An antidote to the present culture of cynicism and ennui, Living in the Sunlight is based on a simple yet profound notion that happiness is contagious and grows by sharing. This book, and the method of putting it into practice, is rooted in a most radical idea, that the point of life is joy. Highly recommended.

- Gordan Djurdjevic, author of *India and the Occult*, and co-translator of *Sayings of Gorakhnāth*

ORA ET LABORA

https://ora-et-labora.site/

Distributed across three volumes, wide-ranging and highly eclectic essays from around the world, *Ora Et Labora* gathers together the research and findings of the practitioner-scholars of Thelema.

ISBN 978-0645103908   Vol I

In the Weaves of the Order · Typology of Will in writings of Aleister Crowley, Meister Eckhart and Carl Gustav Jung · An Analysis of Liber Librae · When meditation goes bad · Health in Thelema: The Stone of the Wise & The Holy Guardian Angel · Eros daimon mediator and Electoral College · On the Epiclesis · Secret Light: Reflections on the Rosy Cross · Eucharist: From Self to God · The Proof is in the Pudding · Baphomet

ISBN 978-0645103915   Vol II

Āmi Satya: Hallaj, Crowley, and the Baul Fakirs of Bengal · Carl Kellner · Freemasonry, the OTO, and Crowley · Aleister Crowley: a K2 Letter · The Spiritual Heritage from Egypt · Notes towards a preliminary analysis of a peculiar motif in the Stele of Ankh-af-na-khonsu · The Birth of the New Aeon: Magick And Mysticism of Thelema from the Perspective of Postmodern A/Theology · Crowley, Conspiracy, Moral Panic and the Media · The Will of the Aeon

ISBN 978-0645103922   Vol III

Alba ad Rubrum: Waratah Blossoms · Lord of Life & Joy · The 'Occult Macrohistory' of Aleister Crowley · Mundus Imaginalis, the Stone of the Wise · Bread and Salt: To be taken with a grain of salt · Initiation and the Hermetic Tradition · The mantras and the spells: Language and magick · "Anything can be Animated": The Visionary Cinema of Jordan Belson and its Esoteric Core · Occultists, Nazis, Atlanteans and Alawites. Vril and the Occult Revival · 'That I may follow and dispel the night': Wagner's Parsifal and Liber XV · A Crack in Everything : Finitude and the Ceremony of the Introit · An Examination of the Symbolism of the Gnostic Mass Temple · Temple Theology in the Gnostic Mass · Apokalypsis II: Temple mysticism in the New Aeon : An Introduction · The Island of Flames and the spiritual heart. A reflective commentary on Rev. Cosmé Hallelujah's "Notes towards a preliminary analysis of a peculiar motif in the Stele of Ankh-af-na-khonsu" · Excursus on Notes towards a preliminary analysis of a particular motif in the Stele of Ankh-af-na-khonsu

THE BEST OF OZ

https://thebestofoz.com/

After 13 years and 50 Issues, OTO Grand Lodge of Australia is making its member-only OZ magazine available to the public in this 'best of' compilation. Inspiring and provocative, OZ chronicles the birth and early development of the Australian Grand Lodge experiment in thought leadership, scholarship, culture and magical design.

ISBN 978-0646815770

Origins of the modern O.T.O in Australia · Aurora Australis: topological reflections on the modern M.M.M. in Australia · 'New Commentary' Theology: Notes towards reorganising the EGC Part 1 & Part 2 · 'From the GM' (AUGL in Japan) · Toiling in the (local) fields of Our Lord · Remembering Parsi Krumm-Heller (1925-2008 e.v.) Obituary · Grand Master Shiva's Introduction to J. Daniel Gunther's 'Initiation in the Aeon of the Child: the Path of the Great Return' · Veni Cooper-Mathieson · Woman Girt with a Sword · EGC Retreat Keynote Address · Our Church – the Clarity of Vocation · Shadow of the Thelemites: the Abbot, the Abbey and the Nightmare · In the Flesh – Manifesting Liber 194 · Battle of the Ants · Apokalypsis 418 – The Temple of Christ, the Angelic priesthood and the Great Return of the Queen of Heaven · Temple Mount: The Oriental Templar crusade for Verità · Living In The Sunlight

If you want
FREEDOM
You must fight for it

If you want
TO FIGHT
You must organise

If you want
TO ORGANISE
Join us

ORDO TEMPLI ORIENTIS
Grand Lodge of Australia

• SYDNEY • MELBOURNE • BRISBANE •
• HOBART • PERTH • ADELAIDE •

www.otoaustralia.org.au

ORDO TEMPLI ORIENTIS
International Contact

www.oto.org

The OTO does not include the A∴A∴ with which body it is, however, in close alliance. While the curricula of A∴A∴ and OTO interpenetrate at points, this is more by nature than design, and the exception, not the rule. The respective systems and their methods are distinct. One follows the Path in Eternity. The other, the Path of the Great Return. The Grand Lodge of Australia openly supports the work of the Great Order by providing resources to its Outer College, hosting lecture tours to Australia by its senior instructors, and collaborating on joint projects and learning events.

Those of you whose will is to communicate with the A∴A∴ should apply by letter to the Cancellarius of the A∴A∴

www.outercol.org

secretary@outercol.org

Printed by BoD™in Norderstedt, Germany